THE wallflower

YAMATONADESHIKO SHICHIHENGE

21

Tomoko Hayakawa

Translated and adapted by
David Ury

Lettered by
North Market Street Graphics

KC
KODANSHA
COMICS

The Wallflower volume 21 is a work of fiction. Names, characters, places, and incidents are the products of the author's imagination or are used fictitiously. Any resemblance to actual events, locales, or persons, living or dead, is entirely coincidental.

A Kodansha Comics Trade Paperback Original.

Published in the United States by Kodansha Comics, an imprint of Kodansha USA Publishing, LLC., New York.

Publication rights for this English edition arranged through Kodansha Ltd., Tokyo.

First published in Japan in 2008 by Kodansha Ltd., Tokyo,
as *Yamatonadeshiko Shichihenge*, volume 21.

ISBN 978-1-61262-333-7

Printed in Canada.

www.kodanshacomics.com

9 8 7 6 5 4 3 2 1

Translator/Adapter—David Ury
Lettering—North Market Street Graphics

Contents

A Note from the Author

KYAA, FOR SOME REASON, I WAS ASKED TO DO A ROMANCE
STORY. HALFWAY THROUGH, I REALLY STARTED TO REGRET
IT. I'M JUST NO GOOD AT WRITING ROMANCE. I REALLY
WORRIED ABOUT HOW TO RESOLVE THE STORY, AND WELL...
THIS IS WHAT I ENDED UP WITH. WHAT ON EARTH WILL
HAPPEN TO SUNAKO NEXT? I HOPE YOU'LL STICK AROUND
AND FIND OUT.

—Tomoko Hayakawa

Honorifics Explained

Throughout the Kodansha Comics books, you will find Japanese honorifics left intact in the translations. For those not familiar with how the Japanese use honorifics and, more important, how they differ from American honorifics, we present this brief overview.

Politeness has always been a critical facet of Japanese culture. Ever since the feudal era, when Japan was a highly stratified society, use of honorifics—which can be defined as polite speech that indicates relationship or status—has played an essential role in the Japanese language. When addressing someone in Japanese, an honorific usually takes the form of a suffix attached to one's name (example: "Asuna-san"), is used as a title at the end of one's name, or appears in place of the name itself (example: "Negi-sensei," or simply "Sensei!").

Honorifics can be expressions of respect or endearment. In the context of manga and anime, honorifics give insight into the nature of the relationship between characters. Many English translations leave out these important honorifics and therefore distort the feel of the original Japanese. Because Japanese honorifics contain nuances that English honorifics lack, it is our policy at Kodansha not to translate them. Here, instead, is a guide to some of the honorifics you may encounter in Kodansha Comics.

-san: This is the most common honorific and is equivalent to Mr., Miss, Ms., or Mrs. It is the all-purpose honorific and can be used in any situation where politeness is required.

-sama: This is one level higher than "-san" and is used to confer great respect.

-dono: This comes from the word "tono," which means "lord." It is an even higher level than "-sama" and confers utmost respect.

-kun: This suffix is used at the end of boys' names to express familiarity or endearment. It is also sometimes used by men among friends, or when addressing someone younger or of a lower station.

-chan: This is used to express endearment, mostly toward girls. It is also used for little boys, pets, and even among lovers. It gives a sense of childish cuteness.

Bozu: This is an informal way to refer to a boy, similar to the English terms "kid" and "squirt."

**Sempai/
Senpai:** This title suggests that the addressee is one's senior in a group or organization. It is most often used in a school setting, where underclassmen refer to their upperclassmen as "sempai." It can also be used in the workplace, such as when a newer employee addresses an employee who has seniority in the company.

Kohai: This is the opposite of "sempai" and is used toward underclassmen in school or newcomers in the workplace. It connotes that the addressee is of a lower station.

Sensei: Literally meaning "one who has come before," this title is used for teachers, doctors, or masters of any profession or art.

-[blank]: This is usually forgotten in these lists, but it is perhaps the most significant difference between Japanese and English. The lack of honorific means that the speaker has permission to address the person in a very intimate way. Usually, only family, spouses, or very close friends have this kind of permission. Known as *yobisute*, it can be gratifying when someone who has earned the intimacy starts to call one by one's name without an honorific. But when that intimacy hasn't been earned, it can be very insulting.

THE wallflower
YAMATONADESHIKO SHICHIHENGE

ヤマトナデシコ七変化♡

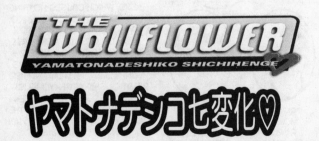

CONTENTS

WALLFLOWER'S BEAUTIFUL CAST OF CHARACTERS (?)

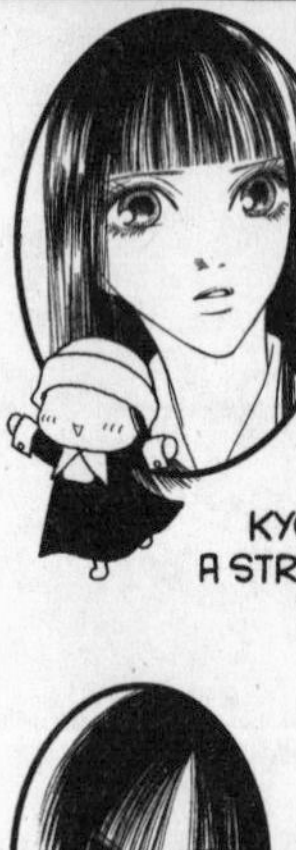

SUNAKO NAKAHARA

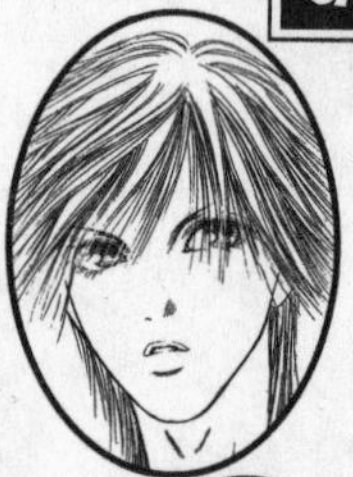

KYOHEI TAKANO–
A STRONG FIGHTER,
"I'M THE KING"

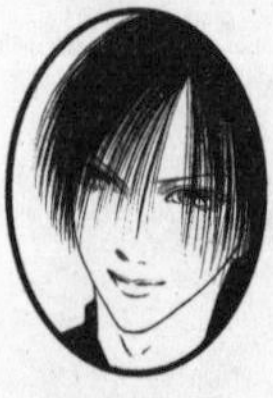

TAKENAGA
ODA–
A CARING
FEMINIST

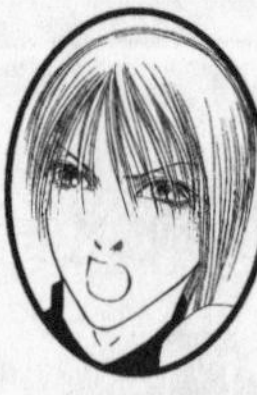

RANMARU
MORII–
A TRUE
LADY'S MAN

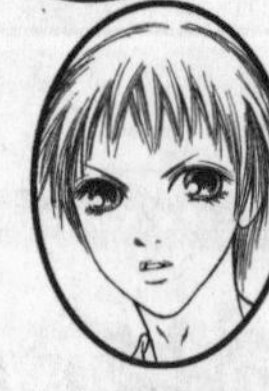

YUKINOJO
TOYAMA–
A GENTLE,
CHEERFUL, AND
VERY EMOTIONAL
GUY

SUNAKO IS A DARK LONER WHO LOVES HORROR MOVIES. WHEN HER AUNT, THE LANDLADY OF A BOARDINGHOUSE, LEAVES TOWN WITH HER BOYFRIEND, SUNAKO IS FORCED TO LIVE WITH FOUR HANDSOME GUYS. SUNAKO'S AUNT MAKES A DEAL WITH THE BOYS, WHICH CAUSES NOTHING BUT HEADACHES FOR SUNAKO. "MAKE SUNAKO INTO A LADY, AND YOU CAN LIVE RENT-FREE FOR THREE YEARS. THE GUYS ARE NOWHERE NEAR TURNING SUNAKO INTO A LADY AND HER RELATIONSHIP WITH KYOHEI ISN'T PROGRESSING AT ALL. THEN AGAIN, IN THE LAST VOLUME, THEY DID BOTH DRAW THE SAME "LUCK IN LOVE" FORTUNE...

Chapter 83 Special Bonus Manga - Come Back, Machiko!

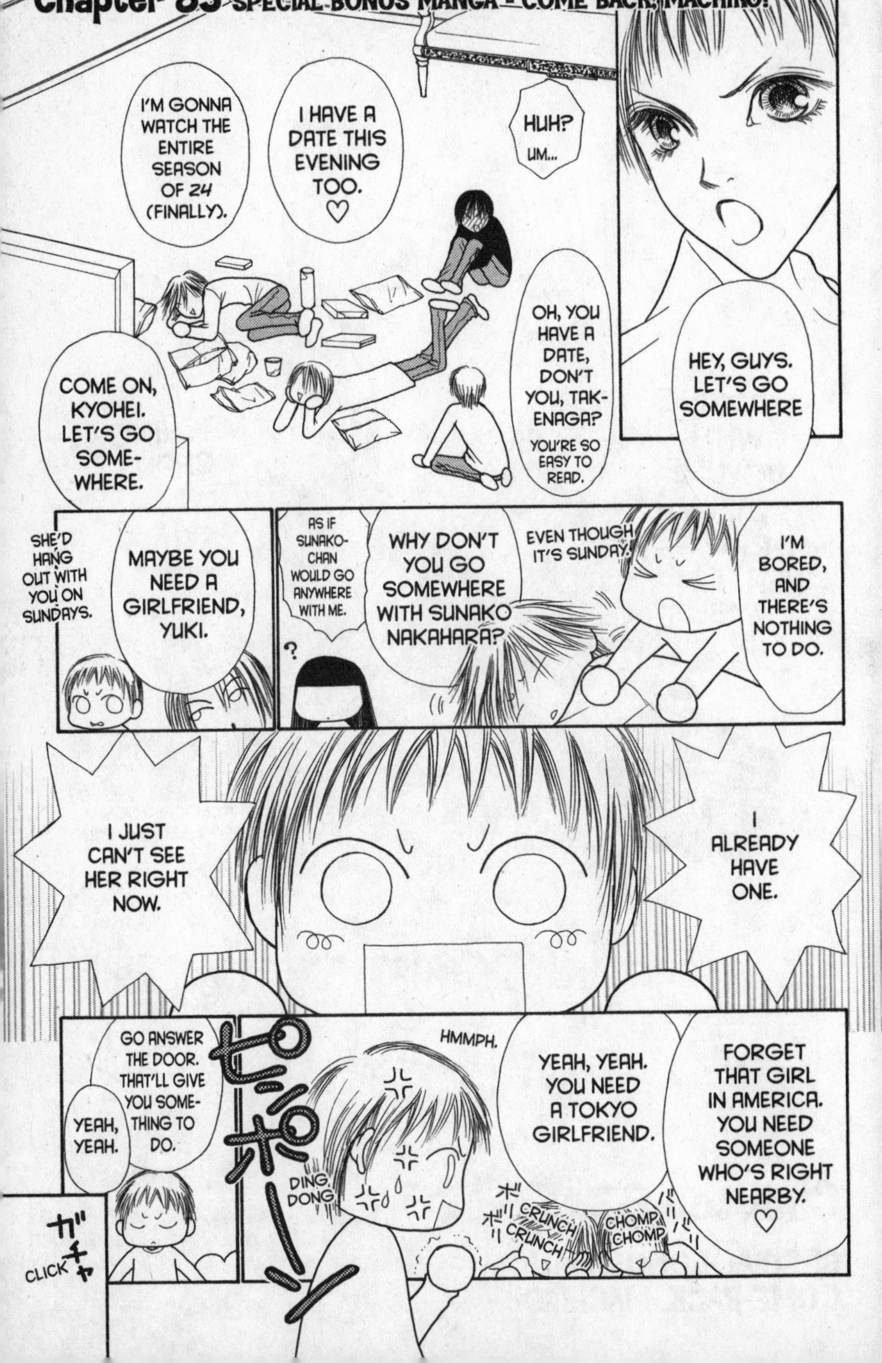

HEY, GUYS. LET'S GO SOMEWHERE
HUH? UM...
OH, YOU HAVE A DATE, DON'T YOU, TAKENAGA? YOU'RE SO EASY TO READ.
I HAVE A DATE THIS EVENING TOO. ♡
I'M GONNA WATCH THE ENTIRE SEASON OF 24 (FINALLY).
COME ON, KYOHEI. LET'S GO SOMEWHERE.
I'M BORED, AND THERE'S NOTHING TO DO.
EVEN THOUGH IT'S SUNDAY.
WHY DON'T YOU GO SOMEWHERE WITH SUNAKO NAKAHARA?
AS IF SUNAKO-CHAN WOULD GO ANYWHERE WITH ME.
?
MAYBE YOU NEED A GIRLFRIEND, YUKI.
SHE'D HANG OUT WITH YOU ON SUNDAYS.
I ALREADY HAVE ONE.
I JUST CAN'T SEE HER RIGHT NOW.
FORGET THAT GIRL IN AMERICA. YOU NEED SOMEONE WHO'S RIGHT NEARBY. ♡
YEAH, YEAH. YOU NEED A TOKYO GIRLFRIEND.
HMMPH.
バリ バリ CHOMP CHOMP
ボリ ボリ CRUNCH CRUNCH
ピンポーン DING DONG
GO ANSWER THE DOOR. THAT'LL GIVE YOU SOMETHING TO DO.
YEAH, YEAH.
ガチャ CLICK

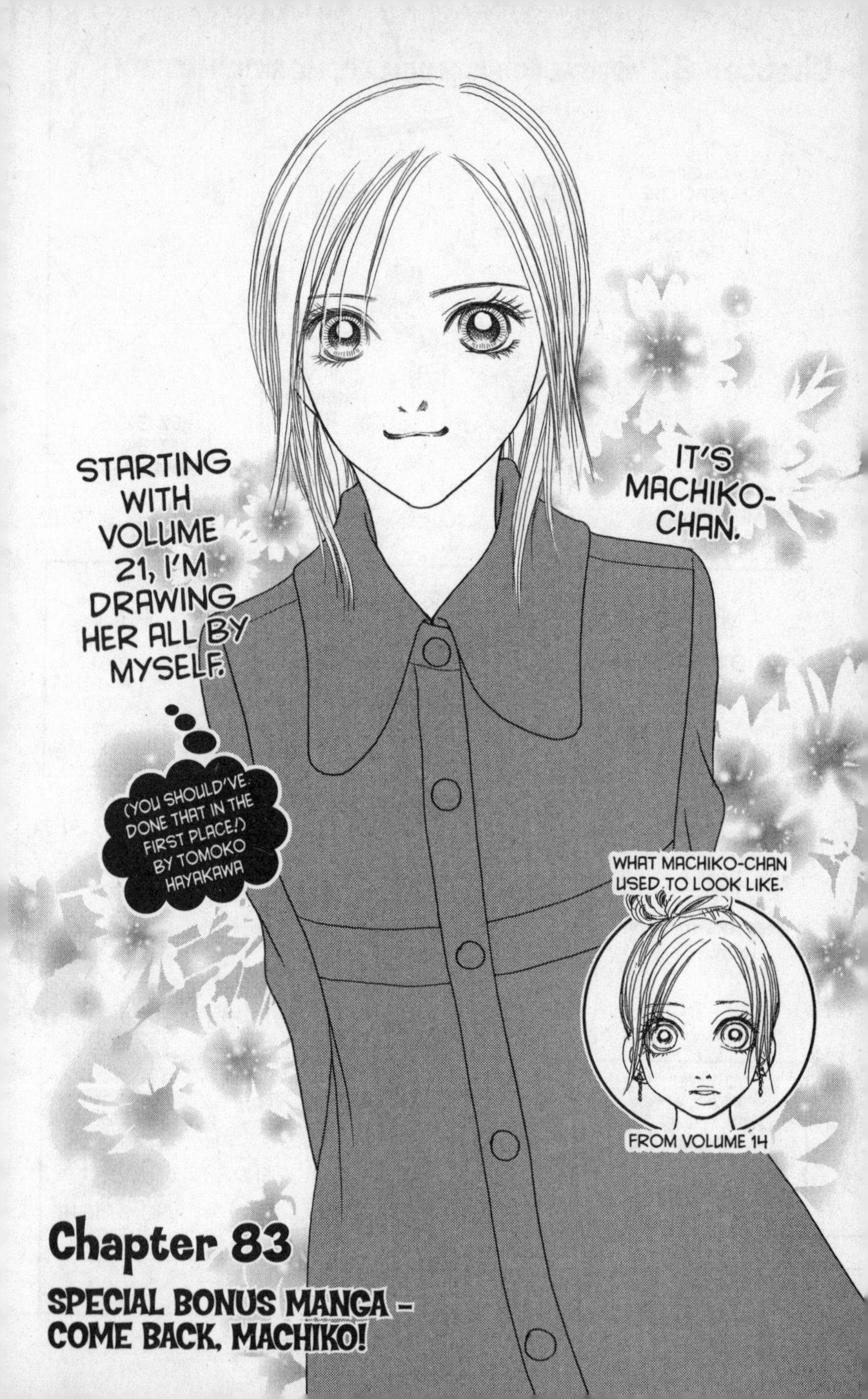
IT'S MACHIKO-CHAN.
STARTING WITH VOLUME 21, I'M DRAWING HER ALL BY MYSELF.
(YOU SHOULD'VE DONE THAT IN THE FIRST PLACE!) BY TOMOKO HAYAKAWA
WHAT MACHIKO-CHAN USED TO LOOK LIKE.
FROM VOLUME 14

Chapter 83

SPECIAL BONUS MANGA – COME BACK, MACHIKO!

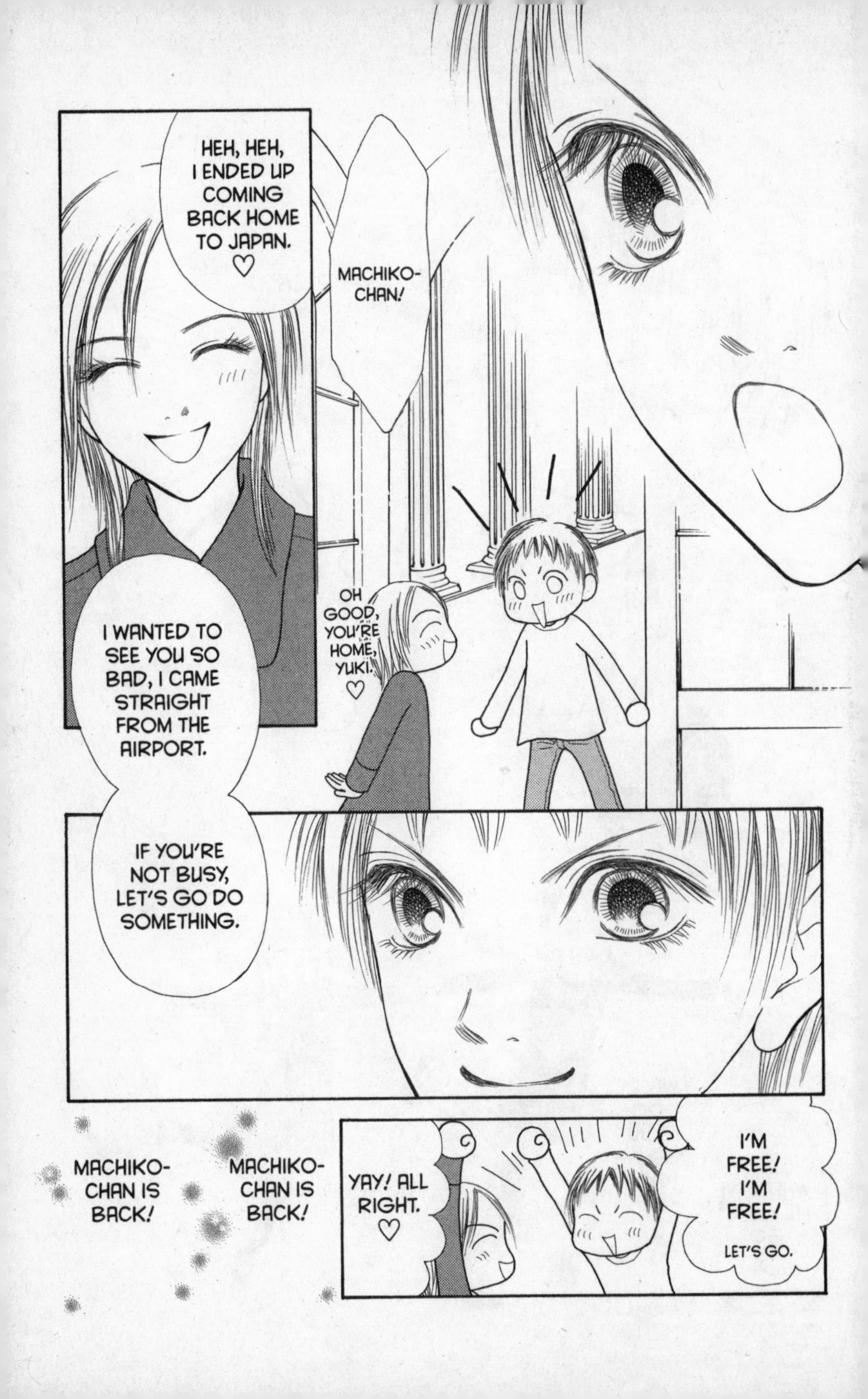
MACHIKO-CHAN!
OH GOOD, YOU'RE HOME, YUKI. ♡
HEH, HEH, I ENDED UP COMING BACK HOME TO JAPAN. ♡
I WANTED TO SEE YOU SO BAD, I CAME STRAIGHT FROM THE AIRPORT.
IF YOU'RE NOT BUSY, LET'S GO DO SOMETHING.
I'M FREE! I'M FREE!
LET'S GO.
YAY! ALL RIGHT. ♡
MACHIKO-CHAN IS BACK!
MACHIKO-CHAN IS BACK!

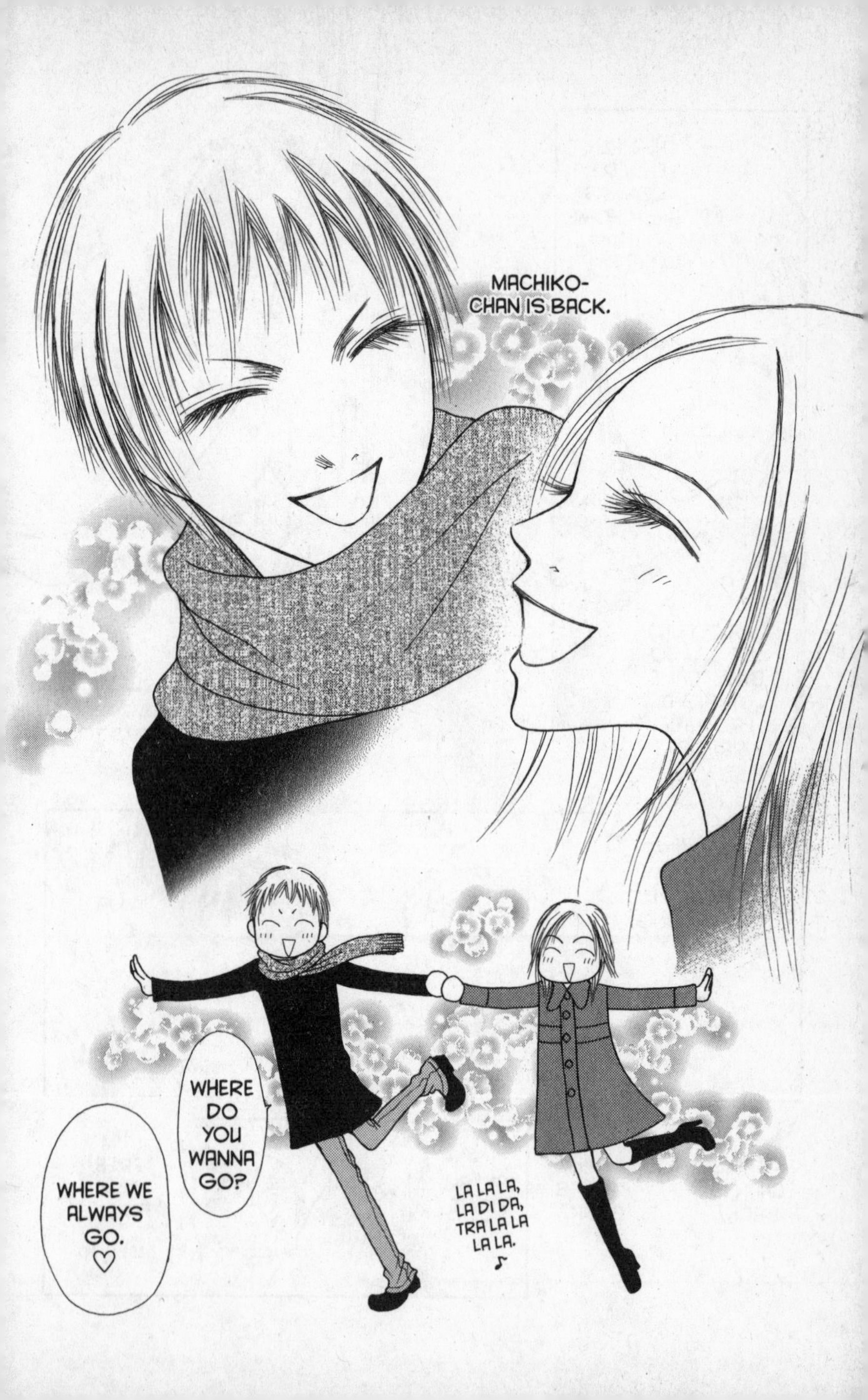
MACHIKO-CHAN IS BACK.
LA LA LA, LA DI DA, TRA LA LA LA LA. ♪
WHERE DO YOU WANNA GO?
WHERE WE ALWAYS GO. ♡

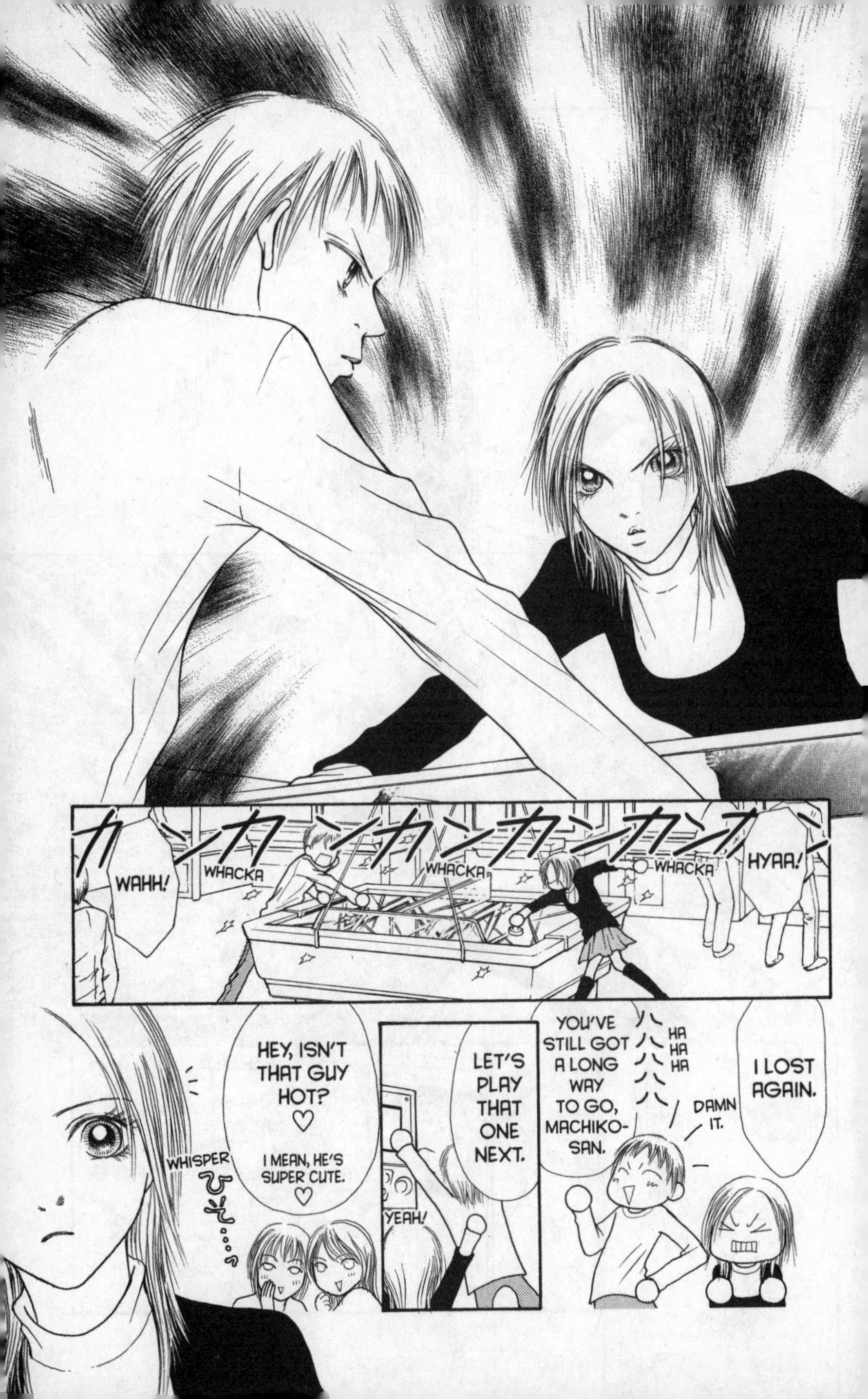
HYAA!
WHACKA
WHACKA
WHACKA
WAHH!
I LOST AGAIN.
DAMN IT.
HA HA HA
ハハハ
YOU'VE STILL GOT A LONG WAY TO GO, MACHIKO-SAN.
LET'S PLAY THAT ONE NEXT.
YEAH!
HEY, ISN'T THAT GUY HOT? ♡
I MEAN, HE'S SUPER CUTE. ♡
WHISPER
ひそ…

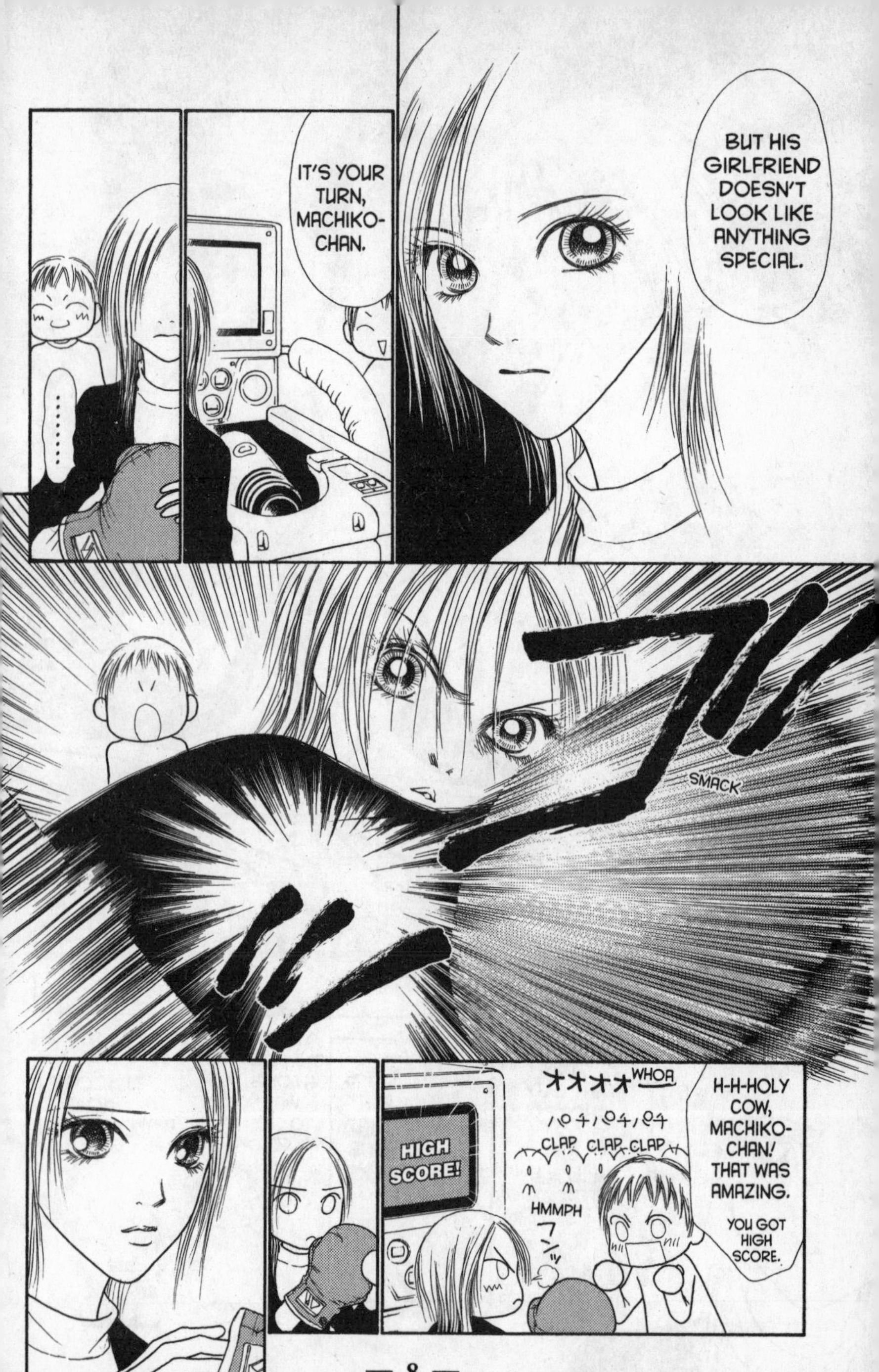

BUT HIS GIRLFRIEND DOESN'T LOOK LIKE ANYTHING SPECIAL.
IT'S YOUR TURN, MACHIKO-CHAN.
……
SMACK
オオオオ WHOA
H-H-HOLY COW, MACHIKO-CHAN! THAT WAS AMAZING.
YOU GOT HIGH SCORE.
パチパチパチ CLAP CLAP CLAP
HMMPH フンッ
HIGH SCORE!

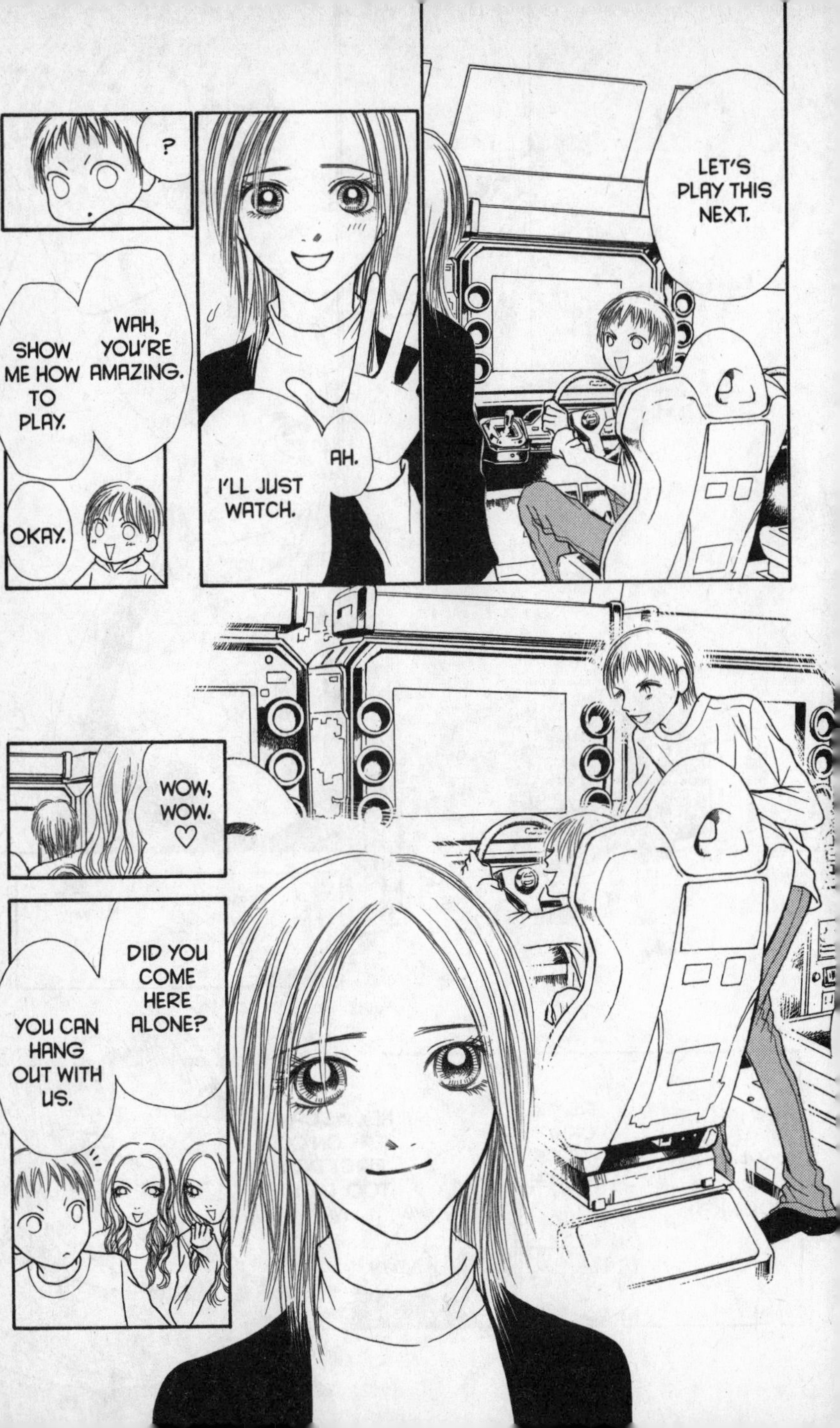
LET'S PLAY THIS NEXT.
AH.
I'LL JUST WATCH.
?
WAH, YOU'RE AMAZING.
SHOW ME HOW TO PLAY.
OKAY.
WOW, WOW. ♥
DID YOU COME HERE ALONE?
YOU CAN HANG OUT WITH US.

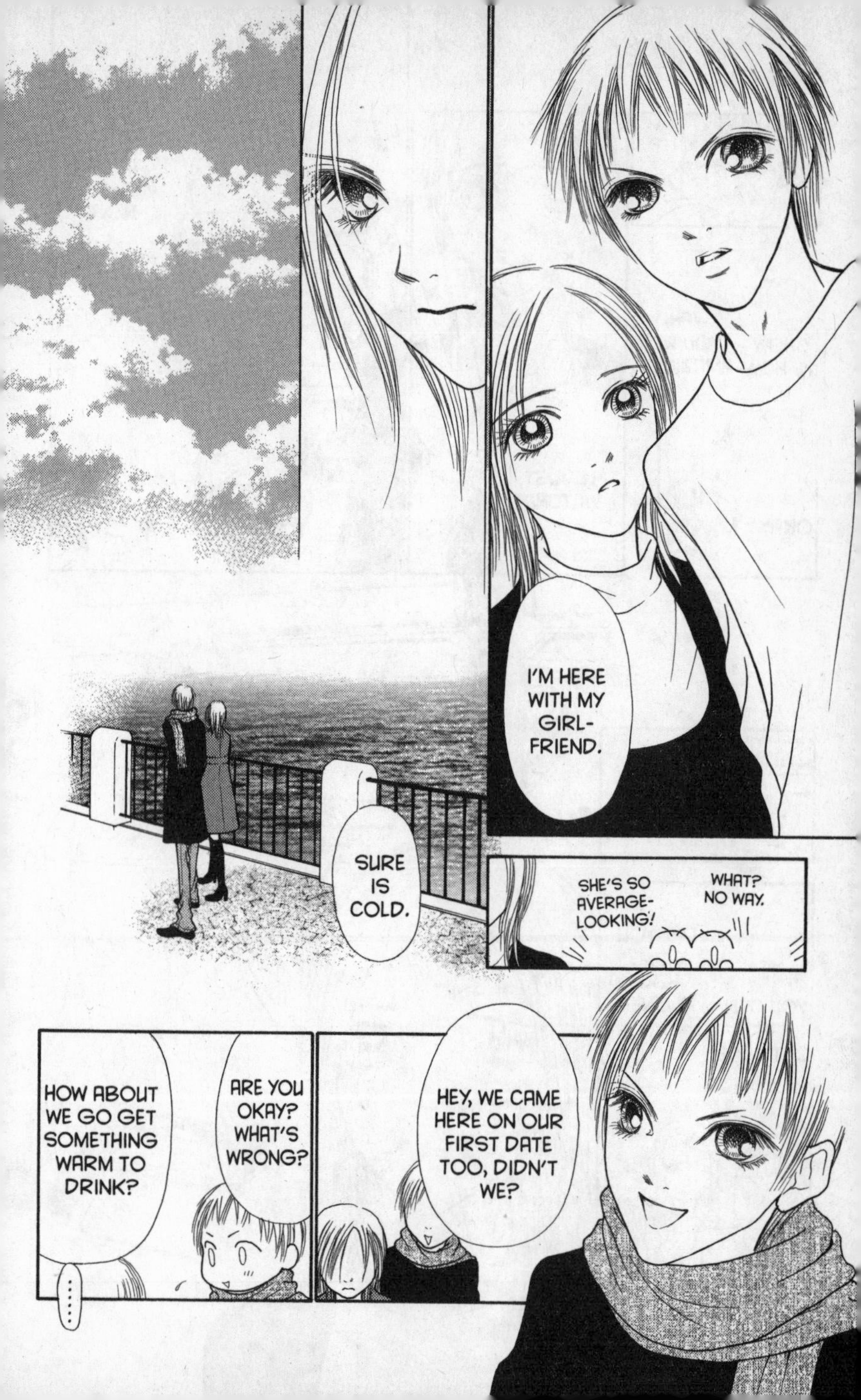
I'M HERE WITH MY GIRL-FRIEND.
WHAT? NO WAY.
SHE'S SO AVERAGE-LOOKING!
SURE IS COLD.
HEY, WE CAME HERE ON OUR FIRST DATE TOO, DIDN'T WE?
ARE YOU OKAY? WHAT'S WRONG?
HOW ABOUT WE GO GET SOMETHING WARM TO DRINK?
……

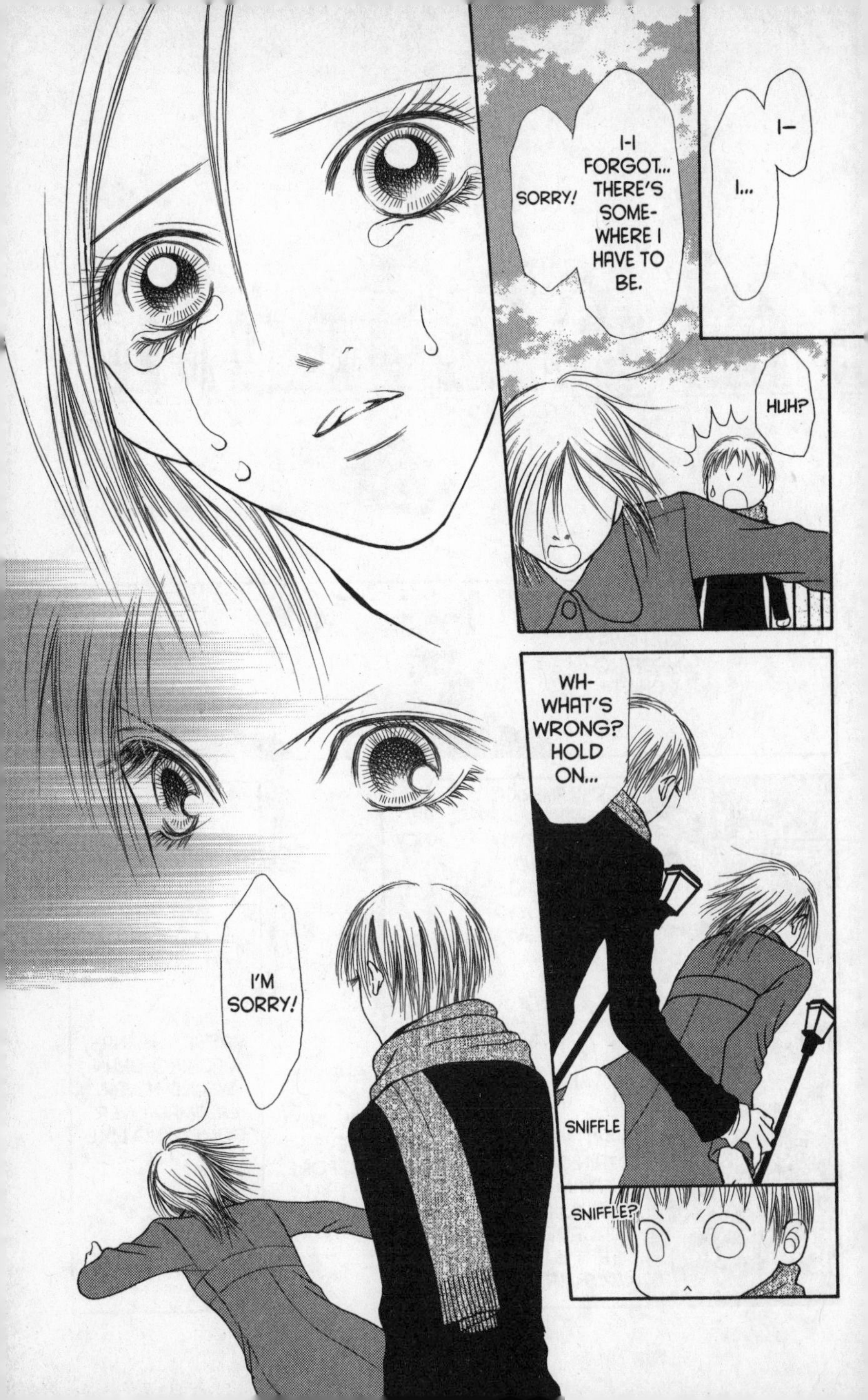
I—
I...
I-I FORGOT... THERE'S SOME-WHERE I HAVE TO BE.
SORRY!
HUH?
WH-WHAT'S WRONG? HOLD ON...
SNIFFLE
SNIFFLE?
I'M SORRY!

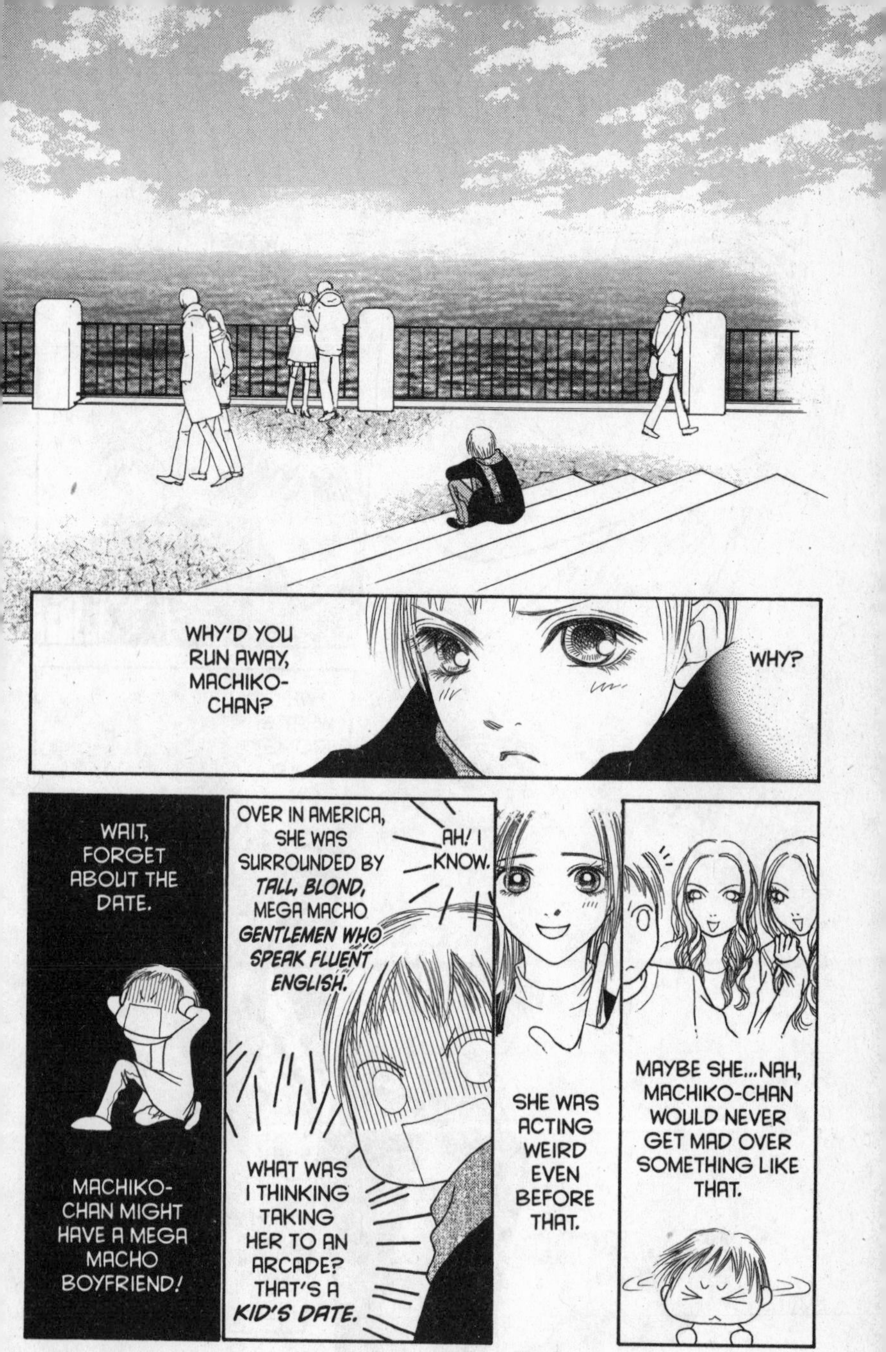
WHY'D YOU RUN AWAY, MACHIKO-CHAN?
WHY?
MAYBE SHE...NAH, MACHIKO-CHAN WOULD NEVER GET MAD OVER SOMETHING LIKE THAT.
SHE WAS ACTING WEIRD EVEN BEFORE THAT.
AH! I KNOW.
OVER IN AMERICA, SHE WAS SURROUNDED BY TALL, BLOND, MEGA MACHO GENTLEMEN WHO SPEAK FLUENT ENGLISH.
WHAT WAS I THINKING TAKING HER TO AN ARCADE? THAT'S A KID'S DATE.
WAIT, FORGET ABOUT THE DATE.
MACHIKO-CHAN MIGHT HAVE A MEGA MACHO BOYFRIEND!

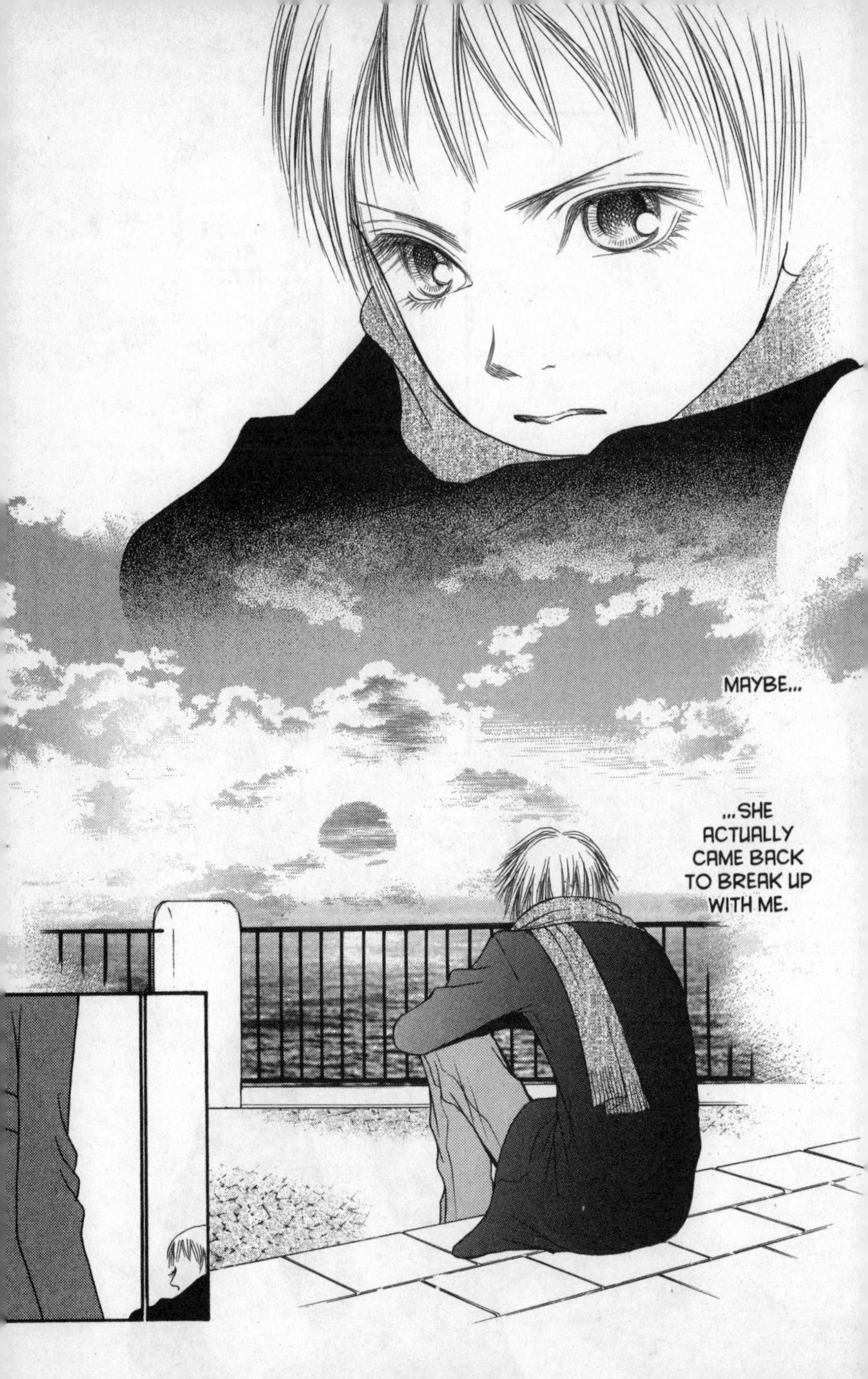

MAYBE...
...SHE ACTUALLY CAME BACK TO BREAK UP WITH ME.

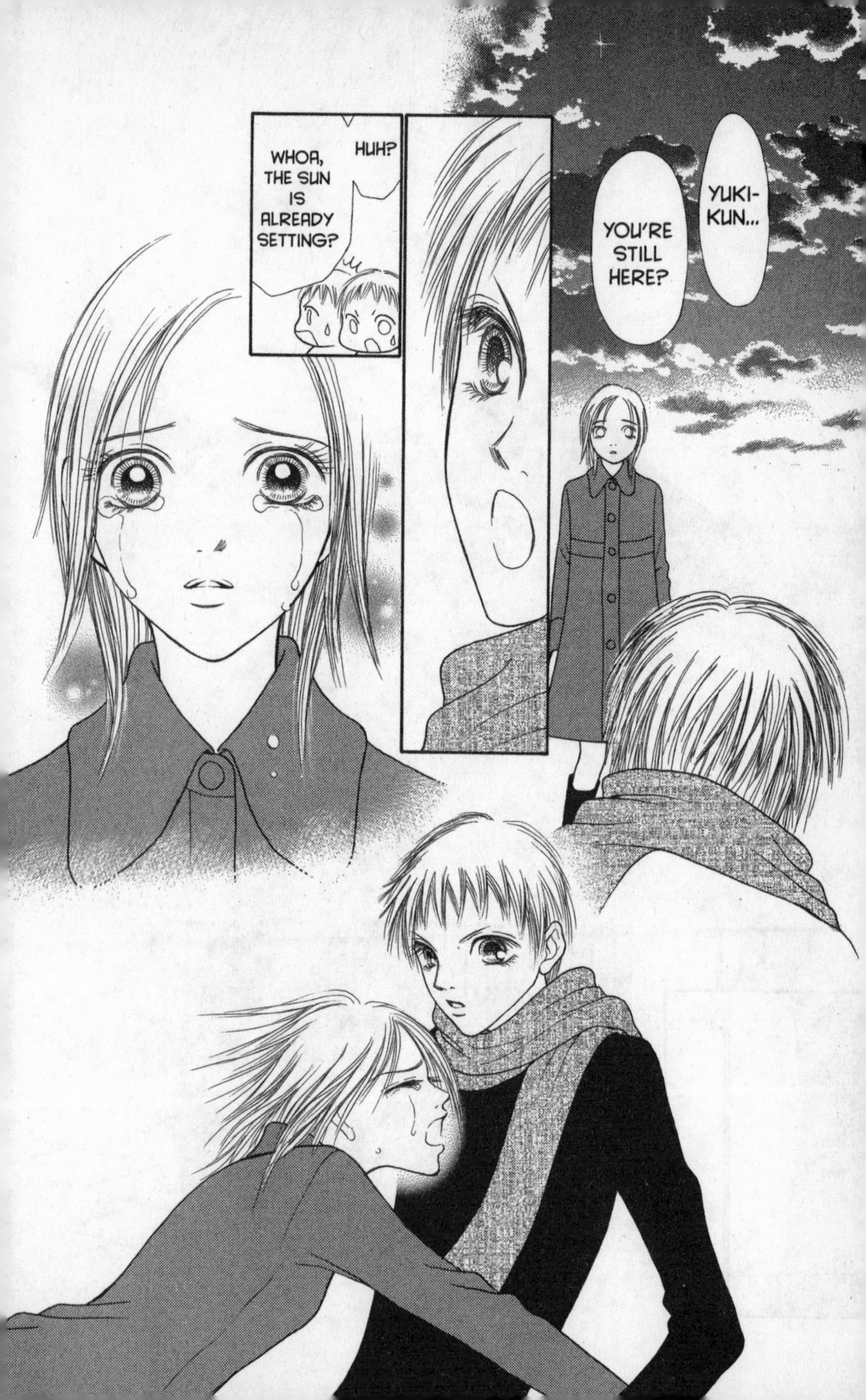
YUKI-KUN...
YOU'RE STILL HERE?
HUH?
WHOA, THE SUN IS ALREADY SETTING?

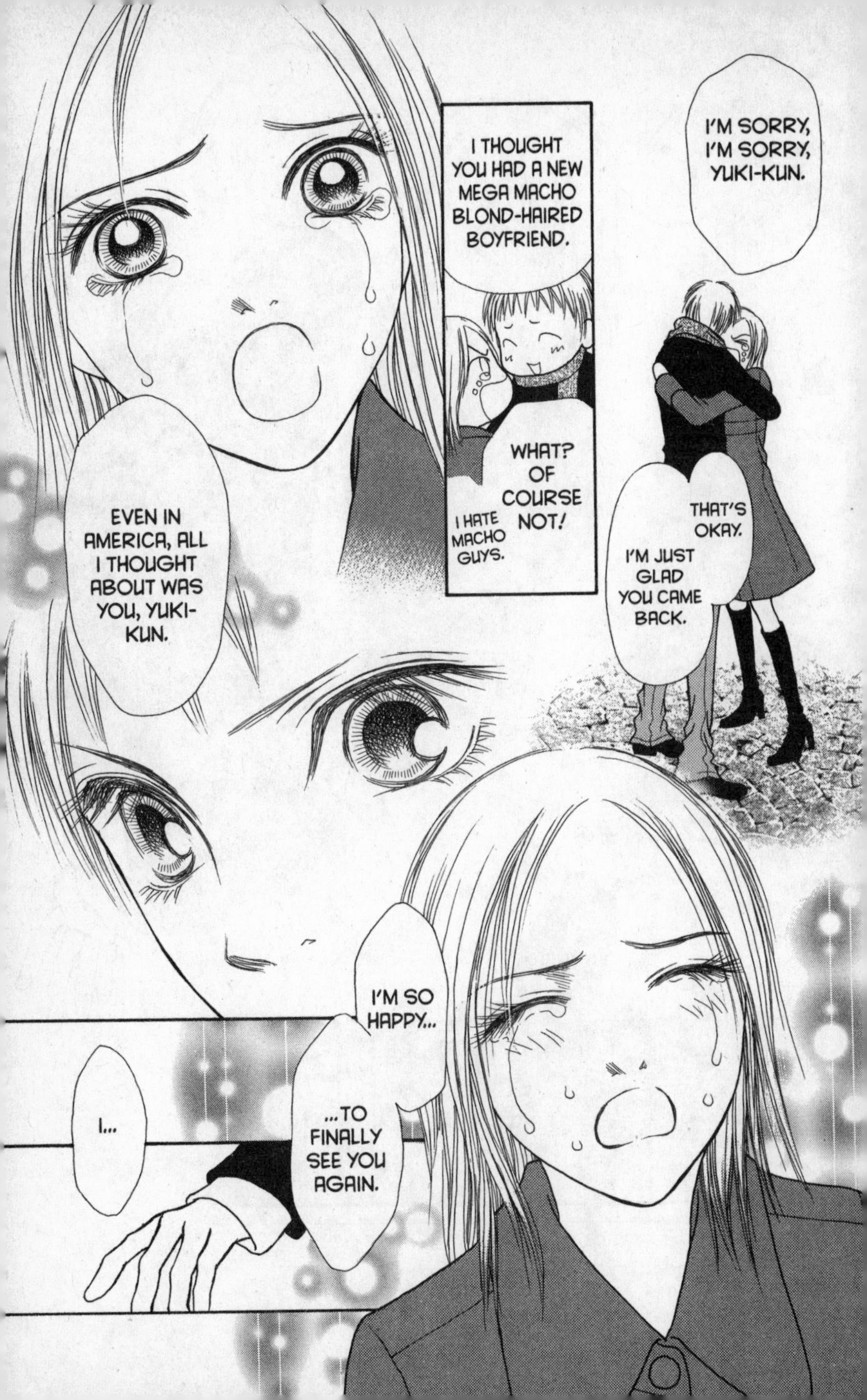
I'M SORRY, I'M SORRY, YUKI-KUN.
THAT'S OKAY.
I'M JUST GLAD YOU CAME BACK.
I THOUGHT YOU HAD A NEW MEGA MACHO BLOND-HAIRED BOYFRIEND.
WHAT? OF COURSE NOT!
I HATE MACHO GUYS.
EVEN IN AMERICA, ALL I THOUGHT ABOUT WAS YOU, YUKI-KUN.
I'M SO HAPPY...
...TO FINALLY SEE YOU AGAIN.
I...

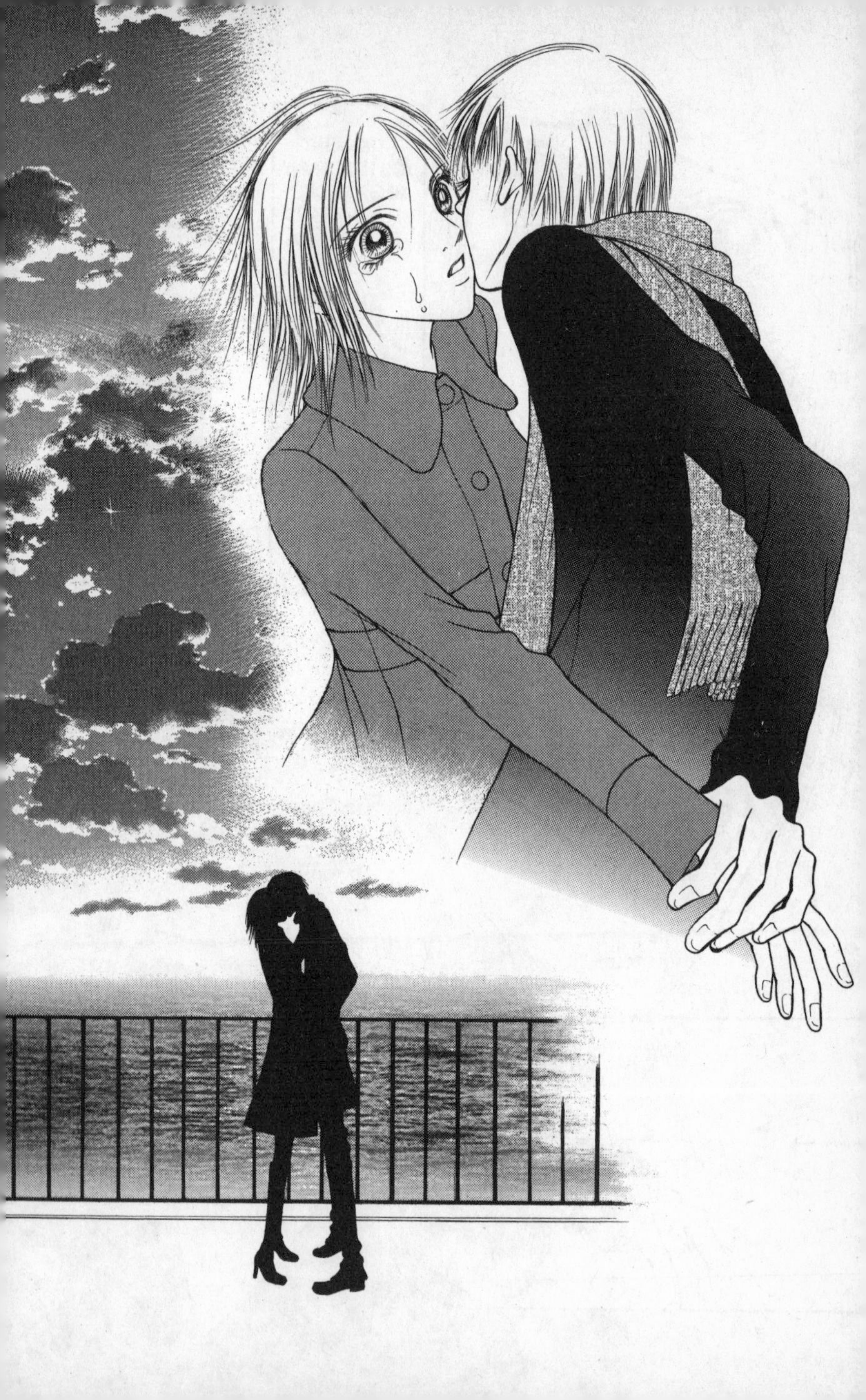

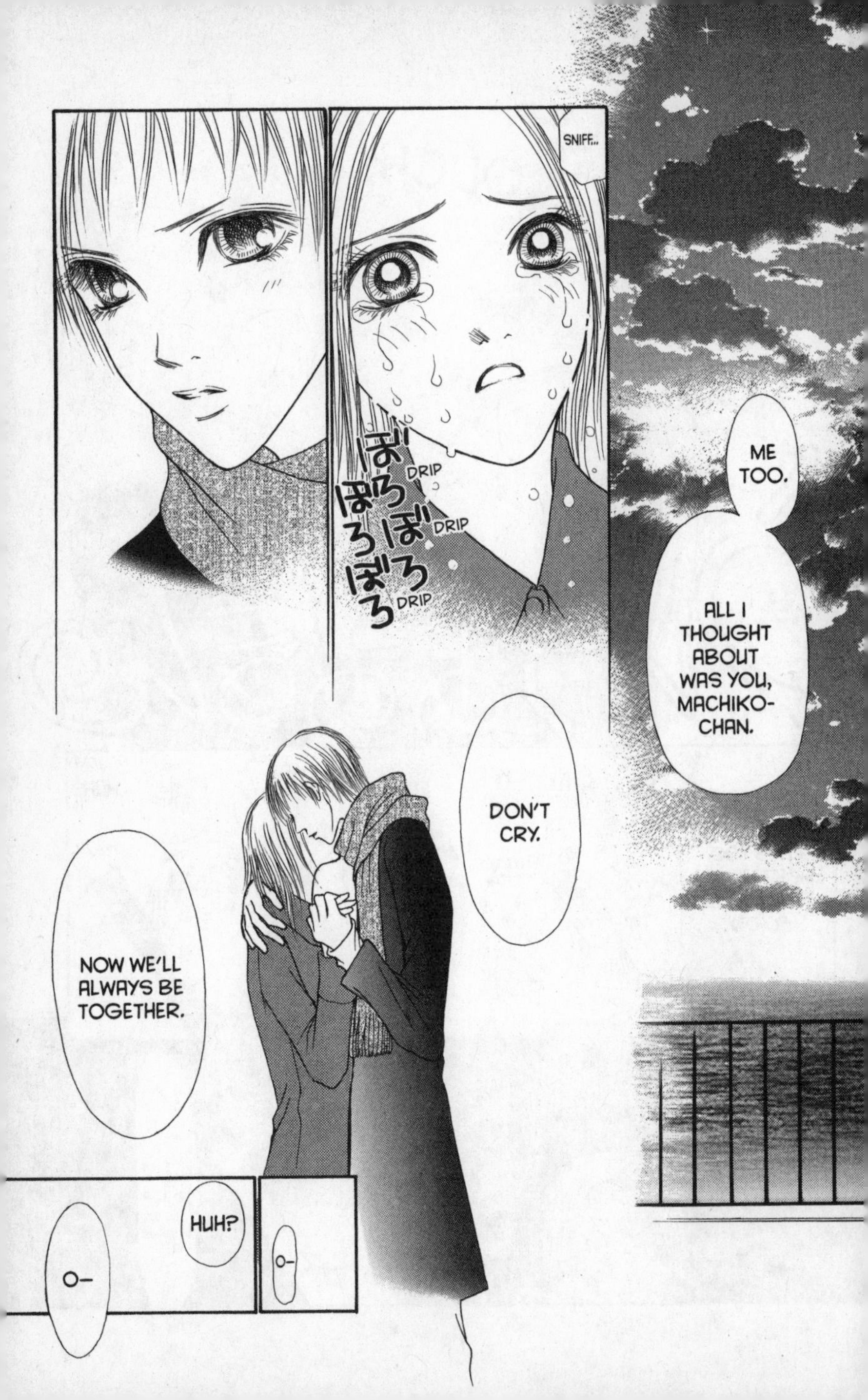
SNIFF...
ぼろぼろぼろ
DRIP
DRIP
DRIP
ぼろぼろぼろ
ME TOO.
ALL I THOUGHT ABOUT WAS YOU, MACHIKO-CHAN.
DON'T CRY.
NOW WE'LL ALWAYS BE TOGETHER.
O–
HUH?
O–

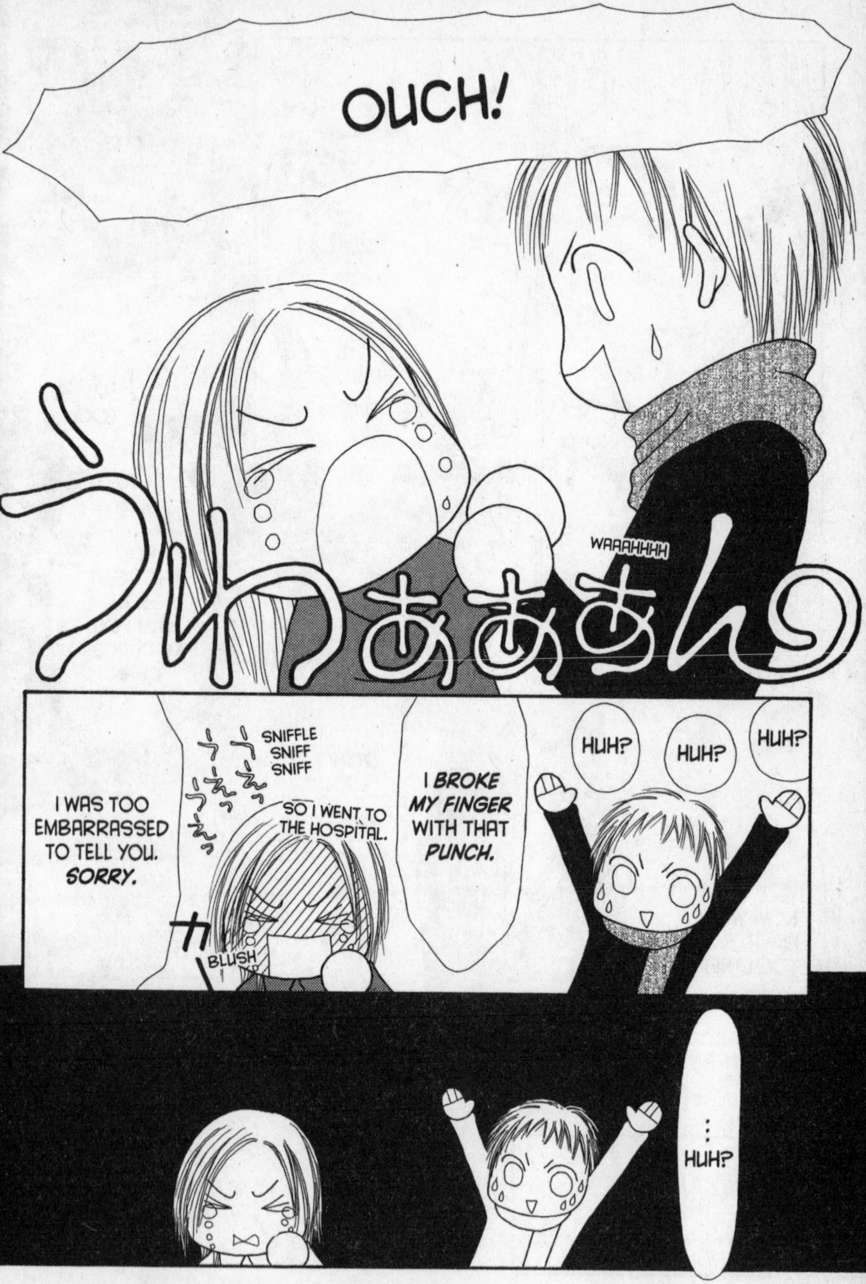
OUCH!
うわあああん
WAAAHHHH
HUH?
HUH?
HUH?
I BROKE MY FINGER WITH THAT PUNCH.
SO I WENT TO THE HOSPITAL.
SNIFFLE SNIFF SNIFF
I WAS TOO EMBARRASSED TO TELL YOU. SORRY.
カ
BLUSH
... HUH?

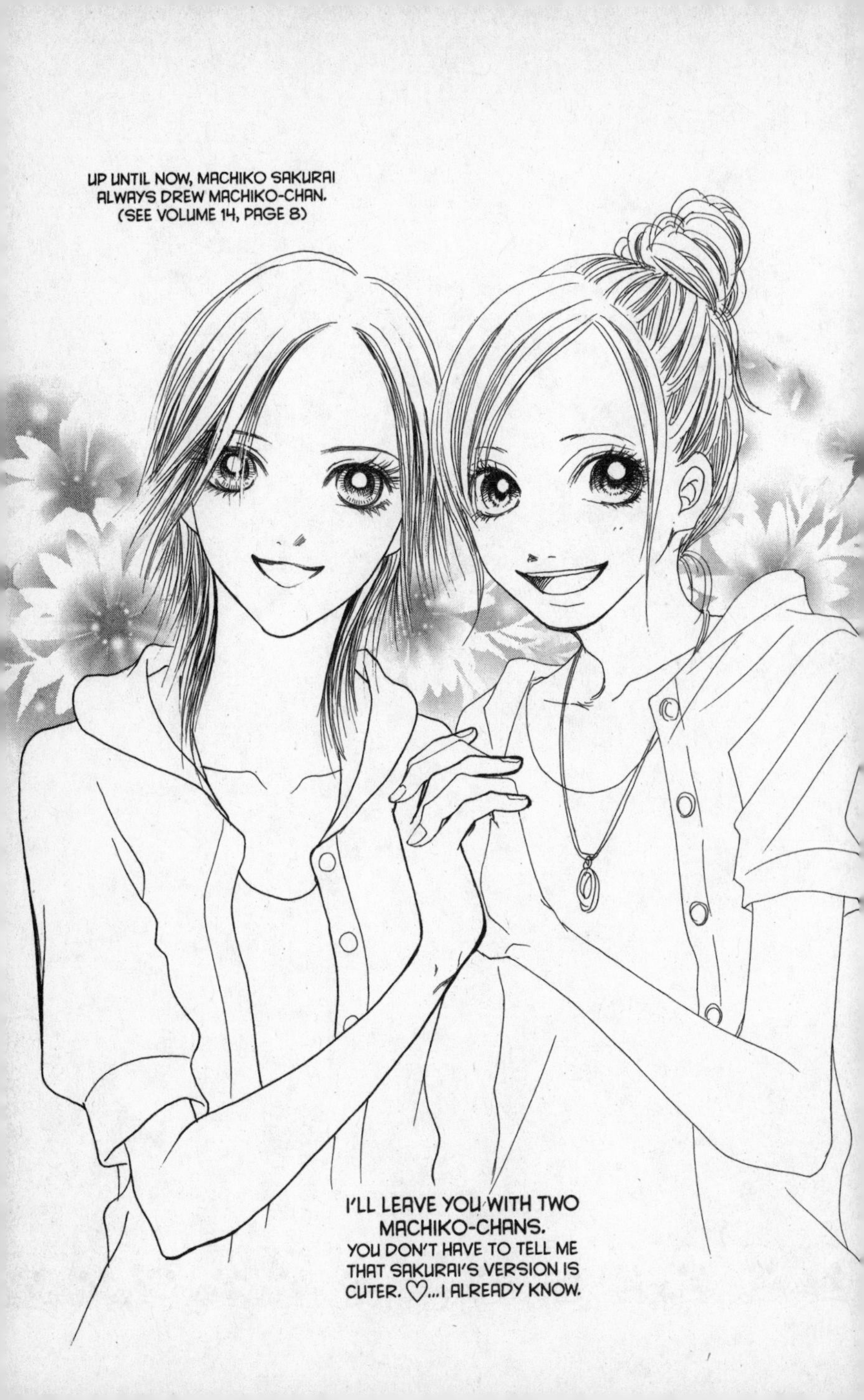
UP UNTIL NOW, MACHIKO SAKURAI ALWAYS DREW MACHIKO-CHAN. (SEE VOLUME 14, PAGE 8)
I'LL LEAVE YOU WITH TWO MACHIKO-CHANS. YOU DON'T HAVE TO TELL ME THAT SAKURAI'S VERSION IS CUTER. ♡...I ALREADY KNOW.

Chapter 84

THE LEGEND OF KYOHEI BEGINS ANEW

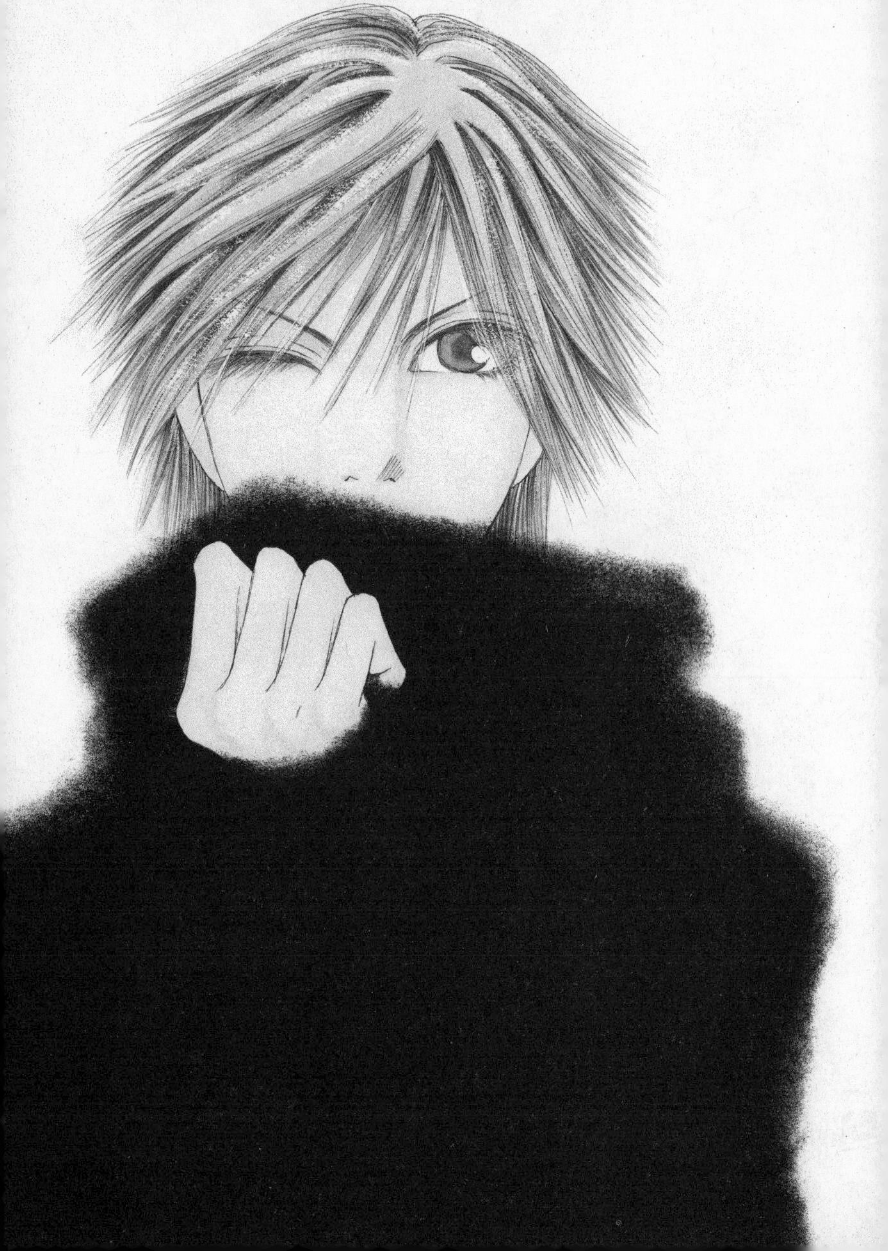

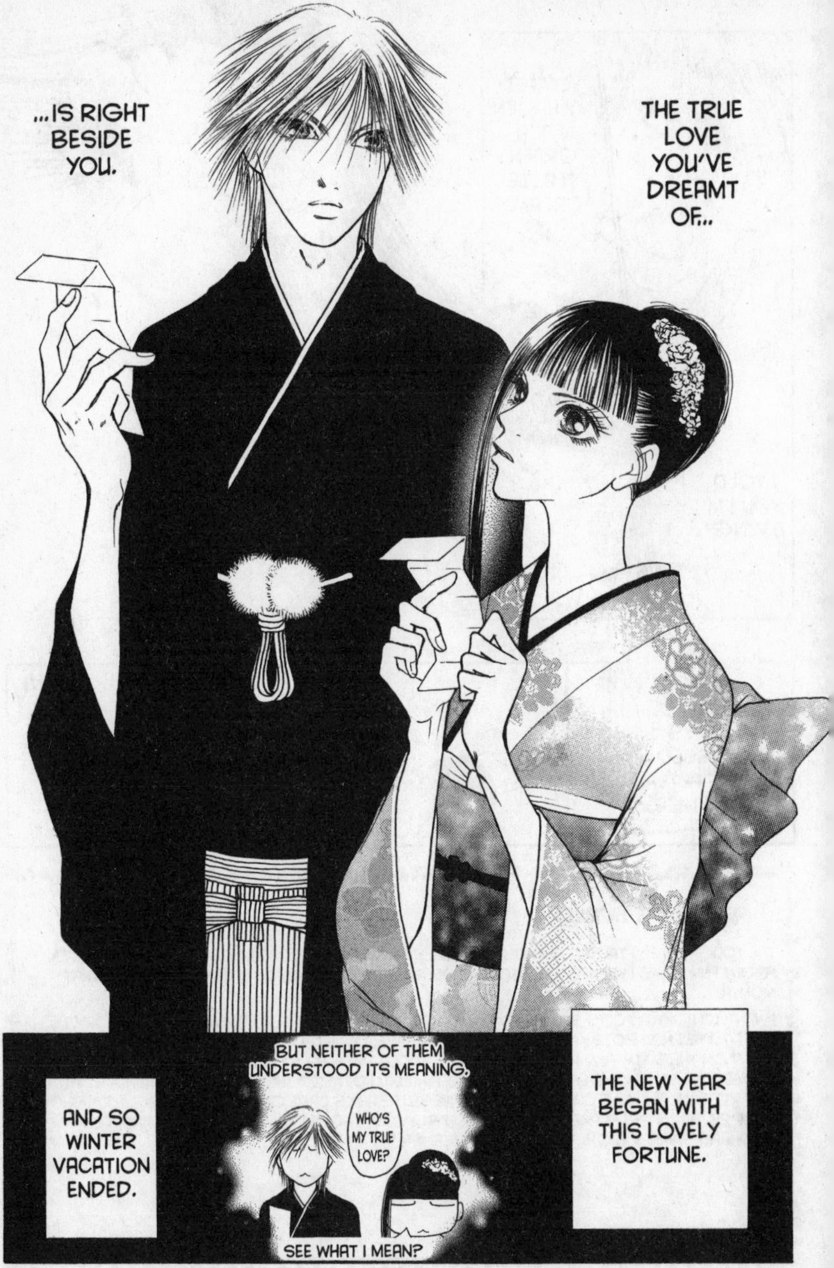
THE TRUE LOVE YOU'VE DREAMT OF...
...IS RIGHT BESIDE YOU.
THE NEW YEAR BEGAN WITH THIS LOVELY FORTUNE.
BUT NEITHER OF THEM UNDERSTOOD ITS MEANING.
WHO'S MY TRUE LOVE?
SEE WHAT I MEAN?
AND SO WINTER VACATION ENDED.

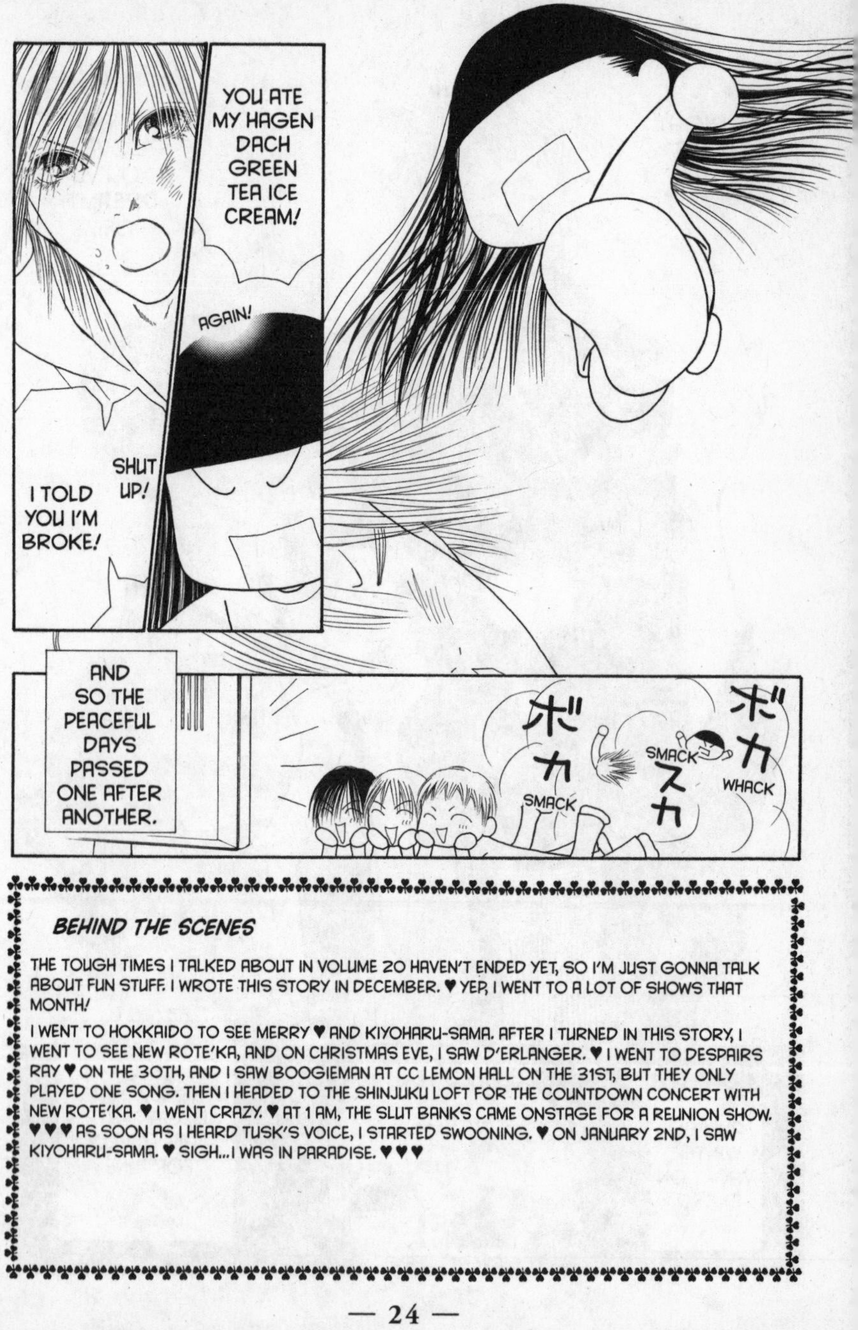
YOU ATE MY HAGEN DACH GREEN TEA ICE CREAM!
AGAIN!
SHUT UP!
I TOLD YOU I'M BROKE!
ボカ
WHACK
スカ
SMACK
ボカ
SMACK
AND SO THE PEACEFUL DAYS PASSED ONE AFTER ANOTHER.

BEHIND THE SCENES

THE TOUGH TIMES I TALKED ABOUT IN VOLUME 20 HAVEN'T ENDED YET, SO I'M JUST GONNA TALK ABOUT FUN STUFF. I WROTE THIS STORY IN DECEMBER. ♥ YEP, I WENT TO A LOT OF SHOWS THAT MONTH!

I WENT TO HOKKAIDO TO SEE MERRY ♥ AND KIYOHARU-SAMA. AFTER I TURNED IN THIS STORY, I WENT TO SEE NEW ROTE'KA, AND ON CHRISTMAS EVE, I SAW D'ERLANGER. ♥ I WENT TO DESPAIRS RAY ♥ ON THE 30TH, AND I SAW BOOGIEMAN AT CC LEMON HALL ON THE 31ST, BUT THEY ONLY PLAYED ONE SONG. THEN I HEADED TO THE SHINJUKU LOFT FOR THE COUNTDOWN CONCERT WITH NEW ROTE'KA. ♥ I WENT CRAZY. ♥ AT 1 AM, THE SLUT BANKS CAME ONSTAGE FOR A REUNION SHOW. ♥ ♥ ♥ AS SOON AS I HEARD TUSK'S VOICE, I STARTED SWOONING. ♥ ON JANUARY 2ND, I SAW KIYOHARU-SAMA. ♥ SIGH...I WAS IN PARADISE. ♥ ♥ ♥

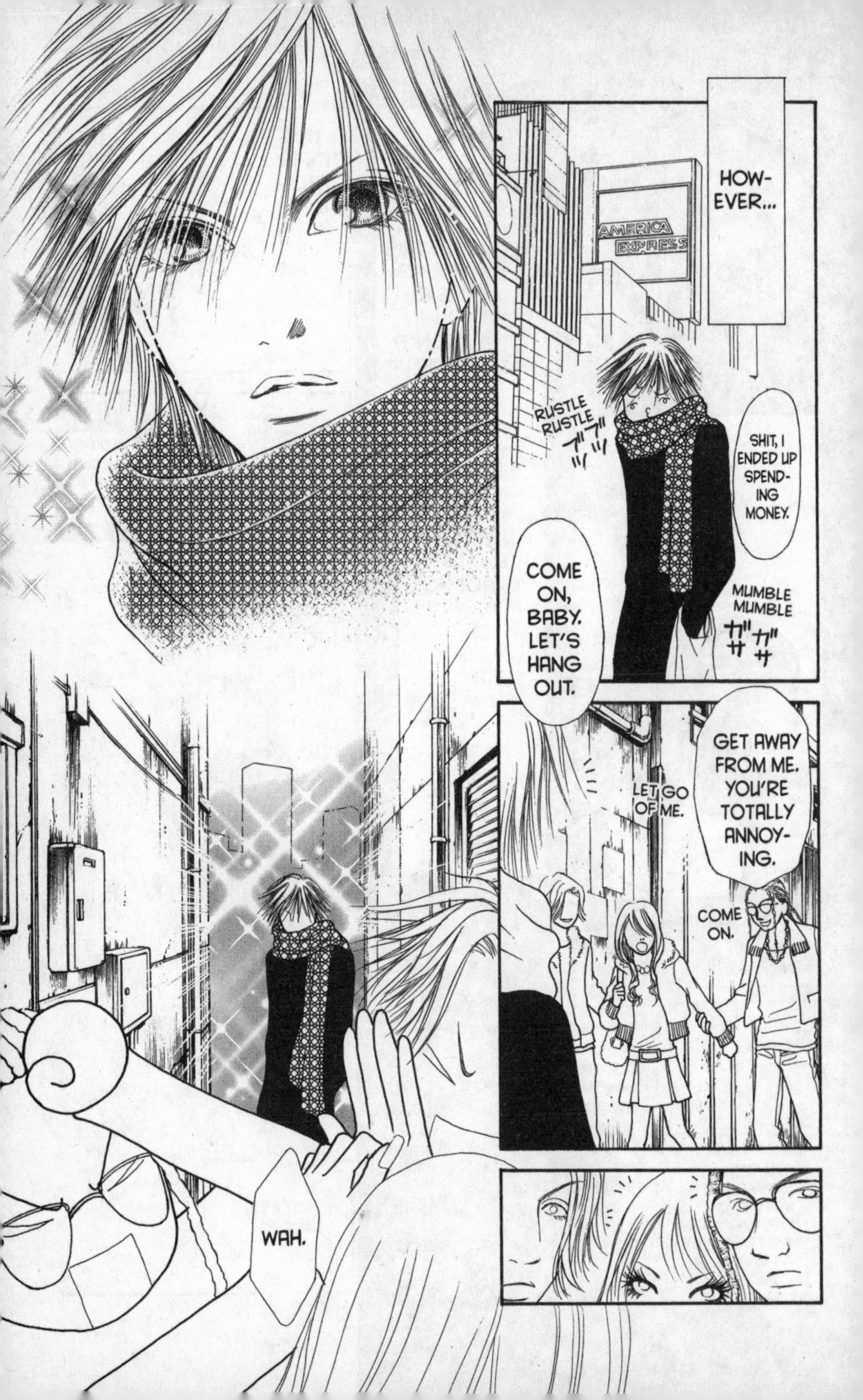
HOW-EVER...
SHIT, I ENDED UP SPEND-ING MONEY.
RUSTLE RUSTLE
MUMBLE MUMBLE
COME ON, BABY. LET'S HANG OUT.
GET AWAY FROM ME. YOU'RE TOTALLY ANNOY-ING.
LET GO OF ME.
COME ON.
WAH.

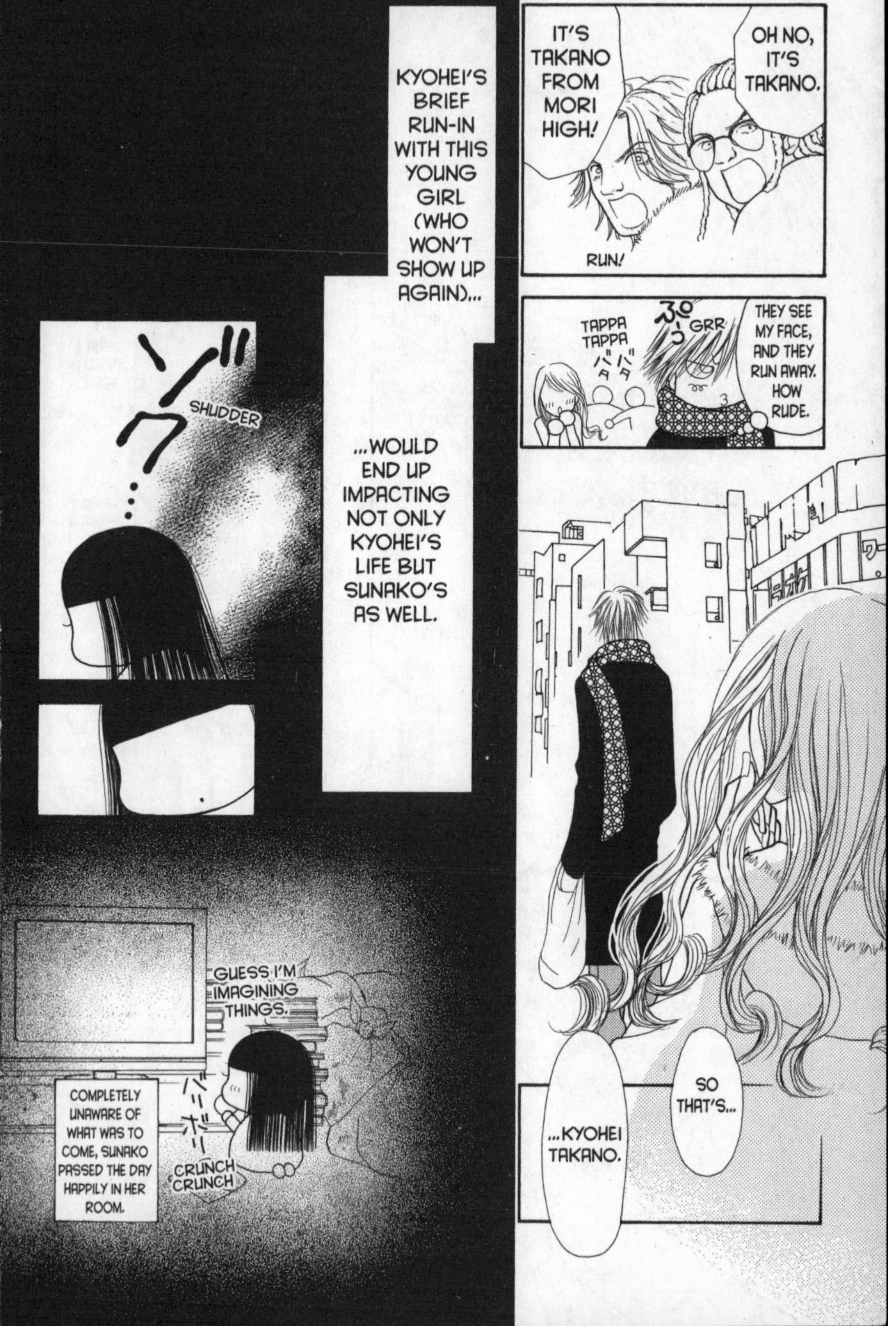
OH NO, IT'S TAKANO.
IT'S TAKANO FROM MORI HIGH!
RUN!
THEY SEE MY FACE, AND THEY RUN AWAY. HOW RUDE.
GRR
TAPPA TAPPA
SO THAT'S...
...KYOHEI TAKANO.
KYOHEI'S BRIEF RUN-IN WITH THIS YOUNG GIRL (WHO WON'T SHOW UP AGAIN)...
...WOULD END UP IMPACTING NOT ONLY KYOHEI'S LIFE BUT SUNAKO'S AS WELL.
SHUDDER
GUESS I'M IMAGINING THINGS.
CRUNCH CRUNCH
COMPLETELY UNAWARE OF WHAT WAS TO COME, SUNAKO PASSED THE DAY HAPPILY IN HER ROOM.

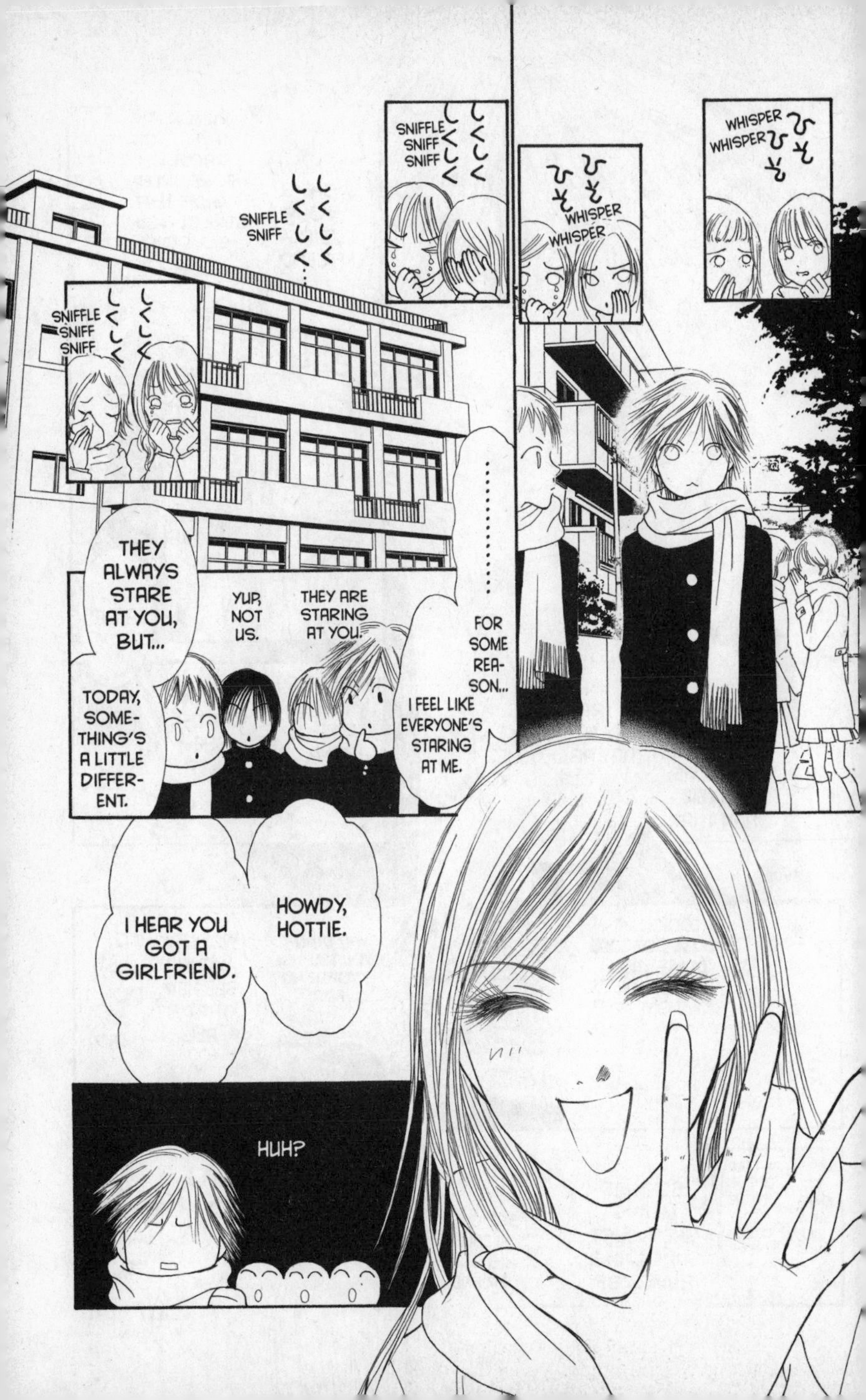
WHISPER WHISPER
ひそひそ
ひそひそ
WHISPER WHISPER
SNIFFLE SNIFF SNIFF
しくしくしくしく
SNIFFLE SNIFF
しくしくしくしく…
SNIFFLE SNIFF SNIFF
しくしくしくしく
……
FOR SOME REA-SON...
I FEEL LIKE EVERYONE'S STARING AT ME.
THEY ARE STARING AT YOU.
YUP, NOT US.
THEY ALWAYS STARE AT YOU, BUT...
TODAY, SOME-THING'S A LITTLE DIFFER-ENT.
HOWDY, HOTTIE.
I HEAR YOU GOT A GIRLFRIEND.
HUH?

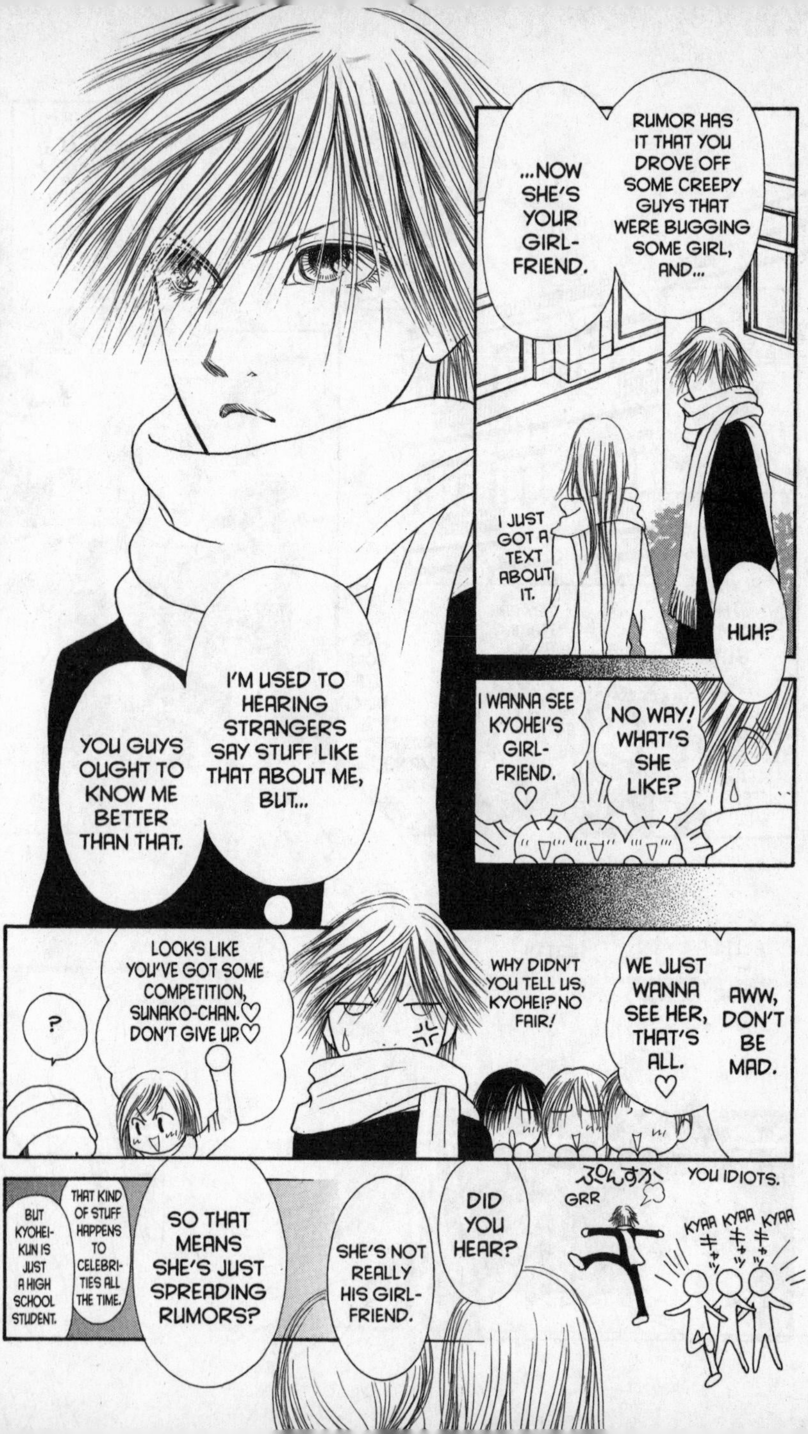
RUMOR HAS IT THAT YOU DROVE OFF SOME CREEPY GUYS THAT WERE BUGGING SOME GIRL, AND...
...NOW SHE'S YOUR GIRL-FRIEND.
I JUST GOT A TEXT ABOUT IT.
HUH?
NO WAY! WHAT'S SHE LIKE?
I WANNA SEE KYOHEI'S GIRL-FRIEND. ♡
I'M USED TO HEARING STRANGERS SAY STUFF LIKE THAT ABOUT ME, BUT...
YOU GUYS OUGHT TO KNOW ME BETTER THAN THAT.
AWW, DON'T BE MAD.
WE JUST WANNA SEE HER, THAT'S ALL. ♡
WHY DIDN'T YOU TELL US, KYOHEI? NO FAIR!
LOOKS LIKE YOU'VE GOT SOME COMPETITION, SUNAKO-CHAN.♡ DON'T GIVE UP.♡
?
YOU IDIOTS.
ぷんすか
GRR
KYAA キャッ
KYAA キャッ
KYAA キャッ
DID YOU HEAR?
SHE'S NOT REALLY HIS GIRL-FRIEND.
SO THAT MEANS SHE'S JUST SPREADING RUMORS?
THAT KIND OF STUFF HAPPENS TO CELEBRI-TIES ALL THE TIME.
BUT KYOHEI-KUN IS JUST A HIGH SCHOOL STUDENT.

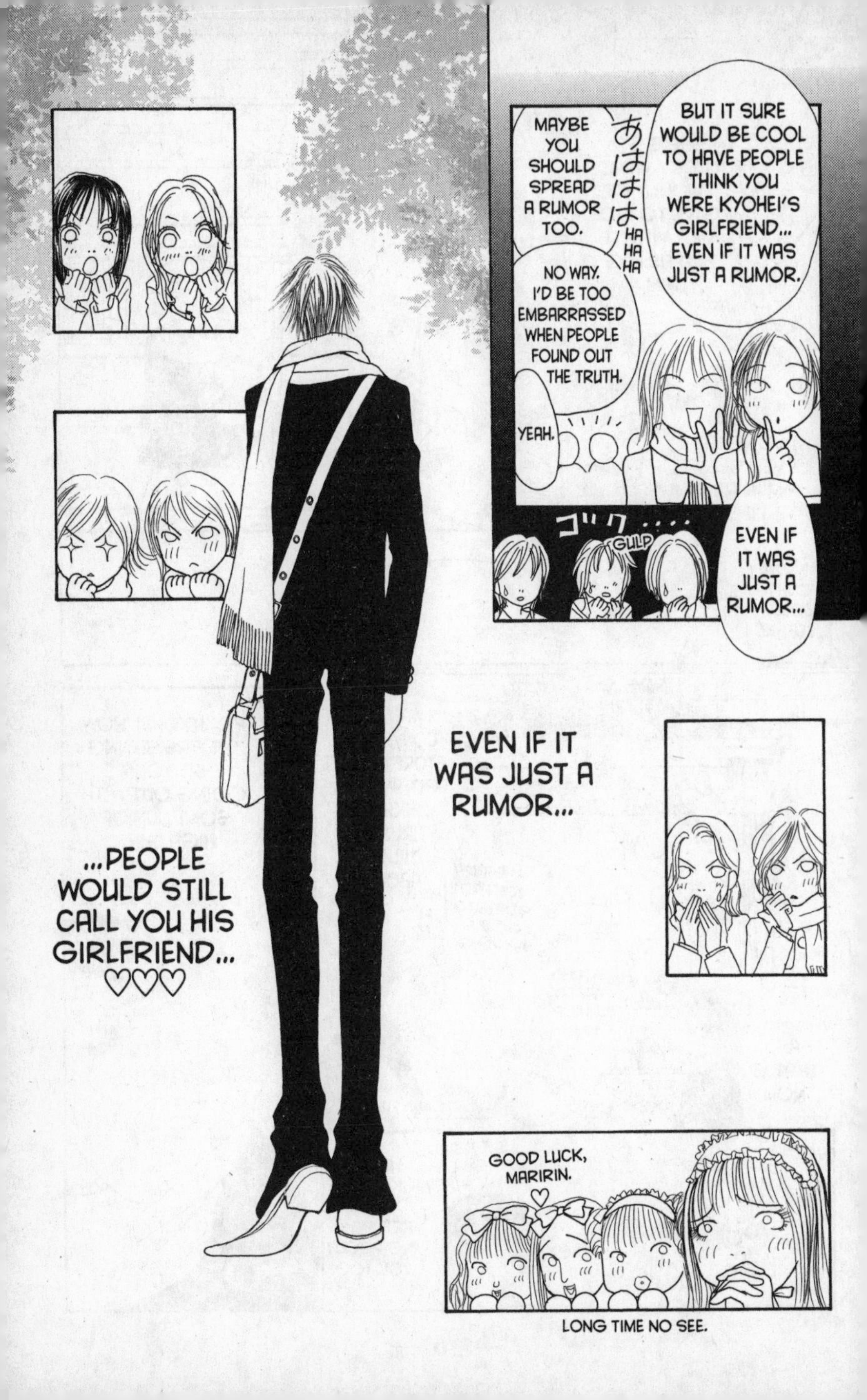
BUT IT SURE WOULD BE COOL TO HAVE PEOPLE THINK YOU WERE KYOHEI'S GIRLFRIEND... EVEN IF IT WAS JUST A RUMOR.
MAYBE YOU SHOULD SPREAD A RUMOR TOO.
あははは HA HA HA
NO WAY. I'D BE TOO EMBARRASSED WHEN PEOPLE FOUND OUT THE TRUTH.
YEAH.
EVEN IF IT WAS JUST A RUMOR...
ゴック GULP
EVEN IF IT WAS JUST A RUMOR...
...PEOPLE WOULD STILL CALL YOU HIS GIRLFRIEND... ♡♡♡
GOOD LUCK, MARIRIN. ♡
LONG TIME NO SEE.

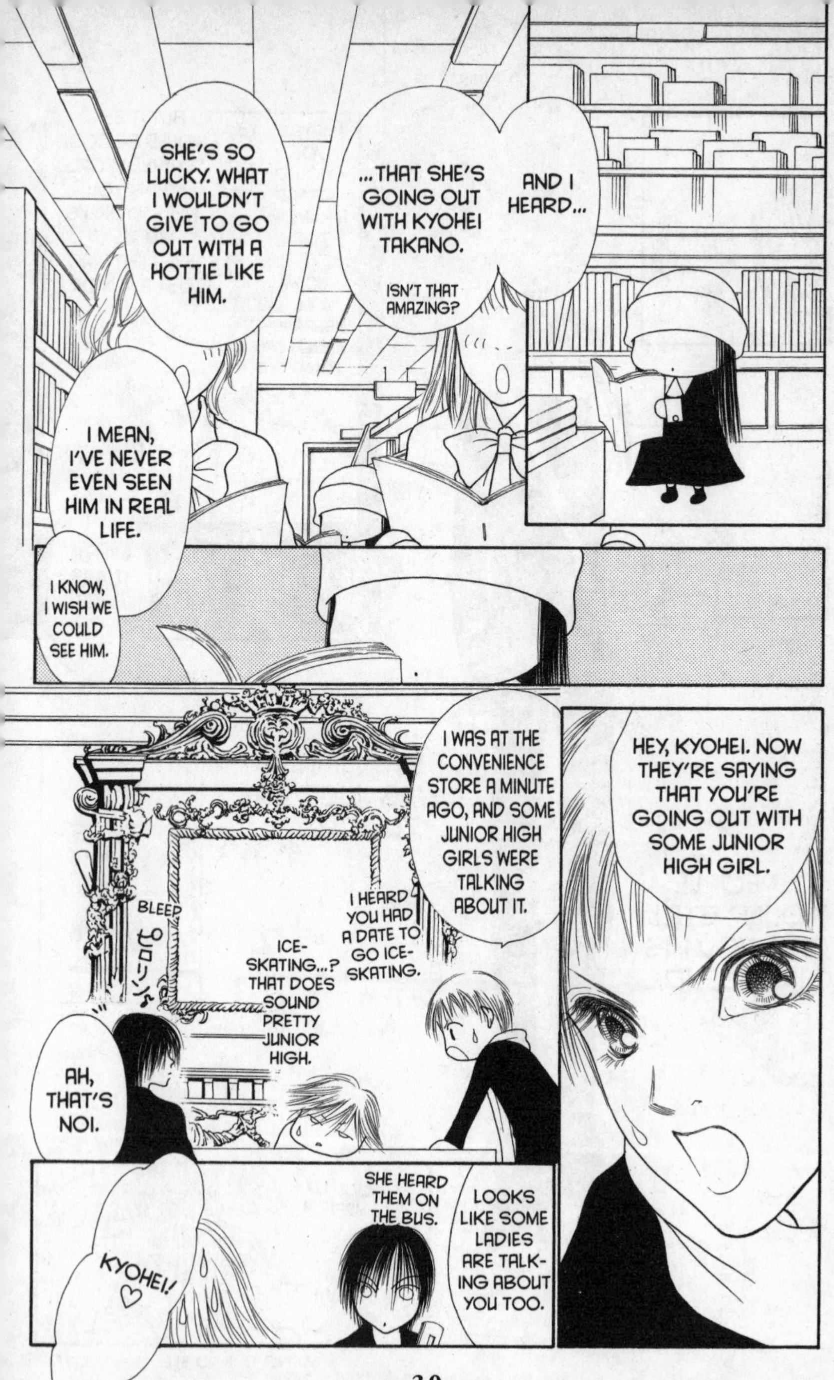
AND I HEARD...
...THAT SHE'S GOING OUT WITH KYOHEI TAKANO.
ISN'T THAT AMAZING?
SHE'S SO LUCKY. WHAT I WOULDN'T GIVE TO GO OUT WITH A HOTTIE LIKE HIM.
I MEAN, I'VE NEVER EVEN SEEN HIM IN REAL LIFE.
I KNOW, I WISH WE COULD SEE HIM.
HEY, KYOHEI. NOW THEY'RE SAYING THAT YOU'RE GOING OUT WITH SOME JUNIOR HIGH GIRL.
I WAS AT THE CONVENIENCE STORE A MINUTE AGO, AND SOME JUNIOR HIGH GIRLS WERE TALKING ABOUT IT.
I HEARD YOU HAD A DATE TO GO ICE-SKATING.
ICE-SKATING...? THAT DOES SOUND PRETTY JUNIOR HIGH.
BLEEP
ピロリン♪
AH, THAT'S NOI.
LOOKS LIKE SOME LADIES ARE TALKING ABOUT YOU TOO.
SHE HEARD THEM ON THE BUS.
KYOHEI! ♡

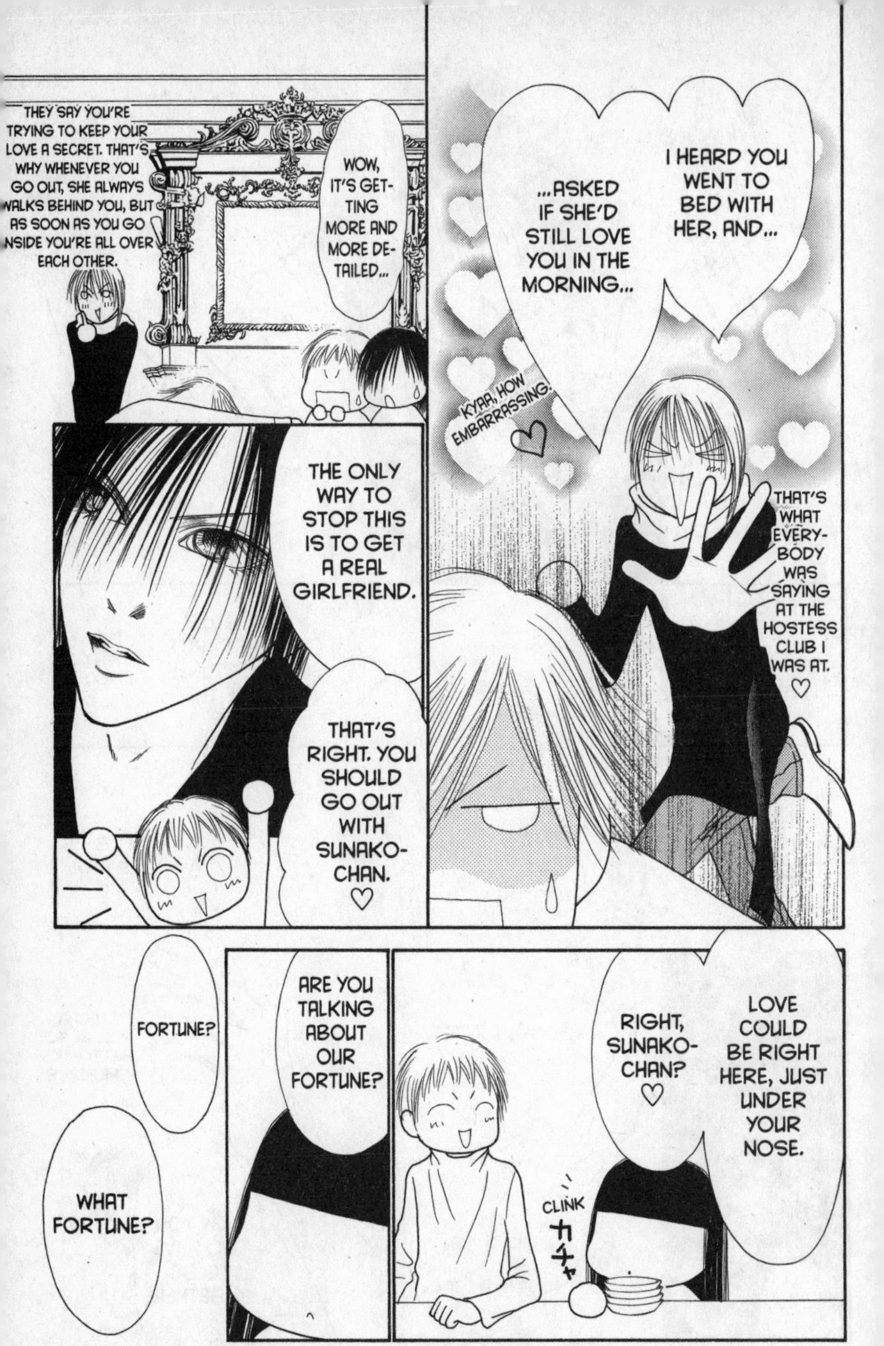
I HEARD YOU WENT TO BED WITH HER, AND...
...ASKED IF SHE'D STILL LOVE YOU IN THE MORNING...
KYAA, HOW EMBARRASSING. ♡
THAT'S WHAT EVERYBODY WAS SAYING AT THE HOSTESS CLUB I WAS AT. ♡
WOW, IT'S GETTING MORE AND MORE DETAILED...
THEY SAY YOU'RE TRYING TO KEEP YOUR LOVE A SECRET. THAT'S WHY WHENEVER YOU GO OUT, SHE ALWAYS WALKS BEHIND YOU, BUT AS SOON AS YOU GO INSIDE YOU'RE ALL OVER EACH OTHER.
THE ONLY WAY TO STOP THIS IS TO GET A REAL GIRLFRIEND.
THAT'S RIGHT. YOU SHOULD GO OUT WITH SUNAKO-CHAN. ♡
LOVE COULD BE RIGHT HERE, JUST UNDER YOUR NOSE.
RIGHT, SUNAKO-CHAN? ♡
CLINK
カチャ
ARE YOU TALKING ABOUT OUR FORTUNE?
FORTUNE?
WHAT FORTUNE?

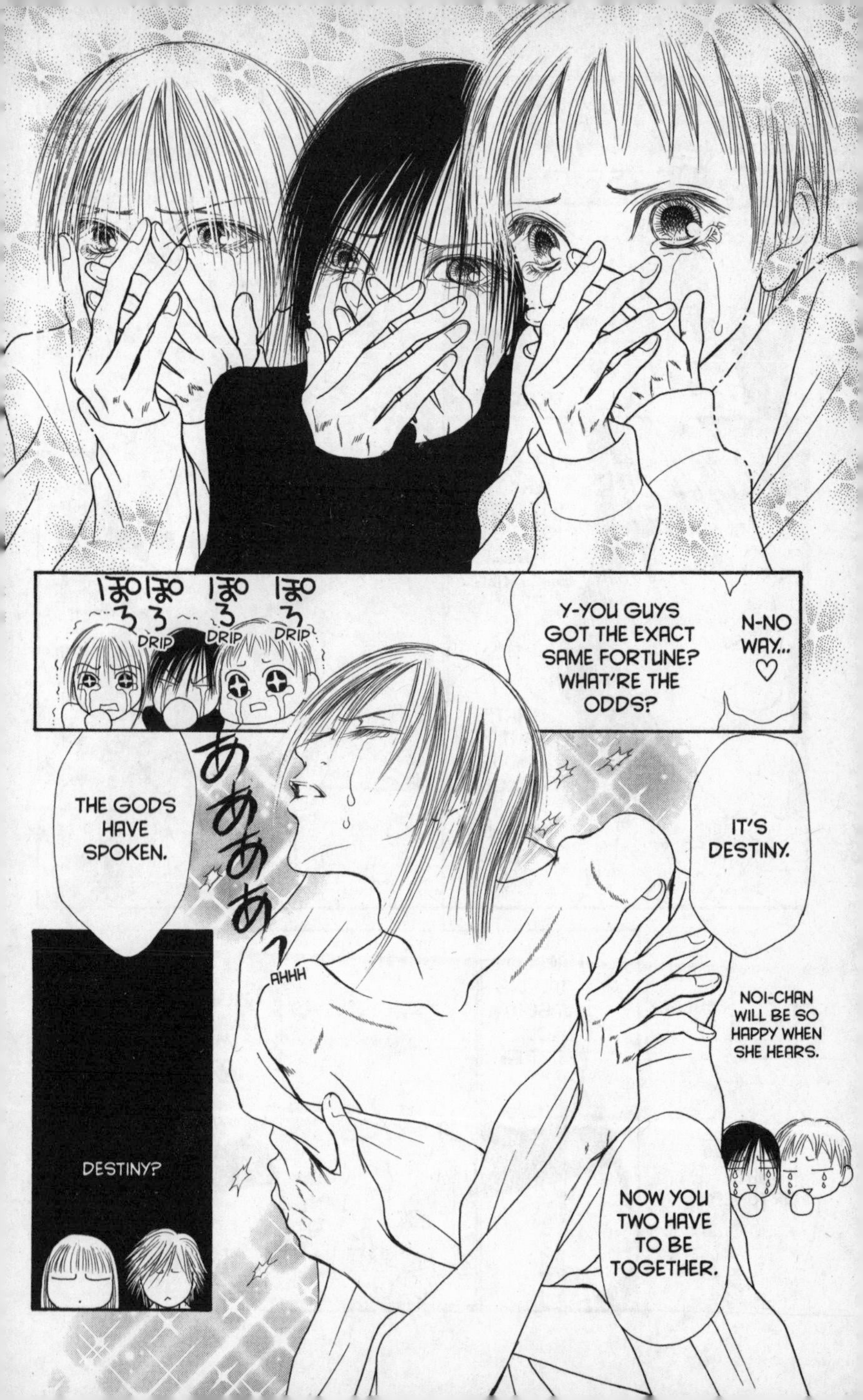
N-NO WAY... ♡
Y-YOU GUYS GOT THE EXACT SAME FORTUNE? WHAT'RE THE ODDS?
ぽろ ぽろ ぽろ ぽろ
DRIP DRIP DRIP
IT'S DESTINY.
THE GODS HAVE SPOKEN.
ああああ
AHHH
NOI-CHAN WILL BE SO HAPPY WHEN SHE HEARS.
NOW YOU TWO HAVE TO BE TOGETHER.
DESTINY?

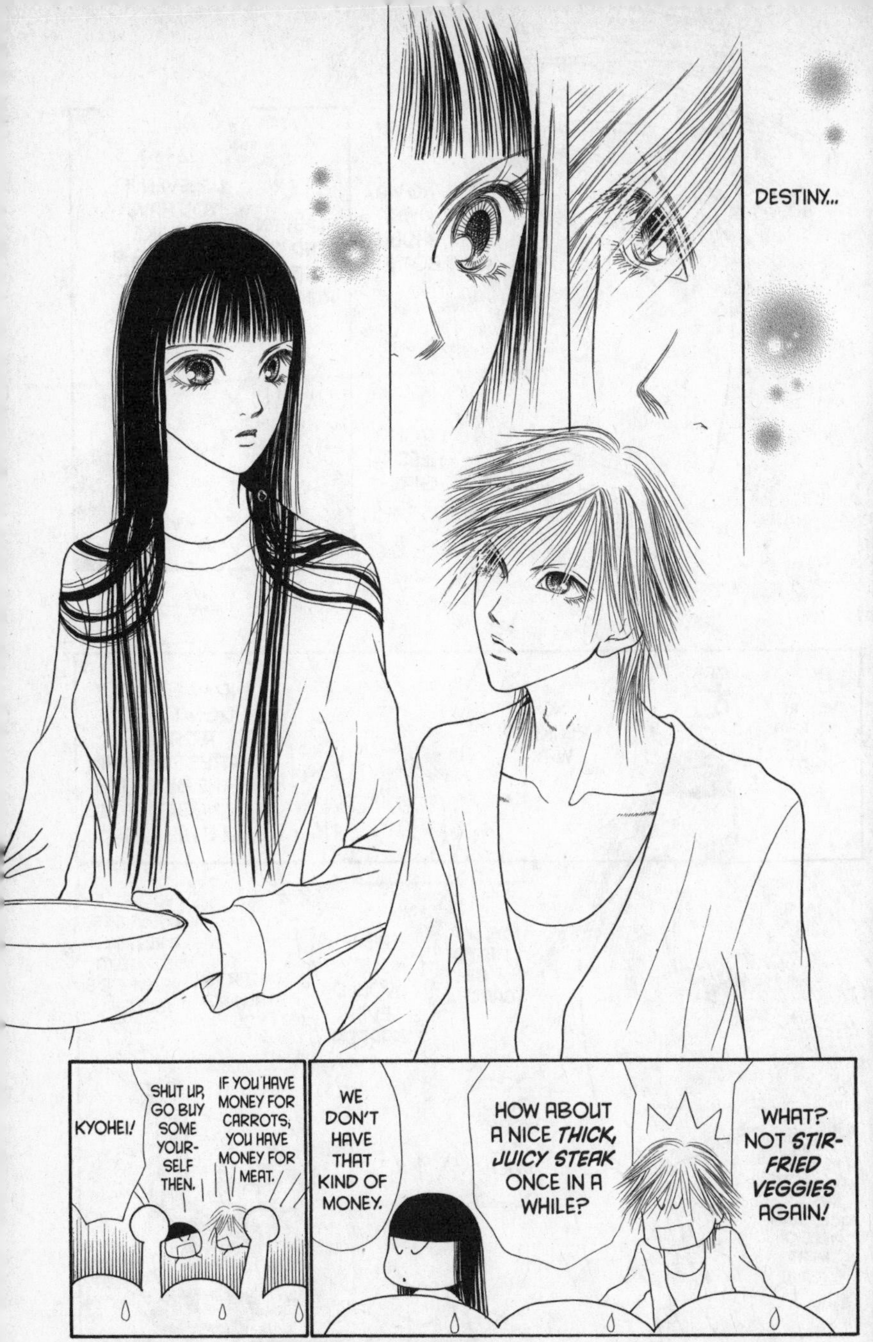
DESTINY...
WHAT? NOT *STIR-FRIED VEGGIES* AGAIN!
HOW ABOUT A NICE *THICK, JUICY STEAK* ONCE IN A WHILE?
WE DON'T HAVE THAT KIND OF MONEY.
IF YOU HAVE MONEY FOR CARROTS, YOU HAVE MONEY FOR MEAT.
SHUT UP, GO BUY SOME YOURSELF THEN.
KYOHEI!

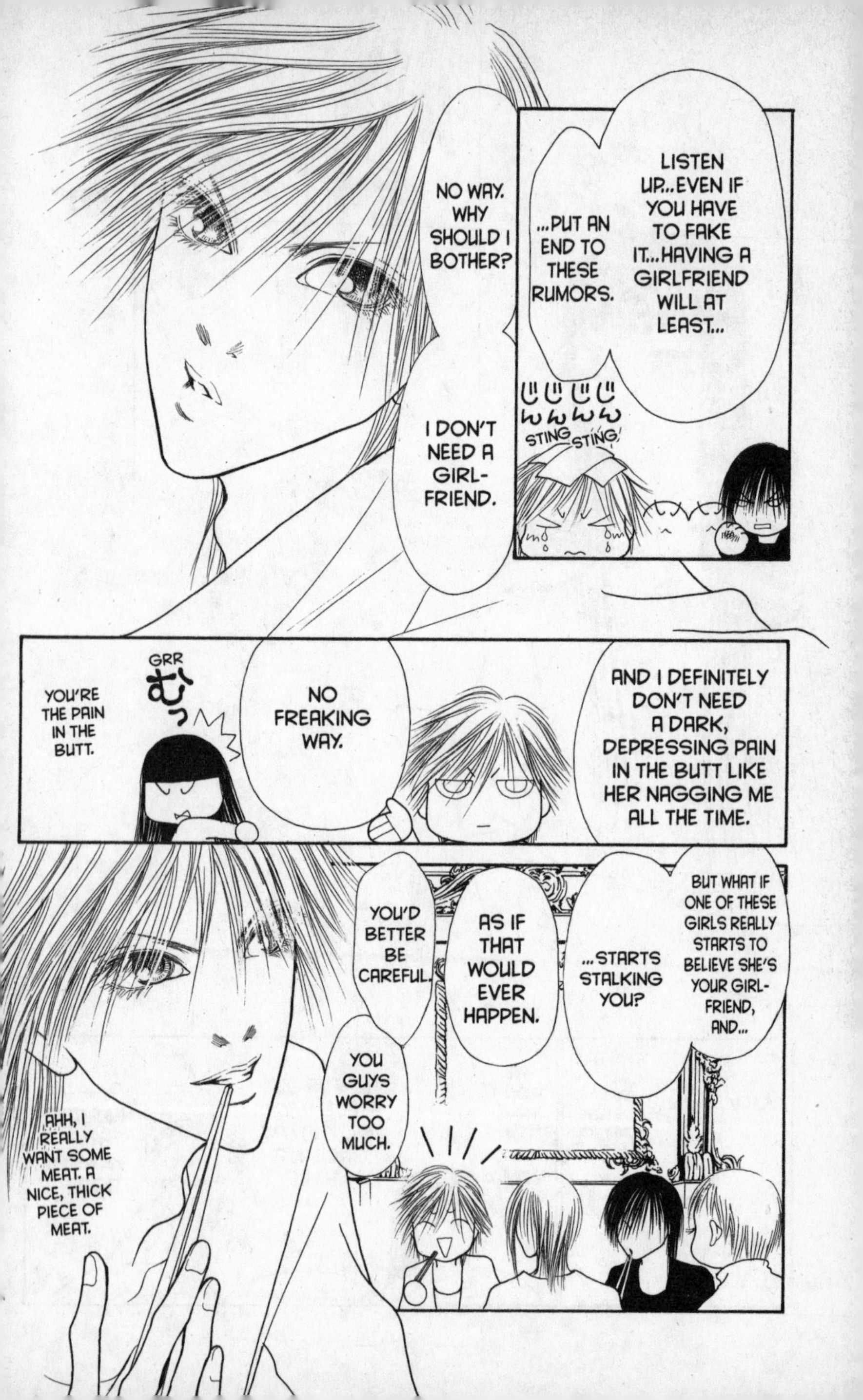
LISTEN UP...EVEN IF YOU HAVE TO FAKE IT...HAVING A GIRLFRIEND WILL AT LEAST...
...PUT AN END TO THESE RUMORS.
STING STING
NO WAY. WHY SHOULD I BOTHER?
I DON'T NEED A GIRL-FRIEND.
AND I DEFINITELY DON'T NEED A DARK, DEPRESSING PAIN IN THE BUTT LIKE HER NAGGING ME ALL THE TIME.
NO FREAKING WAY.
GRR
YOU'RE THE PAIN IN THE BUTT.
BUT WHAT IF ONE OF THESE GIRLS REALLY STARTS TO BELIEVE SHE'S YOUR GIRL-FRIEND, AND...
...STARTS STALKING YOU?
AS IF THAT WOULD EVER HAPPEN.
YOU'D BETTER BE CAREFUL.
YOU GUYS WORRY TOO MUCH.
AHH, I REALLY WANT SOME MEAT. A NICE, THICK PIECE OF MEAT.

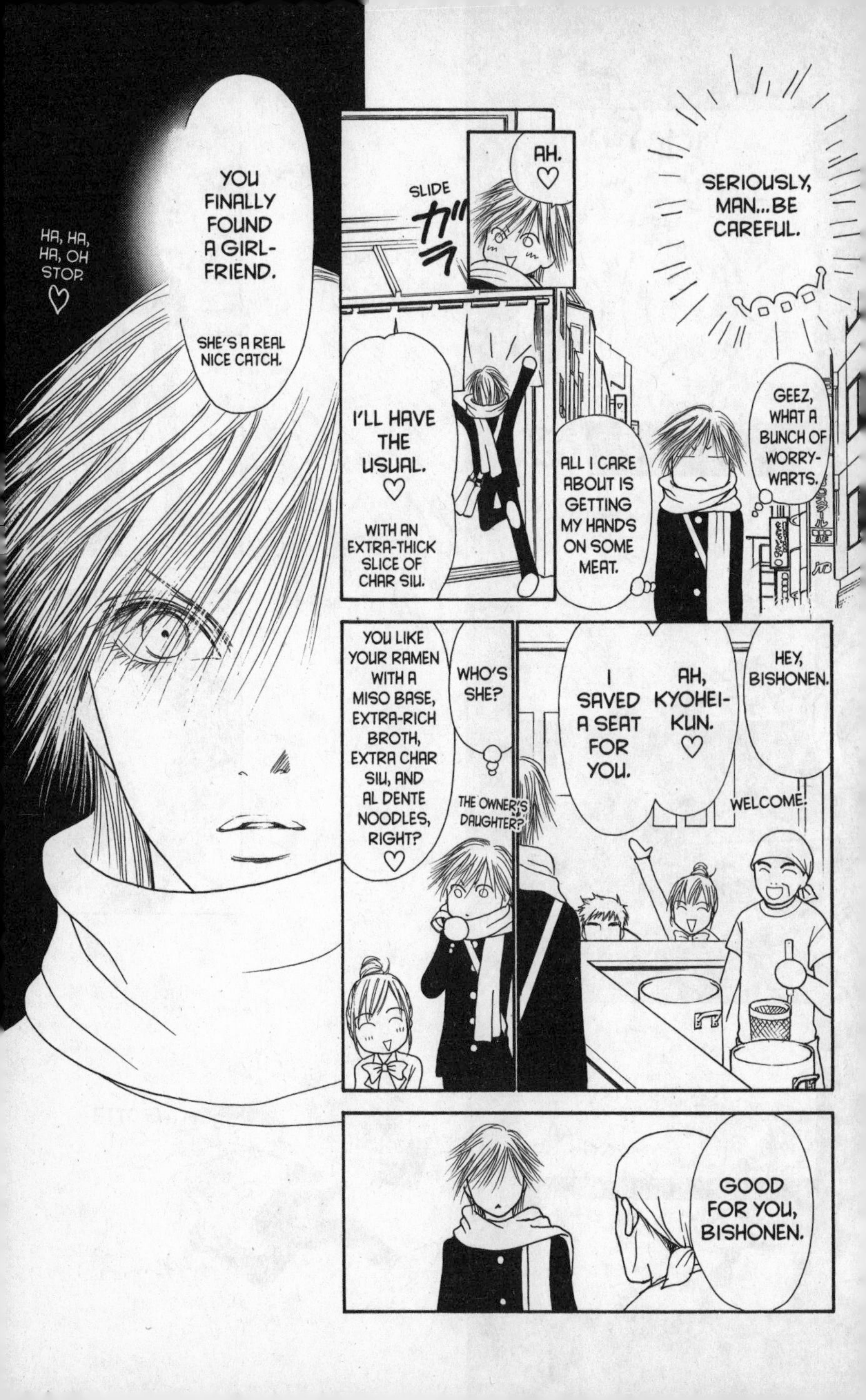
SERIOUSLY, MAN...BE CAREFUL.
GEEZ, WHAT A BUNCH OF WORRY-WARTS.
ALL I CARE ABOUT IS GETTING MY HANDS ON SOME MEAT.
SLIDE
AH. ♡
I'LL HAVE THE USUAL. ♡
WITH AN EXTRA-THICK SLICE OF CHAR SIU.
HEY, BISHONEN.
WELCOME.
AH, KYOHEI-KUN. ♡
I SAVED A SEAT FOR YOU.
WHO'S SHE?
THE OWNER'S DAUGHTER?
YOU LIKE YOUR RAMEN WITH A MISO BASE, EXTRA-RICH BROTH, EXTRA CHAR SIU, AND AL DENTE NOODLES, RIGHT? ♡
GOOD FOR YOU, BISHONEN.
YOU FINALLY FOUND A GIRL-FRIEND.
SHE'S A REAL NICE CATCH.
HA, HA, HA, OH STOP. ♡

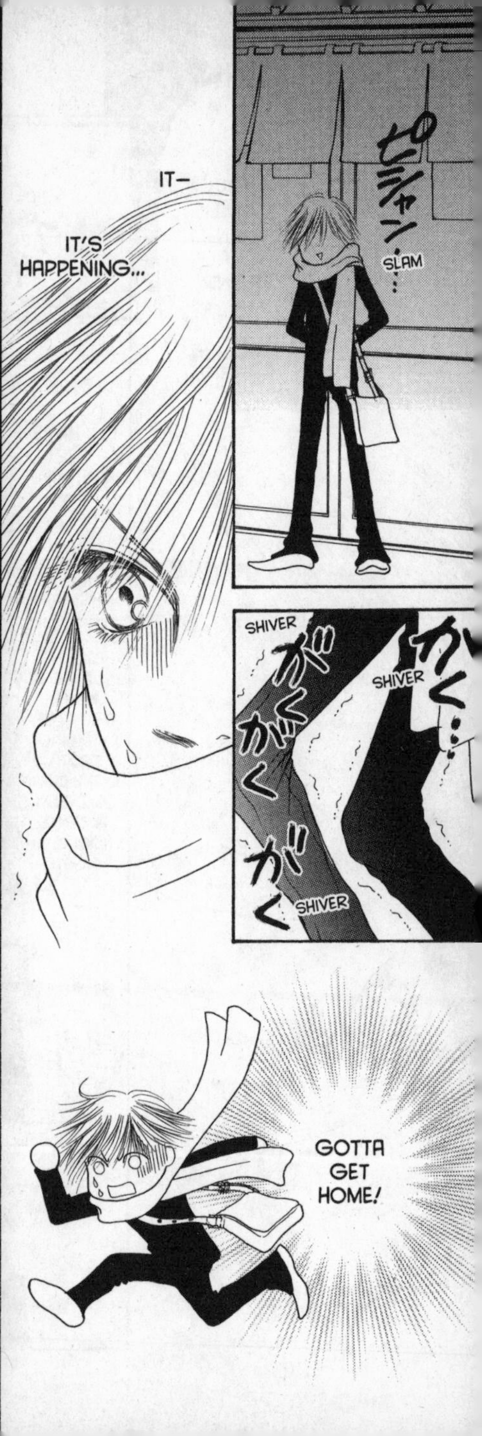
ピシャン
SLAM
がくがく
かく…
SHIVER
SHIVER
がく
SHIVER
IT—
IT'S HAPPENING...
GOTTA GET HOME!

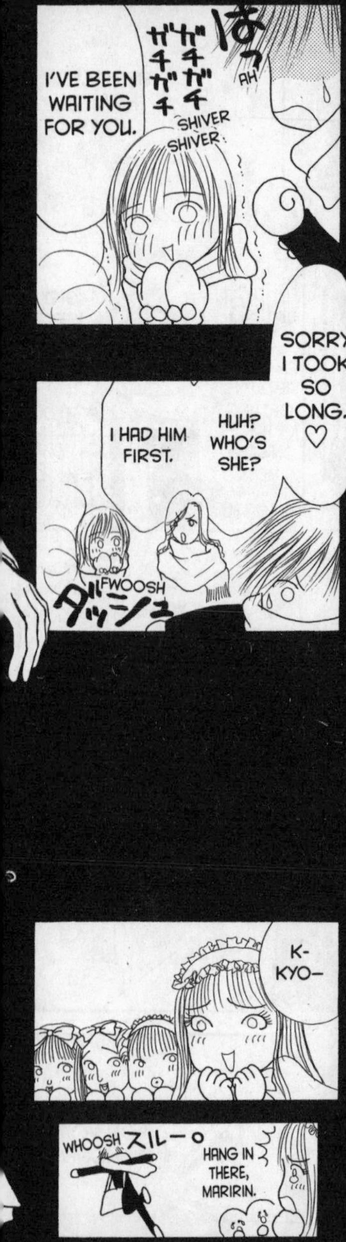
はっ
AH
ガチガチガチガチ
SHIVER SHIVER
I'VE BEEN WAITING FOR YOU.
SORRY I TOOK SO LONG. ♡
HUH? WHO'S SHE?
I HAD HIM FIRST.
ダッシュ
FWOOSH
K-KYO—
スルー。
WHOOSH
HANG IN THERE, MARIRIN.

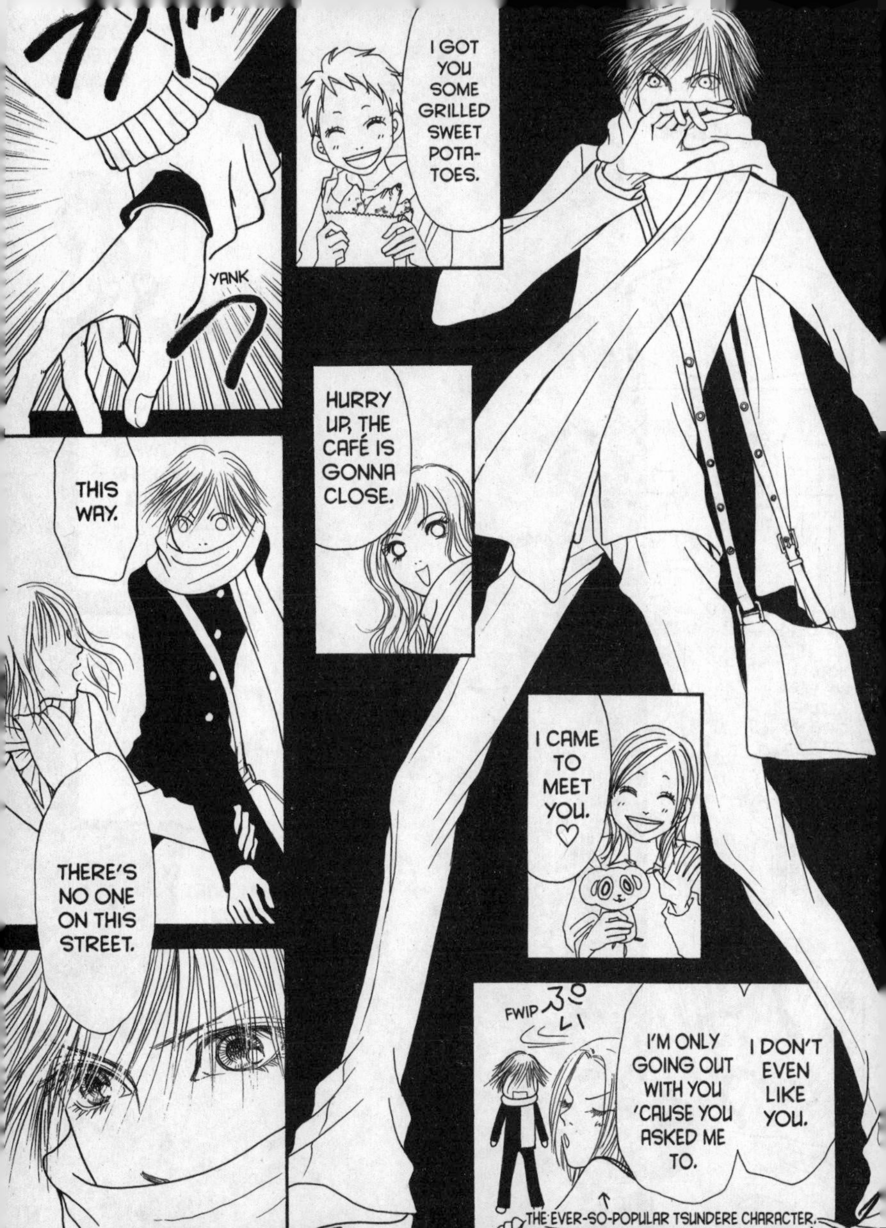
I GOT YOU SOME GRILLED SWEET POTATOES.
HURRY UP, THE CAFÉ IS GONNA CLOSE.
I CAME TO MEET YOU. ♡
I DON'T EVEN LIKE YOU.
I'M ONLY GOING OUT WITH YOU 'CAUSE YOU ASKED ME TO.
FWIP ぷい
THE EVER-SO-POPULAR TSUNDERE CHARACTER.
YANK
THIS WAY.
THERE'S NO ONE ON THIS STREET.

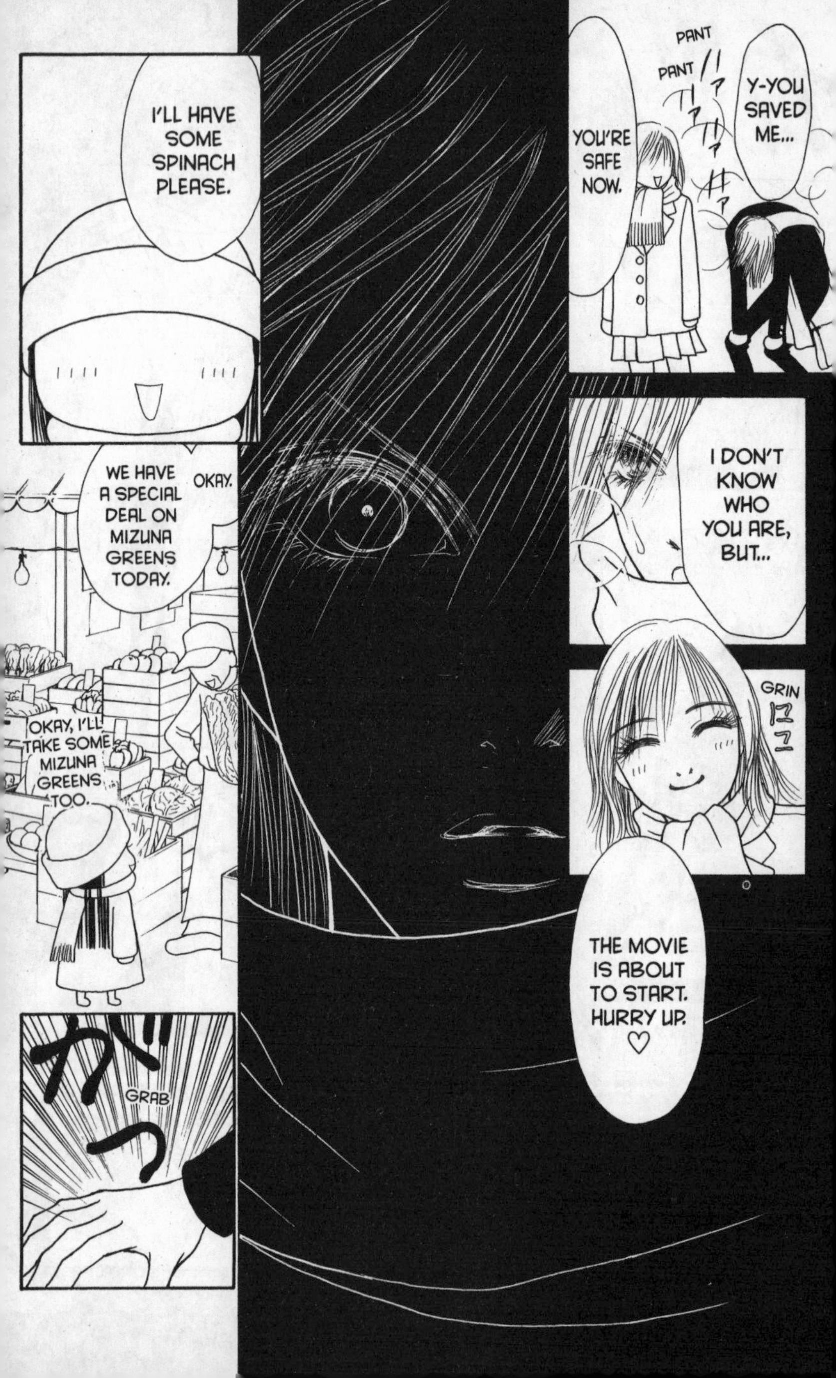
Y-YOU SAVED ME...
PANT PANT
YOU'RE SAFE NOW.
I DON'T KNOW WHO YOU ARE, BUT...
GRIN
THE MOVIE IS ABOUT TO START. HURRY UP. ♡
I'LL HAVE SOME SPINACH PLEASE.
OKAY.
WE HAVE A SPECIAL DEAL ON MIZUNA GREENS TODAY.
OKAY, I'LL TAKE SOME MIZUNA GREENS TOO.
GRAB

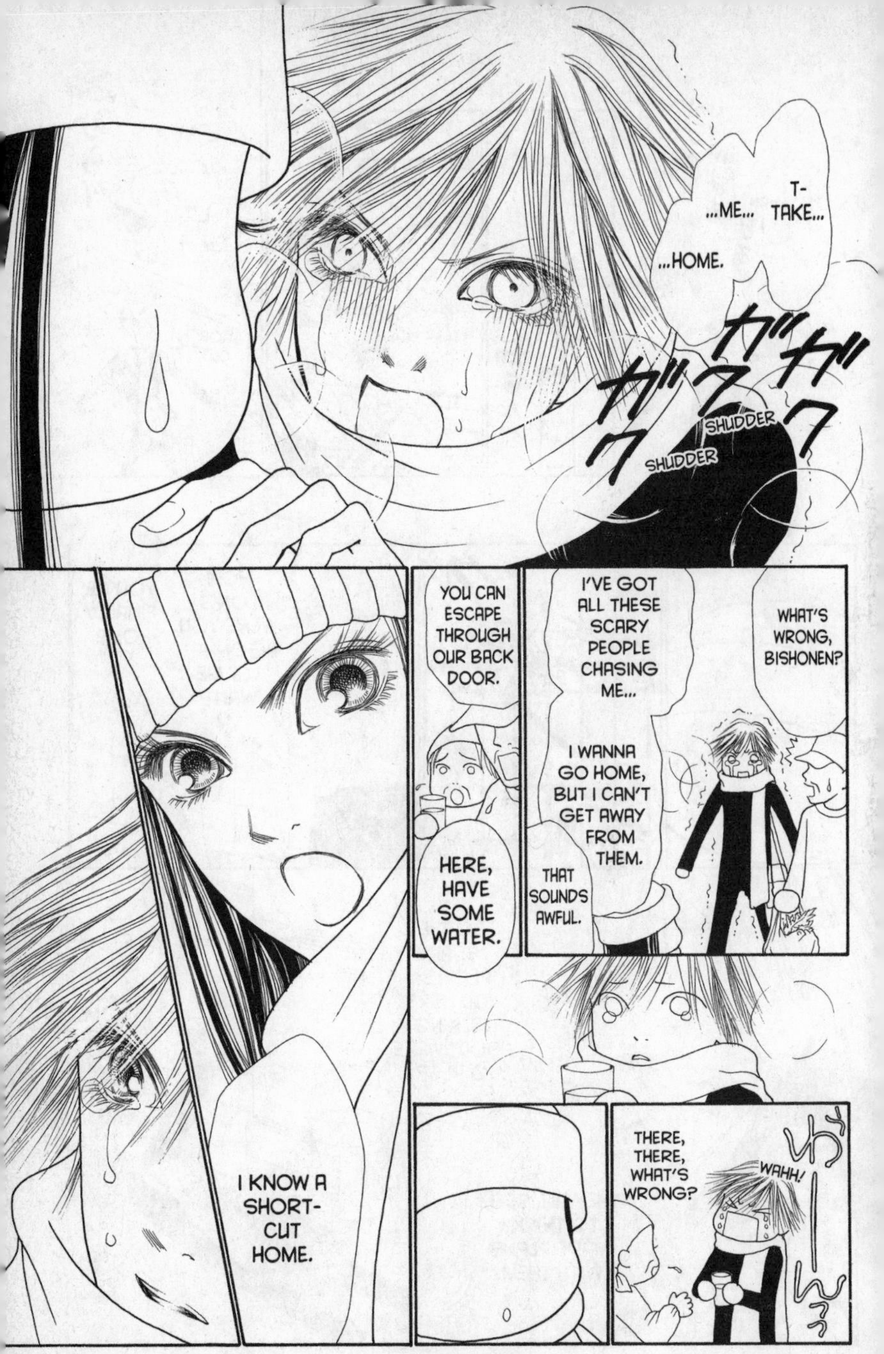
T- TAKE...
...ME...
...HOME.
ガク ガク
SHUDDER
SHUDDER
WHAT'S WRONG, BISHONEN?
I'VE GOT ALL THESE SCARY PEOPLE CHASING ME...
I WANNA GO HOME, BUT I CAN'T GET AWAY FROM THEM.
THAT SOUNDS AWFUL.
YOU CAN ESCAPE THROUGH OUR BACK DOOR.
HERE, HAVE SOME WATER.
うわーん
WAHH!
THERE, THERE, WHAT'S WRONG?
I KNOW A SHORT-CUT HOME.

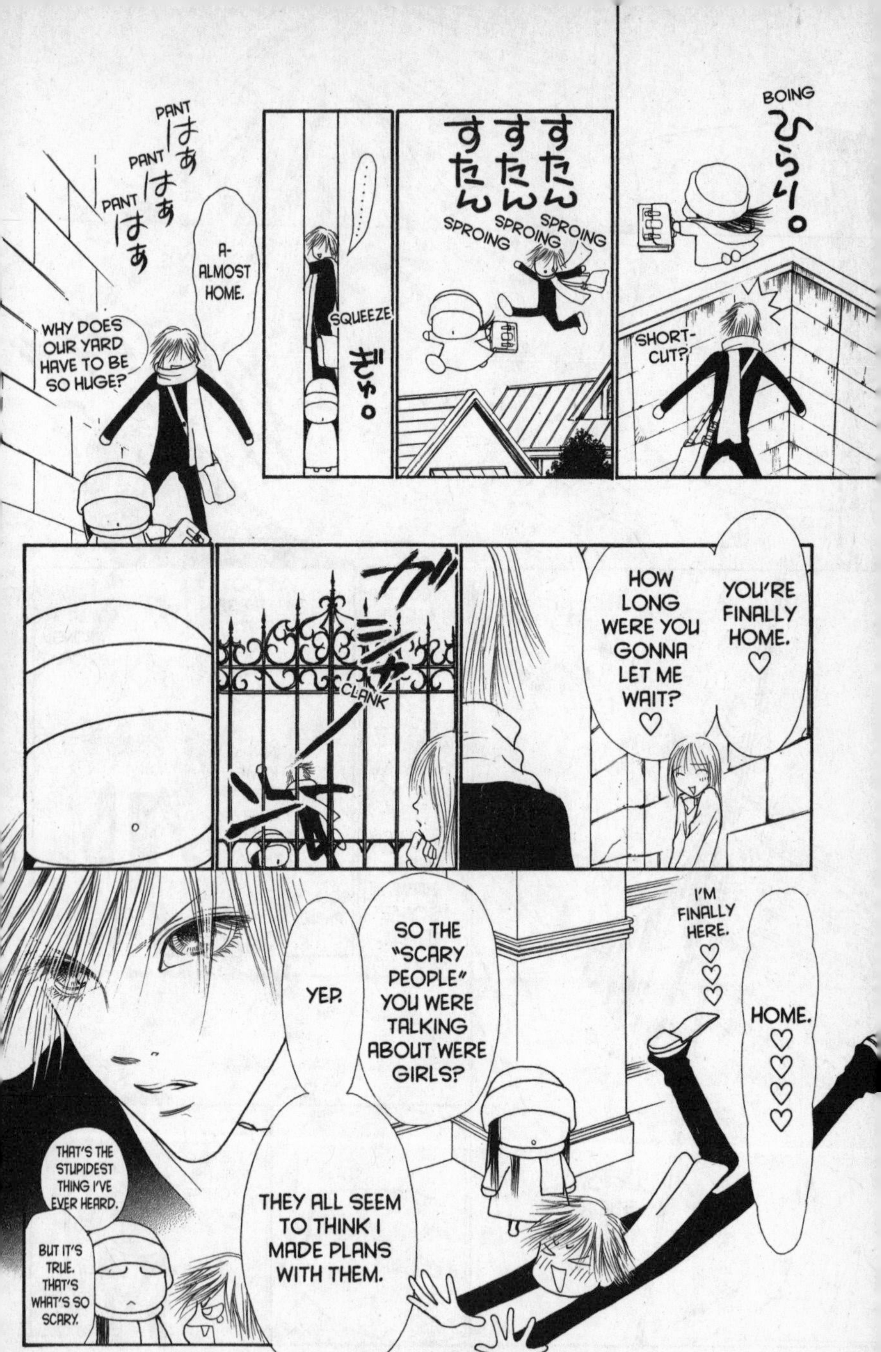
BOING
ひらり。
SHORT-CUT?!
すたん すたん すたん
SPROING SPROING SPROING
......
SQUEEZE
ぎゅ。
PANT はぁ PANT はぁ PANT はぁ
A- ALMOST HOME.
WHY DOES OUR YARD HAVE TO BE SO HUGE?
YOU'RE FINALLY HOME. ♡
HOW LONG WERE YOU GONNA LET ME WAIT? ♡
ガシャ
CLANK
HOME. ♡♡♡♡
I'M FINALLY HERE. ♡♡♡
SO THE "SCARY PEOPLE" YOU WERE TALKING ABOUT WERE GIRLS?
YEP.
THEY ALL SEEM TO THINK I MADE PLANS WITH THEM.
THAT'S THE STUPIDEST THING I'VE EVER HEARD.
BUT IT'S TRUE. THAT'S WHAT'S SO SCARY.

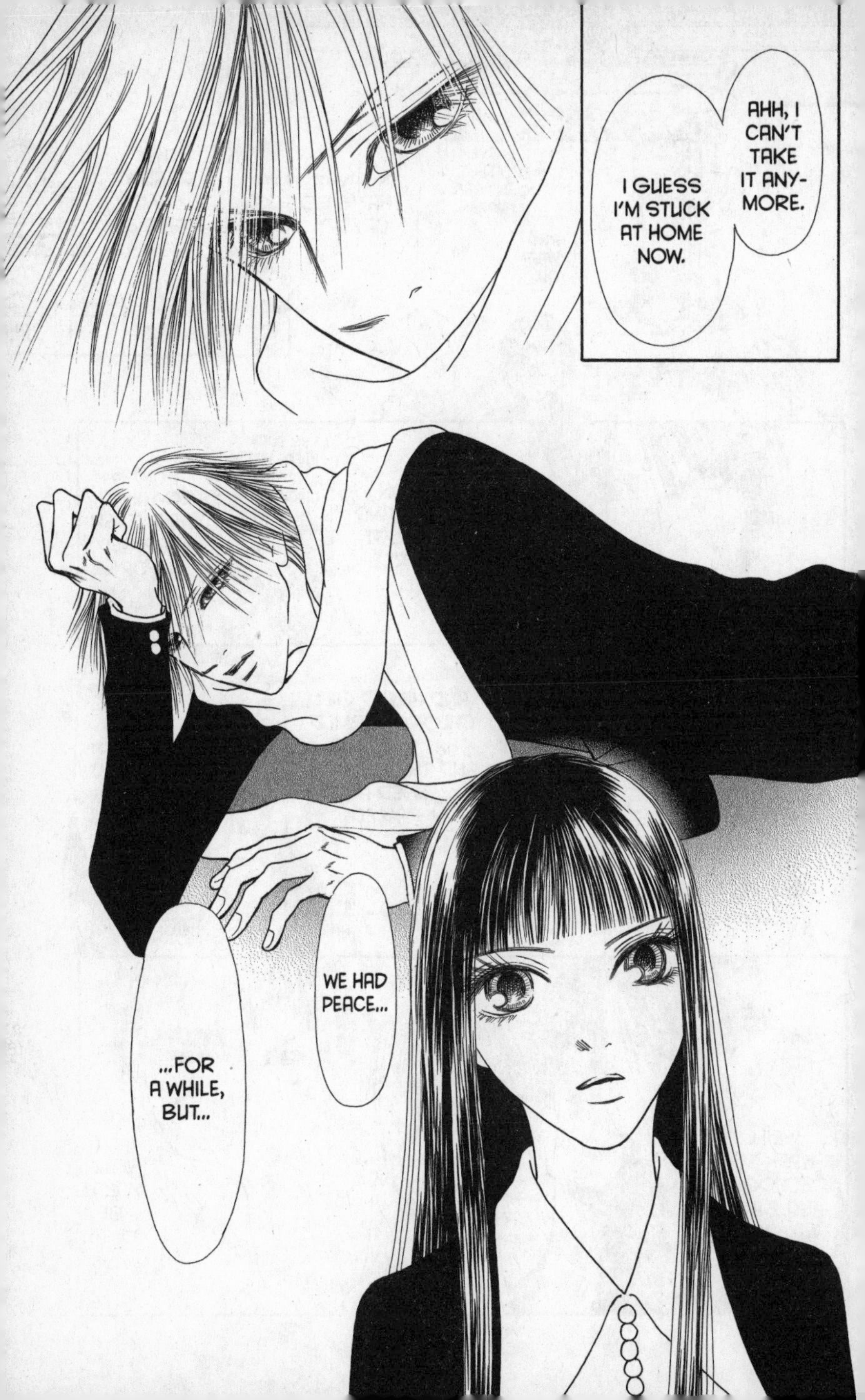
AHH, I CAN'T TAKE IT ANY-MORE.
I GUESS I'M STUCK AT HOME NOW.
WE HAD PEACE...
...FOR A WHILE, BUT...

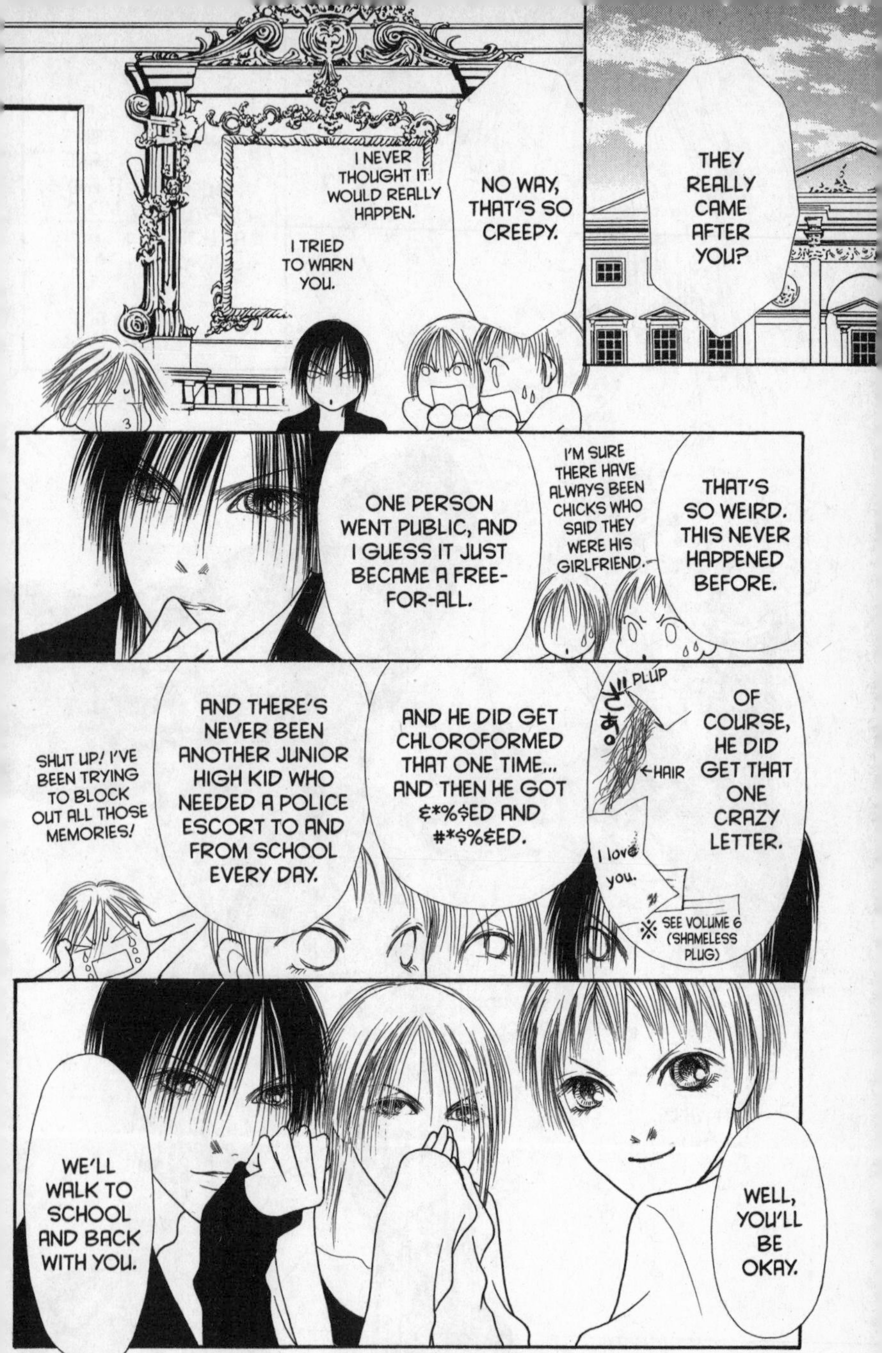
THEY REALLY CAME AFTER YOU?
NO WAY, THAT'S SO CREEPY.
I NEVER THOUGHT IT WOULD REALLY HAPPEN.
I TRIED TO WARN YOU.
THAT'S SO WEIRD. THIS NEVER HAPPENED BEFORE.
I'M SURE THERE HAVE ALWAYS BEEN CHICKS WHO SAID THEY WERE HIS GIRLFRIEND.
ONE PERSON WENT PUBLIC, AND I GUESS IT JUST BECAME A FREE-FOR-ALL.
OF COURSE, HE DID GET THAT ONE CRAZY LETTER.
PLUP
←HAIR
I love you.
※ SEE VOLUME 6 (SHAMELESS PLUG)
AND HE DID GET CHLOROFORMED THAT ONE TIME... AND THEN HE GOT &*%$ED AND #*$%&ED.
AND THERE'S NEVER BEEN ANOTHER JUNIOR HIGH KID WHO NEEDED A POLICE ESCORT TO AND FROM SCHOOL EVERY DAY.
SHUT UP! I'VE BEEN TRYING TO BLOCK OUT ALL THOSE MEMORIES!
WELL, YOU'LL BE OKAY.
WE'LL WALK TO SCHOOL AND BACK WITH YOU.

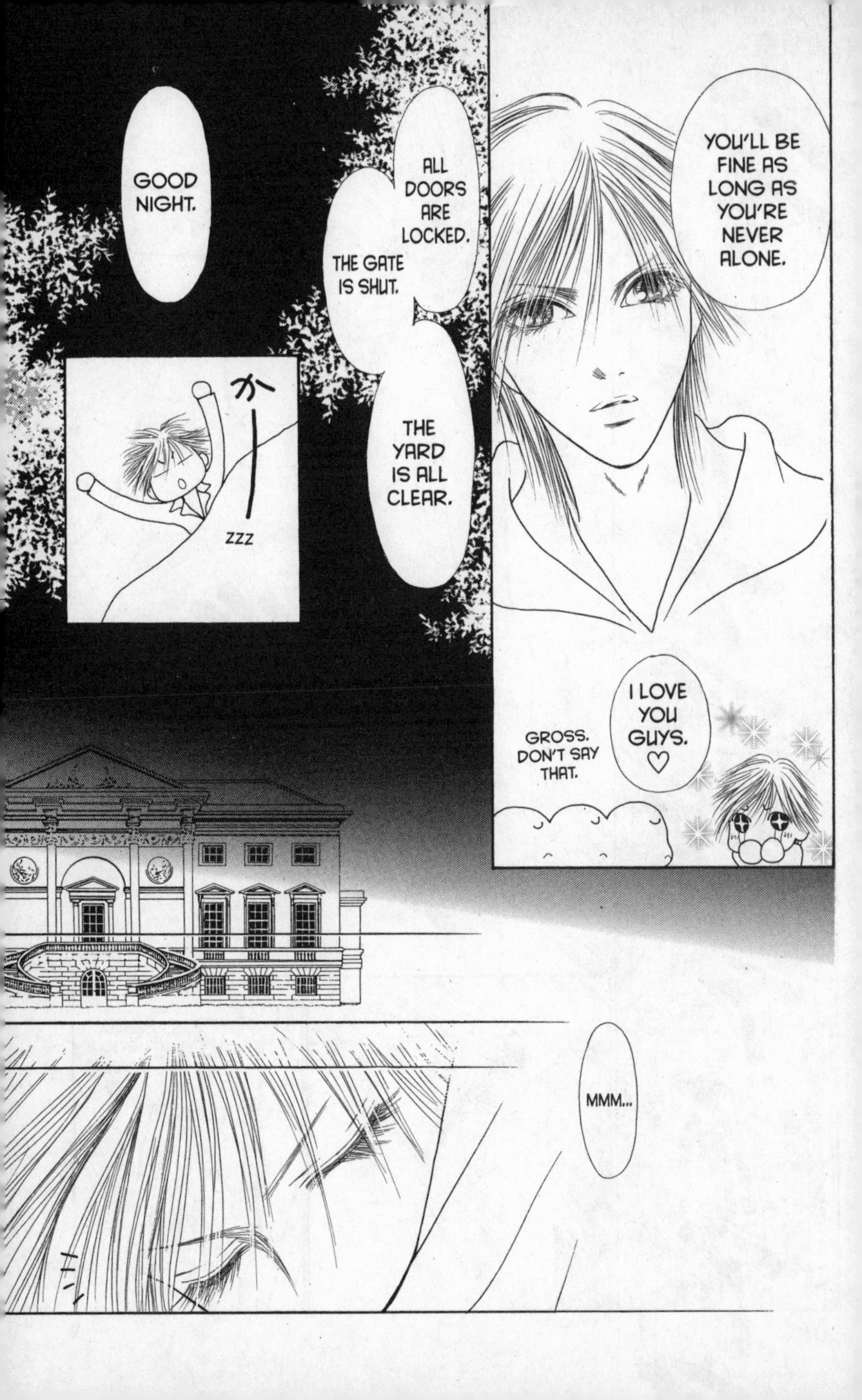
YOU'LL BE FINE AS LONG AS YOU'RE NEVER ALONE.
I LOVE YOU GUYS. ♡
GROSS. DON'T SAY THAT.
ALL DOORS ARE LOCKED.
THE GATE IS SHUT.
THE YARD IS ALL CLEAR.
GOOD NIGHT.
か
ZZZ
MMM...

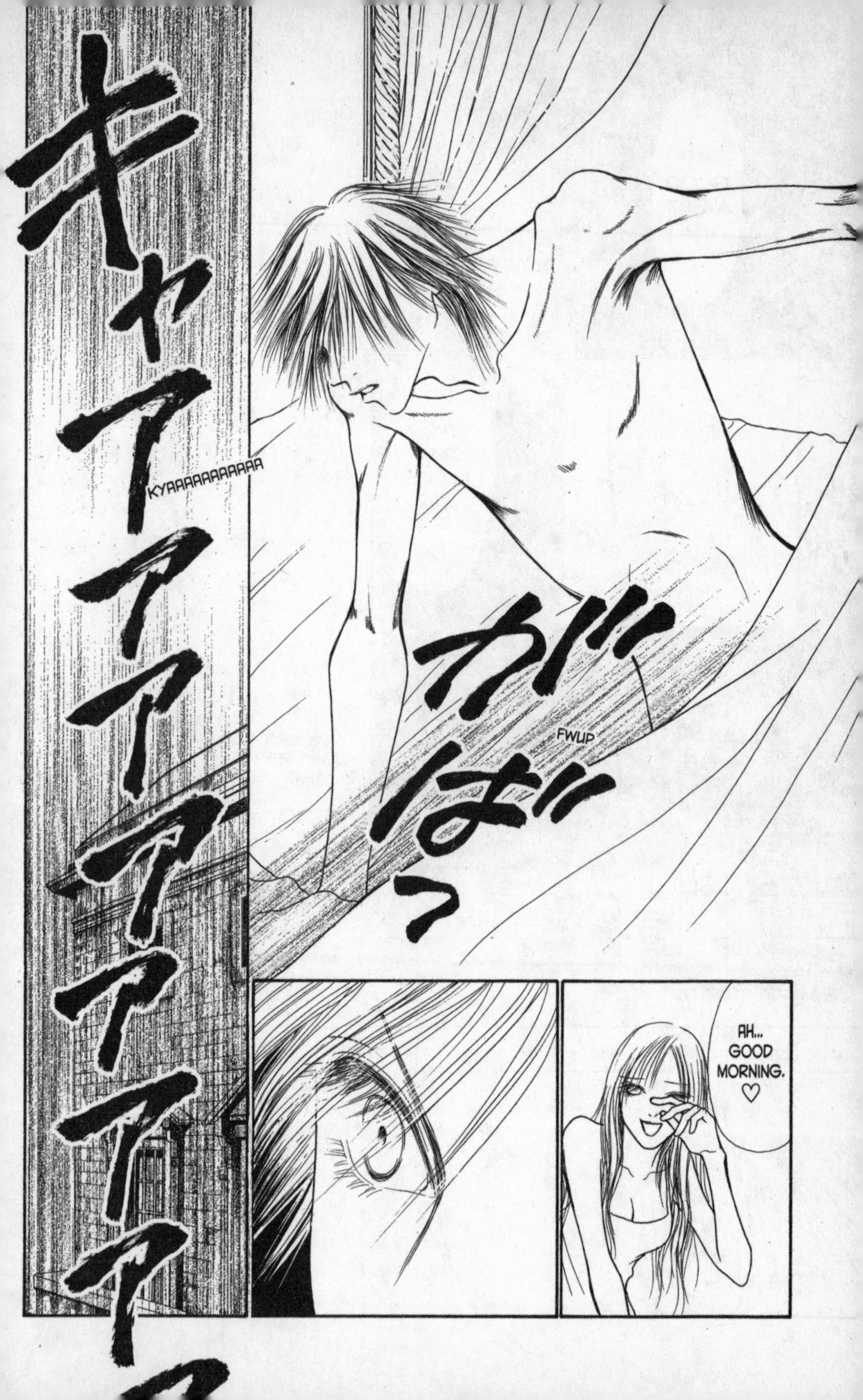
がばっ
FWUP
AH... GOOD MORNING. ♡
キャアアアアアアアッ
KYAAAAAAAAAAA

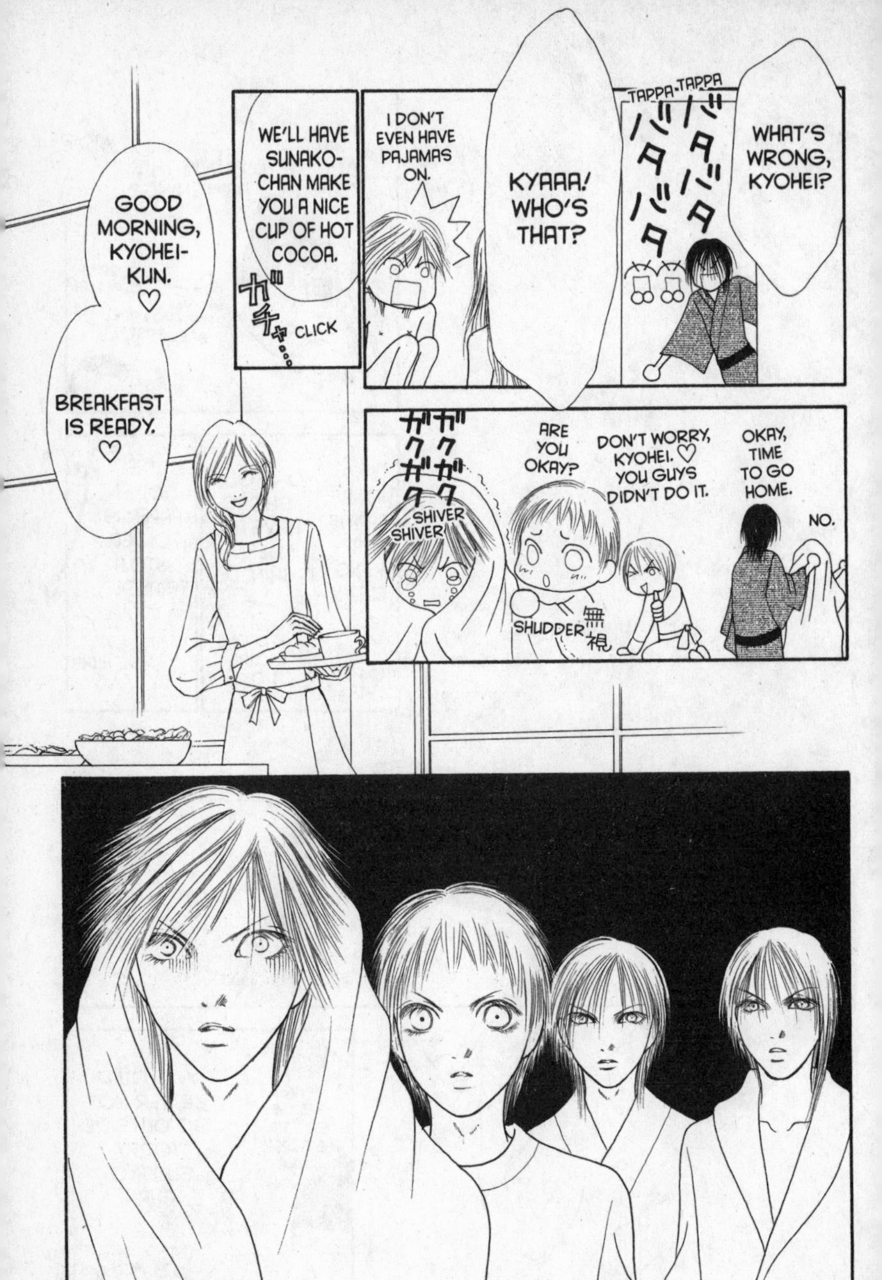
WHAT'S WRONG, KYOHEI?
バタバタ
TAPPA-TAPPA
バタバタ
KYAAA! WHO'S THAT?
I DON'T EVEN HAVE PAJAMAS ON.
WE'LL HAVE SUNAKO-CHAN MAKE YOU A NICE CUP OF HOT COCOA.
ガチャ
CLICK
OKAY, TIME TO GO HOME.
NO.
DON'T WORRY, KYOHEI. ♡ YOU GUYS DIDN'T DO IT.
ARE YOU OKAY?
ガクガク
ガクガク
SHIVER
SHIVER
無視
SHUDDER
GOOD MORNING, KYOHEI-KUN. ♡
BREAKFAST IS READY. ♡

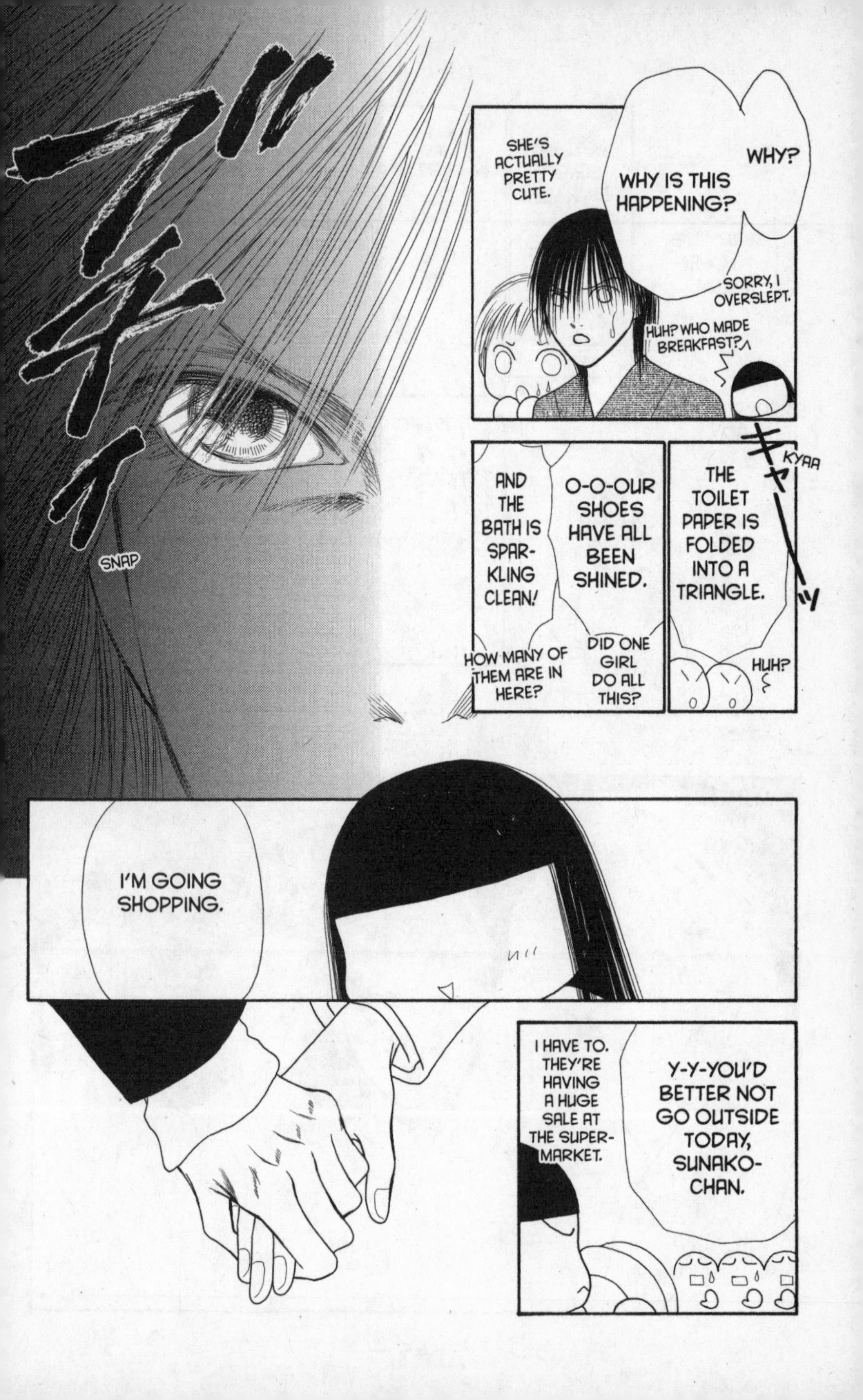
WHY? WHY IS THIS HAPPENING?
SHE'S ACTUALLY PRETTY CUTE.
SORRY, I OVERSLEPT.
HUH? WHO MADE BREAKFAST?
KYAA
THE TOILET PAPER IS FOLDED INTO A TRIANGLE.
HUH?
O-O-OUR SHOES HAVE ALL BEEN SHINED.
AND THE BATH IS SPARKLING CLEAN!
DID ONE GIRL DO ALL THIS?
HOW MANY OF THEM ARE IN HERE?
SNAP
I'M GOING SHOPPING.
Y-Y-YOU'D BETTER NOT GO OUTSIDE TODAY, SUNAKO-CHAN.
I HAVE TO. THEY'RE HAVING A HUGE SALE AT THE SUPERMARKET.

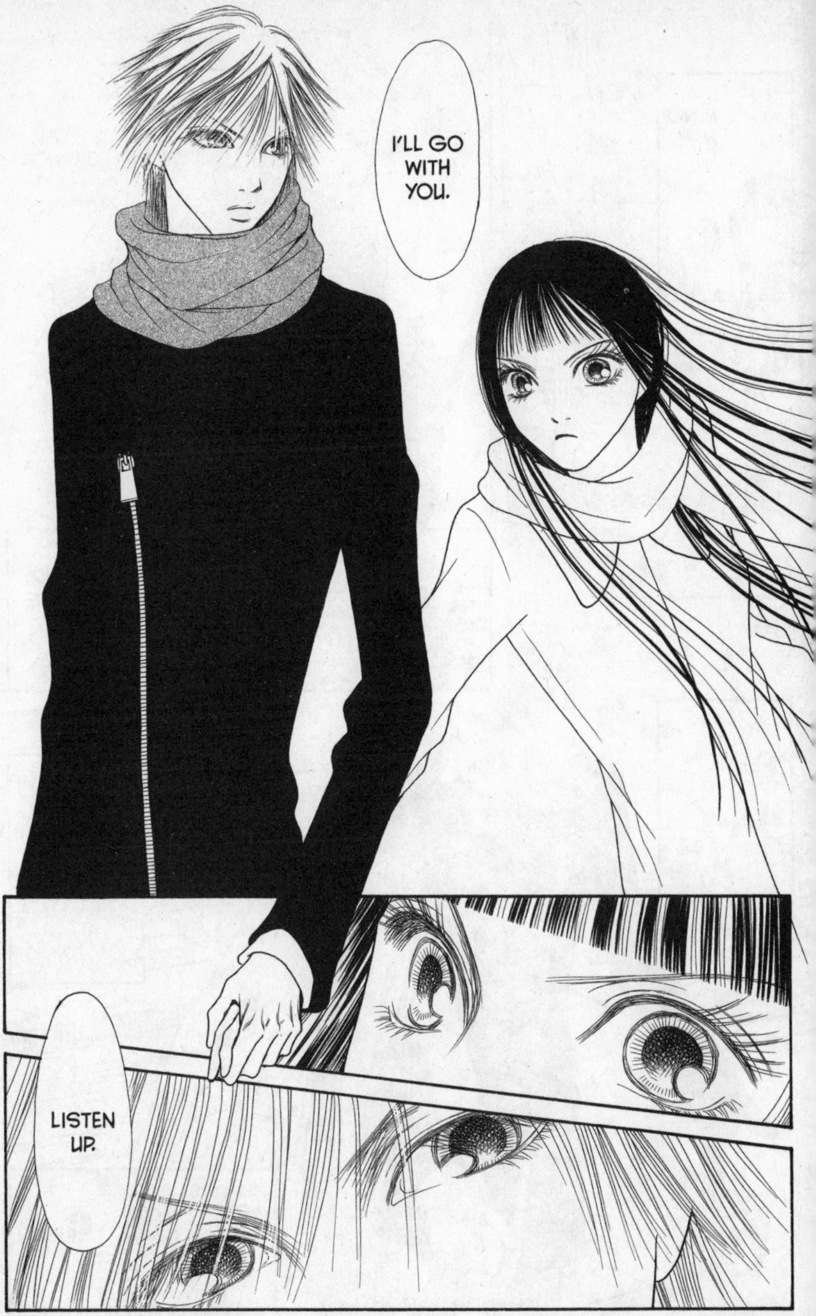
I'LL GO WITH YOU.
LISTEN UP.

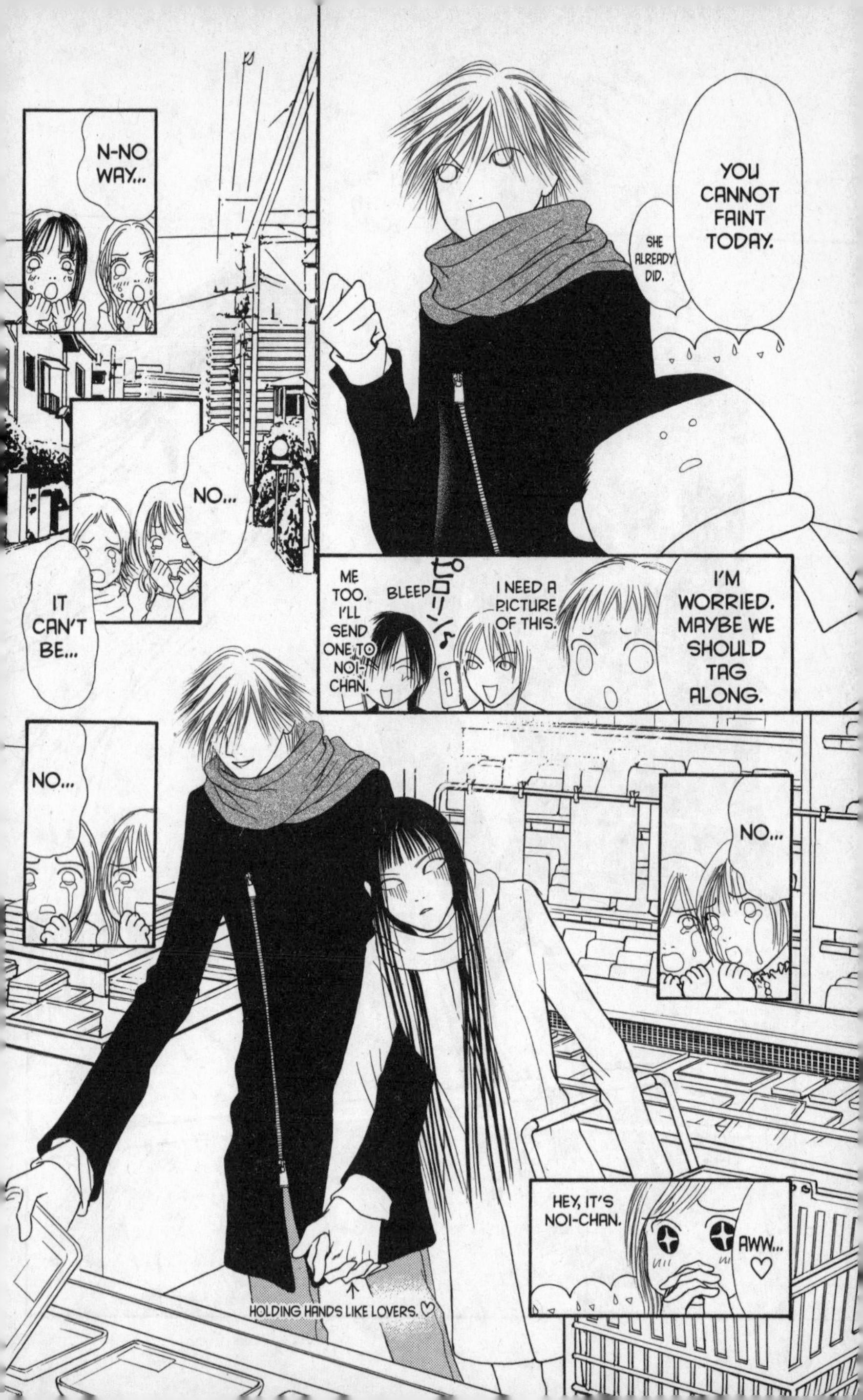
YOU CANNOT FAINT TODAY.
SHE ALREADY DID.
I'M WORRIED. MAYBE WE SHOULD TAG ALONG.
I NEED A PICTURE OF THIS.
ピロリ♪
BLEEP
ME TOO. I'LL SEND ONE TO NOI-CHAN.
N-NO WAY...
NO...
IT CAN'T BE...
NO...
HEY, IT'S NOI-CHAN.
AWW... ♡
NO...
HOLDING HANDS LIKE LOVERS. ♡

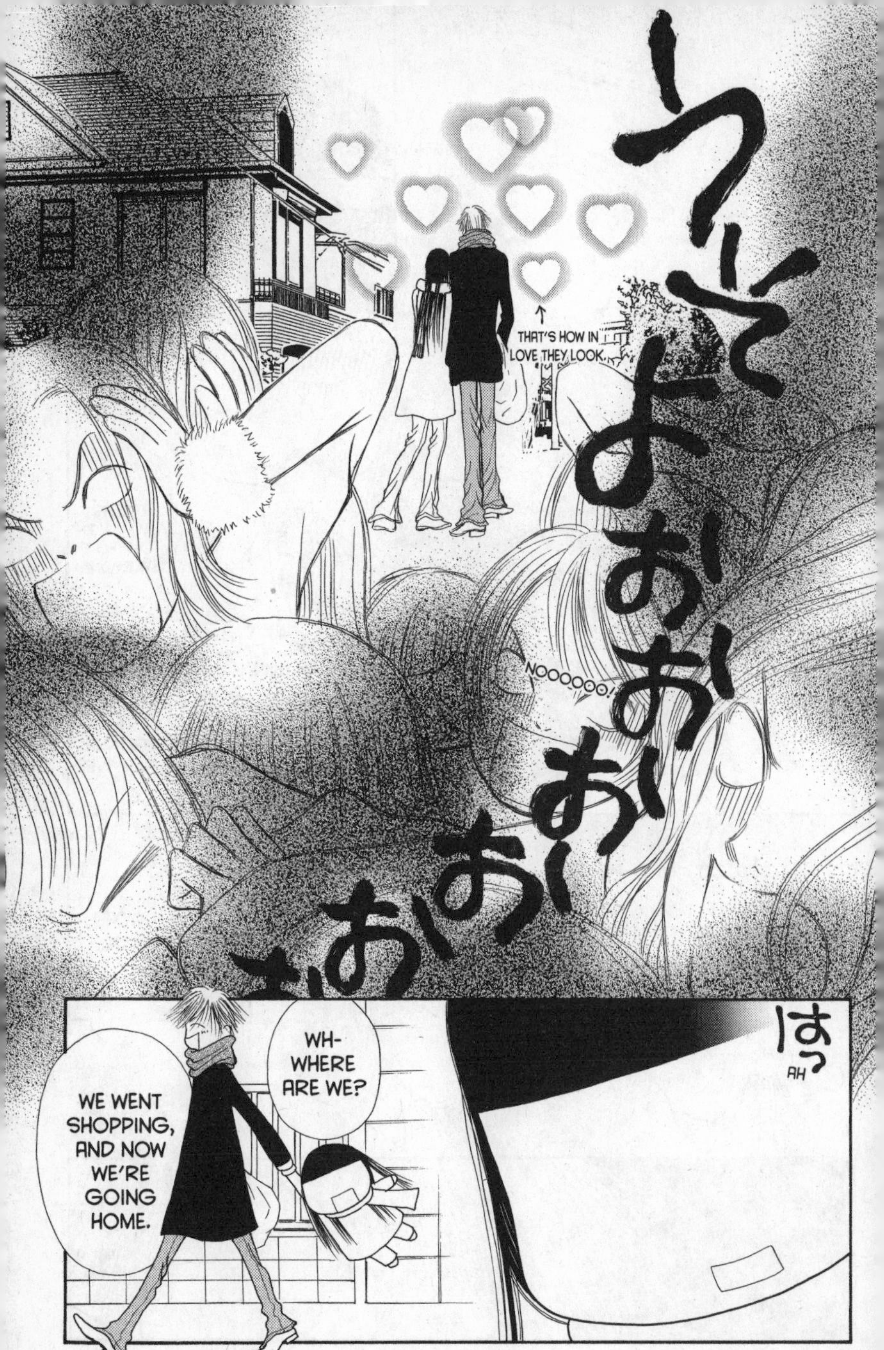
うそよおおおおお
THAT'S HOW IN LOVE THEY LOOK.
NOOOOOOO!
はっ
AH
WH- WHERE ARE WE?
WE WENT SHOPPING, AND NOW WE'RE GOING HOME.

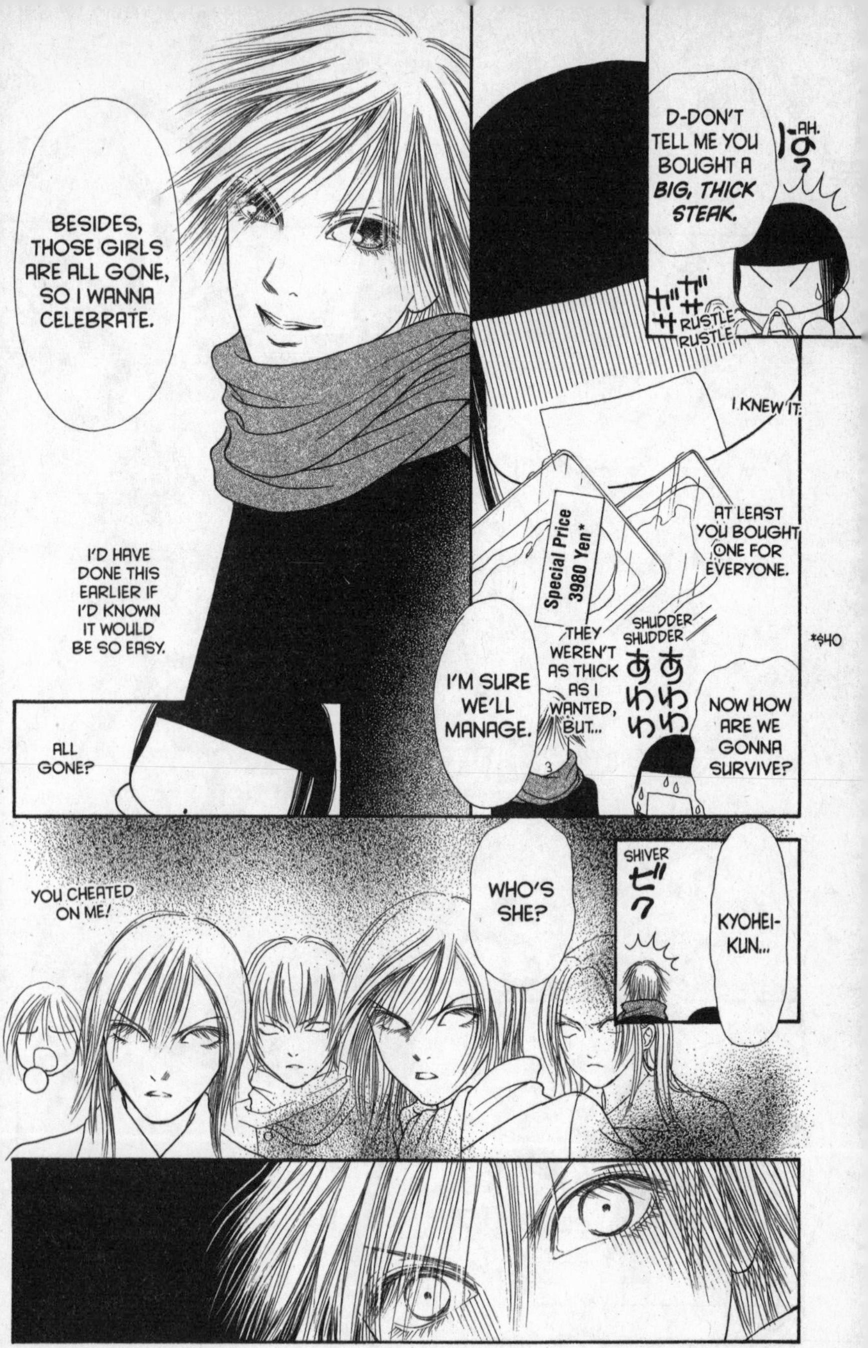
AH.
D-DON'T TELL ME YOU BOUGHT A *BIG, THICK STEAK.*
ガサ ガサ
RUSTLE RUSTLE
I KNEW IT.
AT LEAST YOU BOUGHT ONE FOR EVERYONE.
Special Price 3980 Yen*
*$40
NOW HOW ARE WE GONNA SURVIVE?
あわわ あわわ
SHUDDER SHUDDER
THEY WEREN'T AS THICK AS I WANTED, BUT...
I'M SURE WE'LL MANAGE.
BESIDES, THOSE GIRLS ARE ALL GONE, SO I WANNA CELEBRATE.
I'D HAVE DONE THIS EARLIER IF I'D KNOWN IT WOULD BE SO EASY.
ALL GONE?
KYOHEI-KUN...
SHIVER
WHO'S SHE?
YOU CHEATED ON ME!

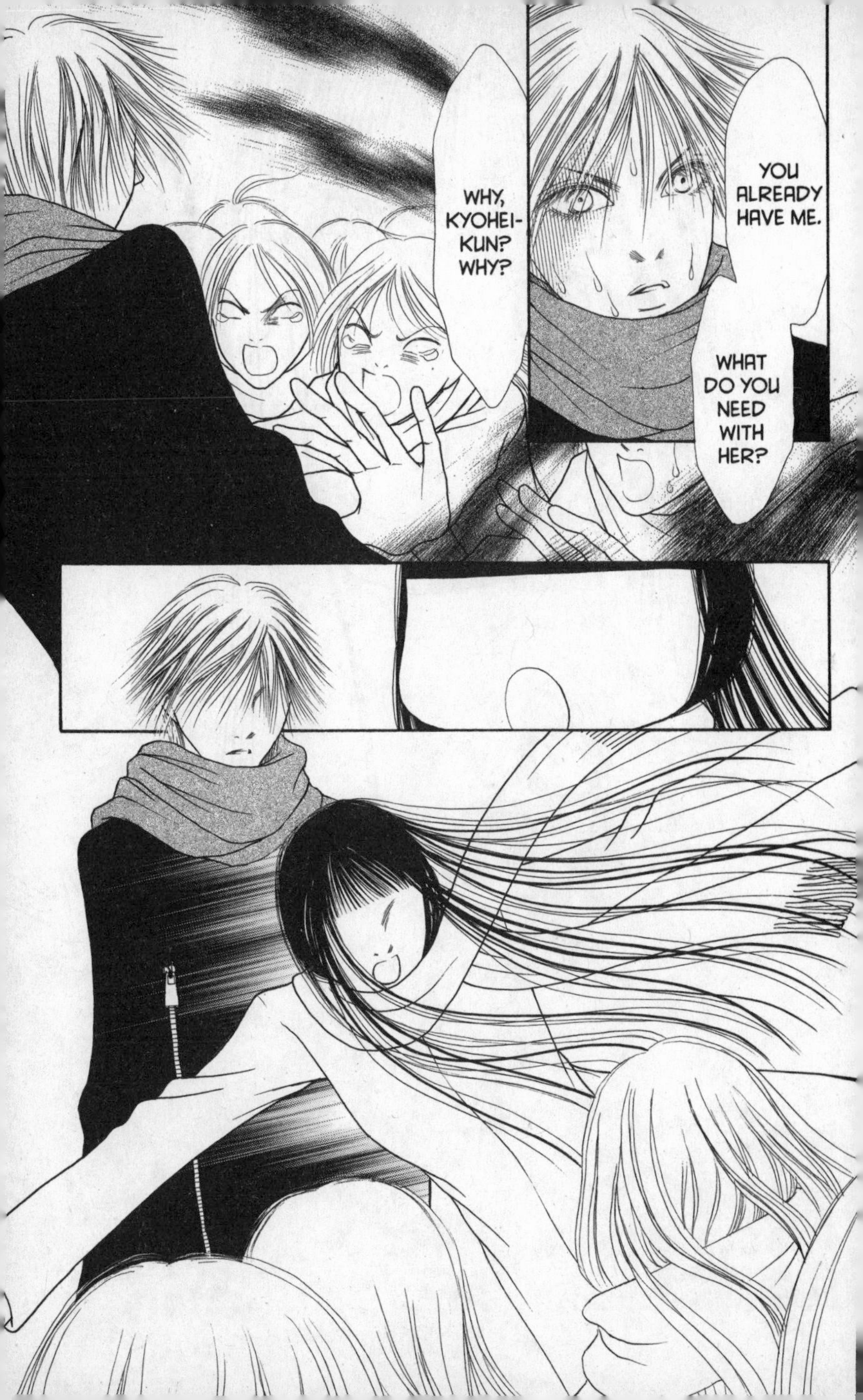
YOU ALREADY HAVE ME.
WHAT DO YOU NEED WITH HER?
WHY, KYOHEI-KUN? WHY?

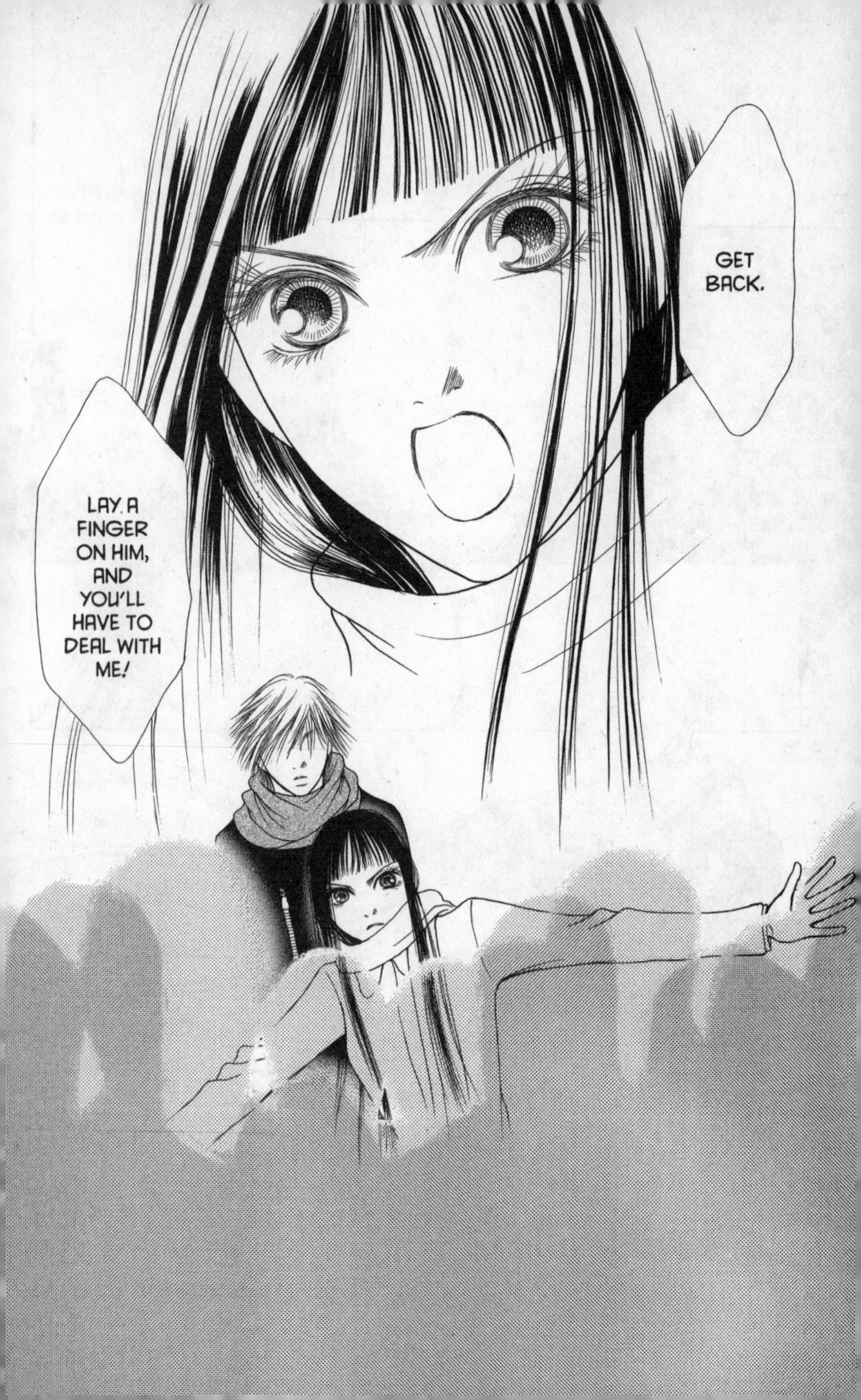
GET BACK.
LAY A FINGER ON HIM, AND YOU'LL HAVE TO DEAL WITH ME!

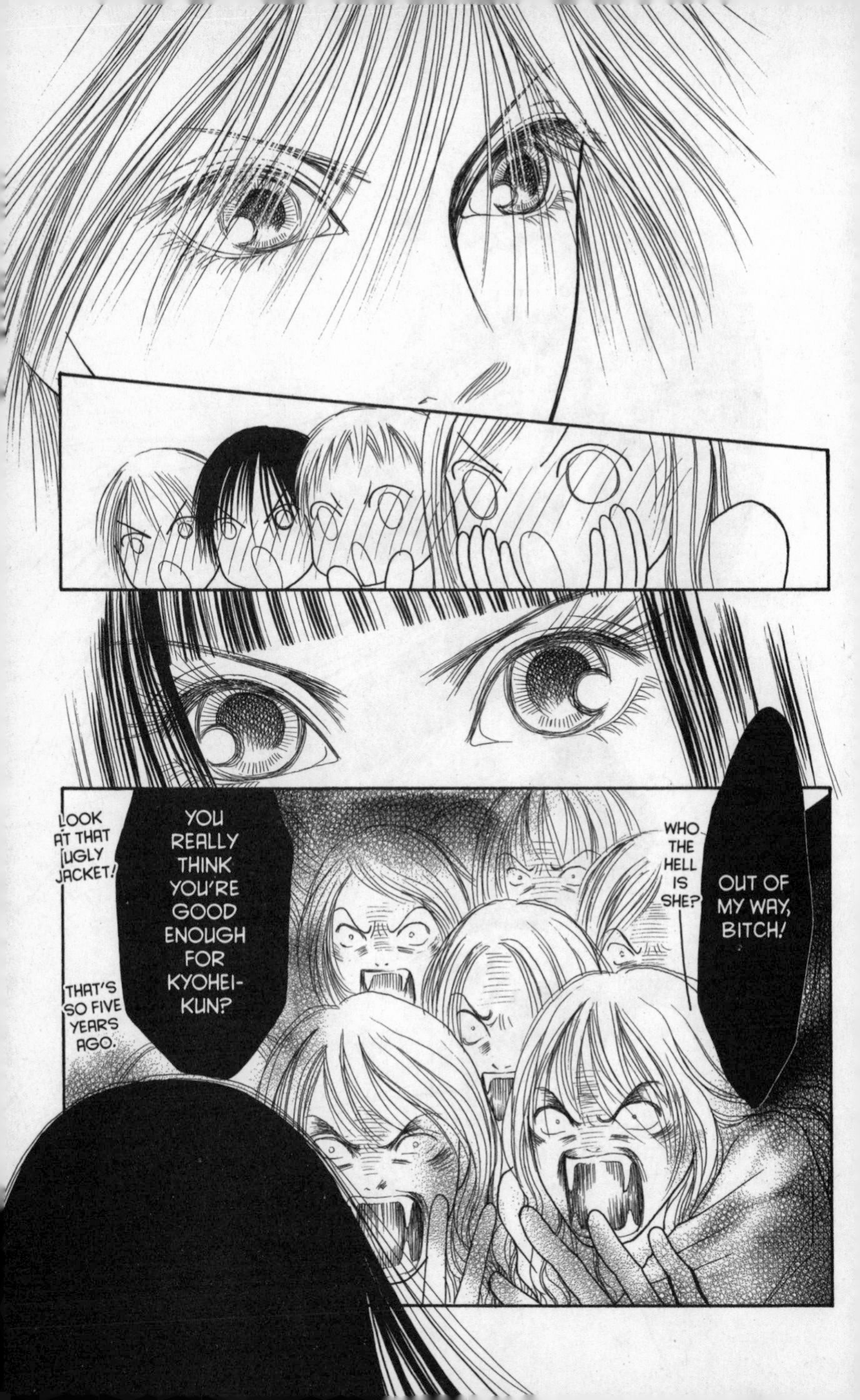
OUT OF MY WAY, BITCH!
WHO THE HELL IS SHE?
YOU REALLY THINK YOU'RE GOOD ENOUGH FOR KYOHEI-KUN?
LOOK AT THAT UGLY JACKET!
THAT'S SO FIVE YEARS AGO.

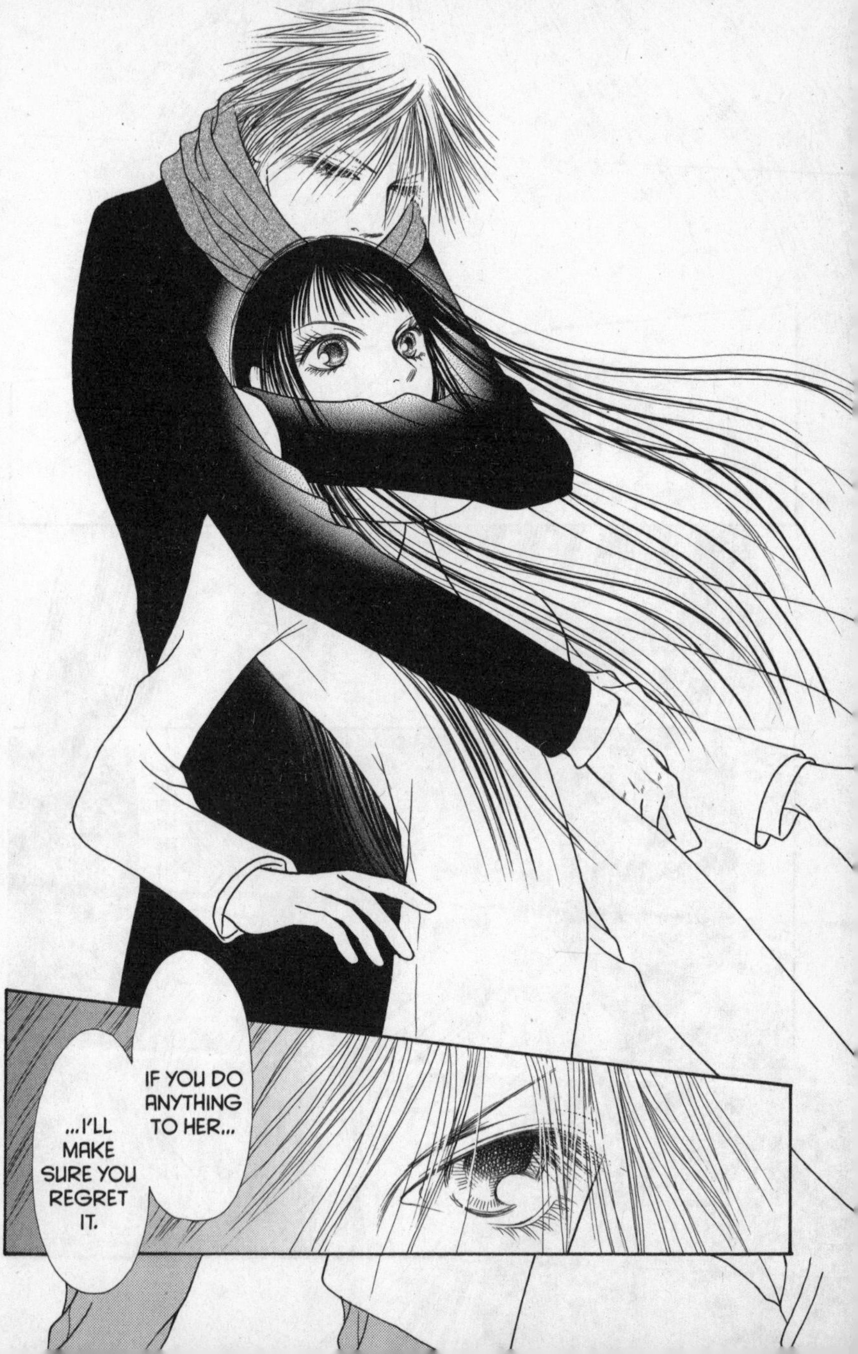
IF YOU DO ANYTHING TO HER...
...I'LL MAKE SURE YOU REGRET IT.

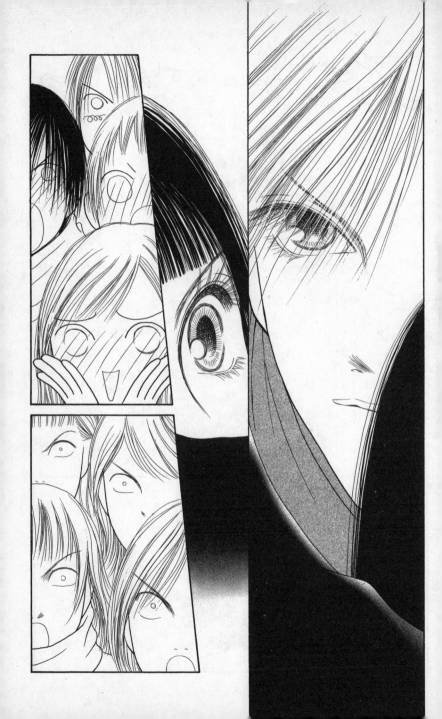

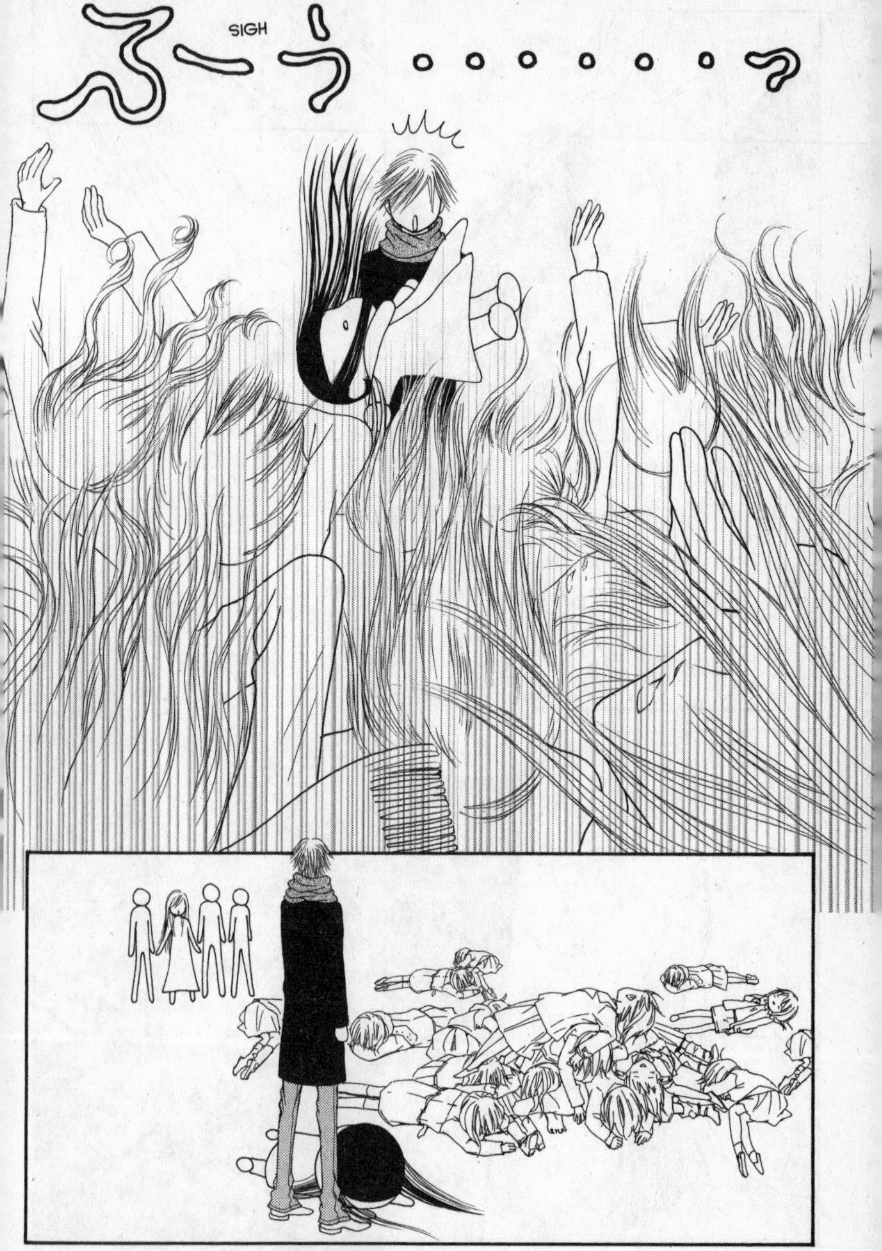
ふーう・・・・・・っ
SIGH

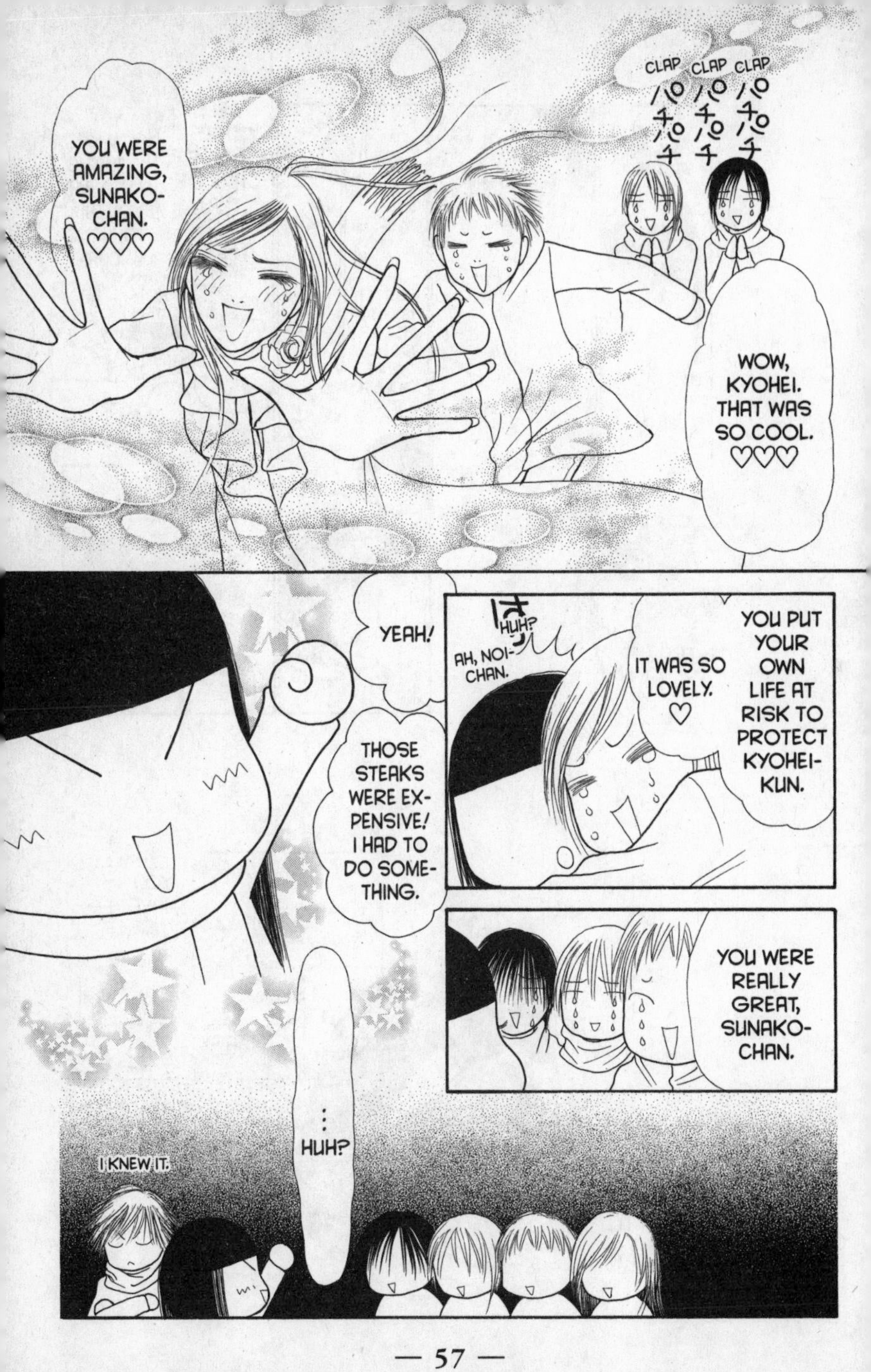
CLAP CLAP CLAP
パチパチ パチパチ パチパチ
WOW, KYOHEI. THAT WAS SO COOL. ♡♡♡
YOU WERE AMAZING, SUNAKO-CHAN. ♡♡♡
YOU PUT YOUR OWN LIFE AT RISK TO PROTECT KYOHEI-KUN.
IT WAS SO LOVELY. ♡
は HUH?
AH, NOI-CHAN.
YOU WERE REALLY GREAT, SUNAKO-CHAN.
YEAH!
THOSE STEAKS WERE EXPENSIVE! I HAD TO DO SOMETHING.
... HUH?
I KNEW IT.

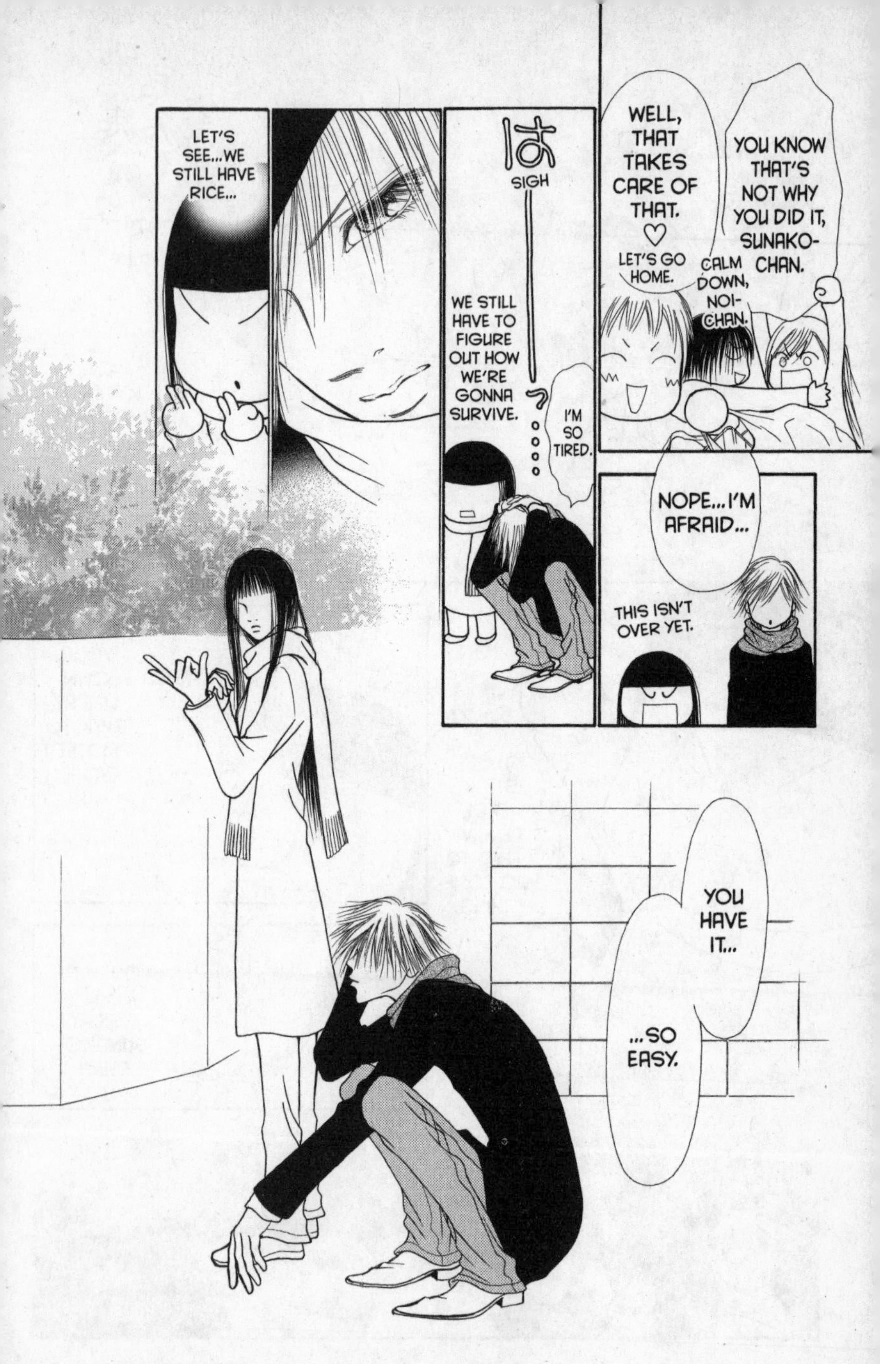
YOU KNOW THAT'S NOT WHY YOU DID IT, SUNAKO-CHAN.
WELL, THAT TAKES CARE OF THAT. ♡
LET'S GO HOME.
CALM DOWN, NOI-CHAN.
NOPE...I'M AFRAID...
THIS ISN'T OVER YET.
は
SIGH
WE STILL HAVE TO FIGURE OUT HOW WE'RE GONNA SURVIVE.
I'M SO TIRED.
LET'S SEE...WE STILL HAVE RICE...
YOU HAVE IT...
...SO EASY.

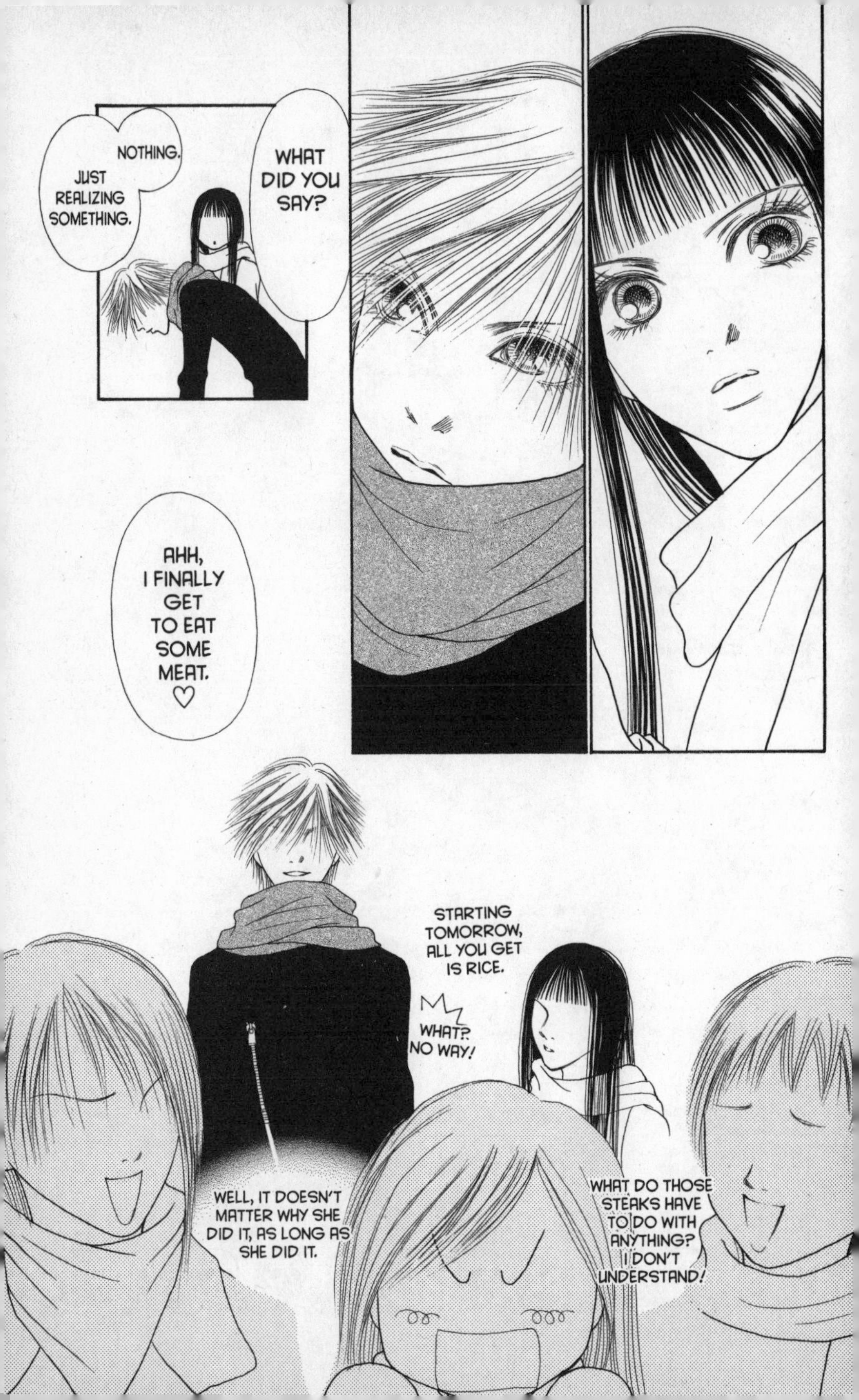
WHAT DID YOU SAY?
NOTHING. JUST REALIZING SOMETHING.
AHH, I FINALLY GET TO EAT SOME MEAT. ♡
STARTING TOMORROW, ALL YOU GET IS RICE.
WHAT? NO WAY!
WHAT DO THOSE STEAKS HAVE TO DO WITH ANYTHING? I DON'T UNDERSTAND!
WELL, IT DOESN'T MATTER WHY SHE DID IT, AS LONG AS SHE DID IT.

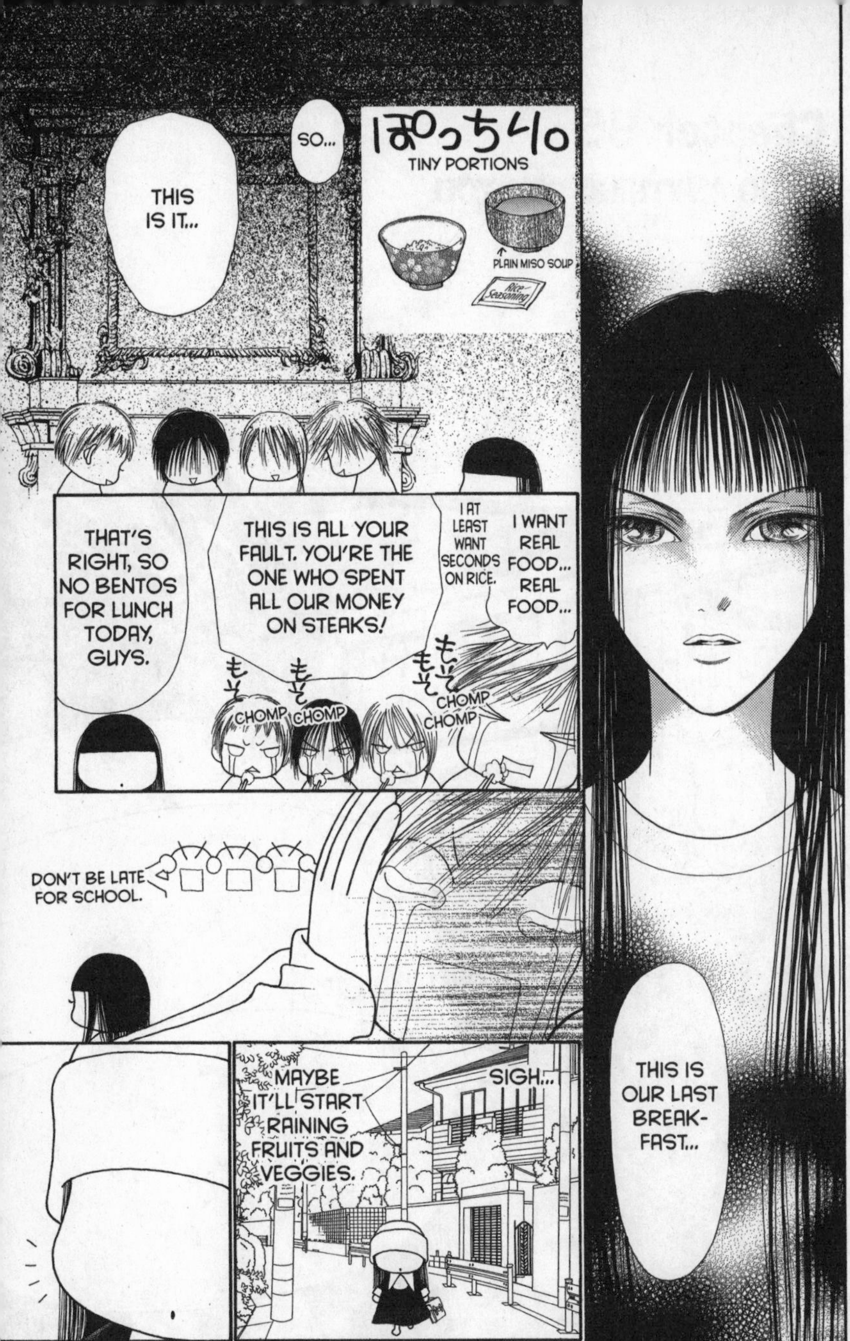

THIS IS OUR LAST BREAKFAST...
ぽっちり。
TINY PORTIONS
PLAIN MISO SOUP
Rice Seasoning
SO...
THIS IS IT...
I WANT REAL FOOD... REAL FOOD...
I AT LEAST WANT SECONDS ON RICE.
THIS IS ALL YOUR FAULT. YOU'RE THE ONE WHO SPENT ALL OUR MONEY ON STEAKS!
THAT'S RIGHT, SO NO BENTOS FOR LUNCH TODAY, GUYS.
もそもそ
CHOMP CHOMP
もそ
CHOMP
もそ
CHOMP
DON'T BE LATE FOR SCHOOL.
SIGH...
MAYBE IT'LL START RAINING FRUITS AND VEGGIES.

Chapter 85 I'D DO ANYTHING FOR YOU

Chapter 85

I'D DO ANYTHING FOR YOU

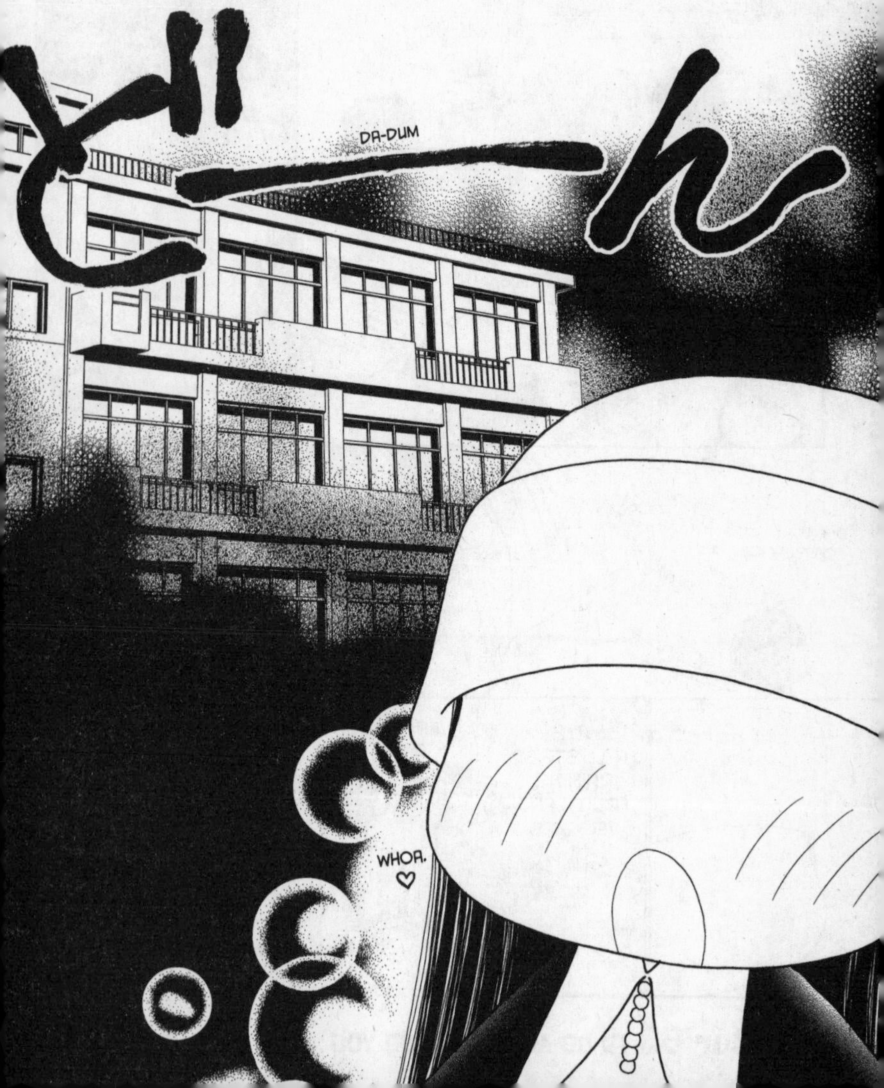
どーん
DA-DUM
WHOA. ♡

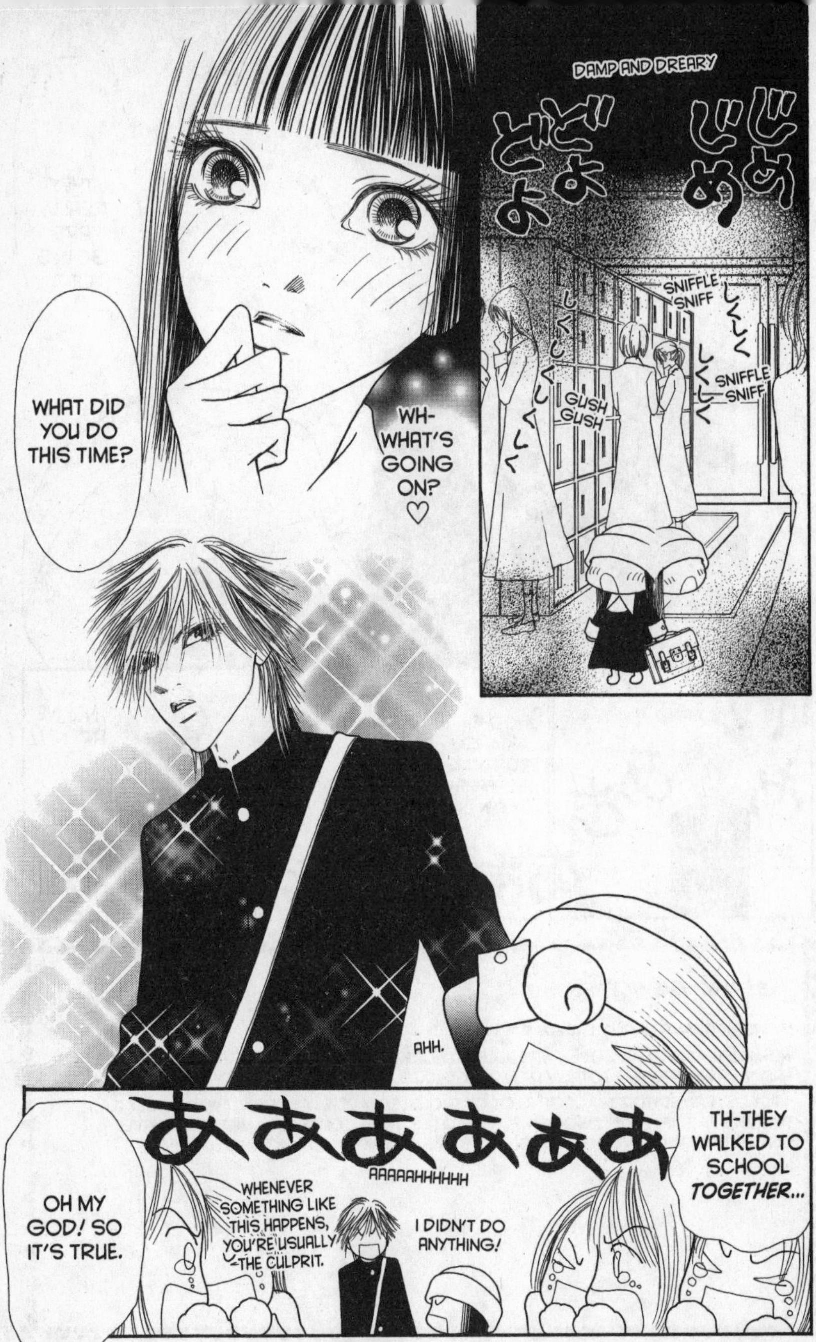
じめじめ
どよどよ
DAMP AND DREARY
SNIFFLE SNIFF
しくしく しくしく
SNIFFLE SNIFF
しくしくしくしく
GUSH GUSH
WH-WHAT'S GOING ON? ♡
WHAT DID YOU DO THIS TIME?
AHH.
あああああああ
AAAAAHHHHHH
TH-THEY WALKED TO SCHOOL *TOGETHER*...
I DIDN'T DO ANYTHING!
WHENEVER SOMETHING LIKE THIS HAPPENS, YOU'RE USUALLY THE CULPRIT.
OH MY GOD! SO IT'S TRUE.

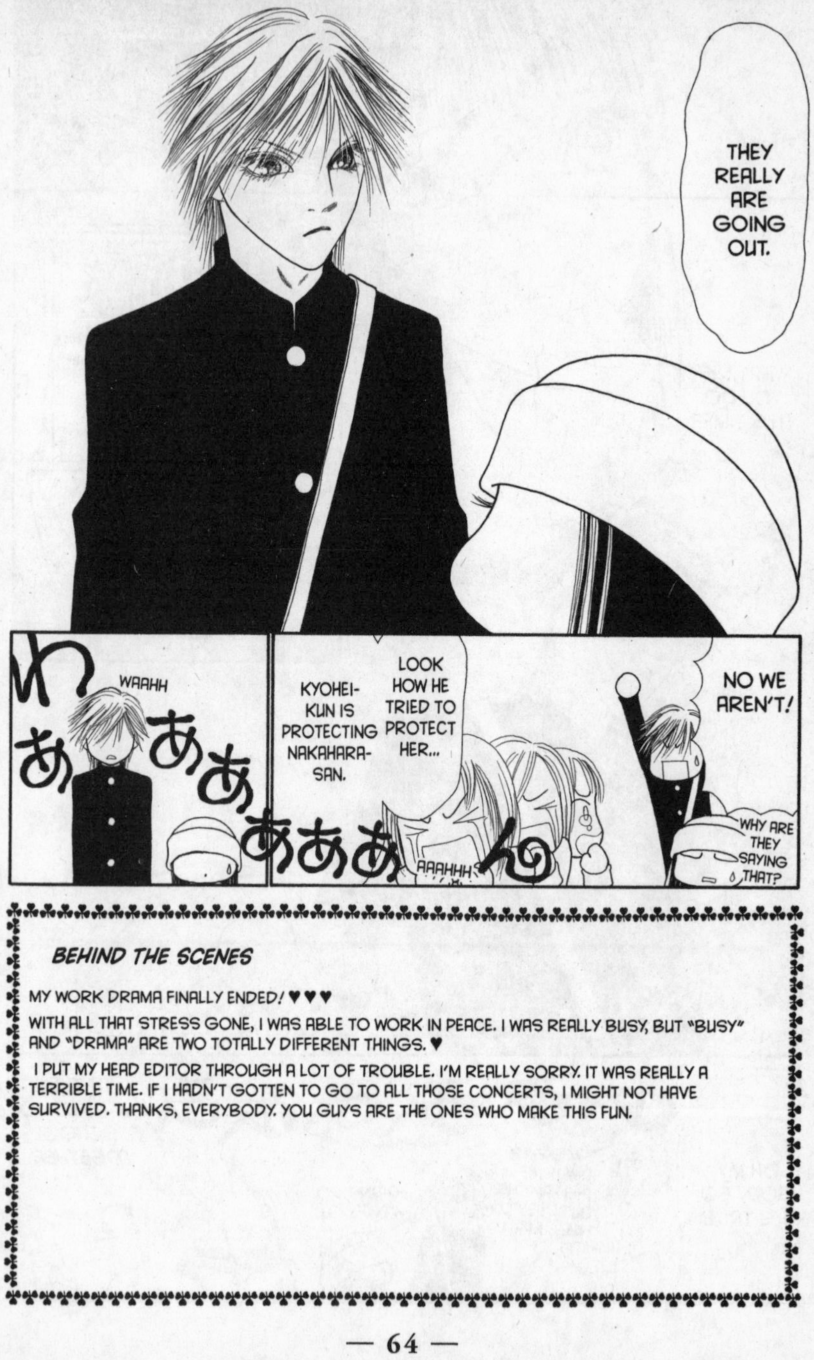
THEY REALLY ARE GOING OUT.
NO WE AREN'T!
WHY ARE THEY SAYING THAT?
LOOK HOW HE TRIED TO PROTECT HER...
KYOHEI-KUN IS PROTECTING NAKAHARA-SAN.
AAAHHH
WAAHH

BEHIND THE SCENES

MY WORK DRAMA FINALLY ENDED! ♥♥♥

WITH ALL THAT STRESS GONE, I WAS ABLE TO WORK IN PEACE. I WAS REALLY BUSY, BUT "BUSY" AND "DRAMA" ARE TWO TOTALLY DIFFERENT THINGS. ♥

I PUT MY HEAD EDITOR THROUGH A LOT OF TROUBLE. I'M REALLY SORRY. IT WAS REALLY A TERRIBLE TIME. IF I HADN'T GOTTEN TO GO TO ALL THOSE CONCERTS, I MIGHT NOT HAVE SURVIVED. THANKS, EVERYBODY. YOU GUYS ARE THE ONES WHO MAKE THIS FUN.

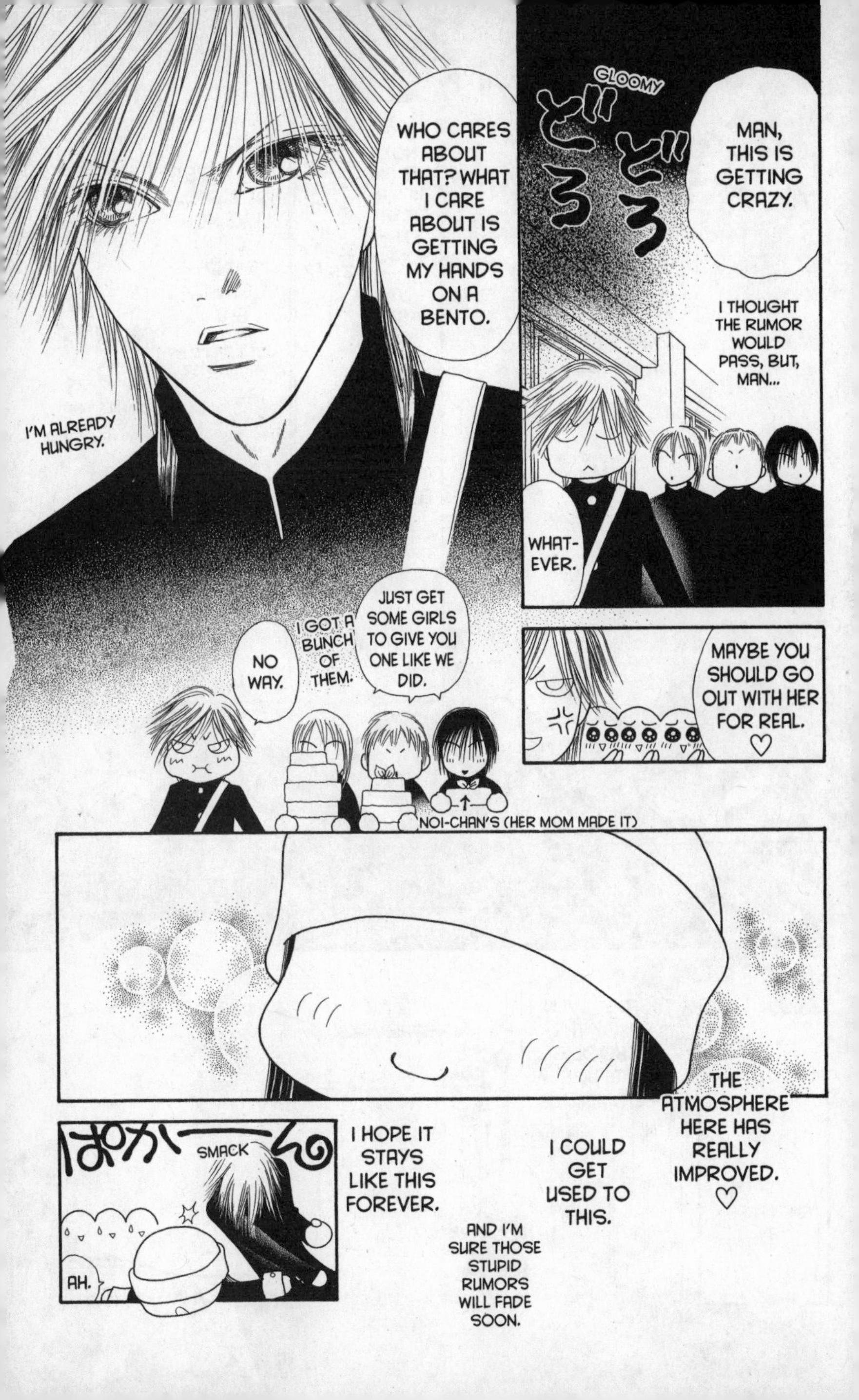
GLOOMY
どろどろ
MAN, THIS IS GETTING CRAZY.
I THOUGHT THE RUMOR WOULD PASS, BUT, MAN...
WHATEVER.
MAYBE YOU SHOULD GO OUT WITH HER FOR REAL. ♡
WHO CARES ABOUT THAT? WHAT I CARE ABOUT IS GETTING MY HANDS ON A BENTO.
I'M ALREADY HUNGRY.
JUST GET SOME GIRLS TO GIVE YOU ONE LIKE WE DID.
I GOT A BUNCH OF THEM.
NO WAY.
NOI-CHAN'S (HER MOM MADE IT)
THE ATMOSPHERE HERE HAS REALLY IMPROVED. ♡
I COULD GET USED TO THIS.
AND I'M SURE THOSE STUPID RUMORS WILL FADE SOON.
I HOPE IT STAYS LIKE THIS FOREVER.
ぱかーん
SMACK
AH.

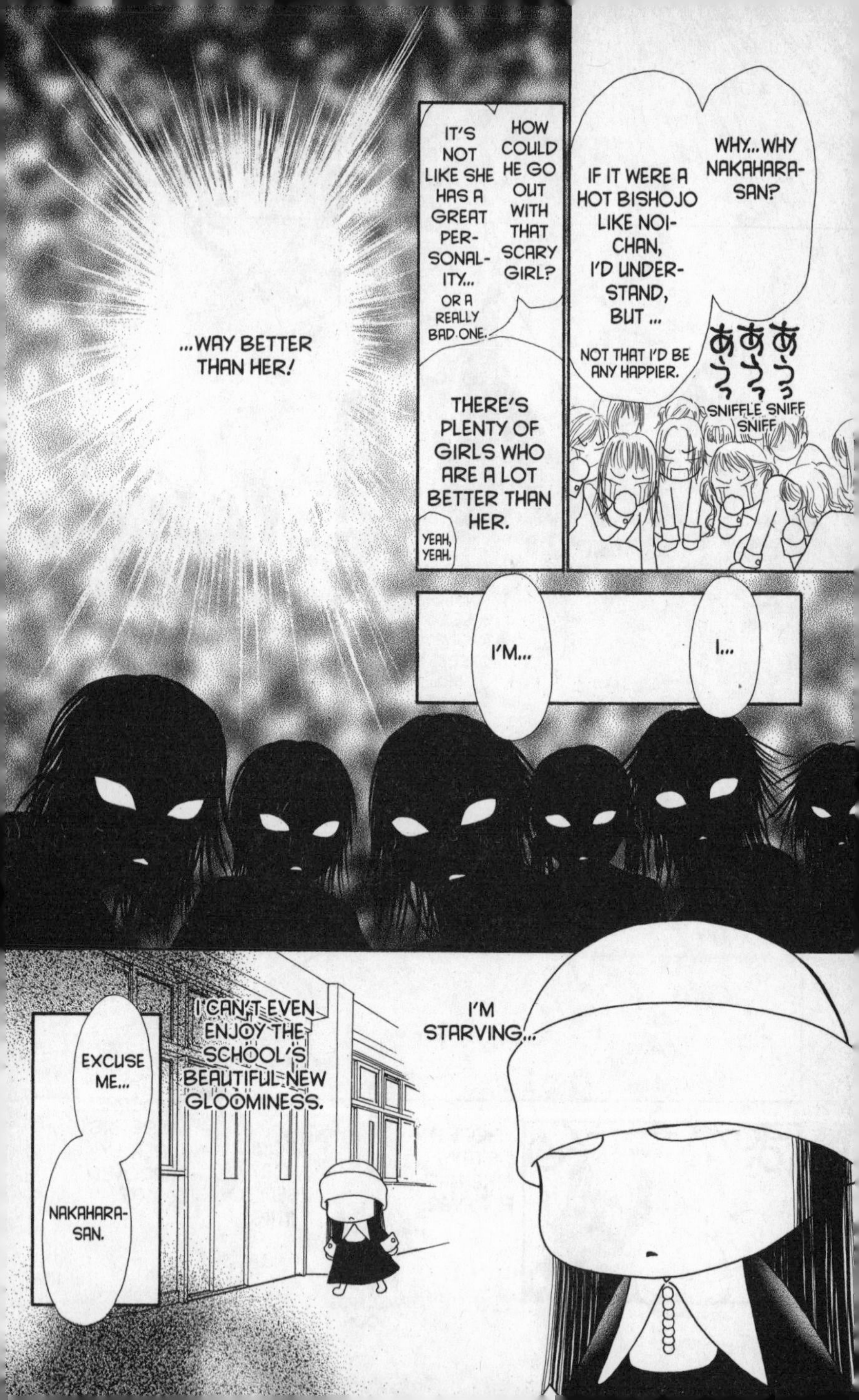

WHY...WHY NAKAHARA-SAN?
IF IT WERE A HOT BISHOJO LIKE NOI-CHAN, I'D UNDERSTAND, BUT ...
NOT THAT I'D BE ANY HAPPIER.
あうぅ あうぅ あうぅ
SNIFFLE SNIFF SNIFF
HOW COULD HE GO OUT WITH THAT SCARY GIRL?
IT'S NOT LIKE SHE HAS A GREAT PERSONALITY... OR A REALLY BAD ONE.
THERE'S PLENTY OF GIRLS WHO ARE A LOT BETTER THAN HER.
YEAH, YEAH.
I...
I'M...
...WAY BETTER THAN HER!
I'M STARVING...
I CAN'T EVEN ENJOY THE SCHOOL'S BEAUTIFUL NEW GLOOMINESS.
EXCUSE ME...
NAKAHARA-SAN.

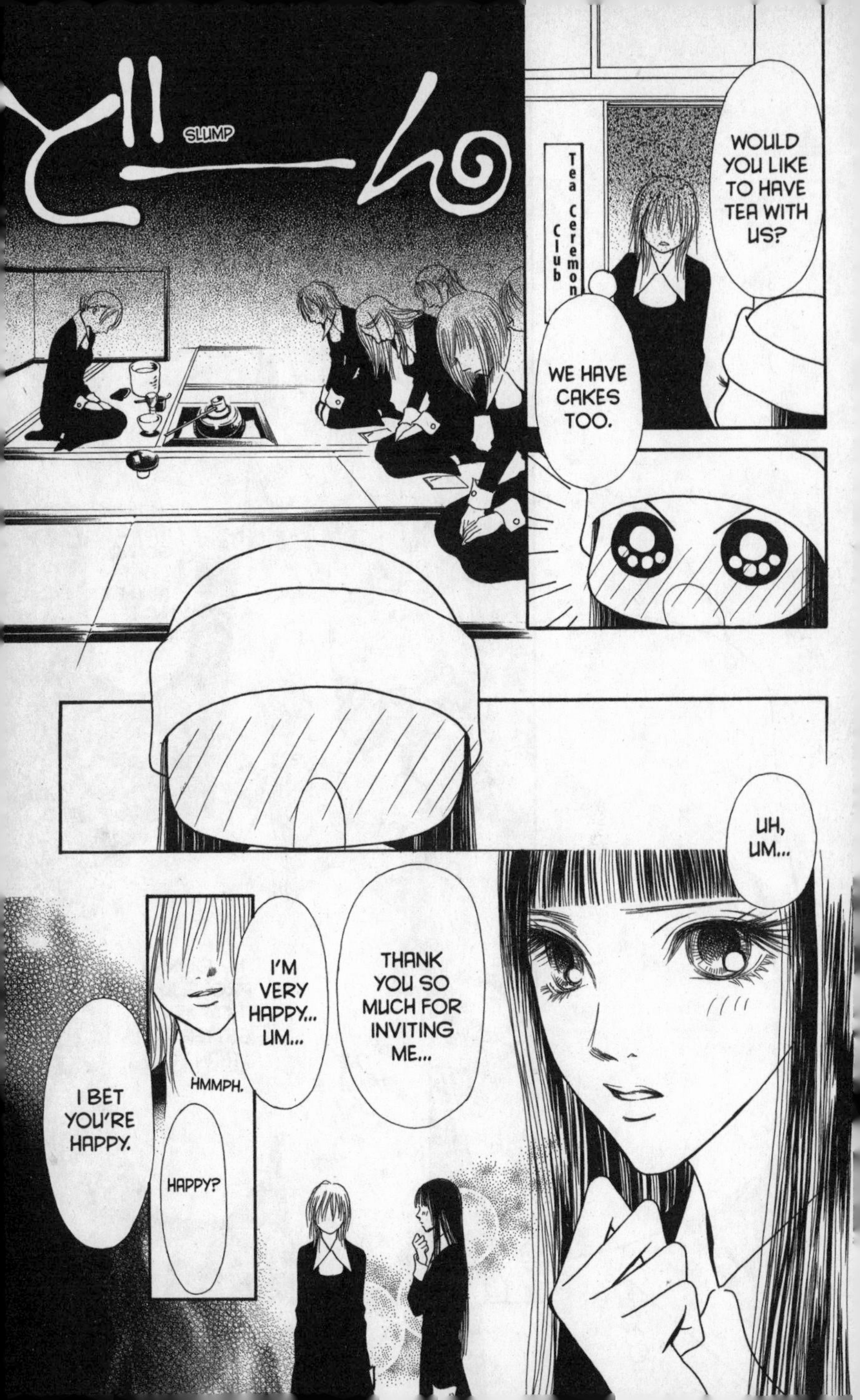
Tea Ceremon Club
WOULD YOU LIKE TO HAVE TEA WITH US?
WE HAVE CAKES TOO.
どーん
SLUMP
UH, UM...
THANK YOU SO MUCH FOR INVITING ME...
I'M VERY HAPPY... UM...
HMMPH.
I BET YOU'RE HAPPY.
HAPPY?

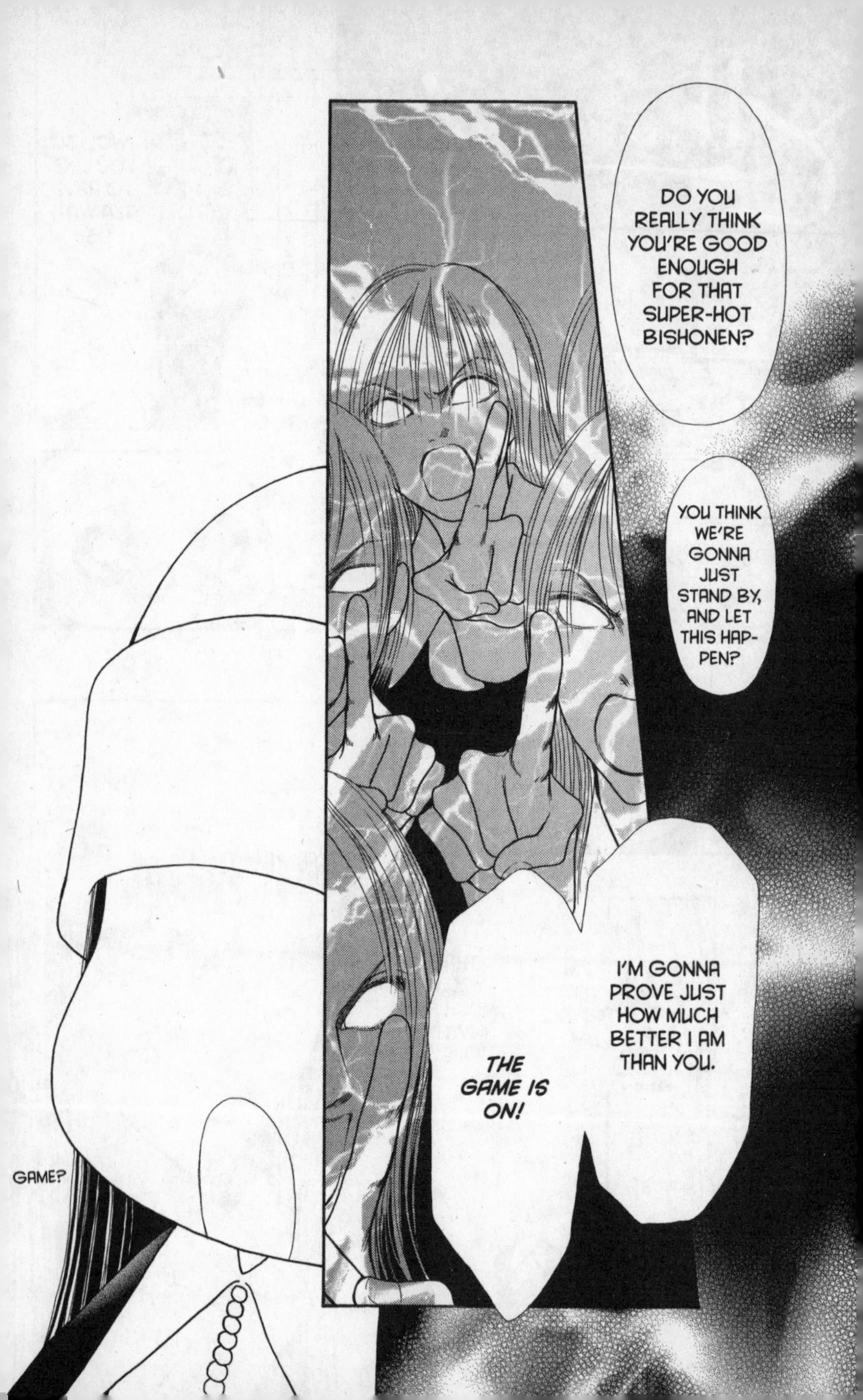
DO YOU REALLY THINK YOU'RE GOOD ENOUGH FOR THAT SUPER-HOT BISHONEN?
YOU THINK WE'RE GONNA JUST STAND BY, AND LET THIS HAP-PEN?
I'M GONNA PROVE JUST HOW MUCH BETTER I AM THAN YOU.
THE GAME IS ON!
GAME?

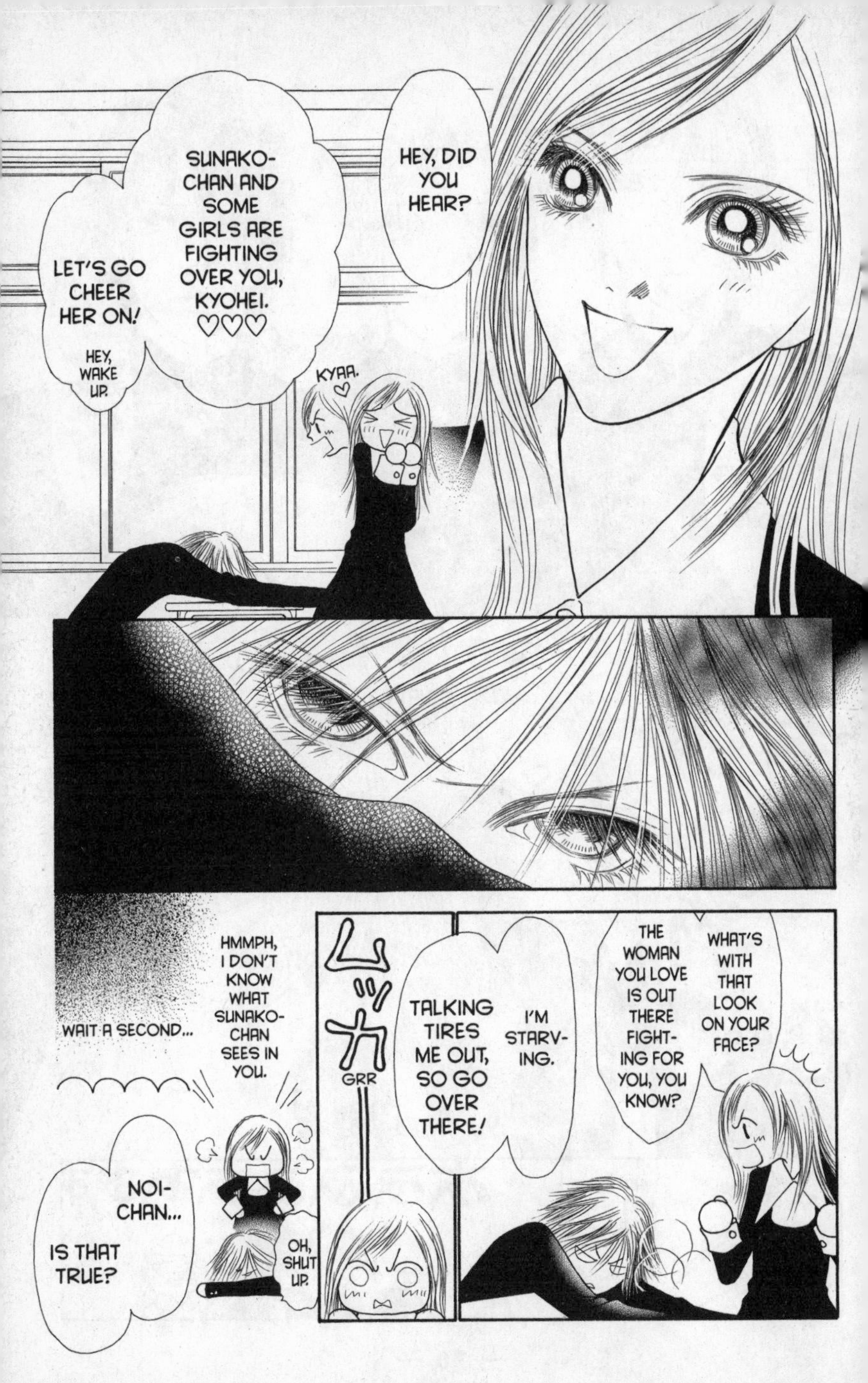
HEY, DID YOU HEAR?
SUNAKO-CHAN AND SOME GIRLS ARE FIGHTING OVER YOU, KYOHEI. ♡♡♡
KYAA. ♡
LET'S GO CHEER HER ON!
HEY, WAKE UP.
WHAT'S WITH THAT LOOK ON YOUR FACE?
THE WOMAN YOU LOVE IS OUT THERE FIGHTING FOR YOU, YOU KNOW?
I'M STARVING.
TALKING TIRES ME OUT, SO GO OVER THERE!
ムッカ
GRR
HMMPH, I DON'T KNOW WHAT SUNAKO-CHAN SEES IN YOU.
WAIT A SECOND...
NOI-CHAN...
IS THAT TRUE?
OH, SHUT UP.

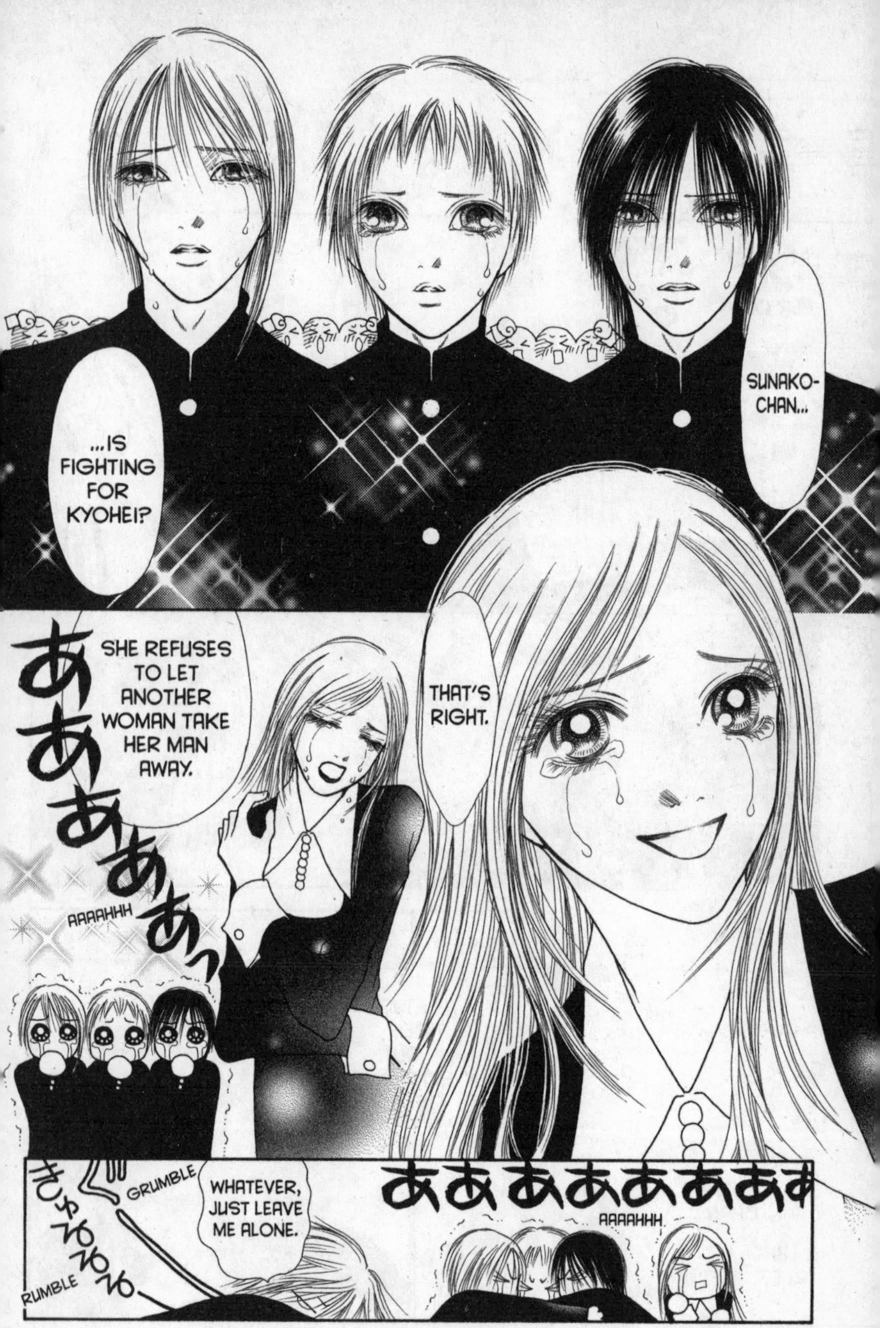
SUNAKO-CHAN...
...IS FIGHTING FOR KYOHEI?
THAT'S RIGHT.
SHE REFUSES TO LET ANOTHER WOMAN TAKE HER MAN AWAY.
ああああっ
AAAAHHH
あああああああああ
AAAAHHH
WHATEVER, JUST LEAVE ME ALONE.
GRUMBLE
RUMBLE

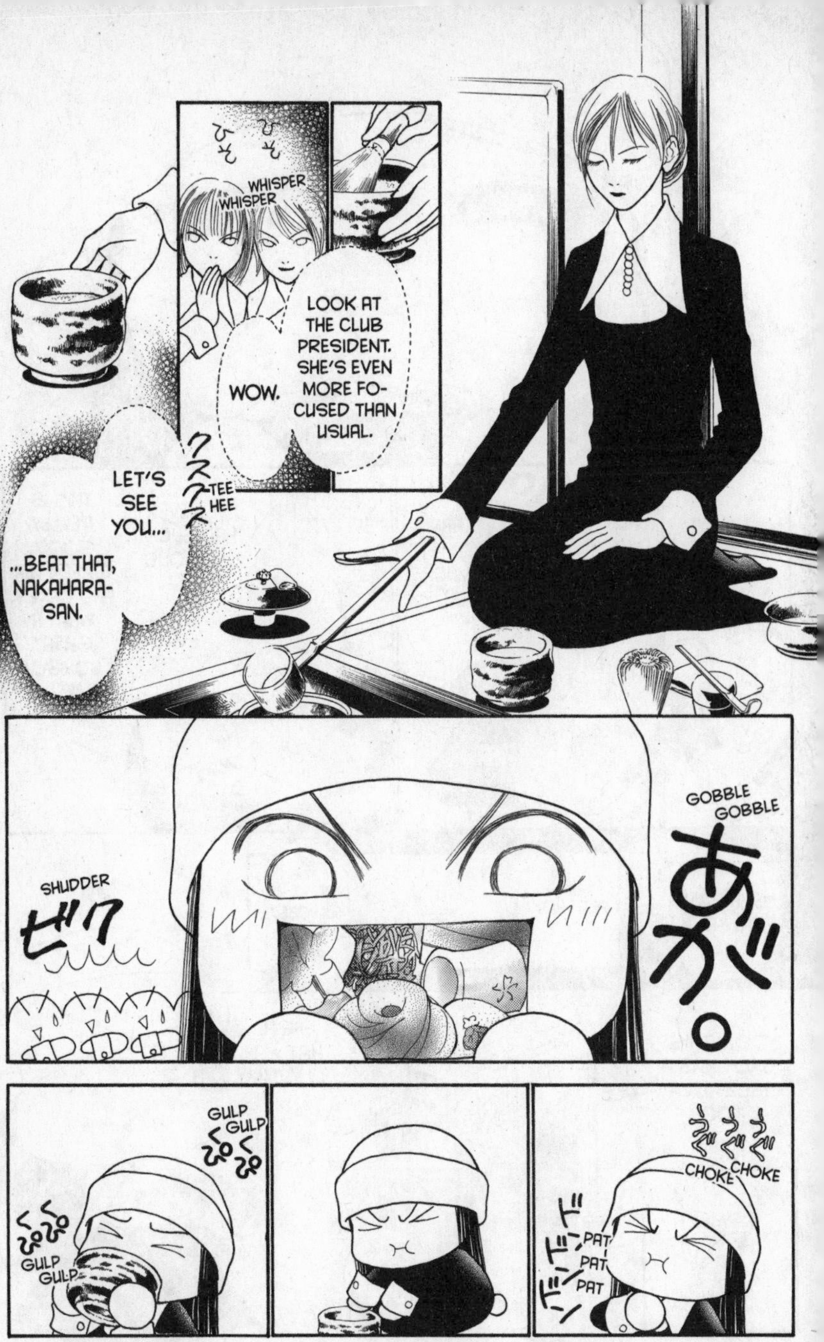
ひそ ひそ
WHISPER WHISPER
WOW.
LOOK AT THE CLUB PRESIDENT. SHE'S EVEN MORE FO-CUSED THAN USUAL.
クスクス
TEE HEE
LET'S SEE YOU...
...BEAT THAT, NAKAHARA-SAN.
GOBBLE GOBBLE
SHUDDER
CHOKE CHOKE
PAT PAT PAT
GULP GULP
GULP GULP

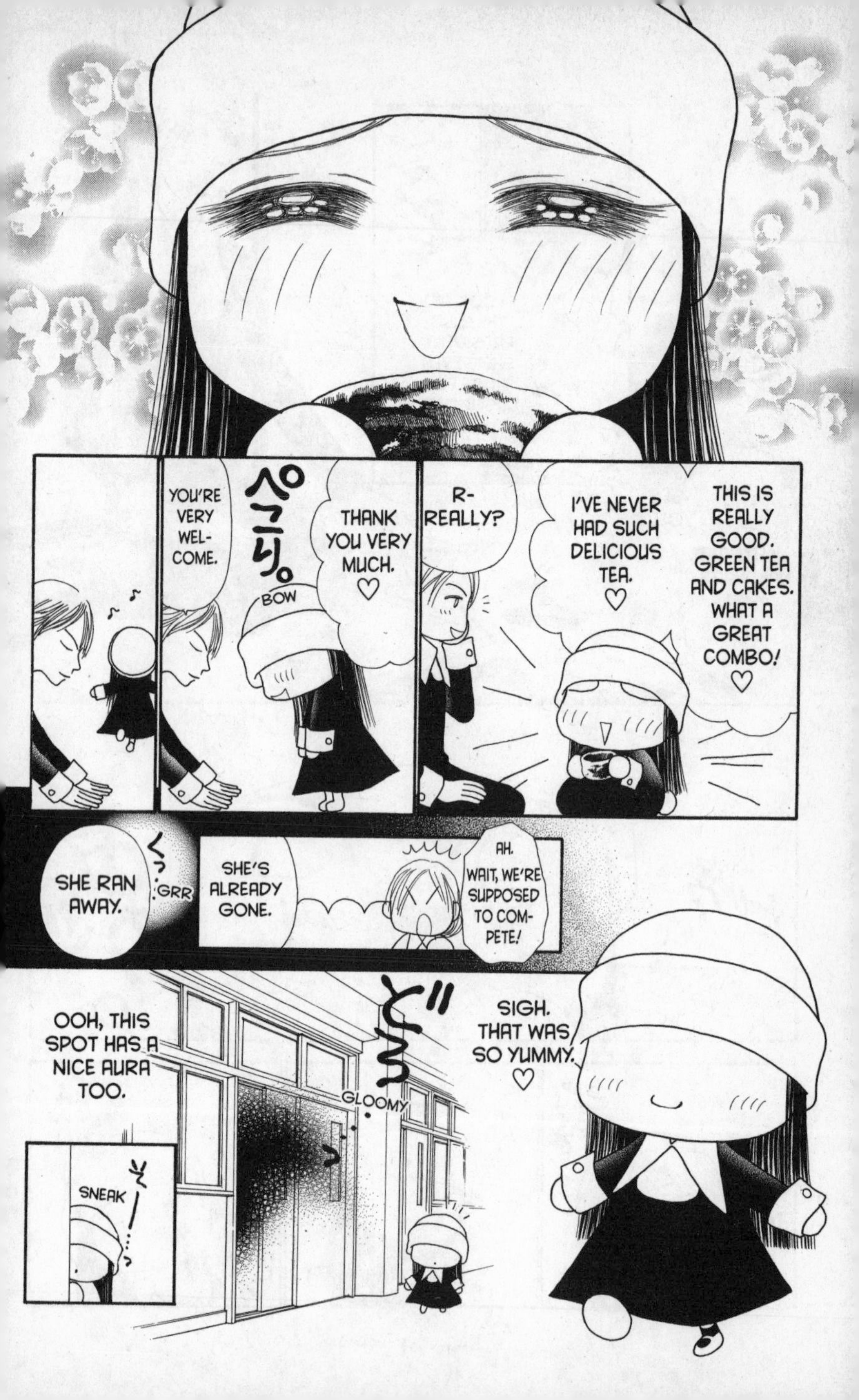
THIS IS REALLY GOOD. GREEN TEA AND CAKES. WHAT A GREAT COMBO! ♡
I'VE NEVER HAD SUCH DELICIOUS TEA. ♡
R- REALLY?
THANK YOU VERY MUCH. ♡
ぺこり。
BOW
YOU'RE VERY WEL- COME.
AH. WAIT, WE'RE SUPPOSED TO COM- PETE!
SHE'S ALREADY GONE.
くっ
GRR
SHE RAN AWAY.
SIGH. THAT WAS SO YUMMY. ♡
どろ
GLOOMY
OOH, THIS SPOT HAS A NICE AURA TOO.
そ～…
SNEAK

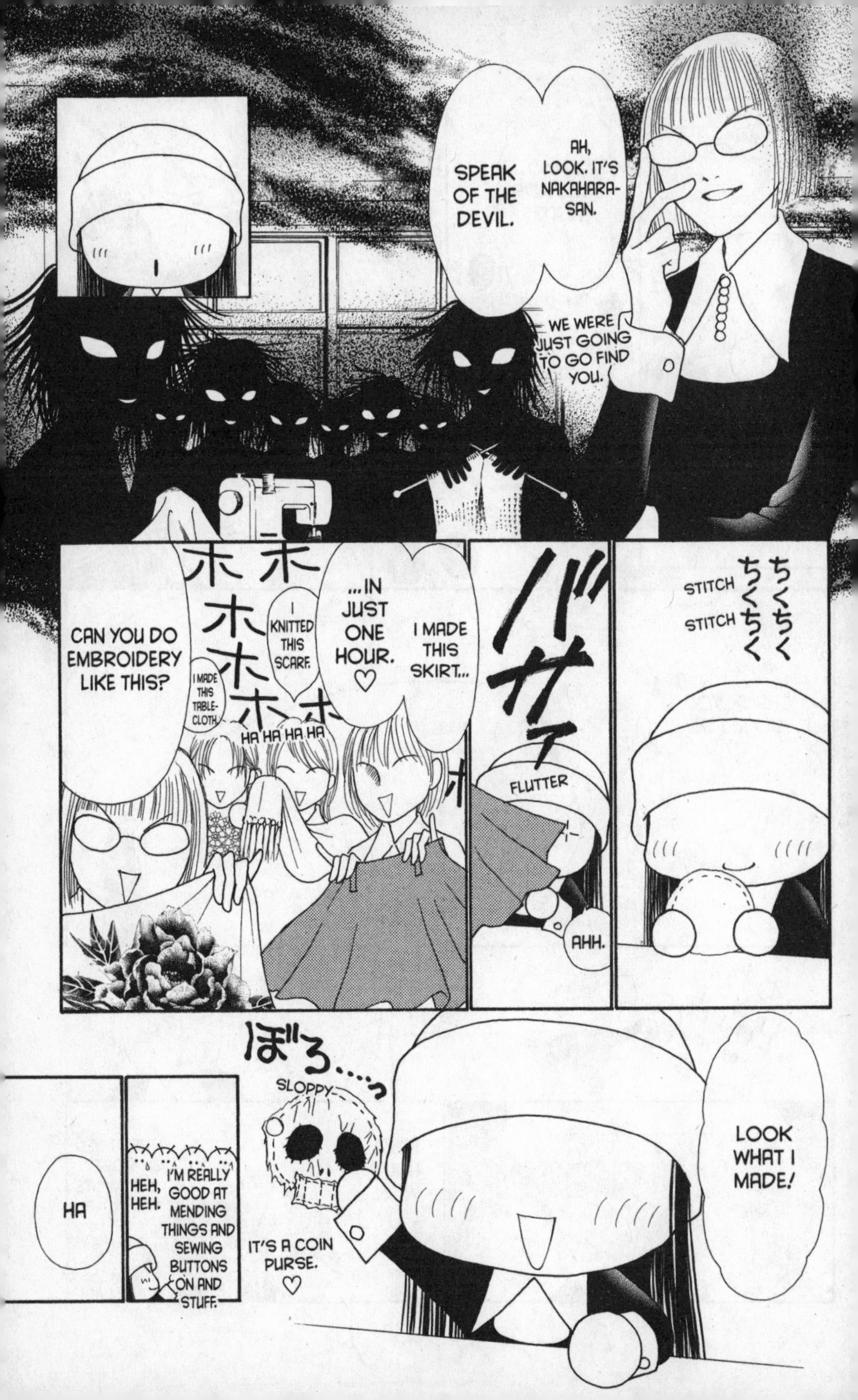
AH, LOOK. IT'S NAKAHARA-SAN.
SPEAK OF THE DEVIL.
WE WERE JUST GOING TO GO FIND YOU.
ちくちく
STITCH
ちくちく
STITCH
バサァ
FLUTTER
AHH.
I MADE THIS SKIRT...
...IN JUST ONE HOUR. ♡
I KNITTED THIS SCARF.
ホホホホホ
I MADE THIS TABLE-CLOTH
HA HA HA HA
CAN YOU DO EMBROIDERY LIKE THIS?
LOOK WHAT I MADE!
ぼろ…
SLOPPY
IT'S A COIN PURSE. ♡
HEH, HEH.
I'M REALLY GOOD AT MENDING THINGS AND SEWING BUTTONS ON AND STUFF.
HA

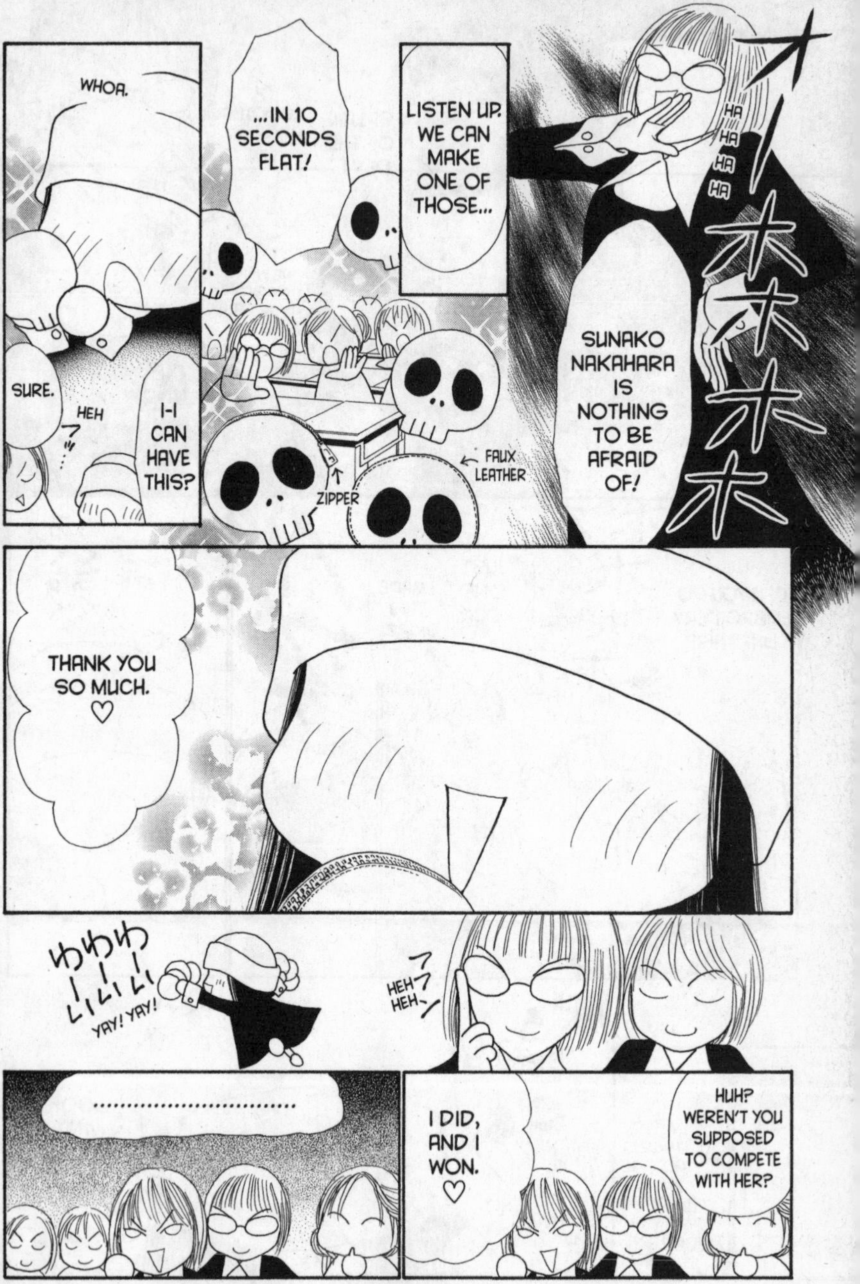

オーホホホホ
HA HA HA HA
SUNAKO NAKAHARA IS NOTHING TO BE AFRAID OF!
LISTEN UP. WE CAN MAKE ONE OF THOSE...
...IN 10 SECONDS FLAT!
FAUX LEATHER
ZIPPER
WHOA.
I-I CAN HAVE THIS?
SURE.
HEH
THANK YOU SO MUCH. ♡
HEH HEH
YAY! YAY!
HUH? WEREN'T YOU SUPPOSED TO COMPETE WITH HER?
I DID, AND I WON. ♡
....

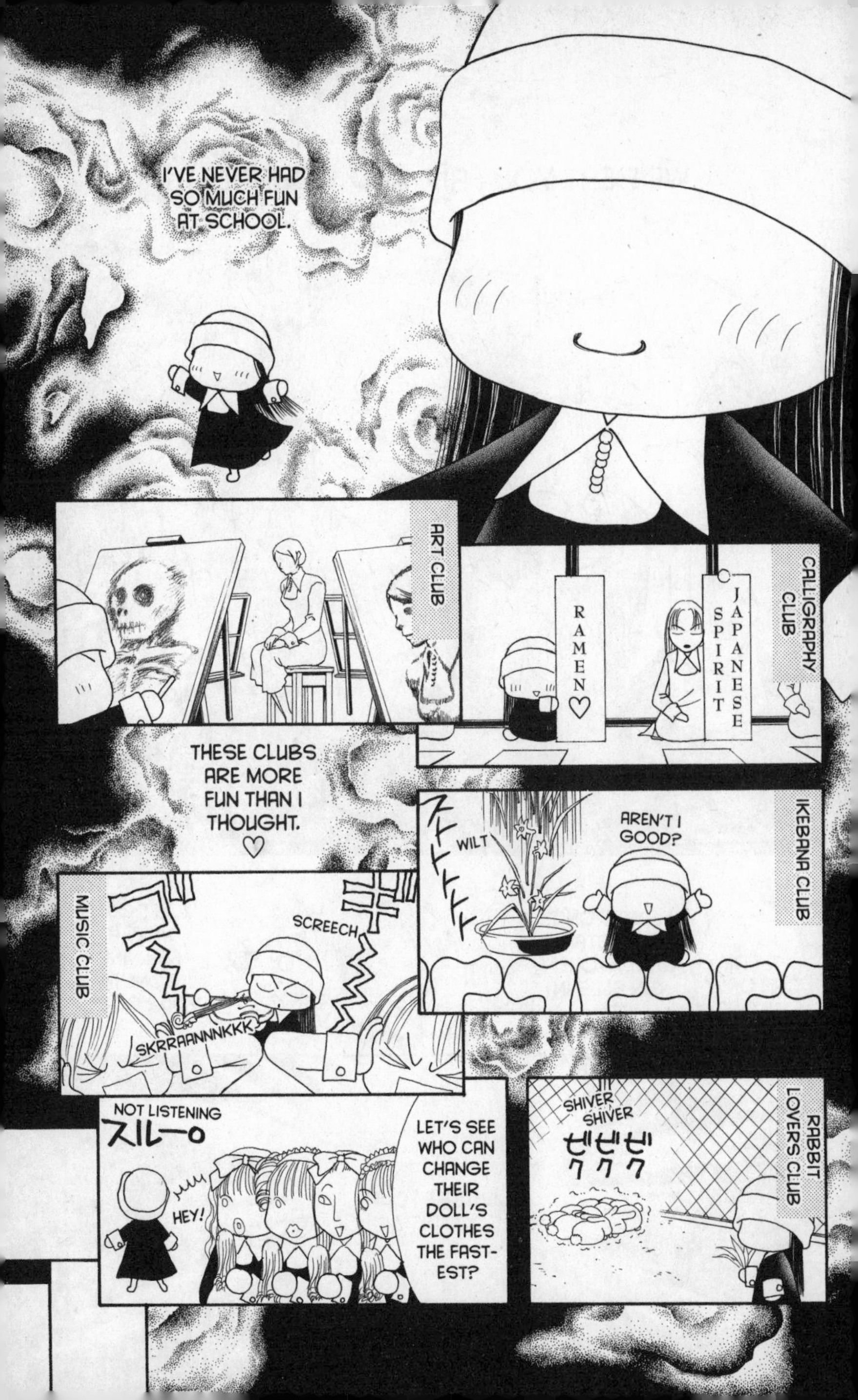
I'VE NEVER HAD SO MUCH FUN AT SCHOOL.
CALLIGRAPHY CLUB
JAPANESE SPIRIT
RAMEN ♡
ART CLUB
THESE CLUBS ARE MORE FUN THAN I THOUGHT. ♡
IKEBANA CLUB
AREN'T I GOOD?
WILT
MUSIC CLUB
SCREECH
SKRRAANNNKKK
RABBIT LOVER'S CLUB
SHIVER SHIVER
ビクビクビク
LET'S SEE WHO CAN CHANGE THEIR DOLL'S CLOTHES THE FAST-EST?
NOT LISTENING
スルー。
HEY!

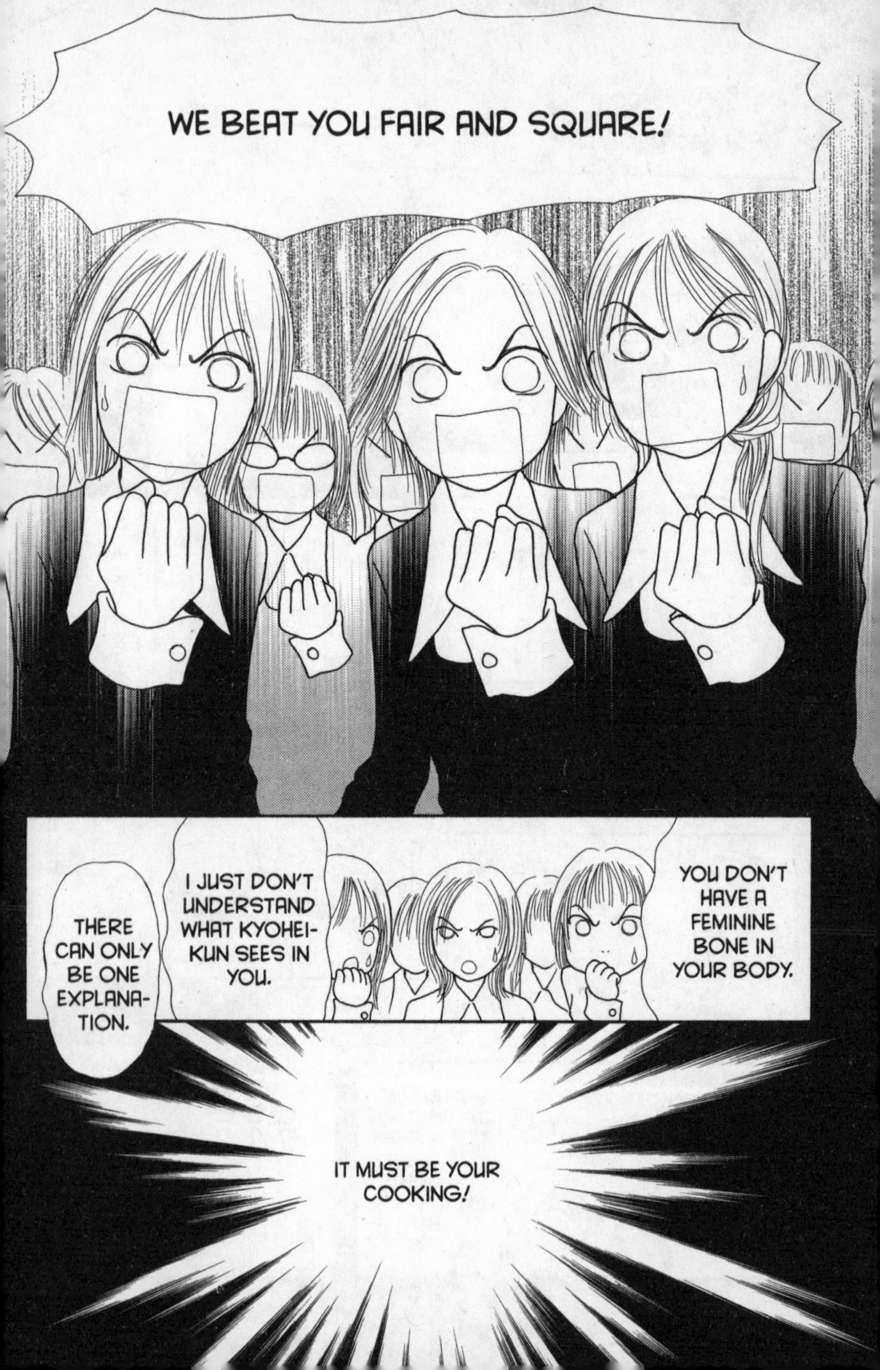
WE BEAT YOU FAIR AND SQUARE!
YOU DON'T HAVE A FEMININE BONE IN YOUR BODY.
I JUST DON'T UNDERSTAND WHAT KYOHEI-KUN SEES IN YOU.
THERE CAN ONLY BE ONE EXPLANATION.
IT MUST BE YOUR COOKING!

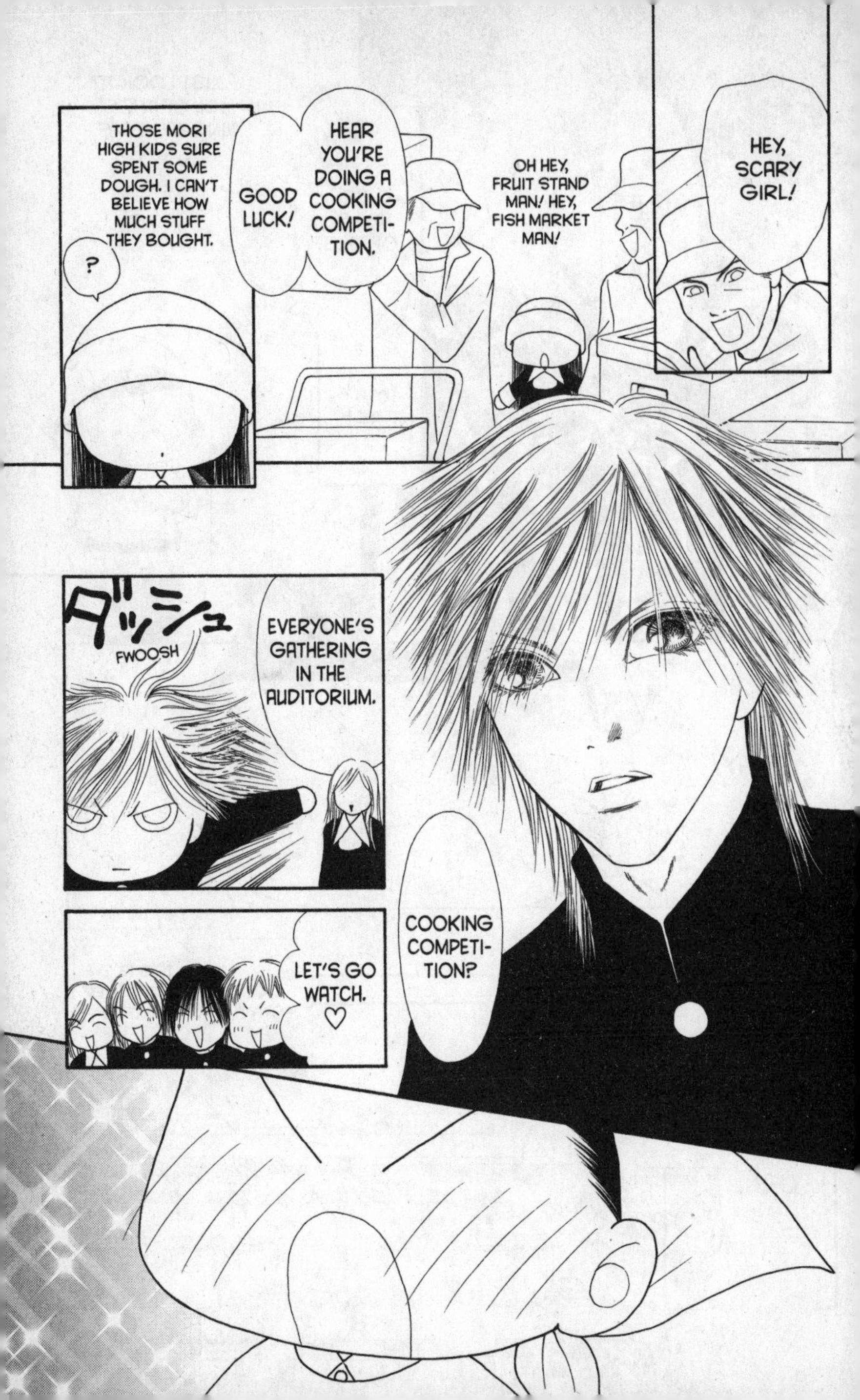
HEY, SCARY GIRL!
OH HEY, FRUIT STAND MAN! HEY, FISH MARKET MAN!
HEAR YOU'RE DOING A COOKING COMPETITION.
GOOD LUCK!
THOSE MORI HIGH KIDS SURE SPENT SOME DOUGH. I CAN'T BELIEVE HOW MUCH STUFF THEY BOUGHT.
?
COOKING COMPETITION?
EVERYONE'S GATHERING IN THE AUDITORIUM.
ダッシュ
FWOOSH
LET'S GO WATCH. ♡

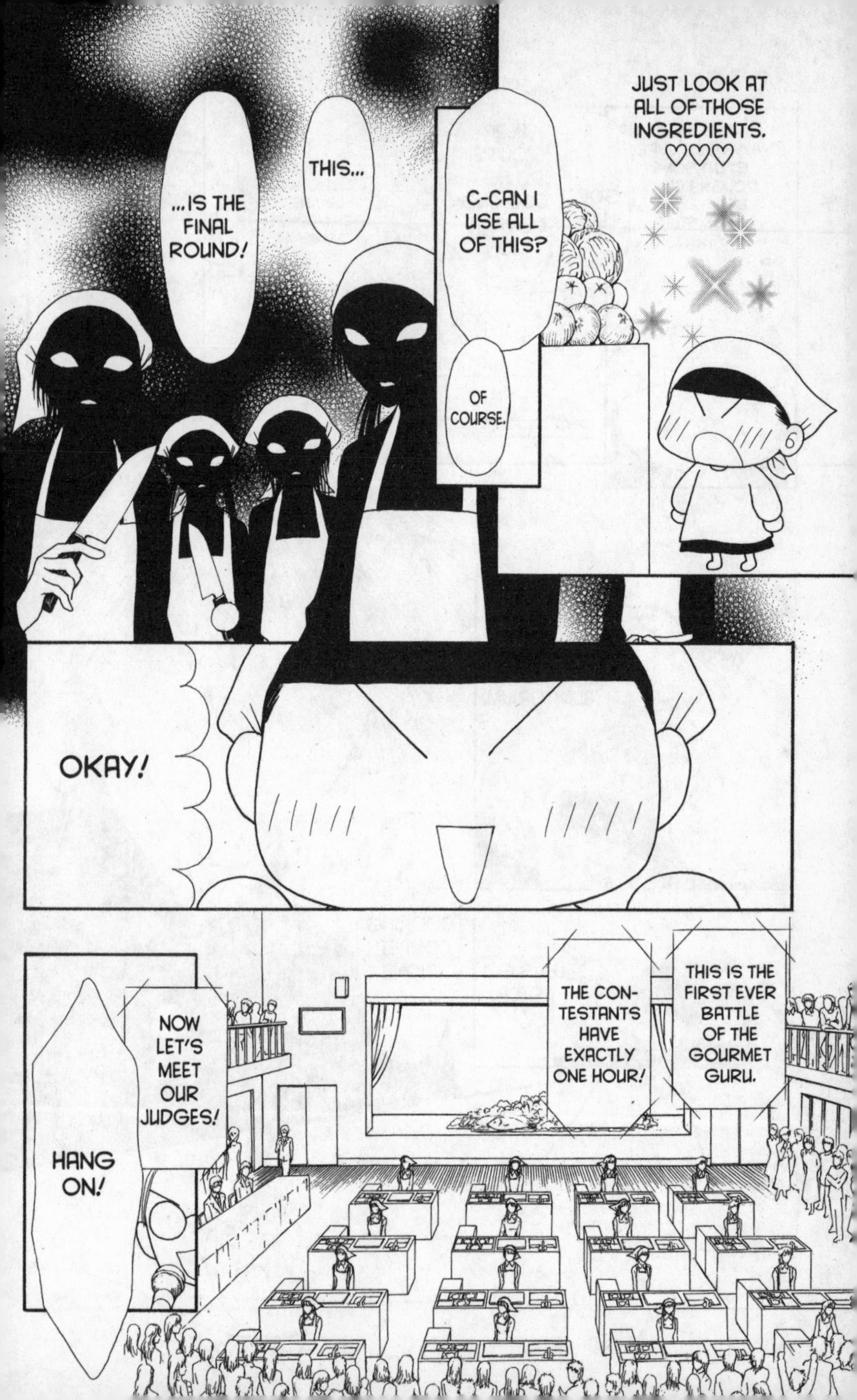
JUST LOOK AT ALL OF THOSE INGREDIENTS. ♡♡♡
C-CAN I USE ALL OF THIS?
OF COURSE.
THIS...
...IS THE FINAL ROUND!
OKAY!
THIS IS THE FIRST EVER BATTLE OF THE GOURMET GURU.
THE CON-TESTANTS HAVE EXACTLY ONE HOUR!
NOW LET'S MEET OUR JUDGES!
HANG ON!

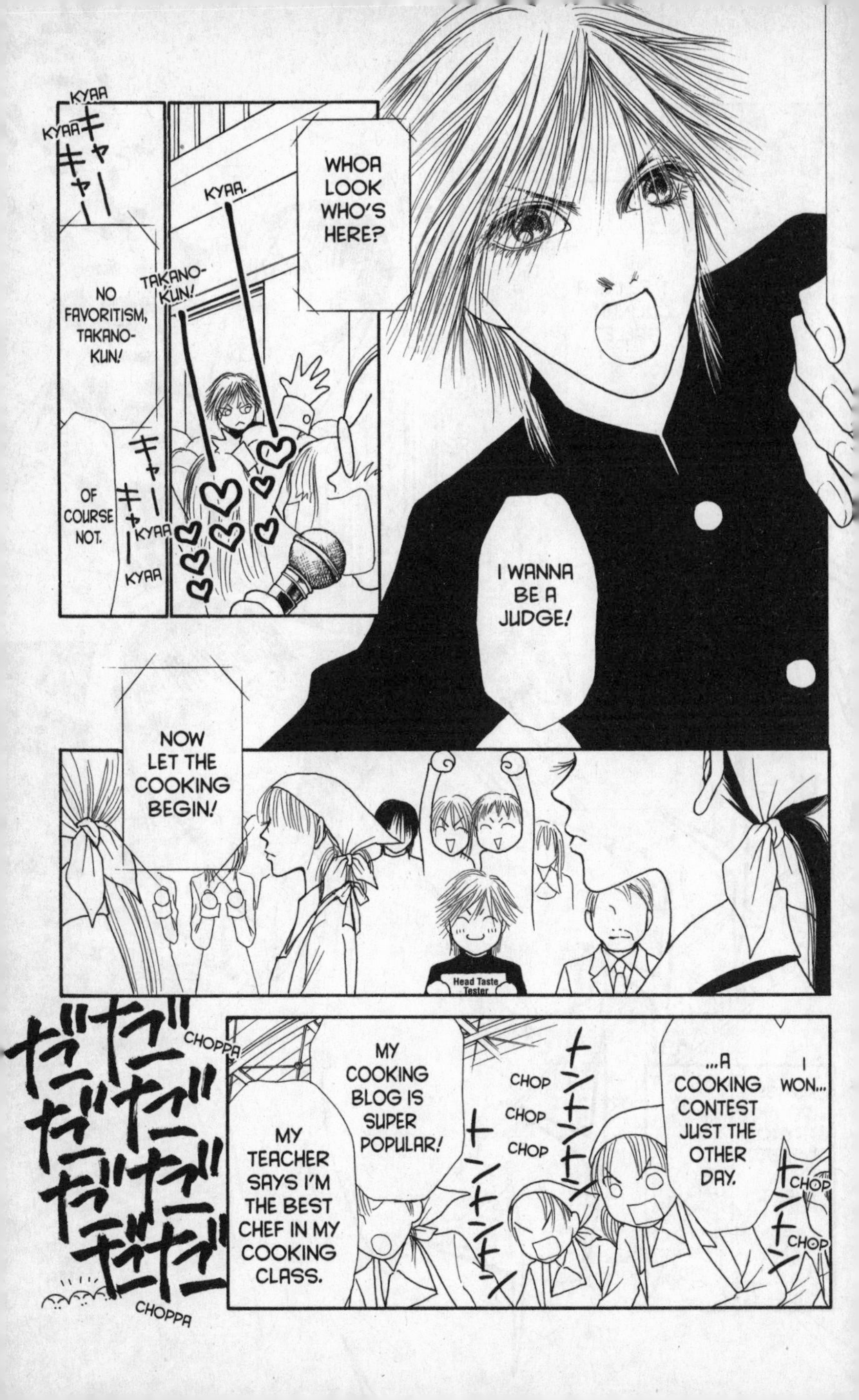

WHOA LOOK WHO'S HERE?
I WANNA BE A JUDGE!
KYAA.
TAKANO-KUN!
キャー
キャー
KYAA
KYAA
キャー
キャー
KYAA
KYAA
NO FAVORITISM, TAKANO-KUN!
OF COURSE NOT.
NOW LET THE COOKING BEGIN!
Head Taste Tester
I WON...
...A COOKING CONTEST JUST THE OTHER DAY.
トントン
CHOP
CHOP
トントントン
CHOP
CHOP
CHOP
MY COOKING BLOG IS SUPER POPULAR!
MY TEACHER SAYS I'M THE BEST CHEF IN MY COOKING CLASS.
だだーだだーだだーだだーだだー
CHOPPA
CHOPPA

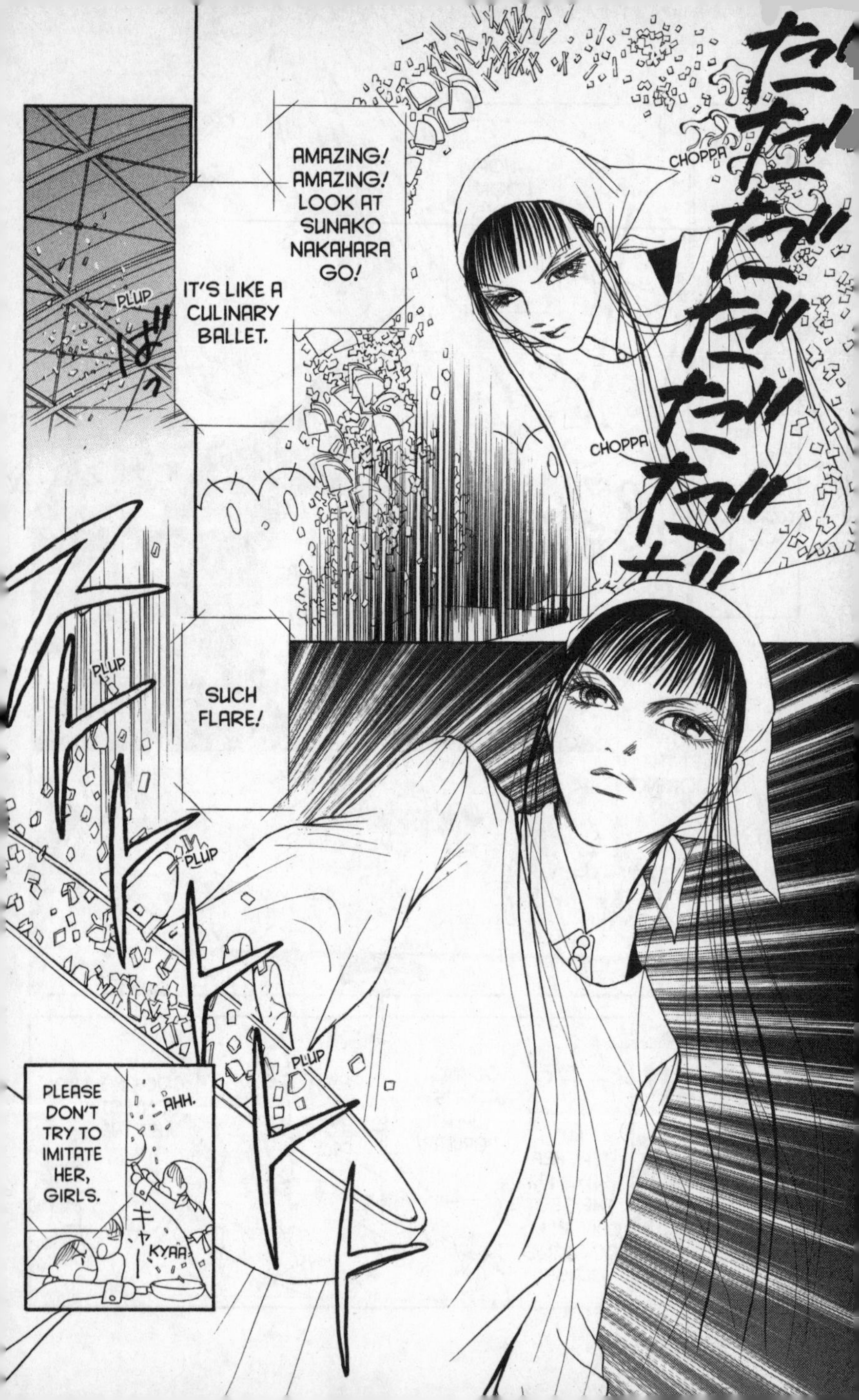

たダダダダ
CHOPPA
CHOPPA
AMAZING! AMAZING! LOOK AT SUNAKO NAKAHARA GO!
IT'S LIKE A CULINARY BALLET.
ばっ
PLUP
SUCH FLARE!
PLUP
PLUP
PLUP
PLEASE DON'T TRY TO IMITATE HER, GIRLS.
AHH.
キャー
KYAA

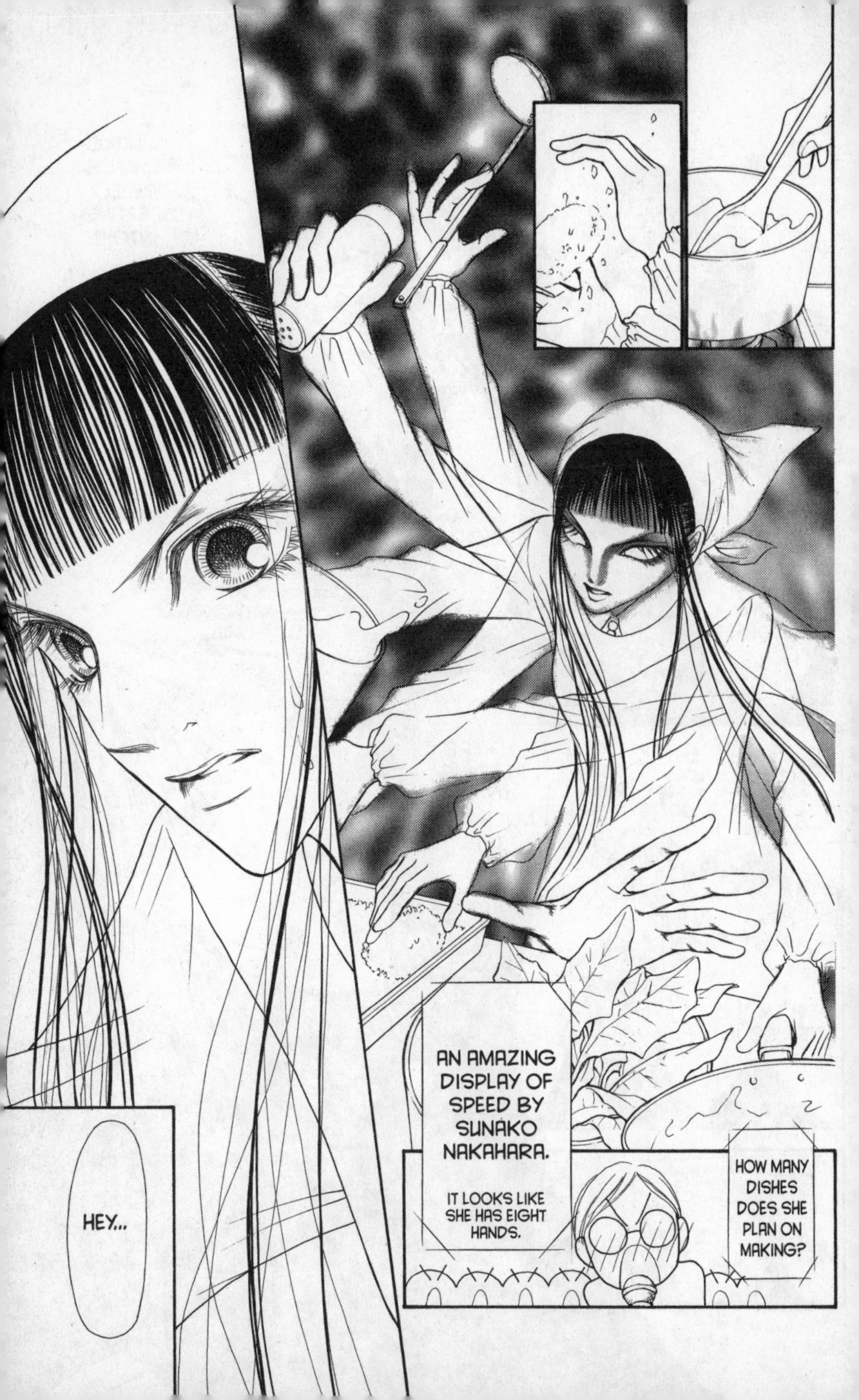
AN AMAZING DISPLAY OF SPEED BY SUNAKO NAKAHARA.
IT LOOKS LIKE SHE HAS EIGHT HANDS.
HOW MANY DISHES DOES SHE PLAN ON MAKING?
HEY...

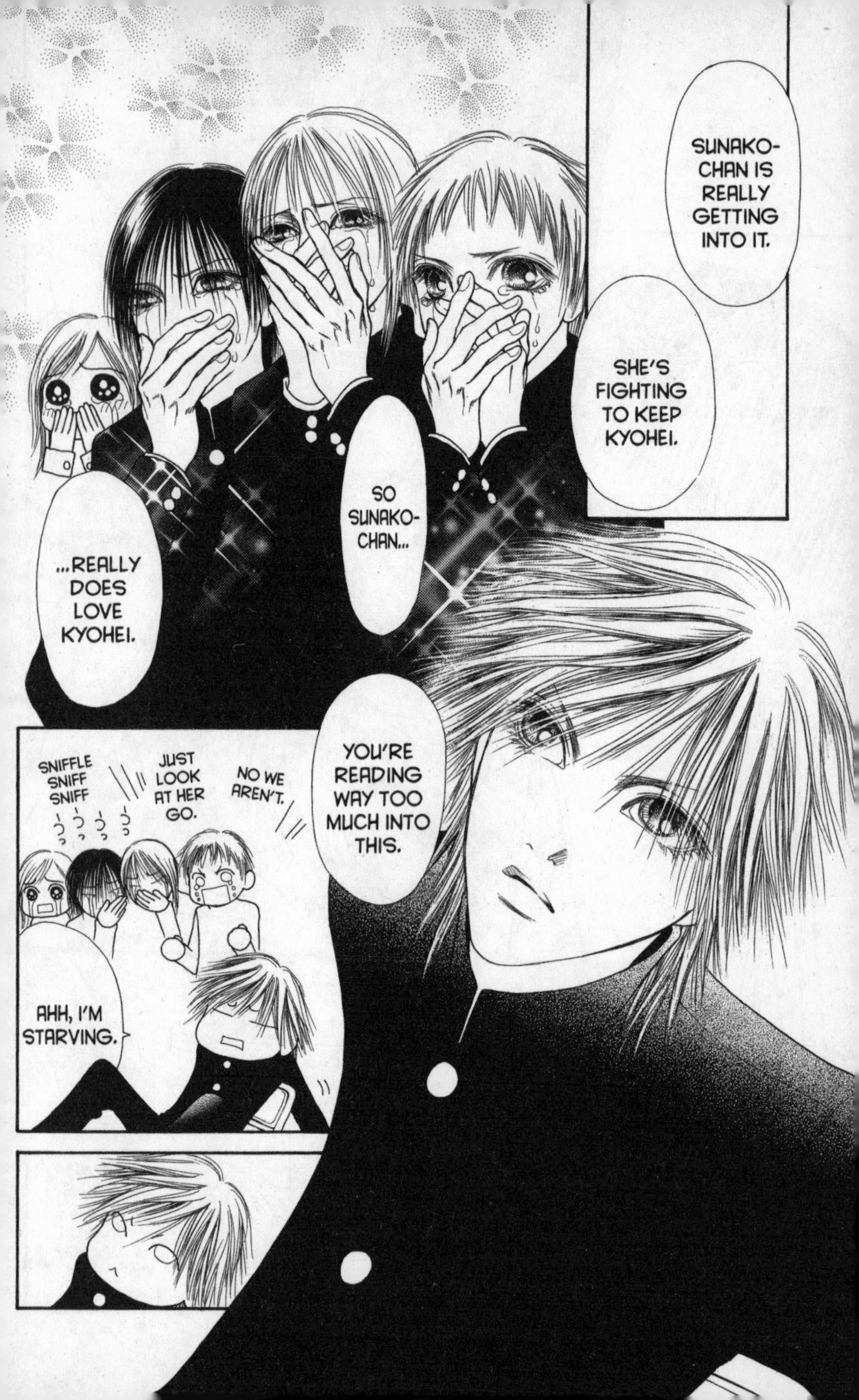

SUNAKO-CHAN IS REALLY GETTING INTO IT.
SHE'S FIGHTING TO KEEP KYOHEI.
SO SUNAKO-CHAN...
...REALLY DOES LOVE KYOHEI.
YOU'RE READING WAY TOO MUCH INTO THIS.
NO WE AREN'T.
JUST LOOK AT HER GO.
SNIFFLE SNIFF SNIFF
AHH, I'M STARVING.

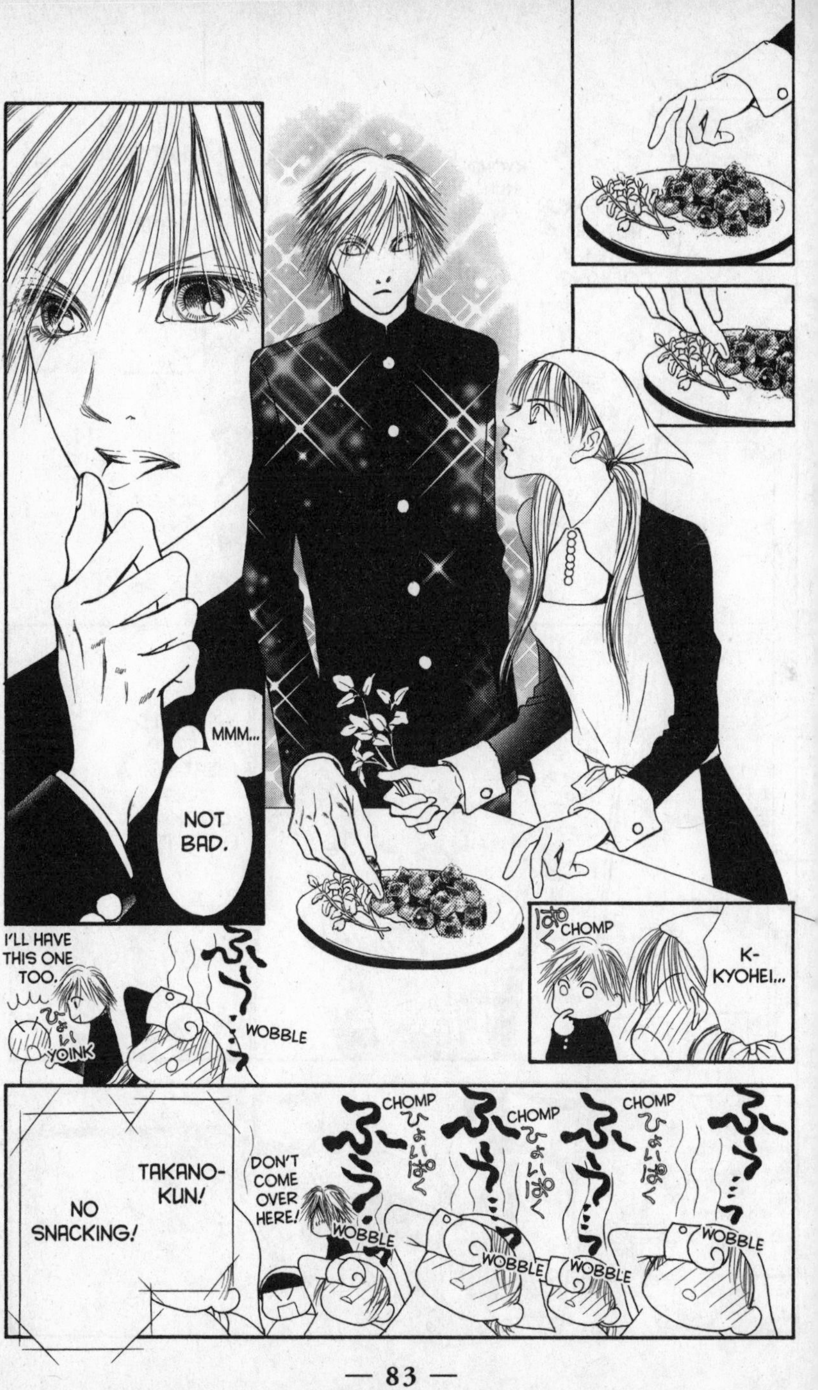
MMM...
NOT BAD.
ぱく
CHOMP
K-KYOHEI...
I'LL HAVE THIS ONE TOO.
ひょい
YOINK
ふら~
WOBBLE
ふら~
WOBBLE
ひょいぱく
CHOMP
ふら~
WOBBLE
ひょいぱく
CHOMP
ふら~
WOBBLE
ひょいぱく
CHOMP
ふら~
WOBBLE
DON'T COME OVER HERE!
TAKANO-KUN!
NO SNACKING!

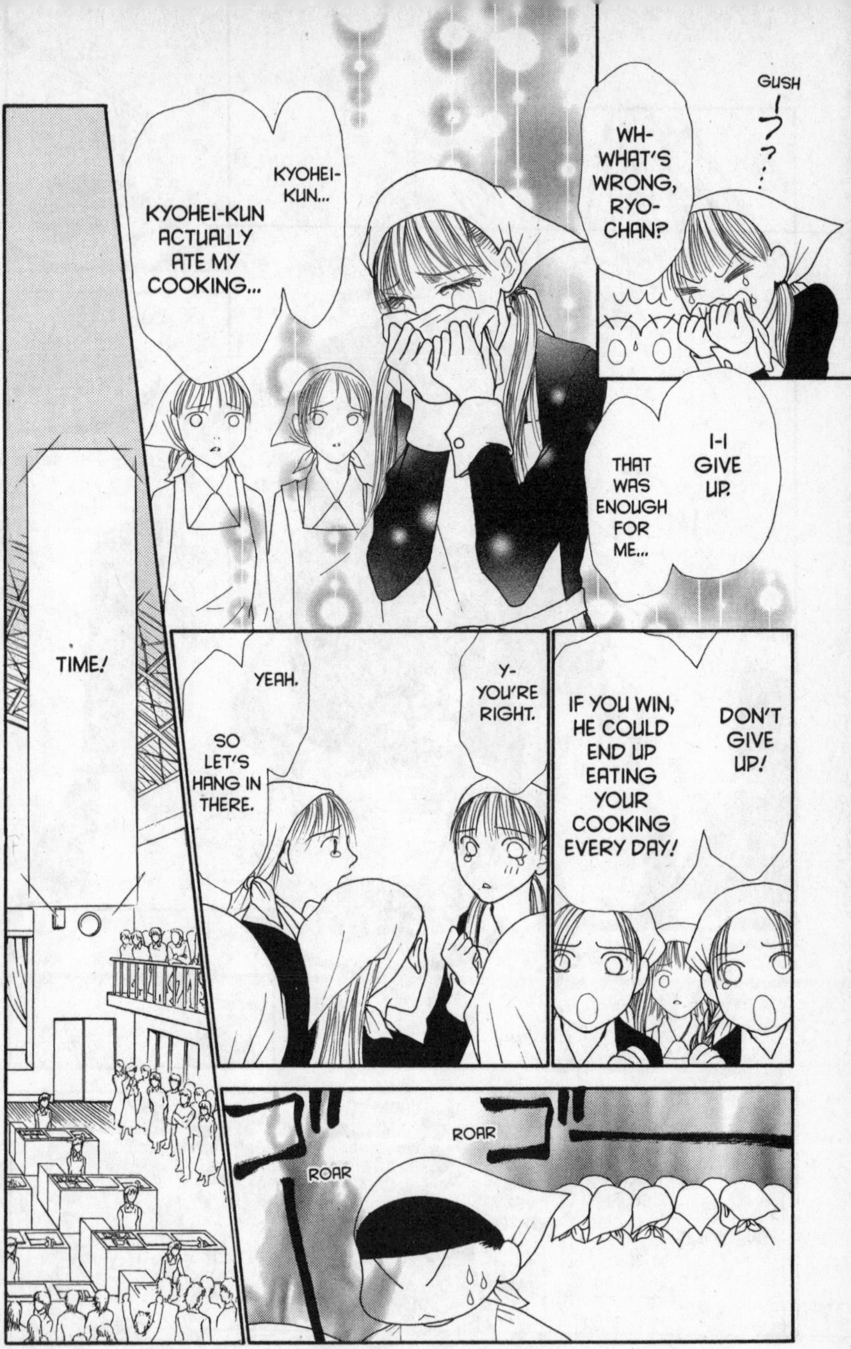
GUSH
WH-WHAT'S WRONG, RYO-CHAN?
KYOHEI-KUN...
KYOHEI-KUN ACTUALLY ATE MY COOKING...
I-I GIVE UP.
THAT WAS ENOUGH FOR ME...
DON'T GIVE UP!
IF YOU WIN, HE COULD END UP EATING YOUR COOKING EVERY DAY!
Y-YOU'RE RIGHT.
YEAH.
SO LET'S HANG IN THERE.
ROAR
ROAR
TIME!

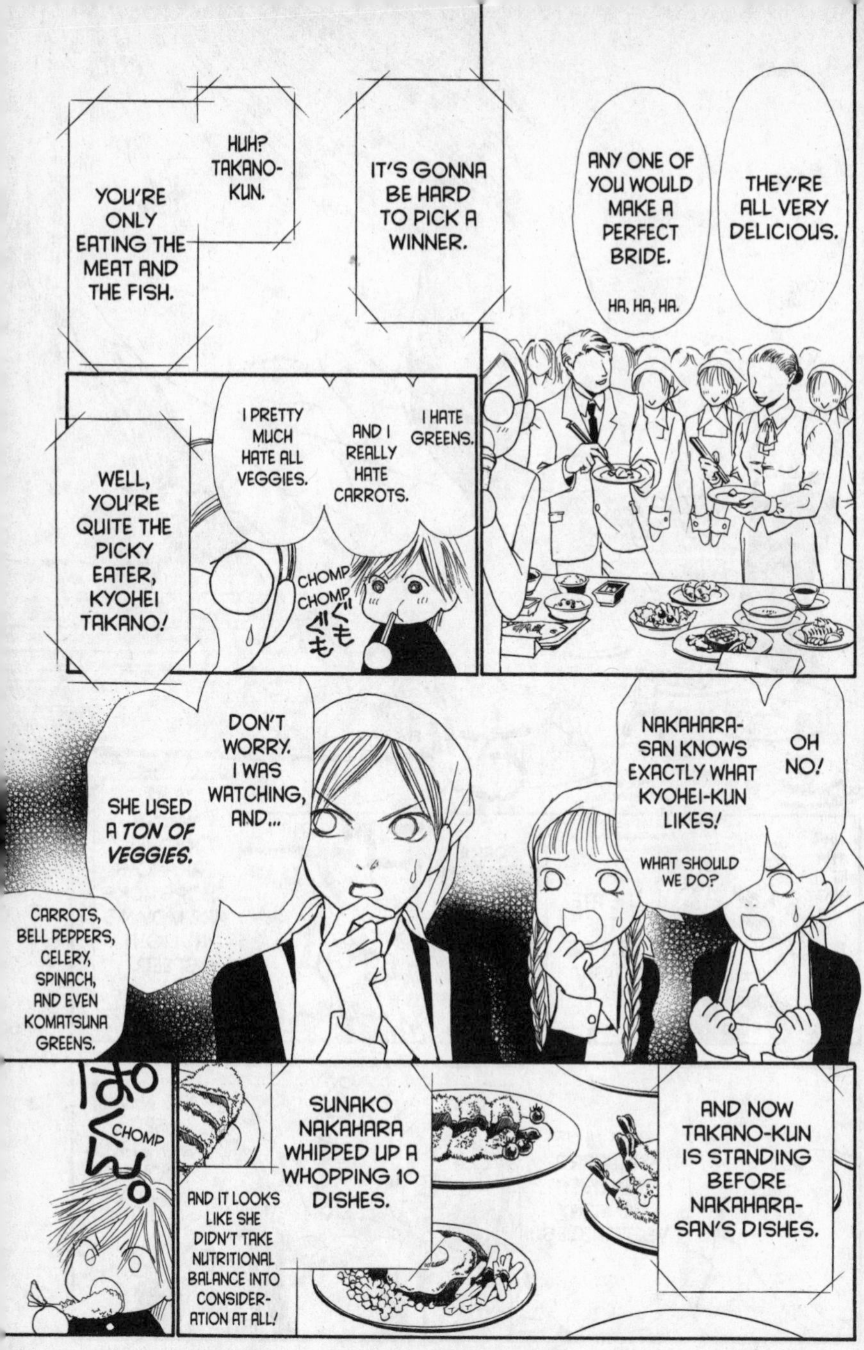
THEY'RE ALL VERY DELICIOUS.
ANY ONE OF YOU WOULD MAKE A PERFECT BRIDE.
HA, HA, HA.
IT'S GONNA BE HARD TO PICK A WINNER.
HUH? TAKANO-KUN.
YOU'RE ONLY EATING THE MEAT AND THE FISH.
I HATE GREENS.
AND I REALLY HATE CARROTS.
I PRETTY MUCH HATE ALL VEGGIES.
CHOMP CHOMP
ぐもぐも
WELL, YOU'RE QUITE THE PICKY EATER, KYOHEI TAKANO!
OH NO!
NAKAHARA-SAN KNOWS EXACTLY WHAT KYOHEI-KUN LIKES!
WHAT SHOULD WE DO?
DON'T WORRY. I WAS WATCHING, AND...
SHE USED A *TON OF VEGGIES.*
CARROTS, BELL PEPPERS, CELERY, SPINACH, AND EVEN KOMATSUNA GREENS.
AND NOW TAKANO-KUN IS STANDING BEFORE NAKAHARA-SAN'S DISHES.
SUNAKO NAKAHARA WHIPPED UP A WHOPPING 10 DISHES.
AND IT LOOKS LIKE SHE DIDN'T TAKE NUTRITIONAL BALANCE INTO CONSIDERATION AT ALL!
ぱくっ。
CHOMP

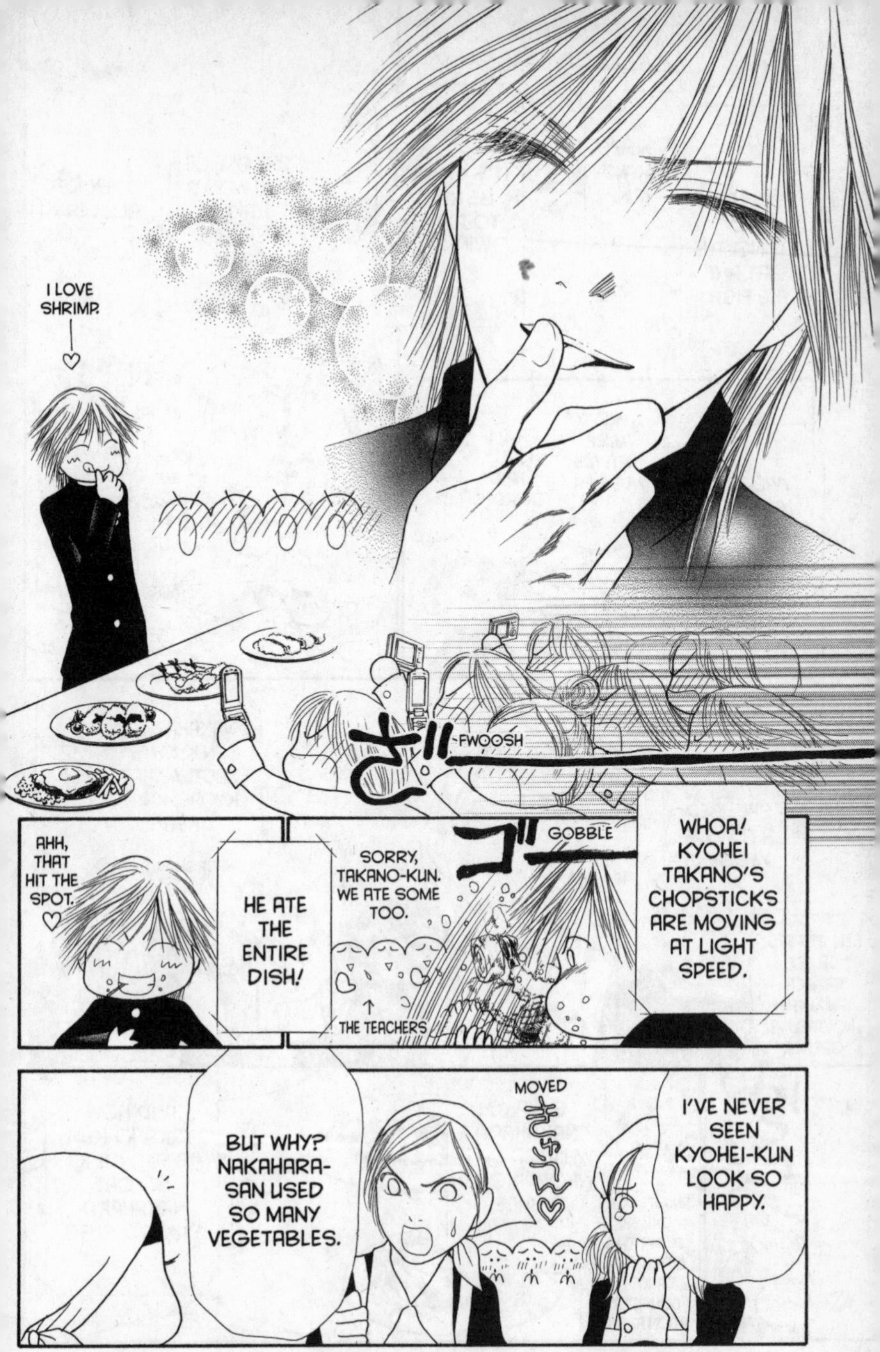
I LOVE SHRIMP.
FWOOSH
WHOA! KYOHEI TAKANO'S CHOPSTICKS ARE MOVING AT LIGHT SPEED.
GOBBLE
SORRY, TAKANO-KUN. WE ATE SOME TOO.
THE TEACHERS
HE ATE THE ENTIRE DISH!
AHH, THAT HIT THE SPOT.
I'VE NEVER SEEN KYOHEI-KUN LOOK SO HAPPY.
MOVED
BUT WHY? NAKAHARA-SAN USED SO MANY VEGETABLES.

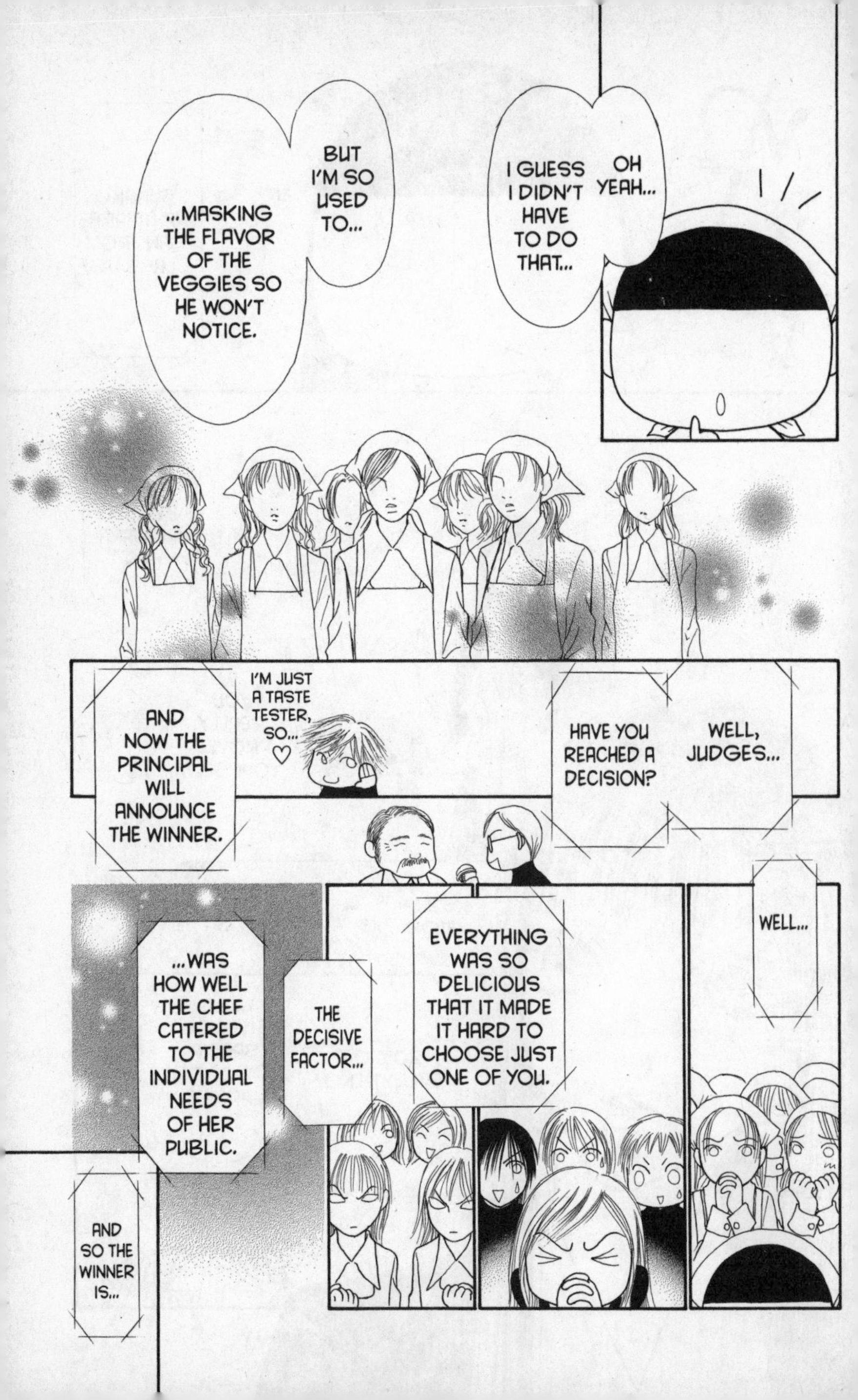
OH YEAH...
I GUESS I DIDN'T HAVE TO DO THAT...
BUT I'M SO USED TO...
...MASKING THE FLAVOR OF THE VEGGIES SO HE WON'T NOTICE.
WELL, JUDGES...
HAVE YOU REACHED A DECISION?
I'M JUST A TASTE TESTER, SO... ♡
AND NOW THE PRINCIPAL WILL ANNOUNCE THE WINNER.
WELL...
EVERYTHING WAS SO DELICIOUS THAT IT MADE IT HARD TO CHOOSE JUST ONE OF YOU.
THE DECISIVE FACTOR...
...WAS HOW WELL THE CHEF CATERED TO THE INDIVIDUAL NEEDS OF HER PUBLIC.
AND SO THE WINNER IS...

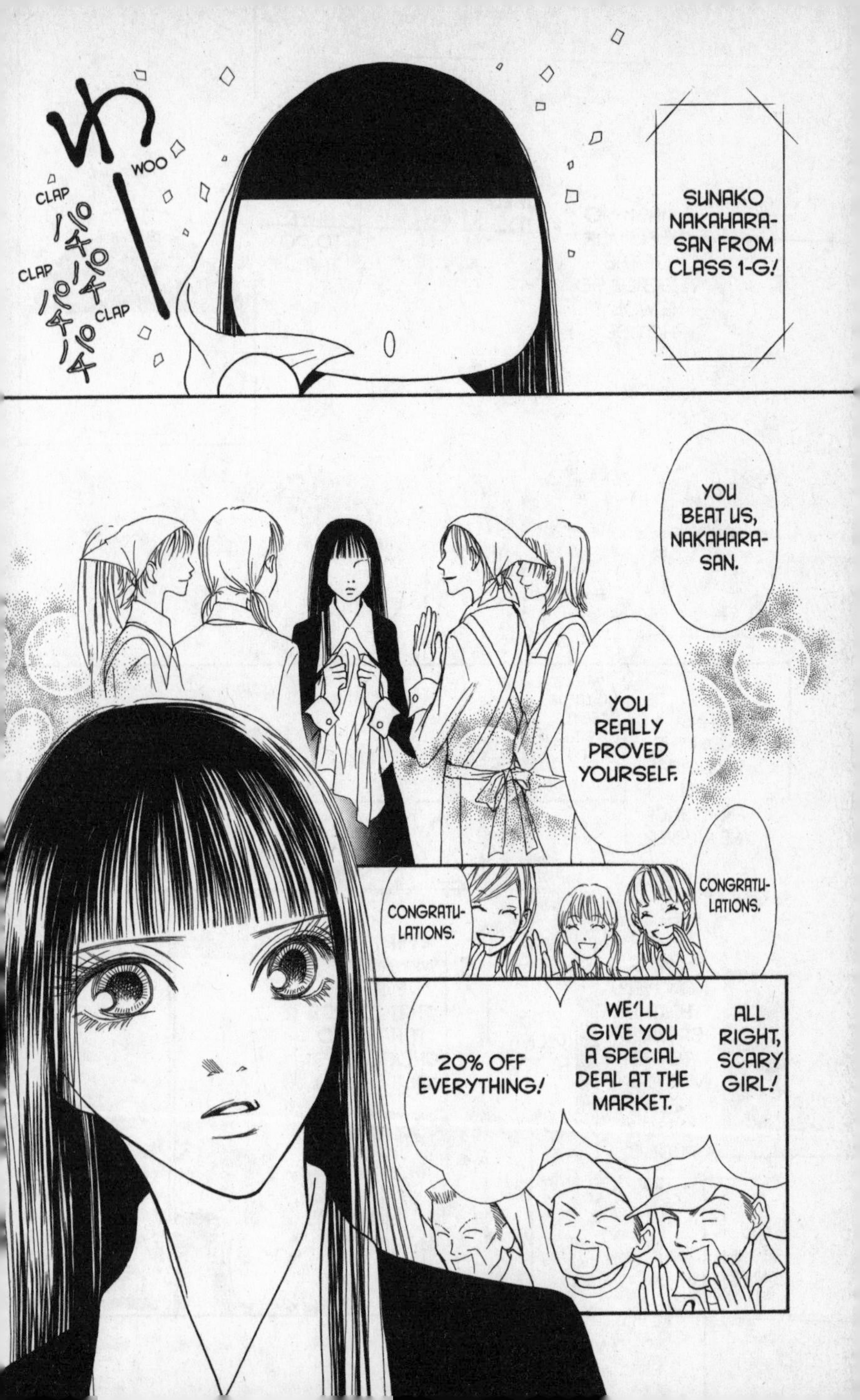

SUNAKO NAKAHARA-SAN FROM CLASS 1-G!
わー
WOO
CLAP
CLAP
CLAP
YOU BEAT US, NAKAHARA-SAN.
YOU REALLY PROVED YOURSELF.
CONGRATULATIONS.
CONGRATULATIONS.
ALL RIGHT, SCARY GIRL!
WE'LL GIVE YOU A SPECIAL DEAL AT THE MARKET.
20% OFF EVERYTHING!

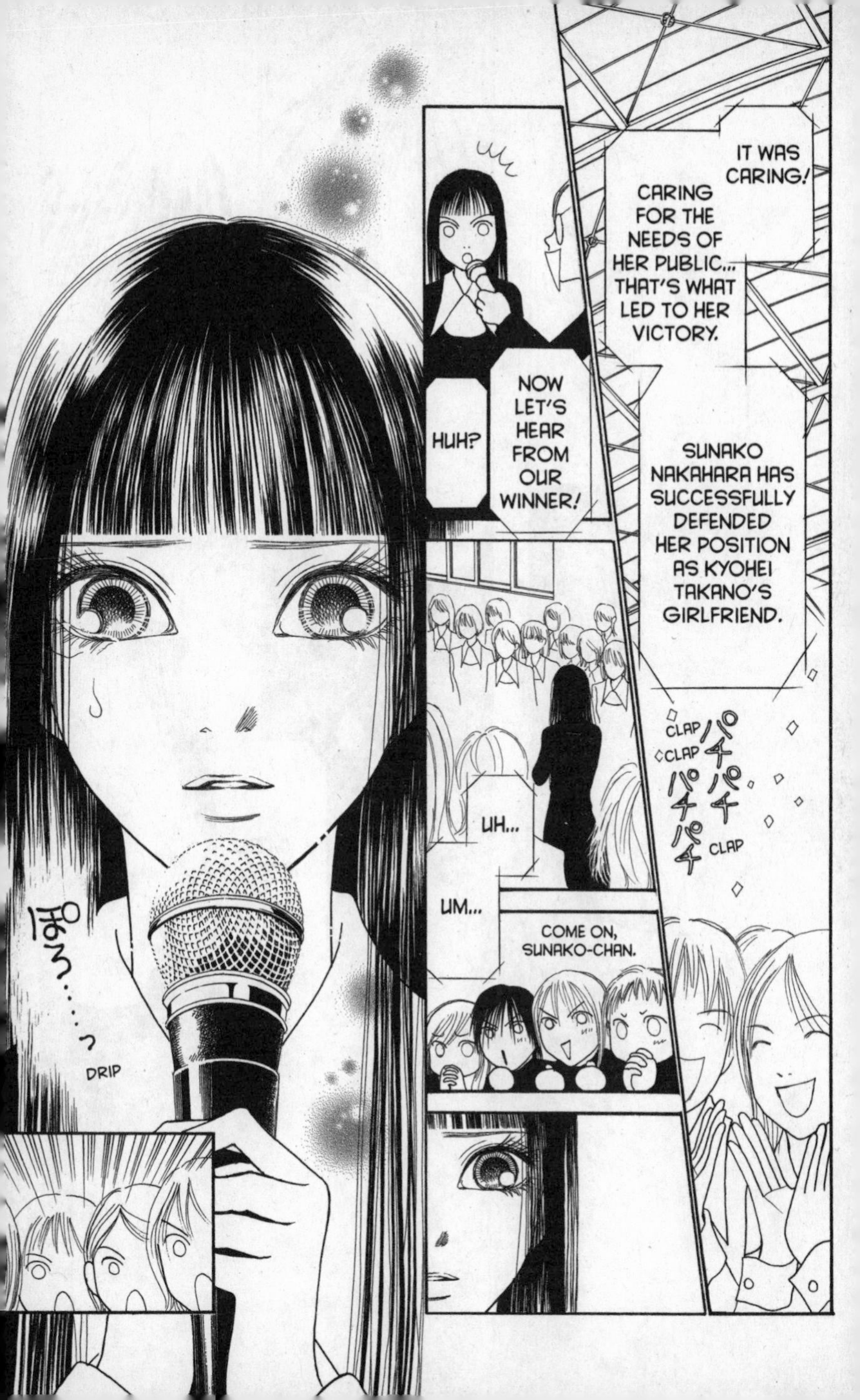
IT WAS CARING!
CARING FOR THE NEEDS OF HER PUBLIC... THAT'S WHAT LED TO HER VICTORY.
NOW LET'S HEAR FROM OUR WINNER!
HUH?
SUNAKO NAKAHARA HAS SUCCESSFULLY DEFENDED HER POSITION AS KYOHEI TAKANO'S GIRLFRIEND.
パチパチ
パチパチ
CLAP
CLAP
CLAP
UH...
UM...
COME ON, SUNAKO-CHAN.
ぽろ…っ
DRIP

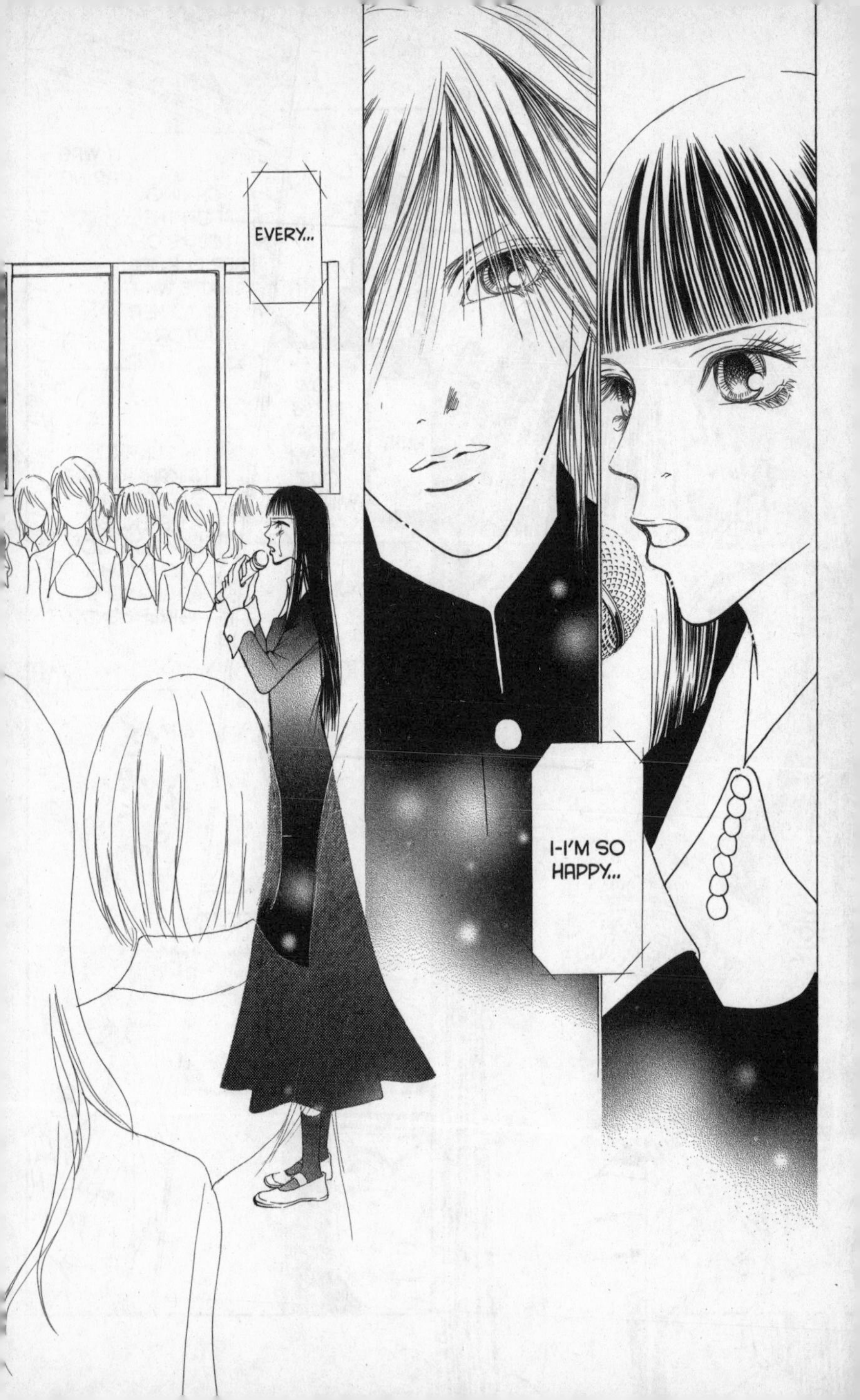
I-I'M SO HAPPY...
EVERY...

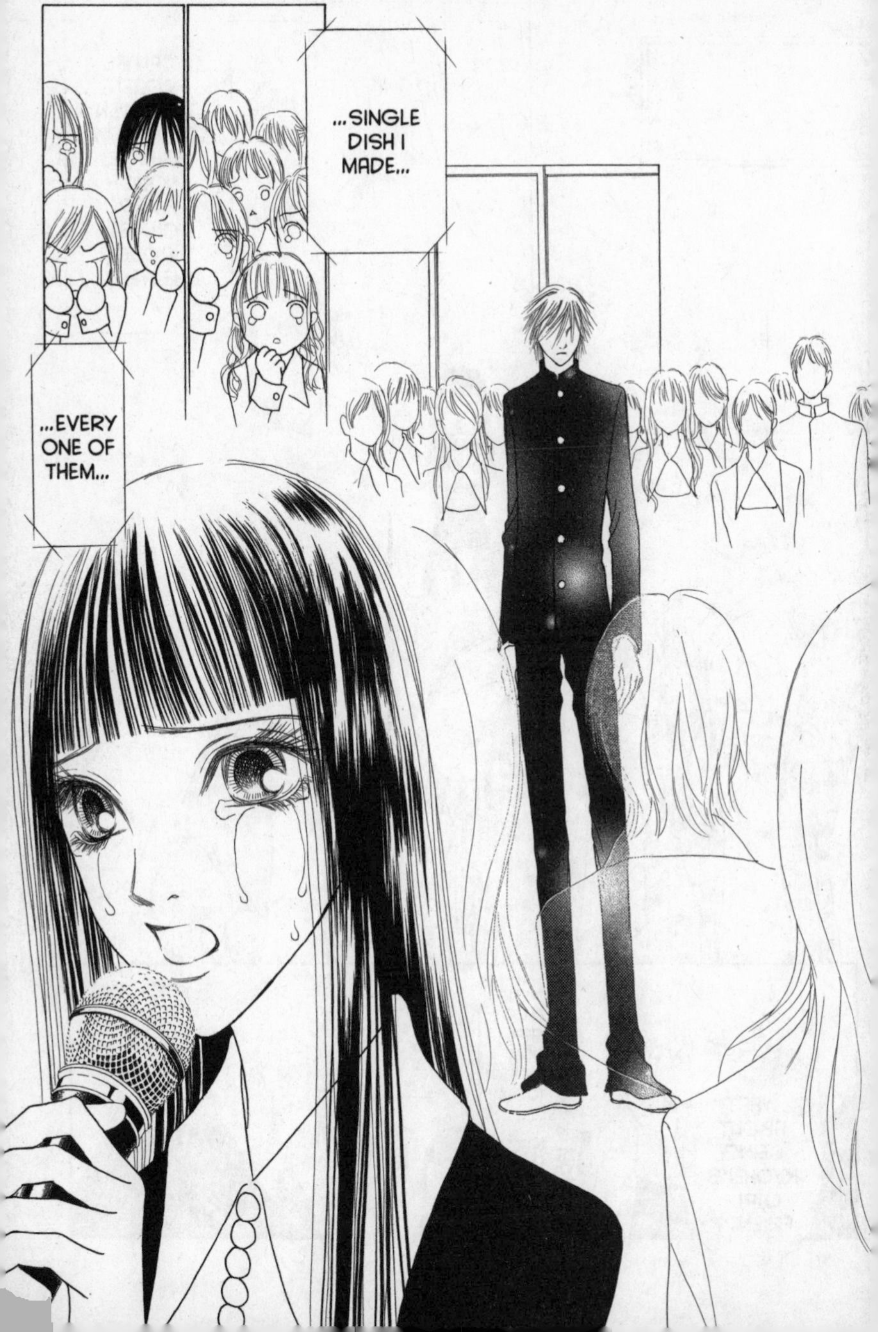
...SINGLE DISH I MADE...
...EVERY ONE OF THEM...

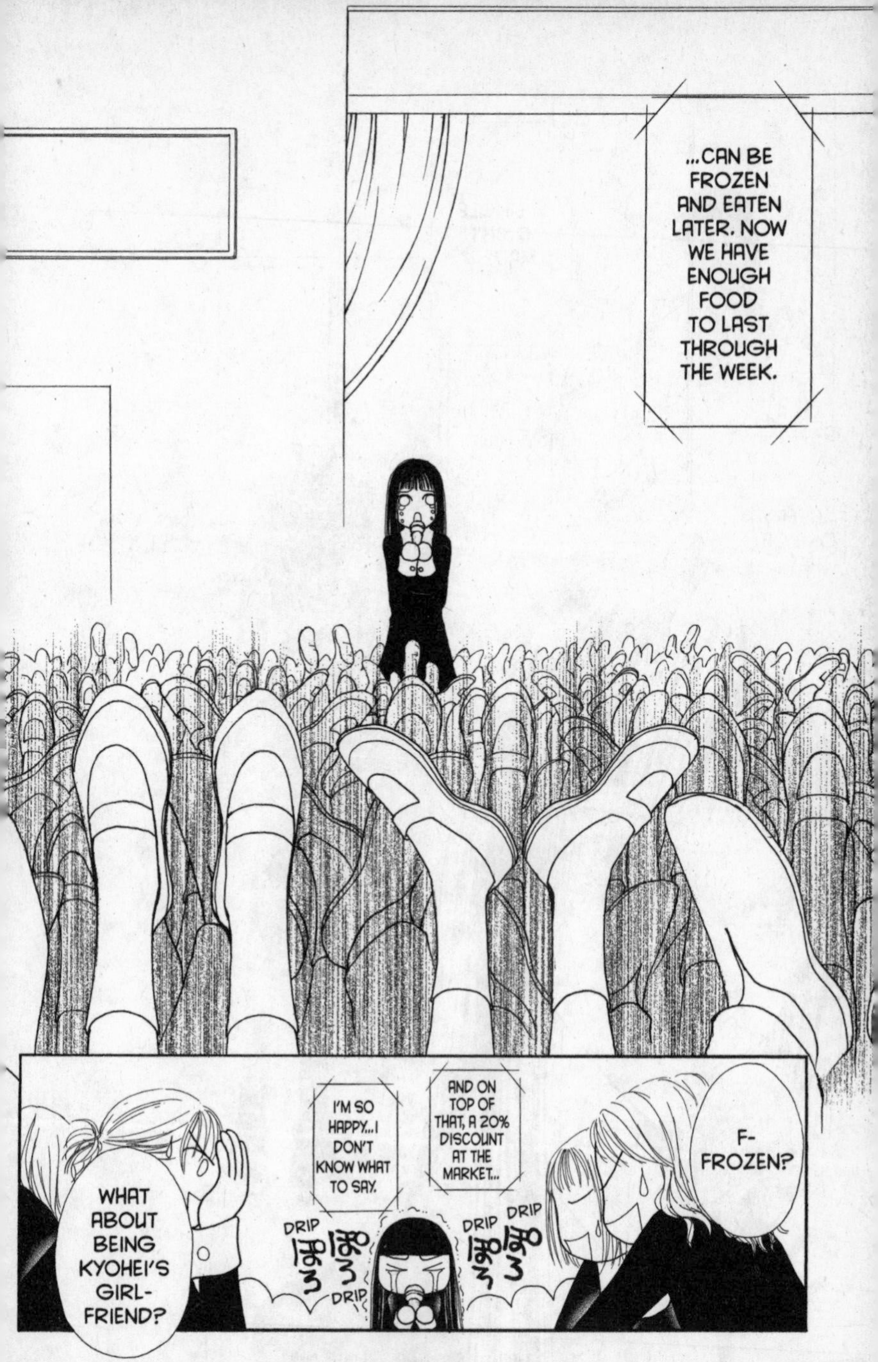
...CAN BE FROZEN AND EATEN LATER. NOW WE HAVE ENOUGH FOOD TO LAST THROUGH THE WEEK.
F-FROZEN?
AND ON TOP OF THAT, A 20% DISCOUNT AT THE MARKET...
DRIP DRIP
I'M SO HAPPY...I DON'T KNOW WHAT TO SAY.
DRIP
DRIP
WHAT ABOUT BEING KYOHEI'S GIRL-FRIEND?

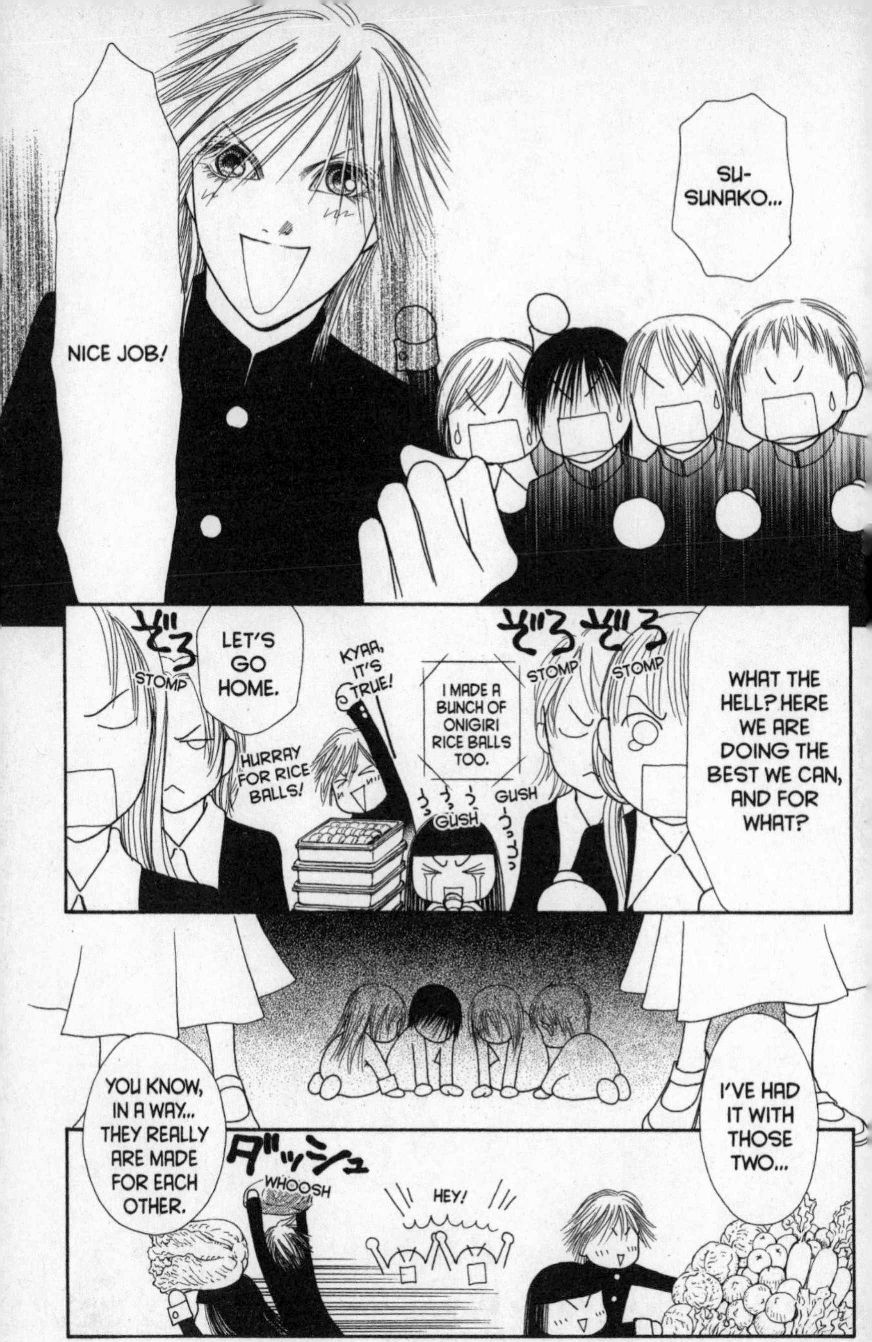
SU-SUNAKO...
NICE JOB!
WHAT THE HELL? HERE WE ARE DOING THE BEST WE CAN, AND FOR WHAT?
ぞろ ぞろ
STOMP
STOMP
I MADE A BUNCH OF ONIGIRI RICE BALLS TOO.
GUSH
GUSH
KYAA, IT'S TRUE!
HURRAY FOR RICE BALLS!
LET'S GO HOME.
ぞろ
STOMP
I'VE HAD IT WITH THOSE TWO...
HEY!
ダッシュ
WHOOSH
YOU KNOW, IN A WAY... THEY REALLY ARE MADE FOR EACH OTHER.

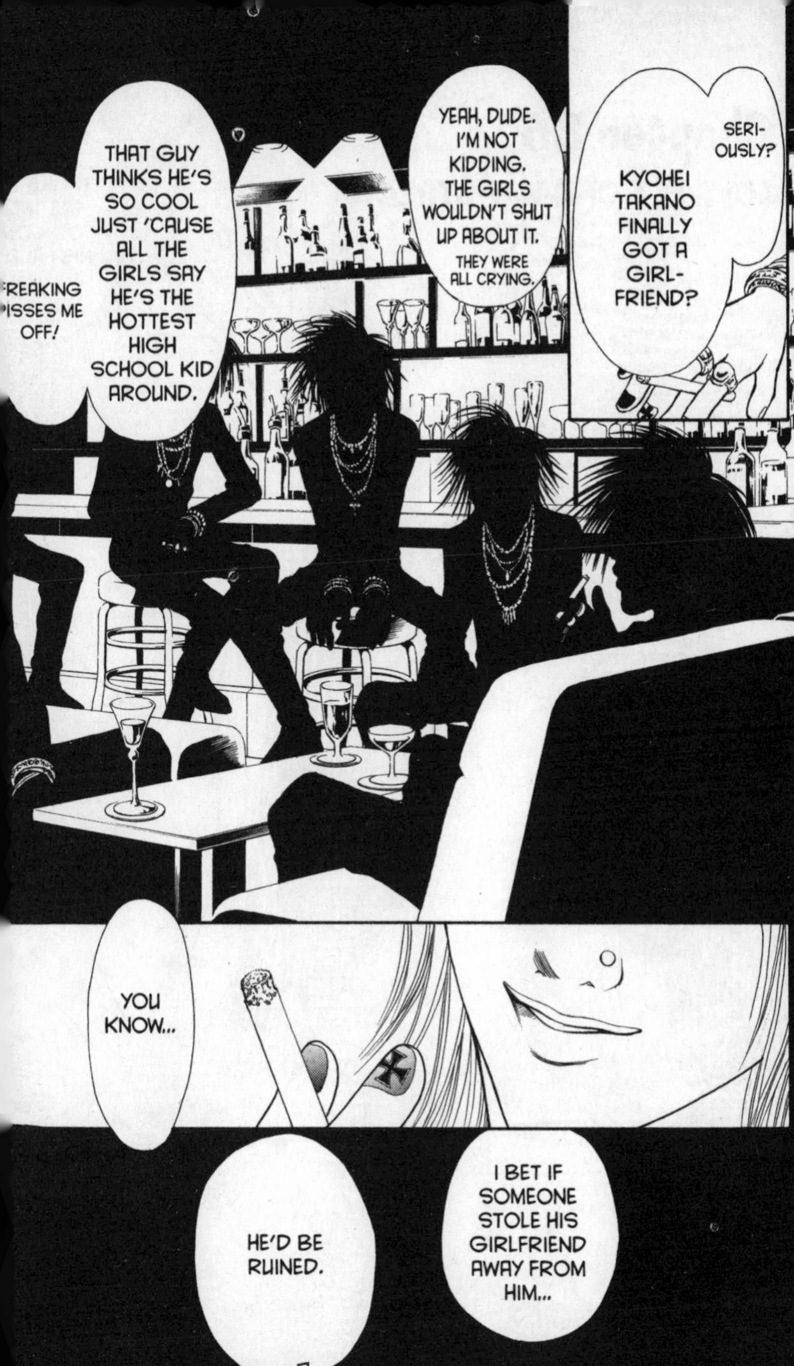
SERI-OUSLY?
KYOHEI TAKANO FINALLY GOT A GIRL-FRIEND?
YEAH, DUDE. I'M NOT KIDDING. THE GIRLS WOULDN'T SHUT UP ABOUT IT.
THEY WERE ALL CRYING.
THAT GUY THINKS HE'S SO COOL JUST 'CAUSE ALL THE GIRLS SAY HE'S THE HOTTEST HIGH SCHOOL KID AROUND.
FREAKING PISSES ME OFF!
YOU KNOW...
I BET IF SOMEONE STOLE HIS GIRLFRIEND AWAY FROM HIM...
HE'D BE RUINED.

Chapter 86 LOVE IS A ONE-WAY STREET

Chapter 86
LOVE IS A ONE-WAY STREET

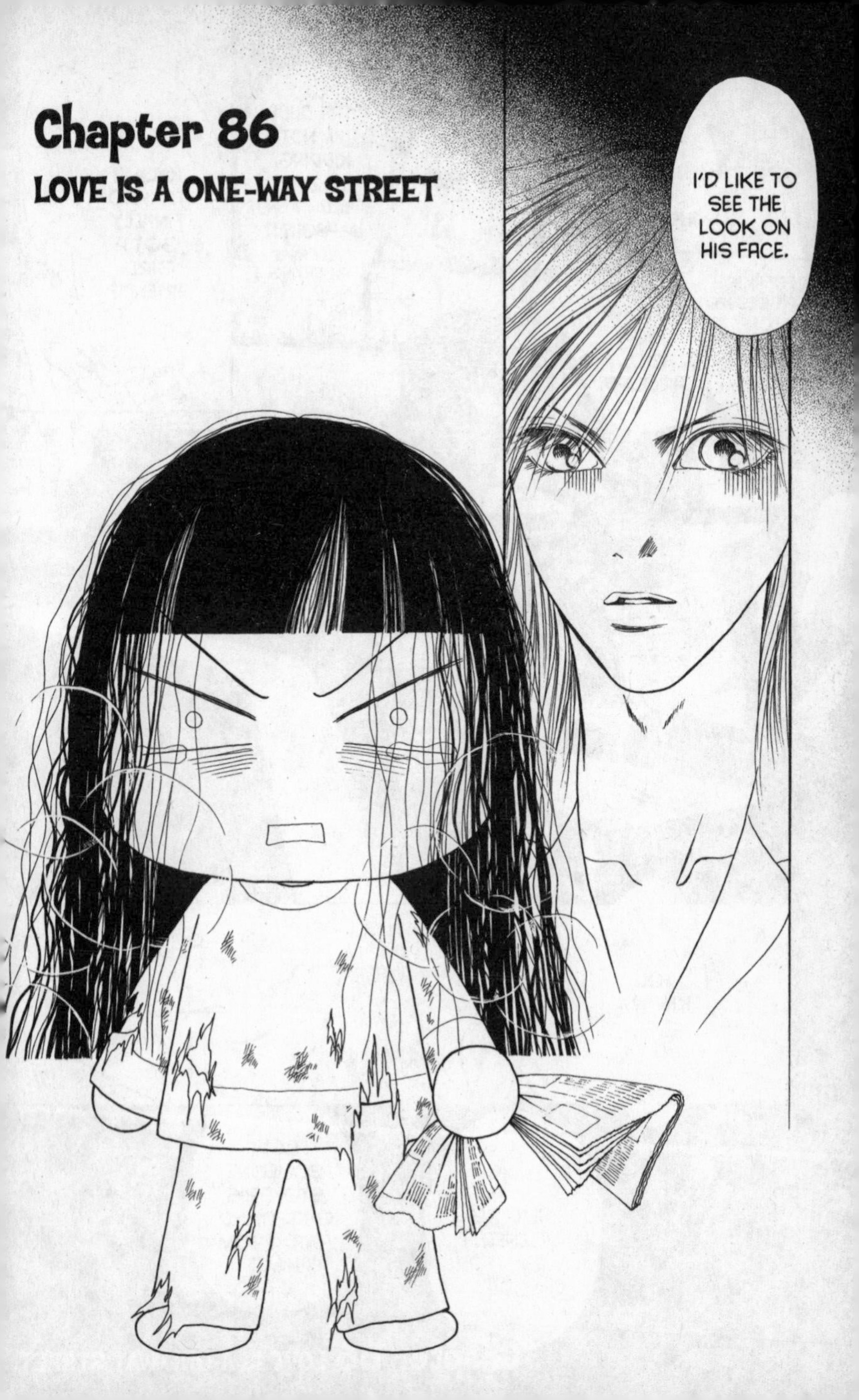
I'D LIKE TO SEE THE LOOK ON HIS FACE.

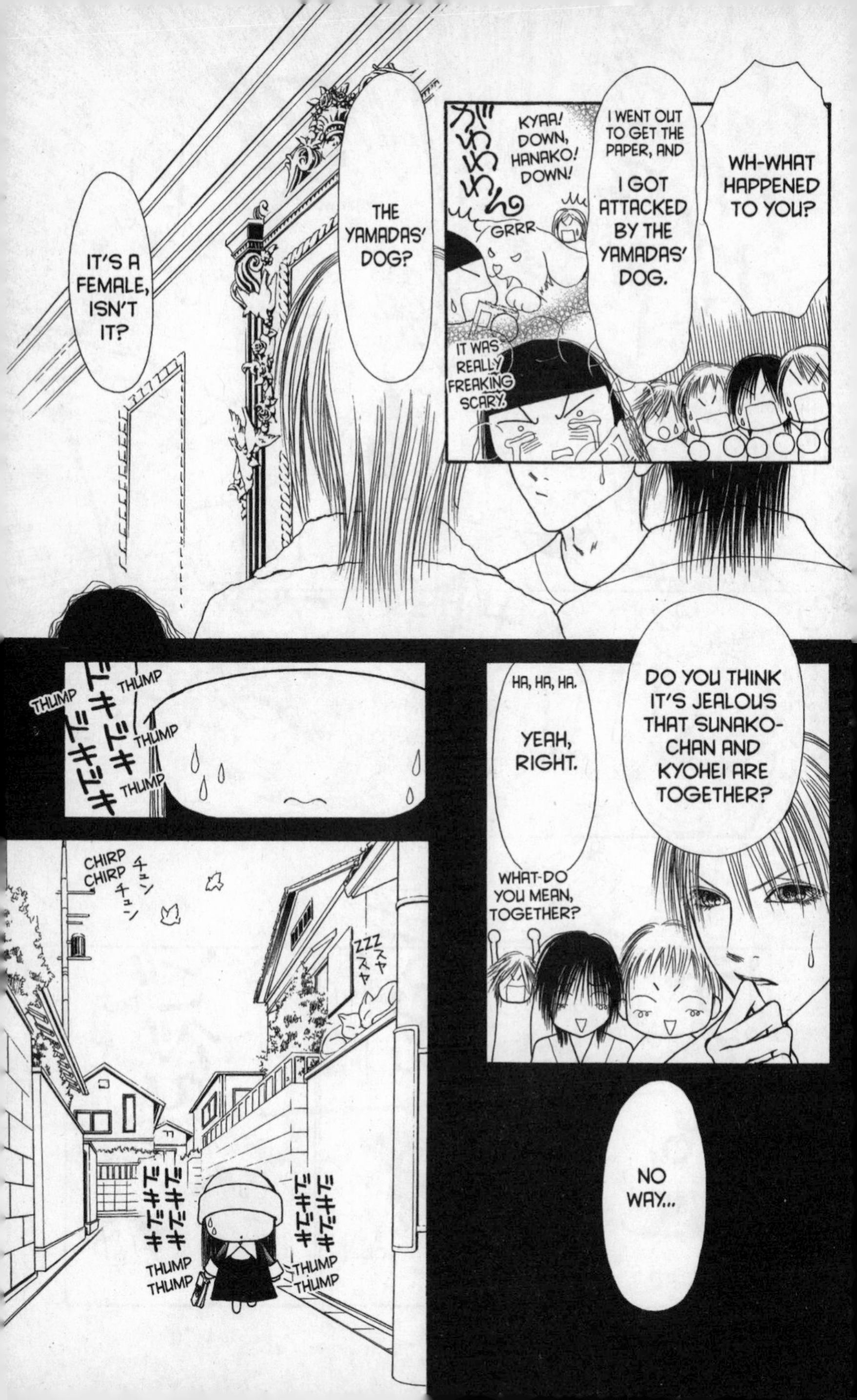
WH-WHAT HAPPENED TO YOU?
I WENT OUT TO GET THE PAPER, AND
I GOT ATTACKED BY THE YAMADAS' DOG.
KYAA! DOWN, HANAKO! DOWN!
GRRR
IT WAS REALLY FREAKING SCARY.
THE YAMADAS' DOG?
IT'S A FEMALE, ISN'T IT?
DO YOU THINK IT'S JEALOUS THAT SUNAKO-CHAN AND KYOHEI ARE TOGETHER?
HA, HA, HA.
YEAH, RIGHT.
WHAT-DO YOU MEAN, TOGETHER?
NO WAY...
ドキドキ
THUMP
ドキドキ
THUMP
THUMP
THUMP
チュン チュン
CHIRP CHIRP
スヤスヤ
ZZZ
ドキドキ
THUMP THUMP
ドキドキ
THUMP THUMP

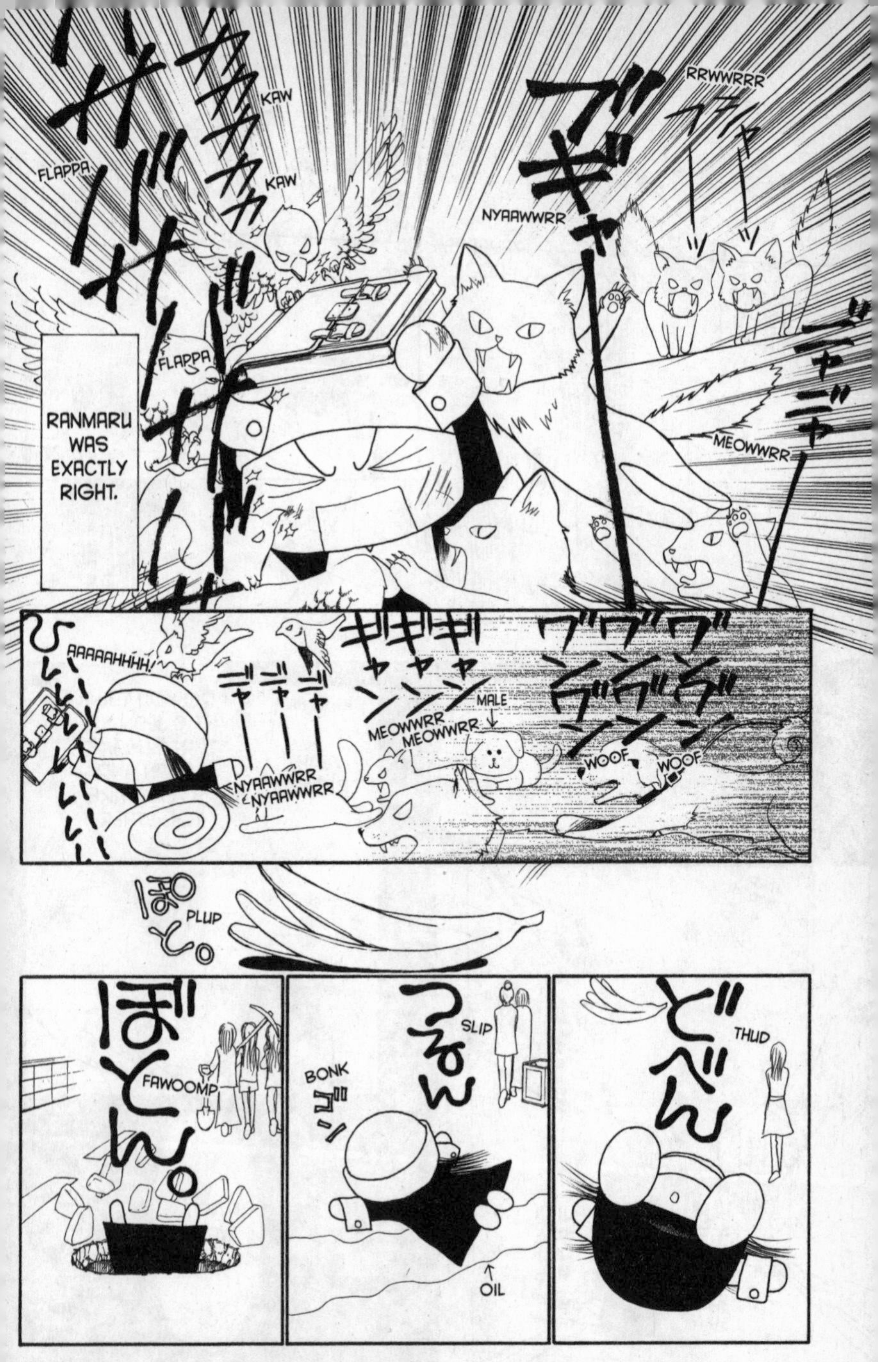
RRWWRRR
NYAAWWRR
MEOWWRR
KAW
KAW
FLAPPA
FLAPPA
RANMARU WAS EXACTLY RIGHT.
WOOF
WOOF
MALE
MEOWWRR
MEOWWRR
NYAAWWRR
NYAAWWRR
AAAAAHHHH!
PLUP
THUD
SLIP
BONK
OIL
FAWOOMP

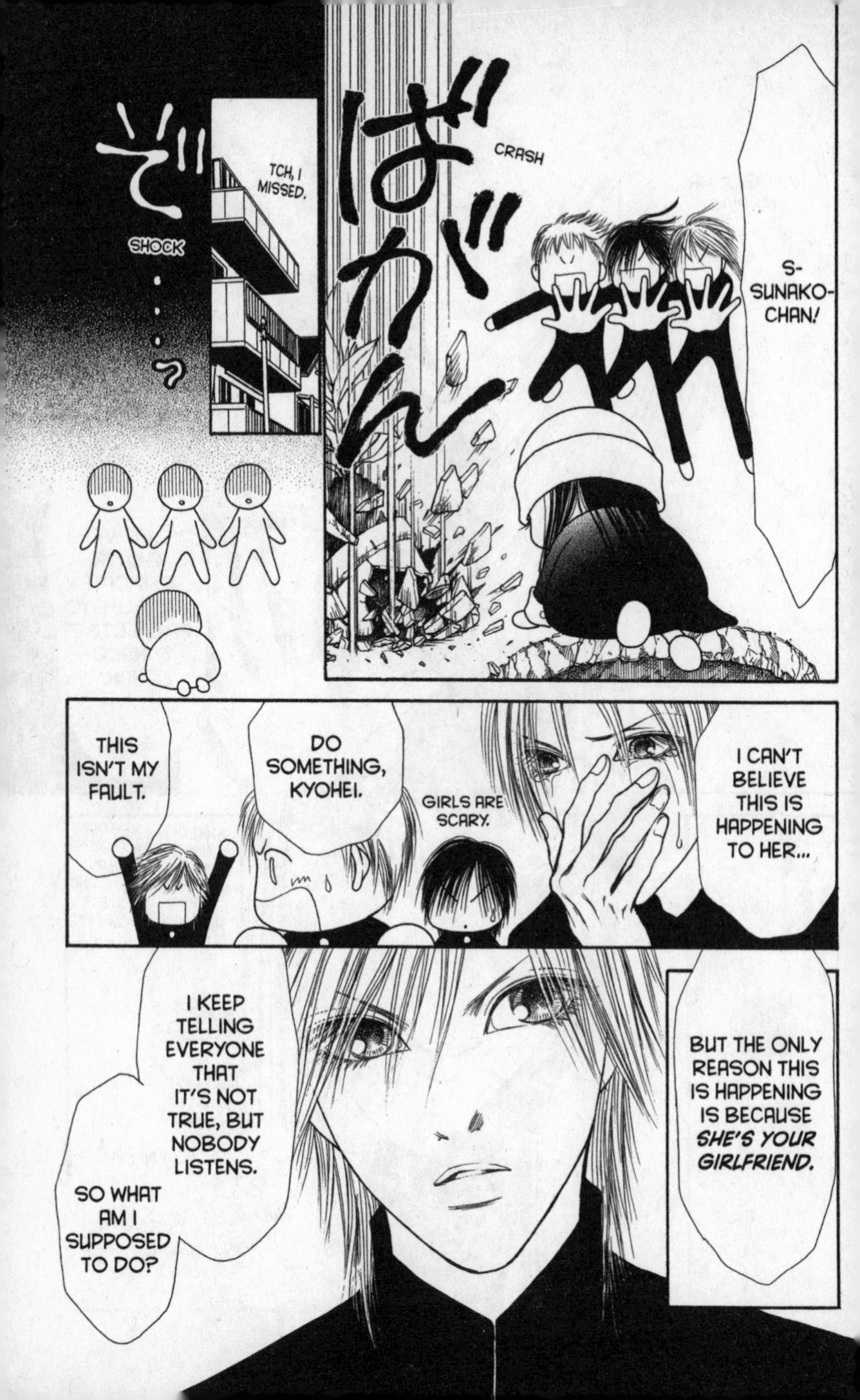
S-SUNAKO-CHAN!
ばがん
CRASH
TCH, I MISSED.
SHOCK
...?
I CAN'T BELIEVE THIS IS HAPPENING TO HER...
GIRLS ARE SCARY.
DO SOMETHING, KYOHEI.
THIS ISN'T MY FAULT.
BUT THE ONLY REASON THIS IS HAPPENING IS BECAUSE *SHE'S YOUR GIRLFRIEND.*
I KEEP TELLING EVERYONE THAT IT'S NOT TRUE, BUT NOBODY LISTENS.
SO WHAT AM I SUPPOSED TO DO?

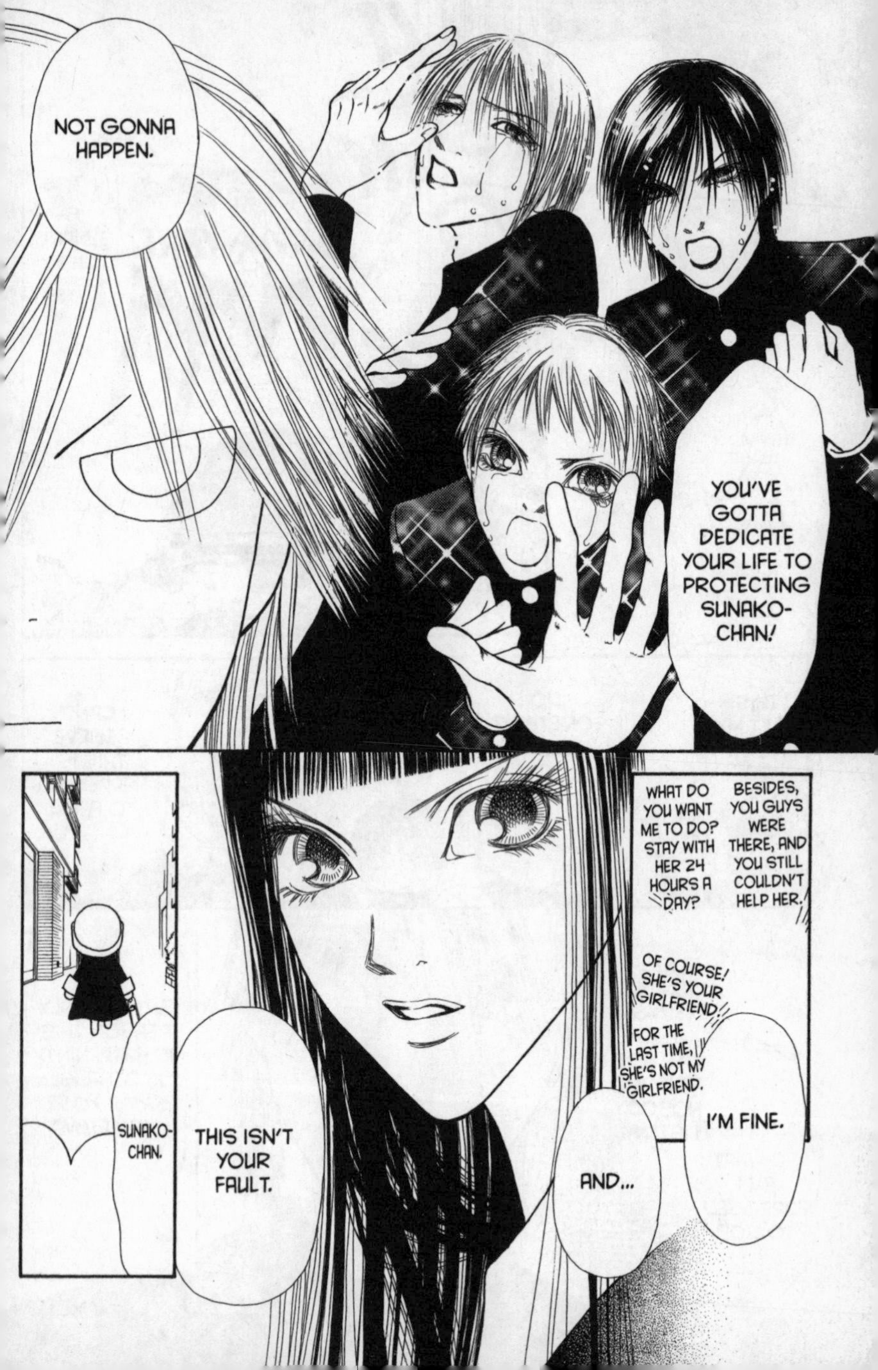
YOU'VE GOTTA DEDICATE YOUR LIFE TO PROTECTING SUNAKO-CHAN!
NOT GONNA HAPPEN.
WHAT DO YOU WANT ME TO DO? STAY WITH HER 24 HOURS A DAY?
BESIDES, YOU GUYS WERE THERE, AND YOU STILL COULDN'T HELP HER.
OF COURSE! SHE'S YOUR GIRLFRIEND!
FOR THE LAST TIME, SHE'S NOT MY GIRLFRIEND.
I'M FINE.
AND...
THIS ISN'T YOUR FAULT.
SUNAKO-CHAN.

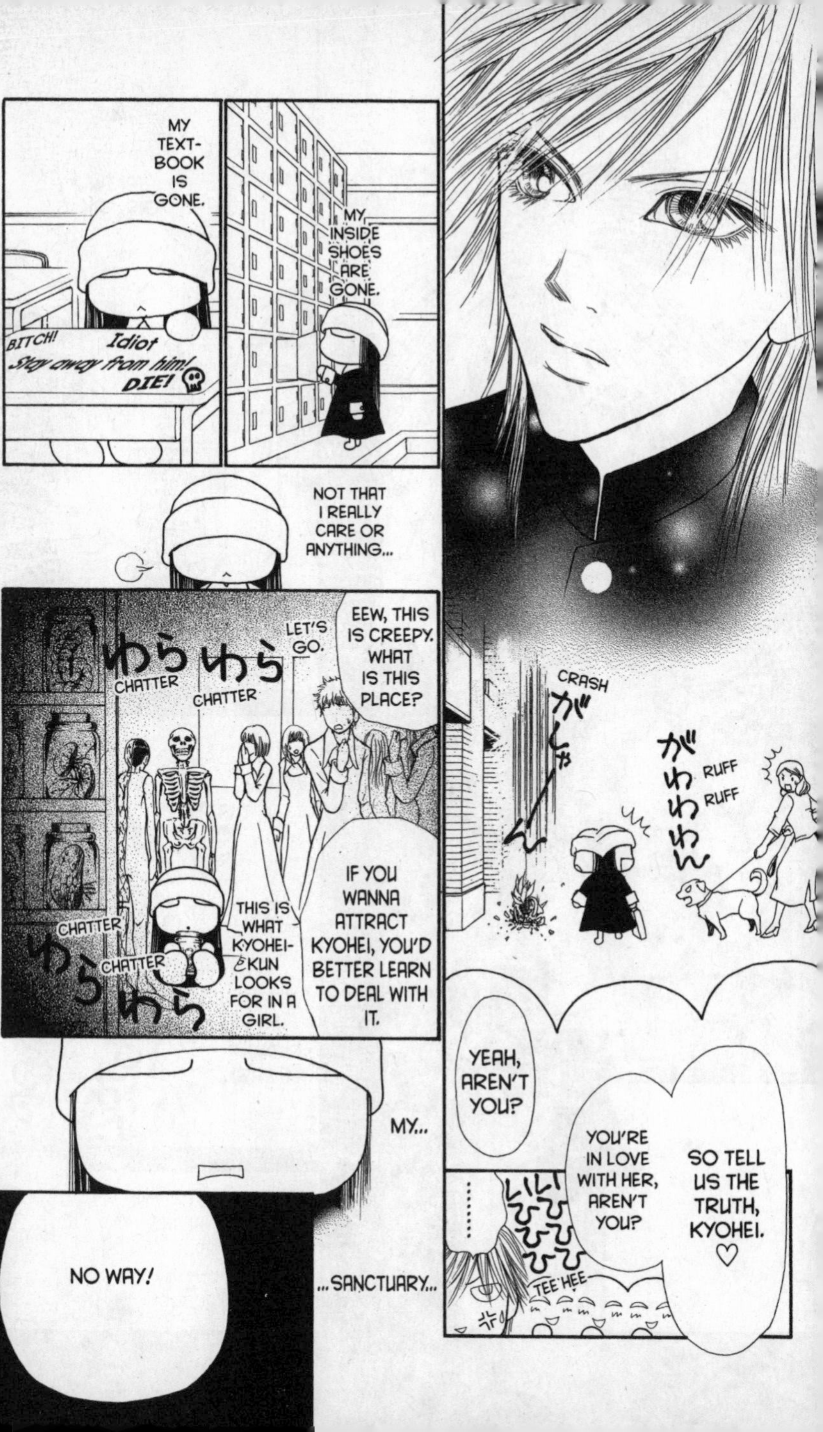
CRASH
RUFF RUFF
SO TELL US THE TRUTH, KYOHEI. ♡
YOU'RE IN LOVE WITH HER, AREN'T YOU?
YEAH, AREN'T YOU?
......
TEE HEE
MY INSIDE SHOES ARE GONE.
MY TEXT-BOOK IS GONE.
BITCH!
Idiot
Stay away from him!
DIE!
NOT THAT I REALLY CARE OR ANYTHING...
EEW, THIS IS CREEPY. WHAT IS THIS PLACE?
LET'S GO.
CHATTER
CHATTER
CHATTER
CHATTER
IF YOU WANNA ATTRACT KYOHEI, YOU'D BETTER LEARN TO DEAL WITH IT.
THIS IS WHAT KYOHEI-KUN LOOKS FOR IN A GIRL.
MY...
...SANCTUARY...
NO WAY!

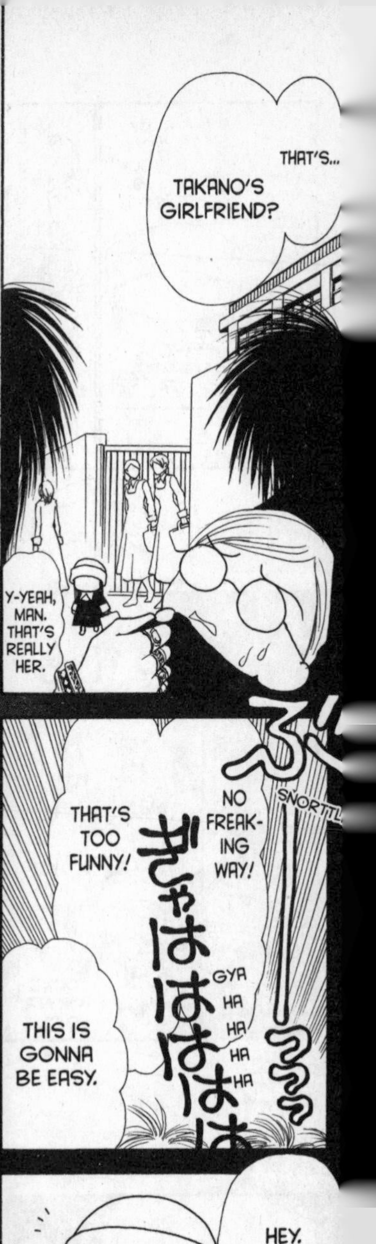
THAT'S...
TAKANO'S GIRLFRIEND?
Y-YEAH, MAN. THAT'S REALLY HER.
ぷ
SNORTL
NO FREAKING WAY!
THAT'S TOO FUNNY!
ぎゃははは
GYA HA HA HA HA
THIS IS GONNA BE EASY.
HEY.
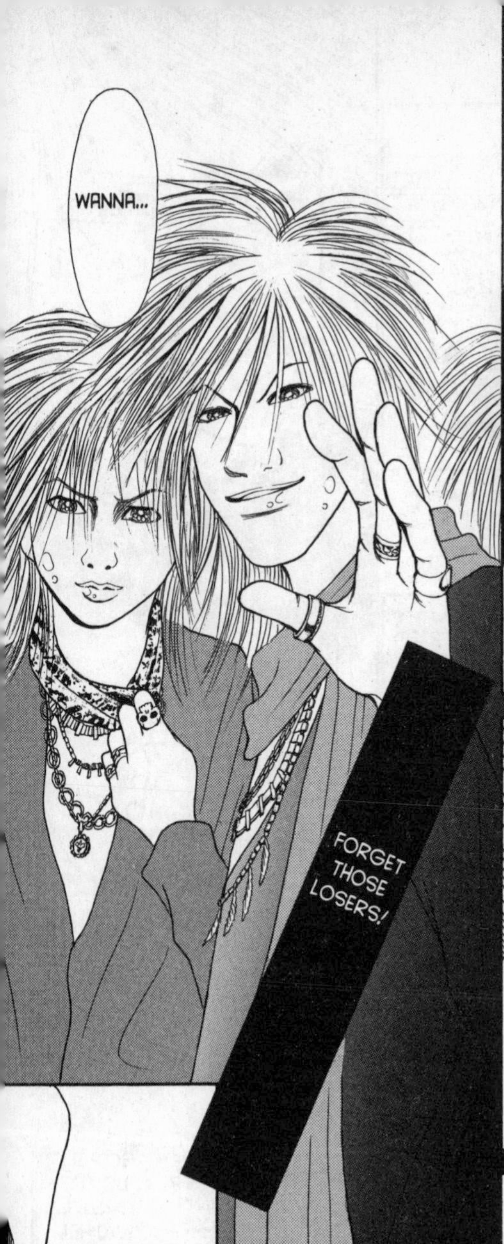
WANNA...
FORGET THOSE LOSERS!

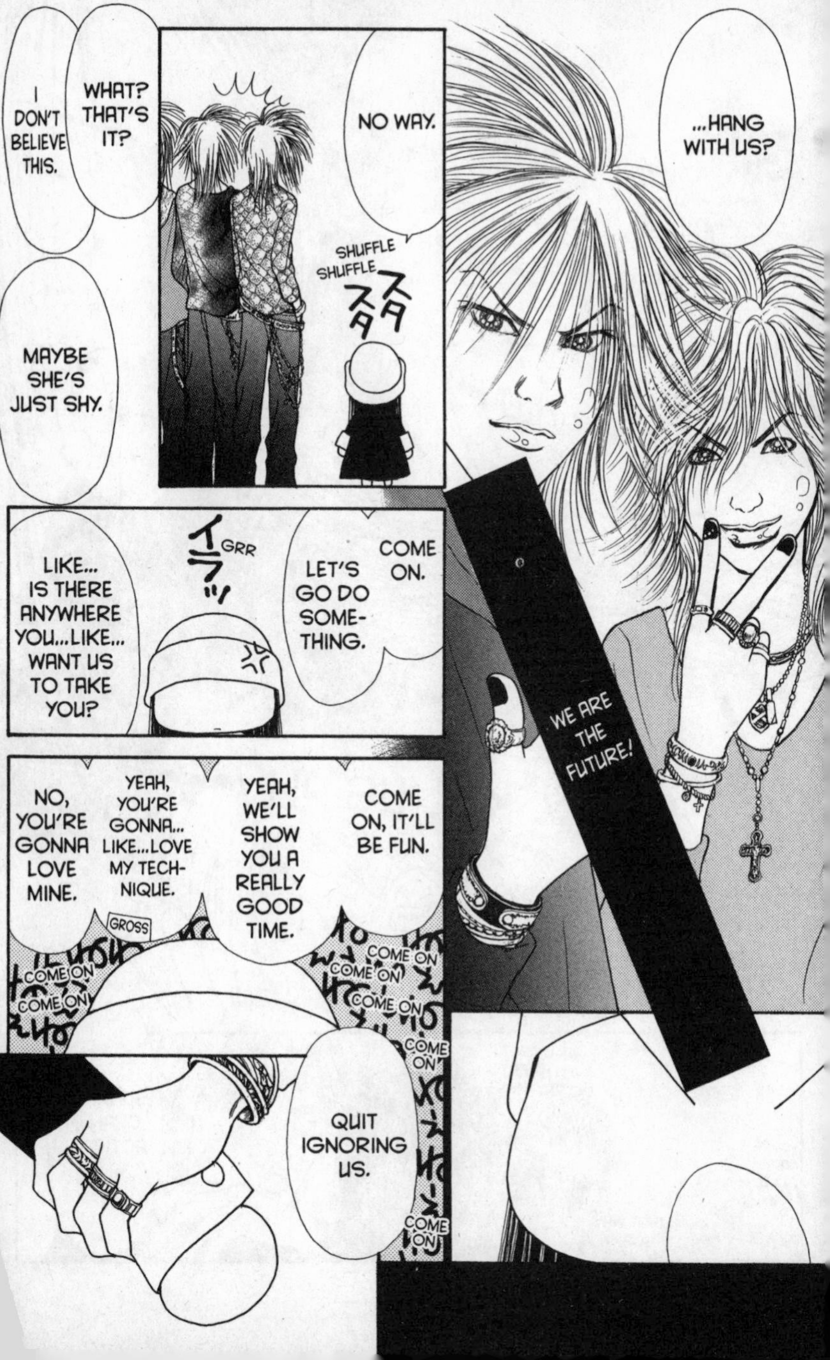
...HANG WITH US?
WE ARE THE FUTURE!
NO WAY.
WHAT? THAT'S IT?
I DON'T BELIEVE THIS.
SHUFFLE SHUFFLE
スタスタ
MAYBE SHE'S JUST SHY.
COME ON.
LET'S GO DO SOME-THING.
イラッ
GRR
LIKE... IS THERE ANYWHERE YOU...LIKE... WANT US TO TAKE YOU?
COME ON, IT'LL BE FUN.
YEAH, WE'LL SHOW YOU A REALLY GOOD TIME.
YEAH, YOU'RE GONNA... LIKE...LOVE MY TECH-NIQUE.
NO, YOU'RE GONNA LOVE MINE.
GROSS
COME ON
COME ON
COME ON
COME ON
COME ON
COME ON
COME ON
QUIT IGNORING US.

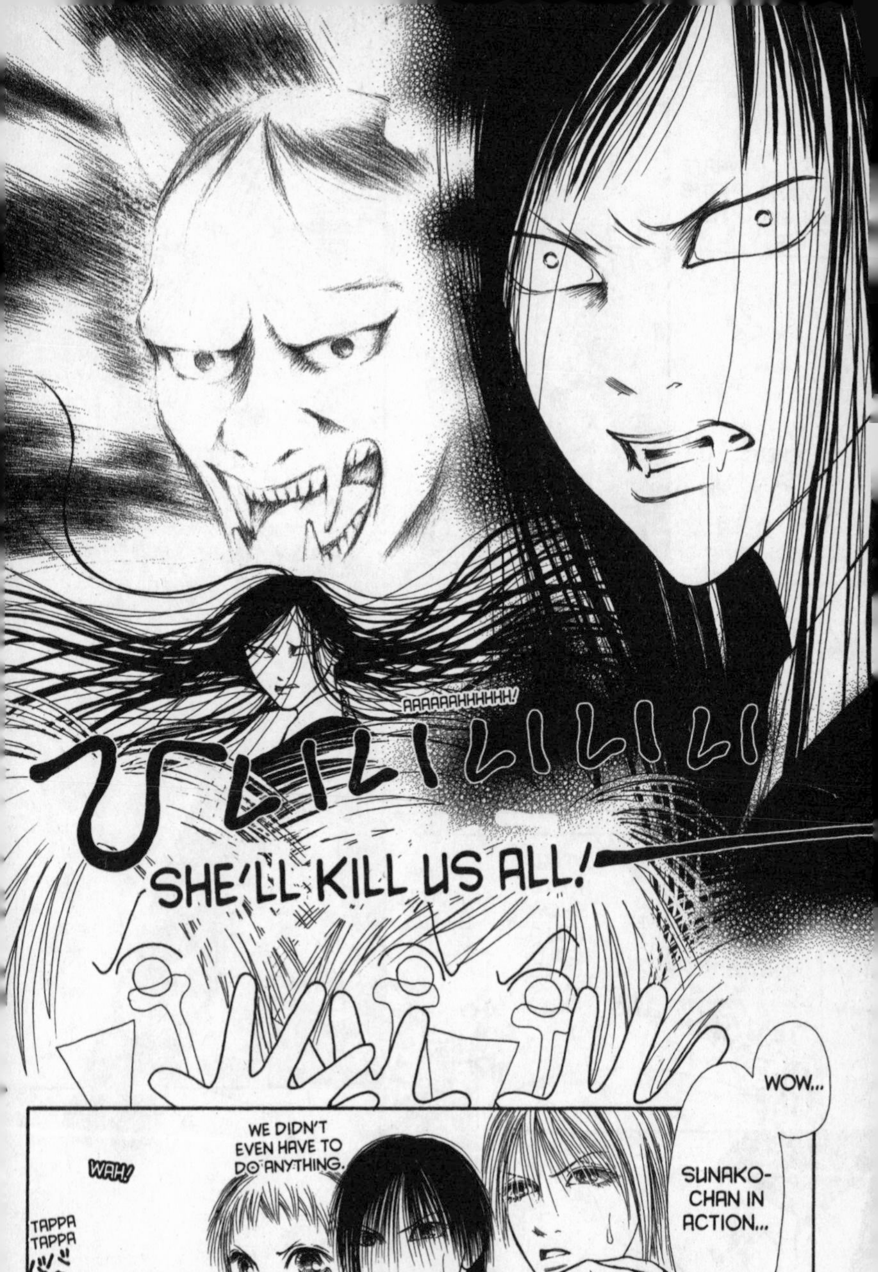
AAAAAAHHHHHH!
SHE'LL KILL US ALL!
WOW...
SUNAKO-CHAN IN ACTION...
WE DIDN'T EVEN HAVE TO DO ANYTHING.
WAH!
THAT WAS SCARY.
TAPPA TAPPA

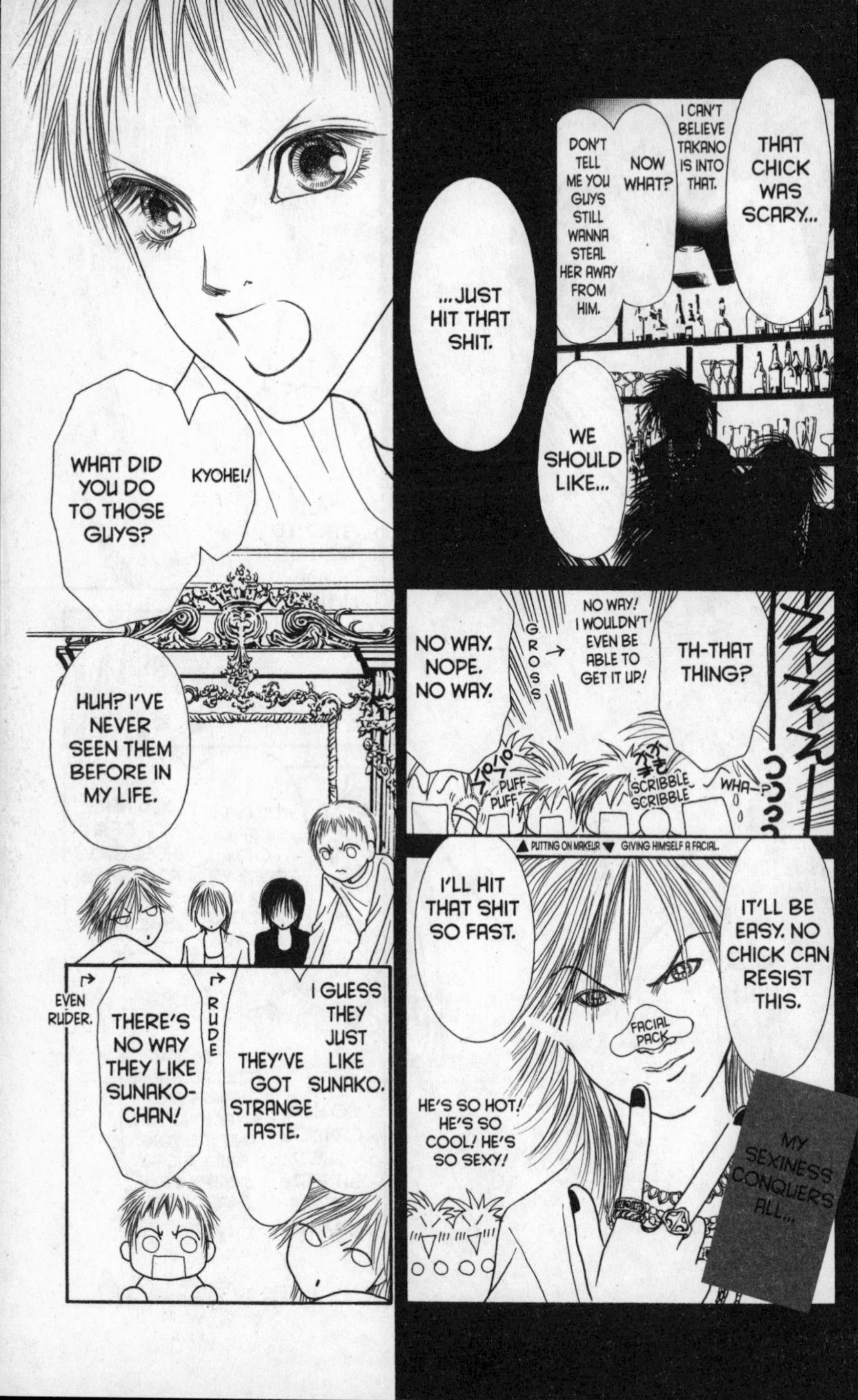
THAT CHICK WAS SCARY...
I CAN'T BELIEVE TAKANO IS INTO THAT.
NOW WHAT?
DON'T TELL ME YOU GUYS STILL WANNA STEAL HER AWAY FROM HIM.
WE SHOULD LIKE...
...JUST HIT THAT SHIT.
TH-THAT THING?
NO WAY! I WOULDN'T EVEN BE ABLE TO GET IT UP!
GROSS
NO WAY. NOPE. NO WAY.
WHA-?
SCRIBBLE SCRIBBLE
PUFF PUFF
▲PUTTING ON MAKEUP ▼GIVING HIMSELF A FACIAL.
IT'LL BE EASY. NO CHICK CAN RESIST THIS.
I'LL HIT THAT SHIT SO FAST.
FACIAL PACK
MY SEXINESS CONQUERS ALL...
HE'S SO HOT! HE'S SO COOL! HE'S SO SEXY!
KYOHEI!
WHAT DID YOU DO TO THOSE GUYS?
HUH? I'VE NEVER SEEN THEM BEFORE IN MY LIFE.
I GUESS THEY JUST LIKE SUNAKO.
THEY'VE GOT STRANGE TASTE.
RUDE
THERE'S NO WAY THEY LIKE SUNAKO-CHAN!
EVEN RUDER.

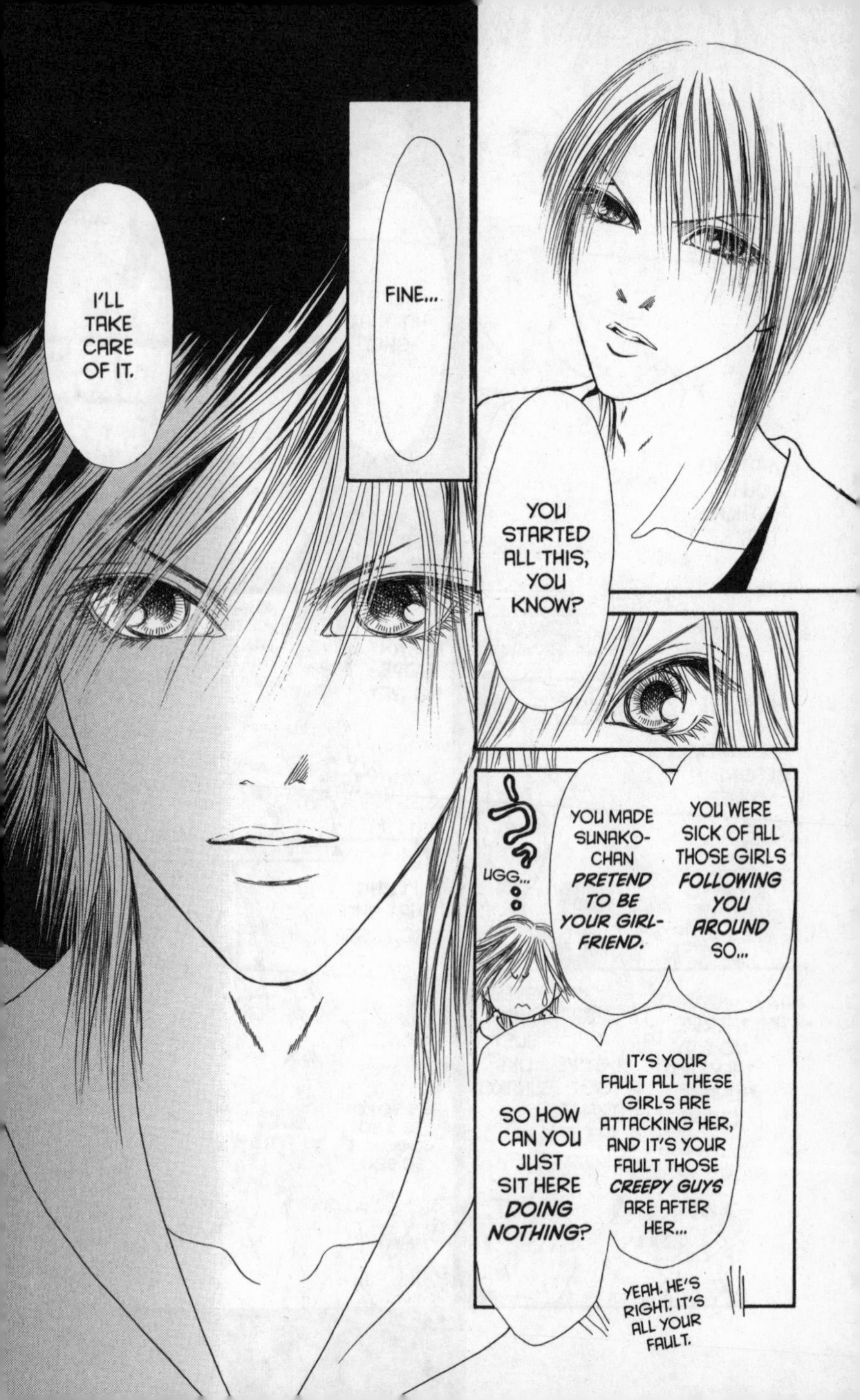

YOU STARTED ALL THIS, YOU KNOW?
YOU WERE SICK OF ALL THOSE GIRLS FOLLOWING YOU AROUND SO...
YOU MADE SUNAKO-CHAN PRETEND TO BE YOUR GIRL-FRIEND.
UGG...
IT'S YOUR FAULT ALL THESE GIRLS ARE ATTACKING HER, AND IT'S YOUR FAULT THOSE CREEPY GUYS ARE AFTER HER...
SO HOW CAN YOU JUST SIT HERE DOING NOTHING?
YEAH. HE'S RIGHT. IT'S ALL YOUR FAULT.
FINE...
I'LL TAKE CARE OF IT.

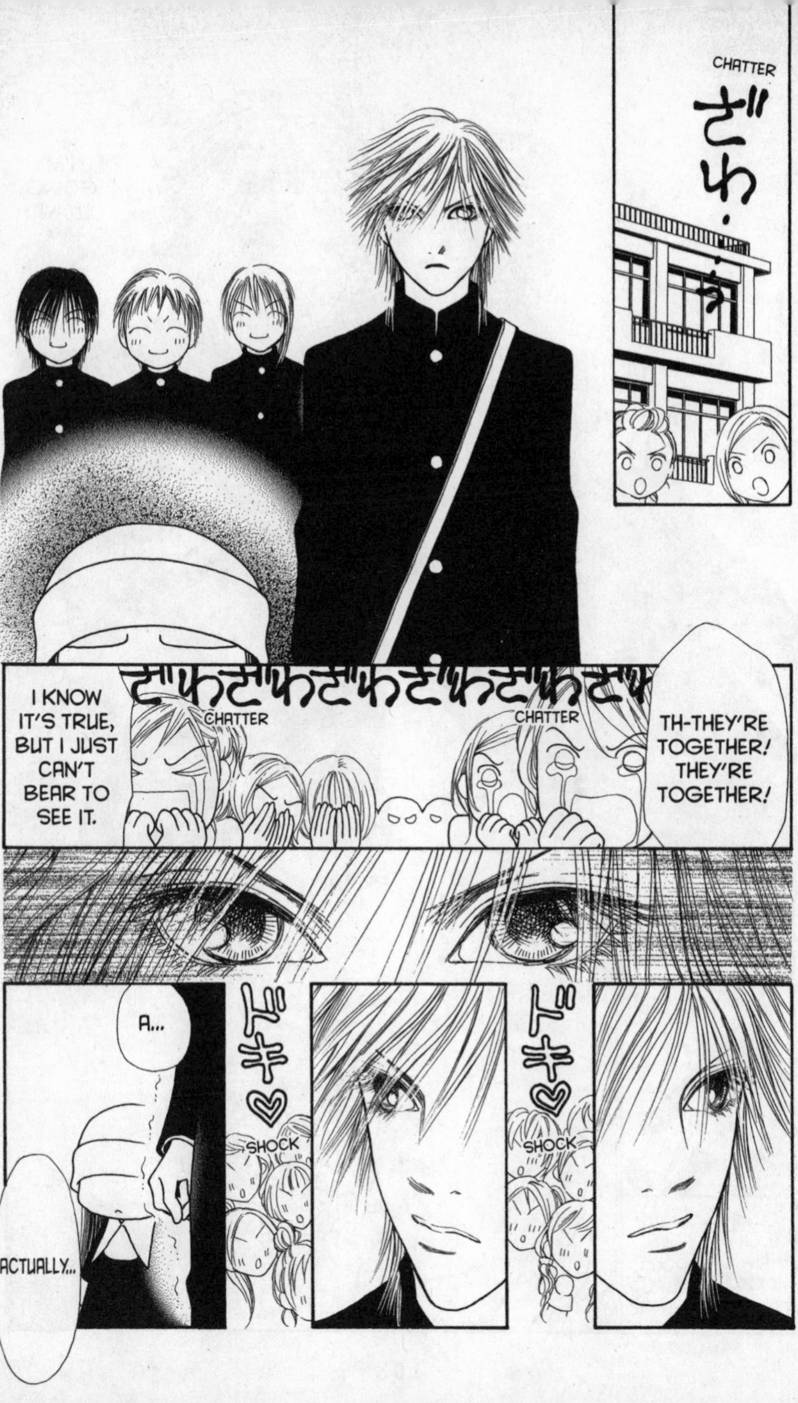
CHATTER
ざわ・・・
TH-THEY'RE TOGETHER! THEY'RE TOGETHER!
ざわざわざわざわざわざわ
CHATTER
CHATTER
I KNOW IT'S TRUE, BUT I JUST CAN'T BEAR TO SEE IT.
ドキ♡
SHOCK
ドキ♡
SHOCK
A...
ACTUALLY...

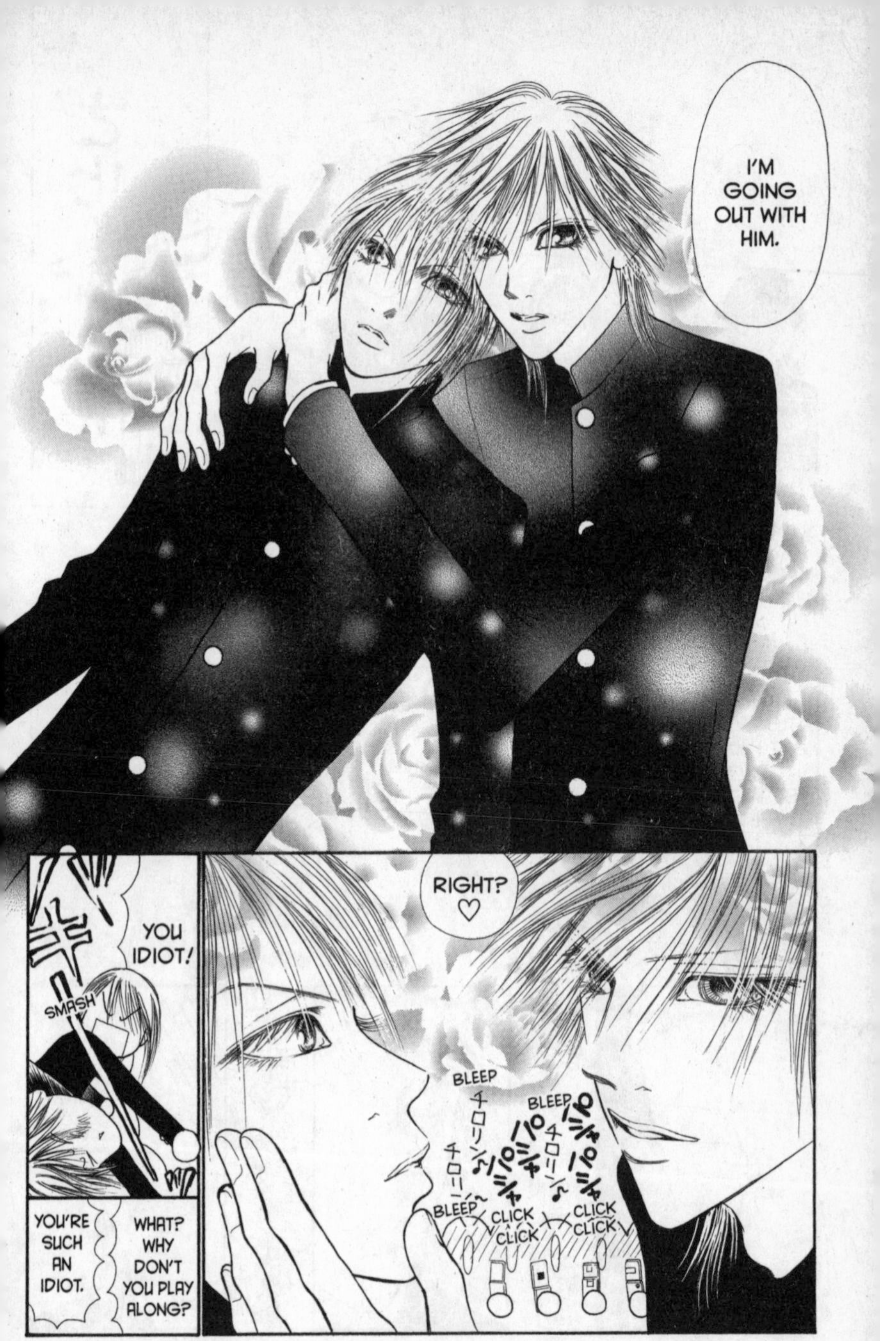
I'M GOING OUT WITH HIM.
RIGHT? ♡
BLEEP
BLEEP
BLEEP
CLICK CLICK
CLICK CLICK
YOU IDIOT!
SMASH
WHAT? WHY DON'T YOU PLAY ALONG?
YOU'RE SUCH AN IDIOT.

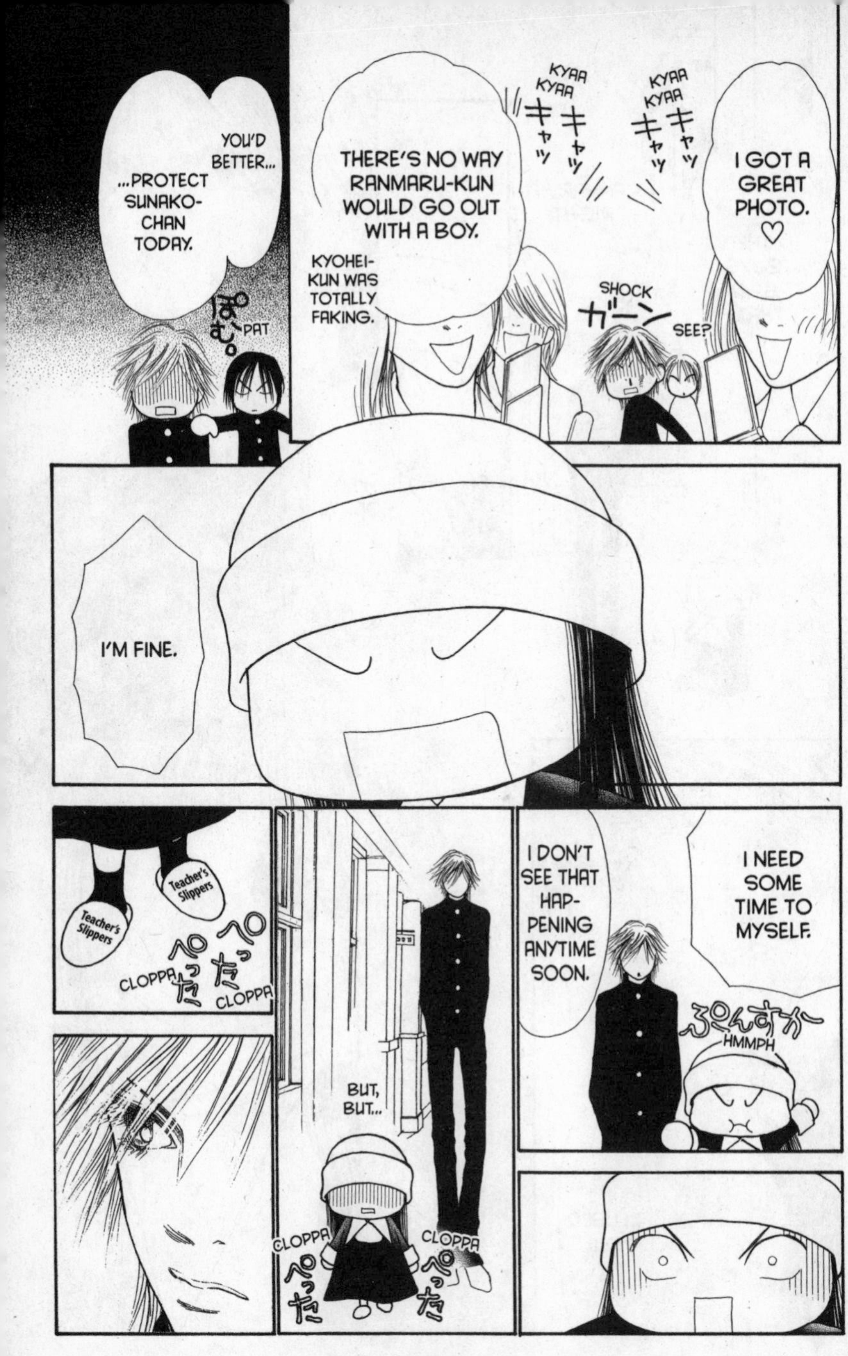
KYAA KYAA
キャッ キャッ
KYAA KYAA
キャッ キャッ
I GOT A GREAT PHOTO. ♡
SHOCK
ガーン
SEE?
THERE'S NO WAY RANMARU-KUN WOULD GO OUT WITH A BOY.
KYOHEI-KUN WAS TOTALLY FAKING.
YOU'D BETTER...
...PROTECT SUNAKO-CHAN TODAY.
ぽむ
PAT
I'M FINE.
I NEED SOME TIME TO MYSELF.
I DON'T SEE THAT HAPPENING ANYTIME SOON.
ぷんすか
HMMPH
BUT, BUT...
CLOPPA
ぺった
CLOPPA
ぺった
Teacher's Slippers
Teacher's Slippers
ぺった
CLOPPA
ぺった
CLOPPA

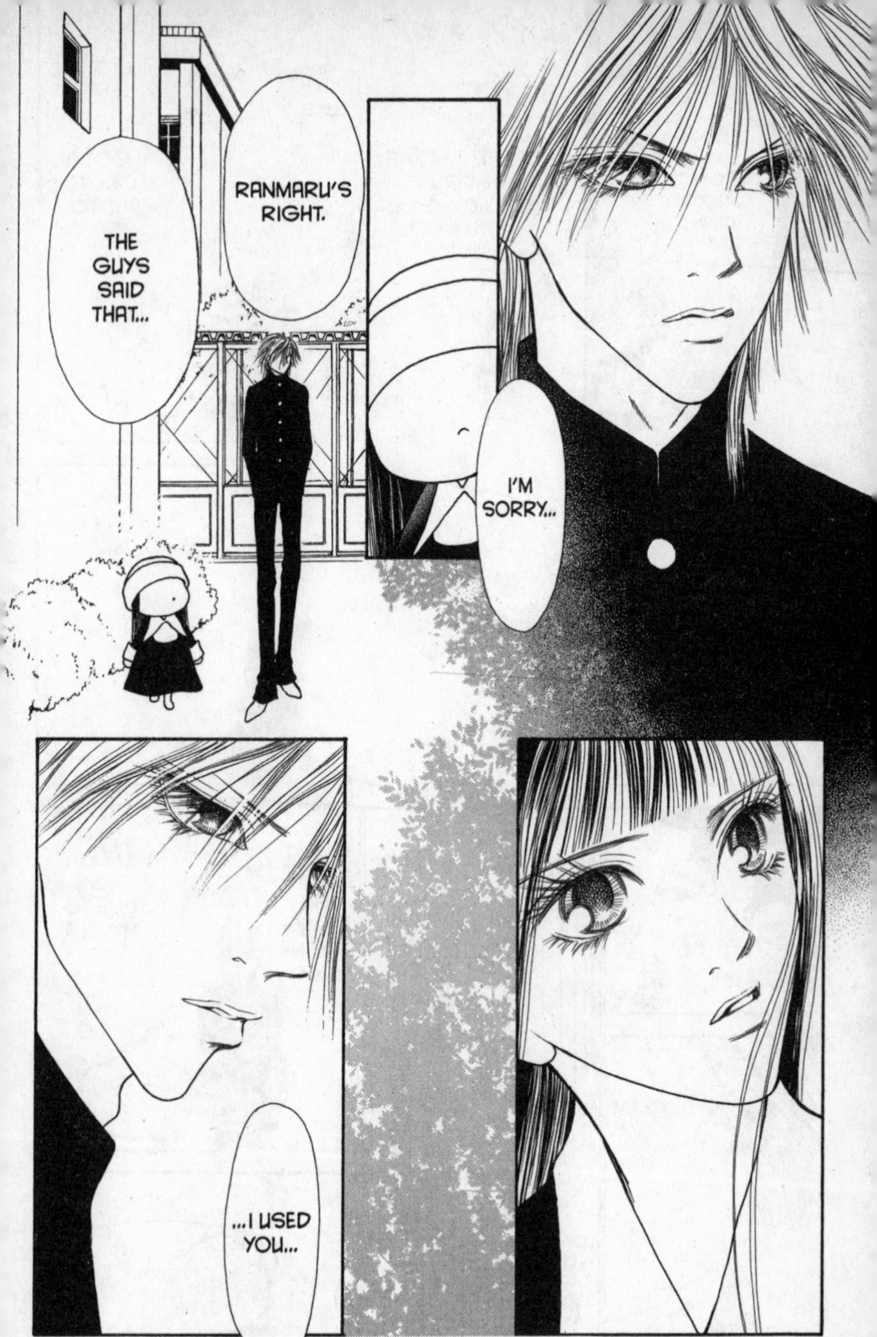
I'M SORRY...
RANMARU'S RIGHT.
THE GUYS SAID THAT...
...I USED YOU...

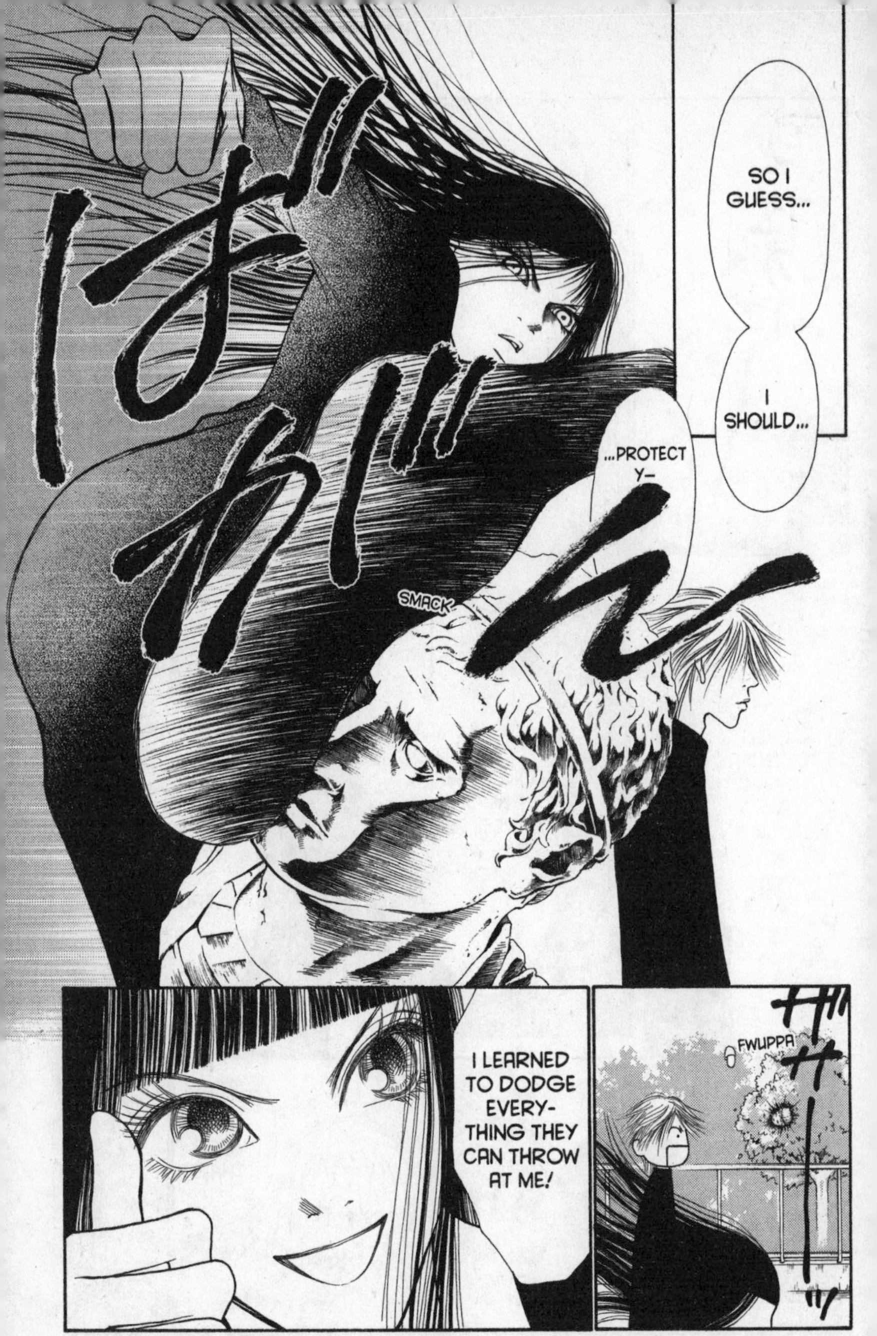
SO I GUESS...
I SHOULD...
...PROTECT Y—
SMACK
FWUPPA
I LEARNED TO DODGE EVERY-THING THEY CAN THROW AT ME!

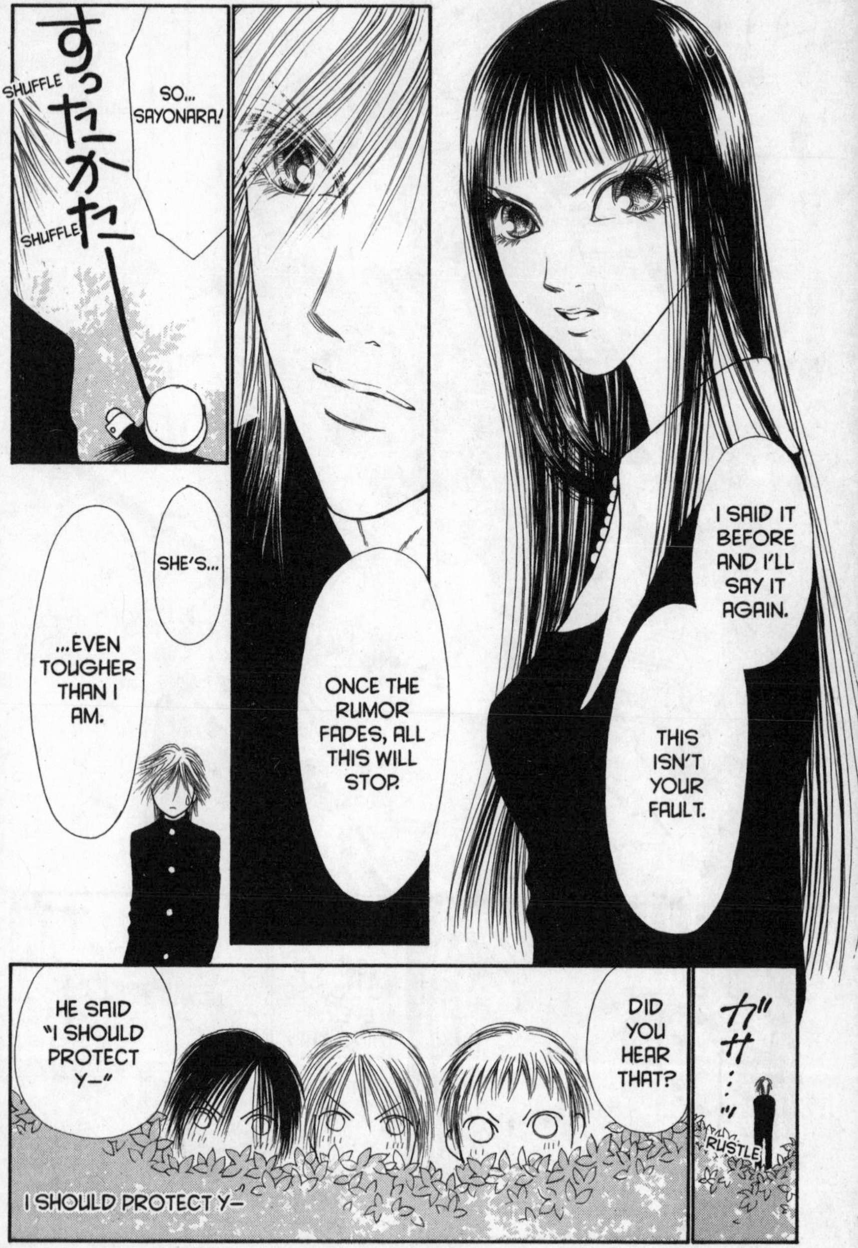
I SAID IT BEFORE AND I'LL SAY IT AGAIN.
THIS ISN'T YOUR FAULT.
ONCE THE RUMOR FADES, ALL THIS WILL STOP.
SO... SAYONARA!
すったかたー
SHUFFLE
SHUFFLE
SHE'S...
...EVEN TOUGHER THAN I AM.
ガサ…
RUSTLE
DID YOU HEAR THAT?
HE SAID "I SHOULD PROTECT Y—"
I SHOULD PROTECT Y—

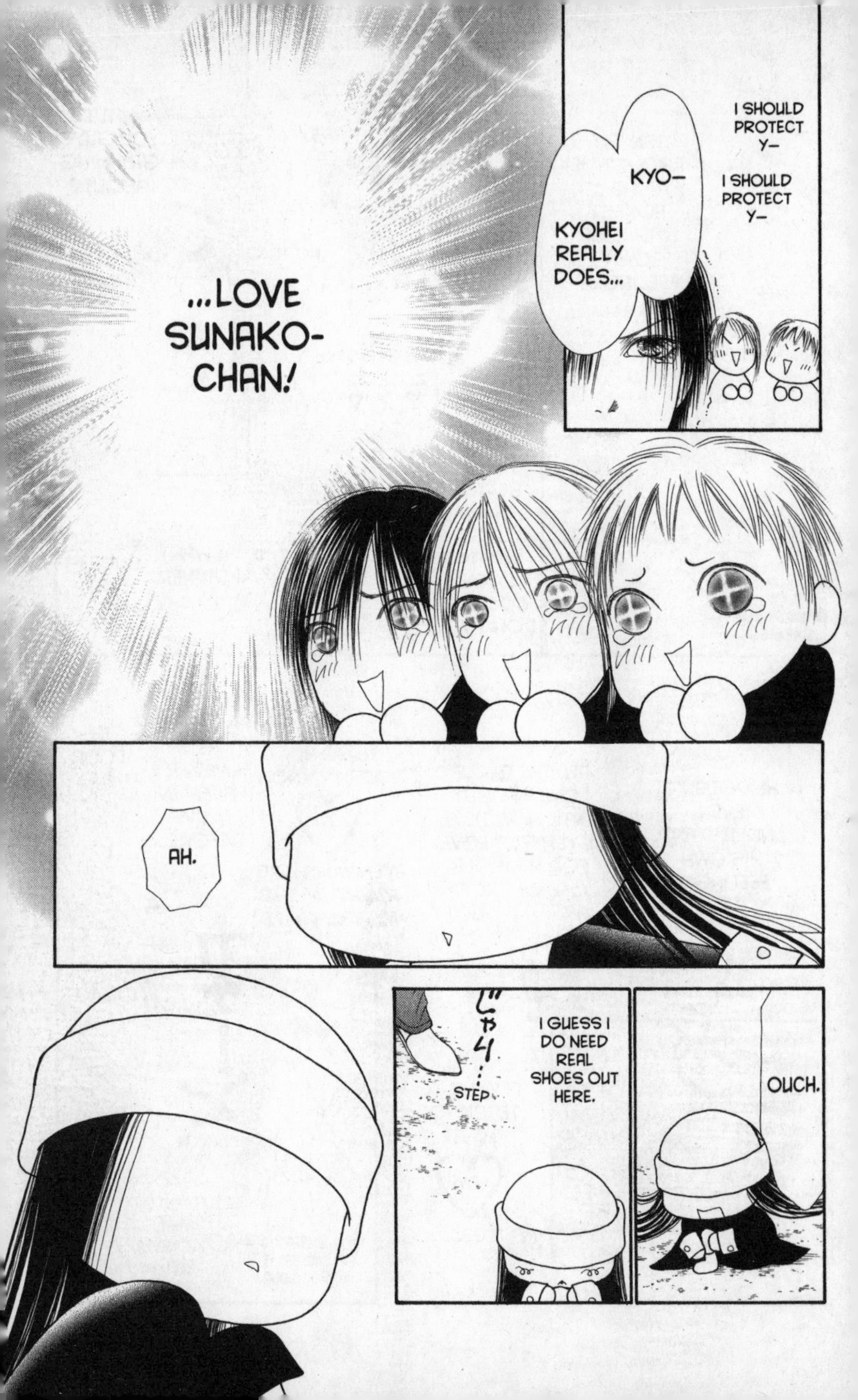
I SHOULD PROTECT Y—
I SHOULD PROTECT Y—
KYO— KYOHEI REALLY DOES...
...LOVE SUNAKO-CHAN!
AH.
OUCH.
I GUESS I DO NEED REAL SHOES OUT HERE.
じゃり…
STEP

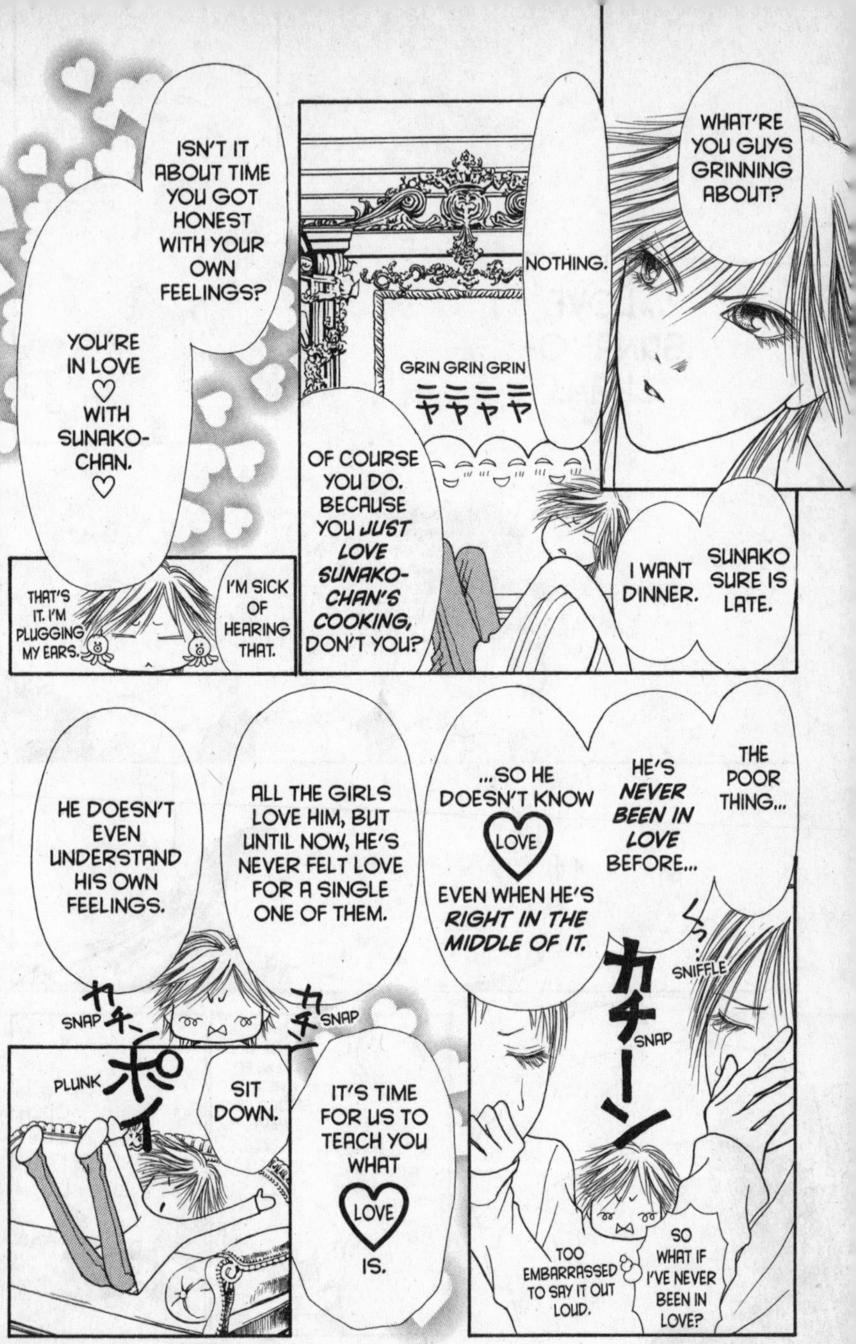

WHAT'RE YOU GUYS GRINNING ABOUT?
NOTHING.
GRIN GRIN GRIN
ニニニニ ヤヤヤヤ
SUNAKO SURE IS LATE.
I WANT DINNER.
OF COURSE YOU DO. BECAUSE YOU *JUST LOVE SUNAKO-CHAN'S COOKING,* DON'T YOU?
ISN'T IT ABOUT TIME YOU GOT HONEST WITH YOUR OWN FEELINGS?
YOU'RE IN LOVE ♡ WITH SUNAKO-CHAN. ♡
I'M SICK OF HEARING THAT.
THAT'S IT. I'M PLUGGING MY EARS.
THE POOR THING...
HE'S *NEVER BEEN IN LOVE* BEFORE...
...SO HE DOESN'T KNOW LOVE EVEN WHEN HE'S *RIGHT IN THE MIDDLE OF IT.*
ALL THE GIRLS LOVE HIM, BUT UNTIL NOW, HE'S NEVER FELT LOVE FOR A SINGLE ONE OF THEM.
HE DOESN'T EVEN UNDERSTAND HIS OWN FEELINGS.
SNIFFLE
カチーン
SNAP
SO WHAT IF I'VE NEVER BEEN IN LOVE?
TOO EMBARRASSED TO SAY IT OUT LOUD.
IT'S TIME FOR US TO TEACH YOU WHAT LOVE IS.
SNAP
SNAP
SIT DOWN.
ポイ
PLUNK

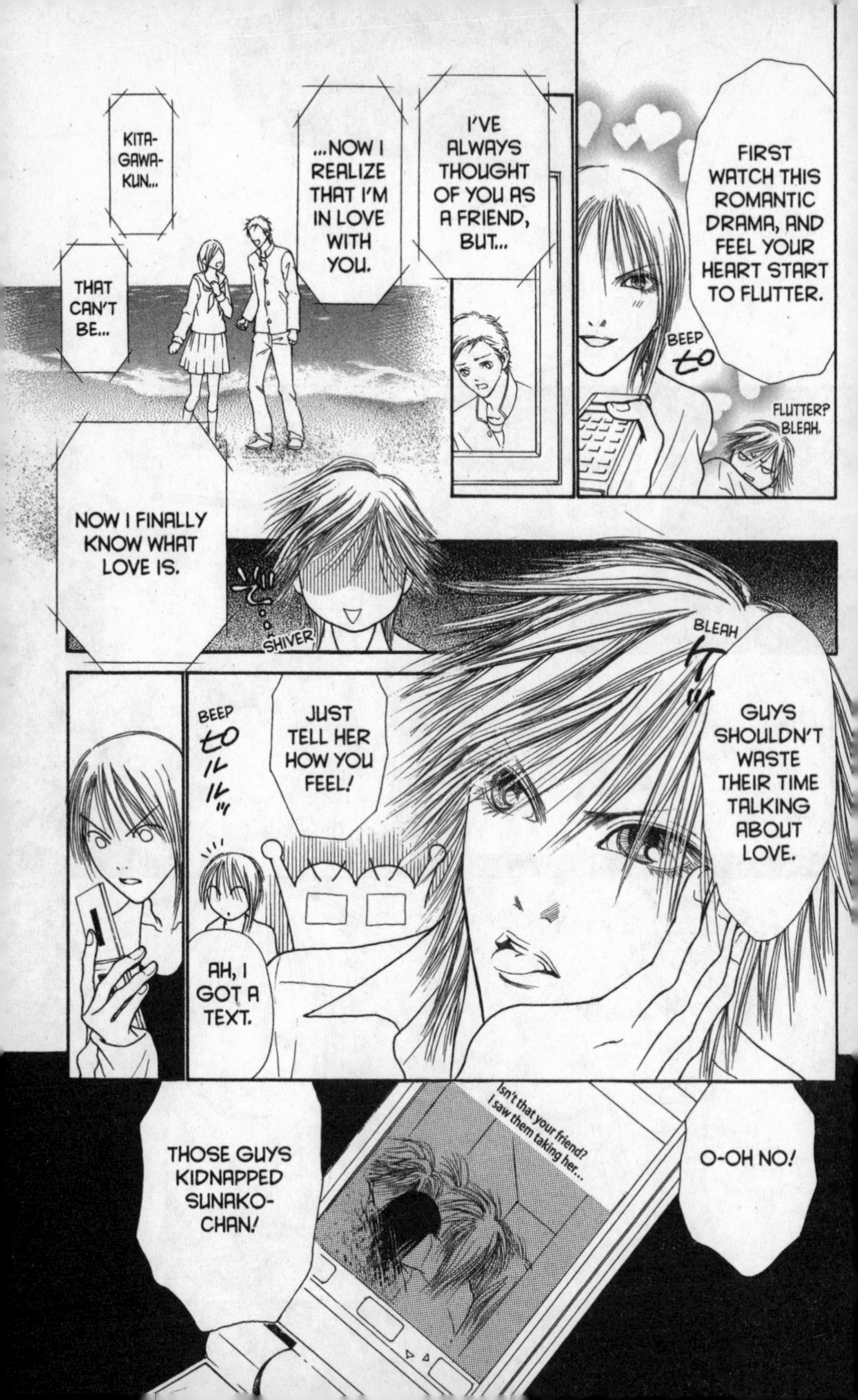
FIRST WATCH THIS ROMANTIC DRAMA, AND FEEL YOUR HEART START TO FLUTTER.
BEEP
FLUTTER? BLEAH.
I'VE ALWAYS THOUGHT OF YOU AS A FRIEND, BUT...
...NOW I REALIZE THAT I'M IN LOVE WITH YOU.
KITA-GAWA-KUN...
THAT CAN'T BE...
NOW I FINALLY KNOW WHAT LOVE IS.
SHIVER
BLEAH
GUYS SHOULDN'T WASTE THEIR TIME TALKING ABOUT LOVE.
JUST TELL HER HOW YOU FEEL!
AH, I GOT A TEXT.
BEEP
O-OH NO!
Isn't that your friend? I saw them taking her...
THOSE GUYS KIDNAPPED SUNAKO-CHAN!

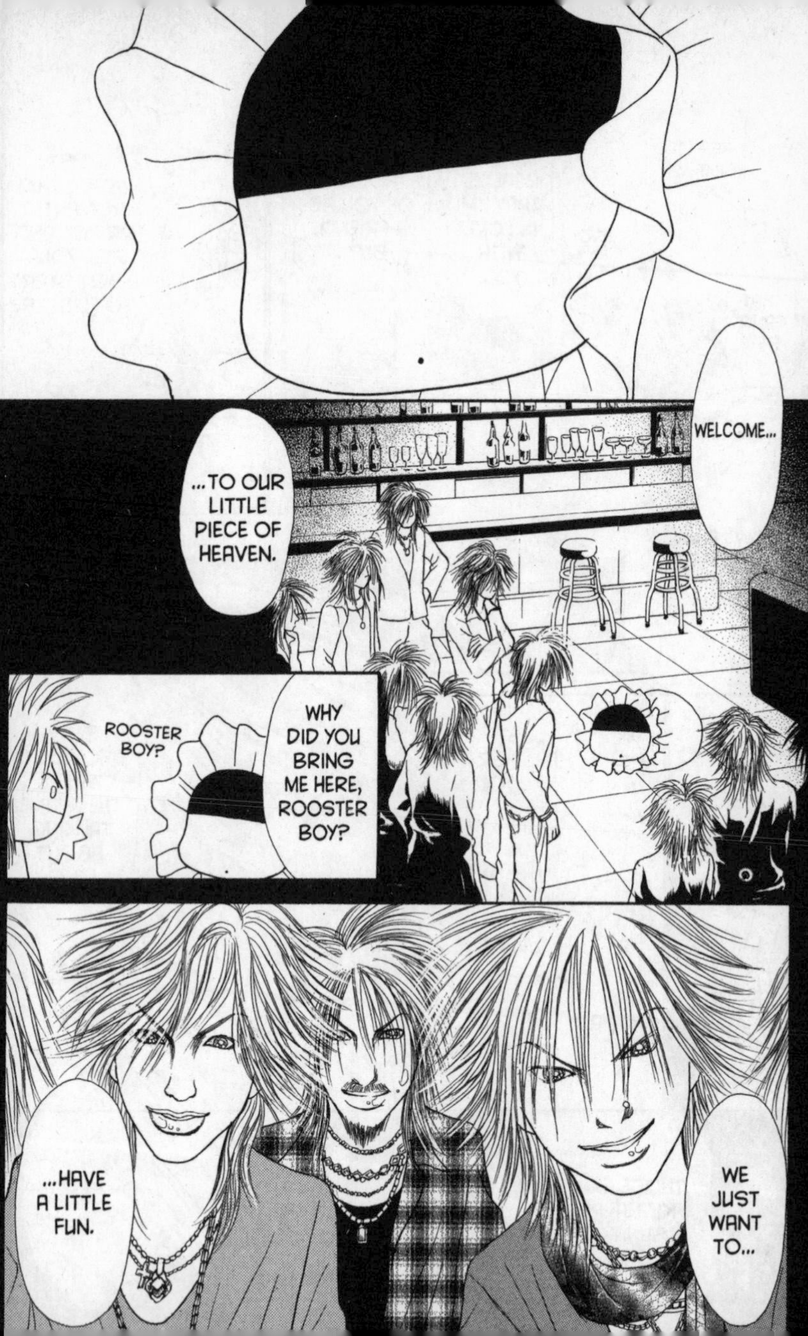
WELCOME...
...TO OUR LITTLE PIECE OF HEAVEN.
WHY DID YOU BRING ME HERE, ROOSTER BOY?
ROOSTER BOY?
WE JUST WANT TO...
...HAVE A LITTLE FUN.

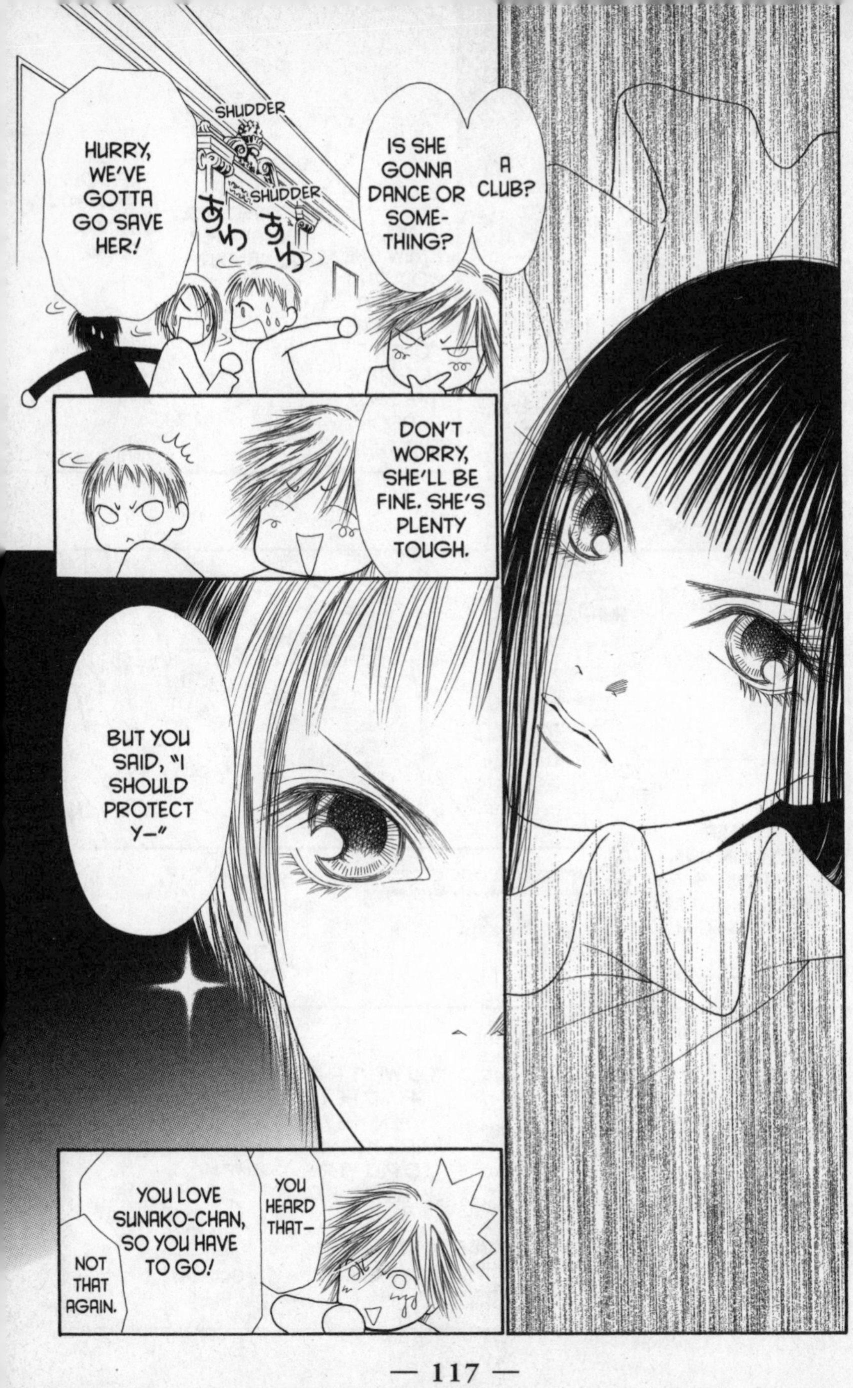
A CLUB?
IS SHE GONNA DANCE OR SOMETHING?
SHUDDER
SHUDDER
HURRY, WE'VE GOTTA GO SAVE HER!
DON'T WORRY, SHE'LL BE FINE. SHE'S PLENTY TOUGH.
BUT YOU SAID, "I SHOULD PROTECT Y—"
YOU HEARD THAT—
YOU LOVE SUNAKO-CHAN, SO YOU HAVE TO GO!
NOT THAT AGAIN.

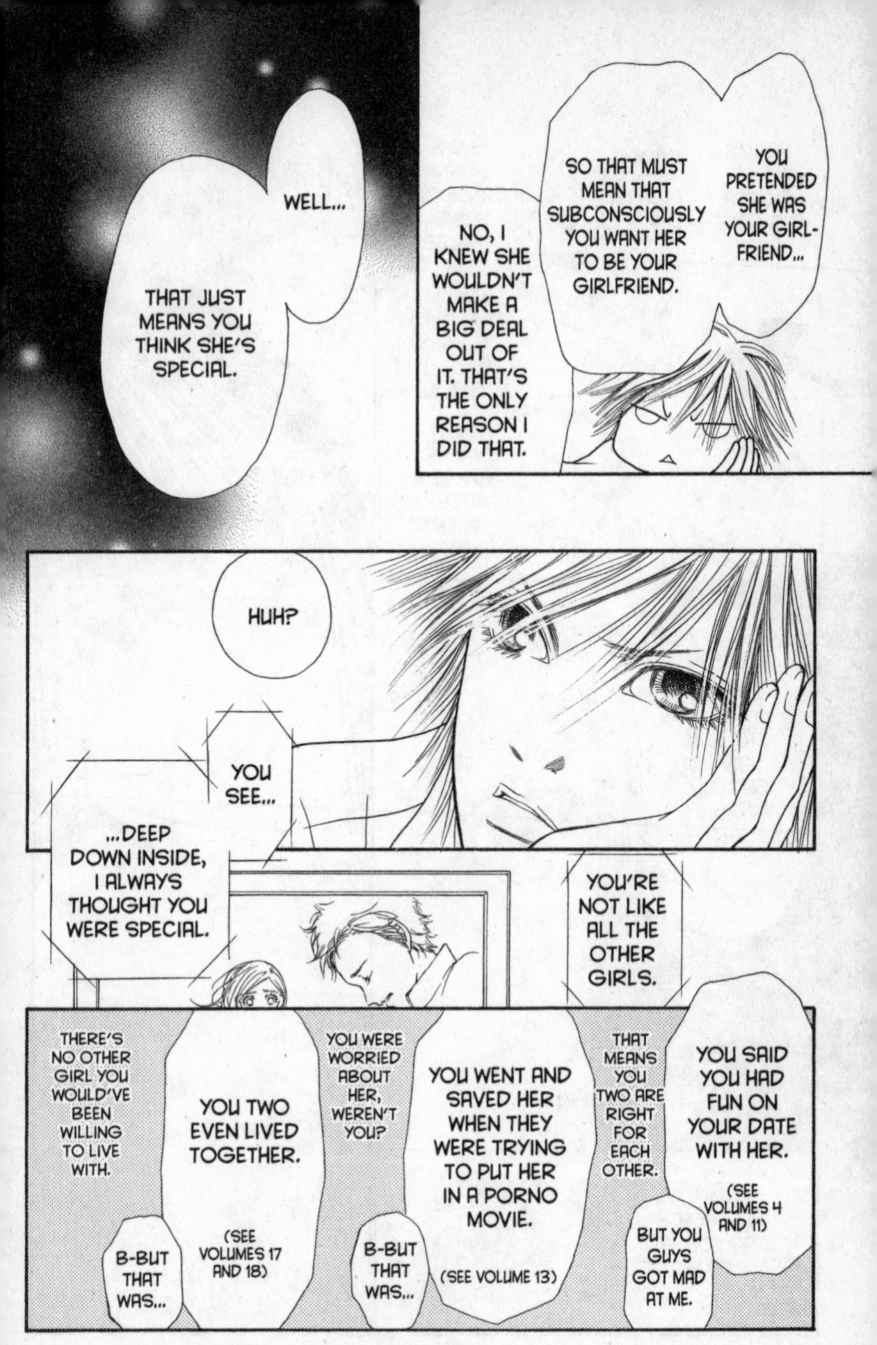
YOU PRETENDED SHE WAS YOUR GIRL-FRIEND...
SO THAT MUST MEAN THAT SUBCONSCIOUSLY YOU WANT HER TO BE YOUR GIRLFRIEND.
NO, I KNEW SHE WOULDN'T MAKE A BIG DEAL OUT OF IT. THAT'S THE ONLY REASON I DID THAT.
WELL...
THAT JUST MEANS YOU THINK SHE'S SPECIAL.
HUH?
YOU SEE...
...DEEP DOWN INSIDE, I ALWAYS THOUGHT YOU WERE SPECIAL.
YOU'RE NOT LIKE ALL THE OTHER GIRLS.
YOU SAID YOU HAD FUN ON YOUR DATE WITH HER.
(SEE VOLUMES 4 AND 11)
BUT YOU GUYS GOT MAD AT ME.
THAT MEANS YOU TWO ARE RIGHT FOR EACH OTHER.
YOU WENT AND SAVED HER WHEN THEY WERE TRYING TO PUT HER IN A PORNO MOVIE.
(SEE VOLUME 13)
YOU WERE WORRIED ABOUT HER, WEREN'T YOU?
B-BUT THAT WAS...
YOU TWO EVEN LIVED TOGETHER.
(SEE VOLUMES 17 AND 18)
THERE'S NO OTHER GIRL YOU WOULD'VE BEEN WILLING TO LIVE WITH.
B-BUT THAT WAS...

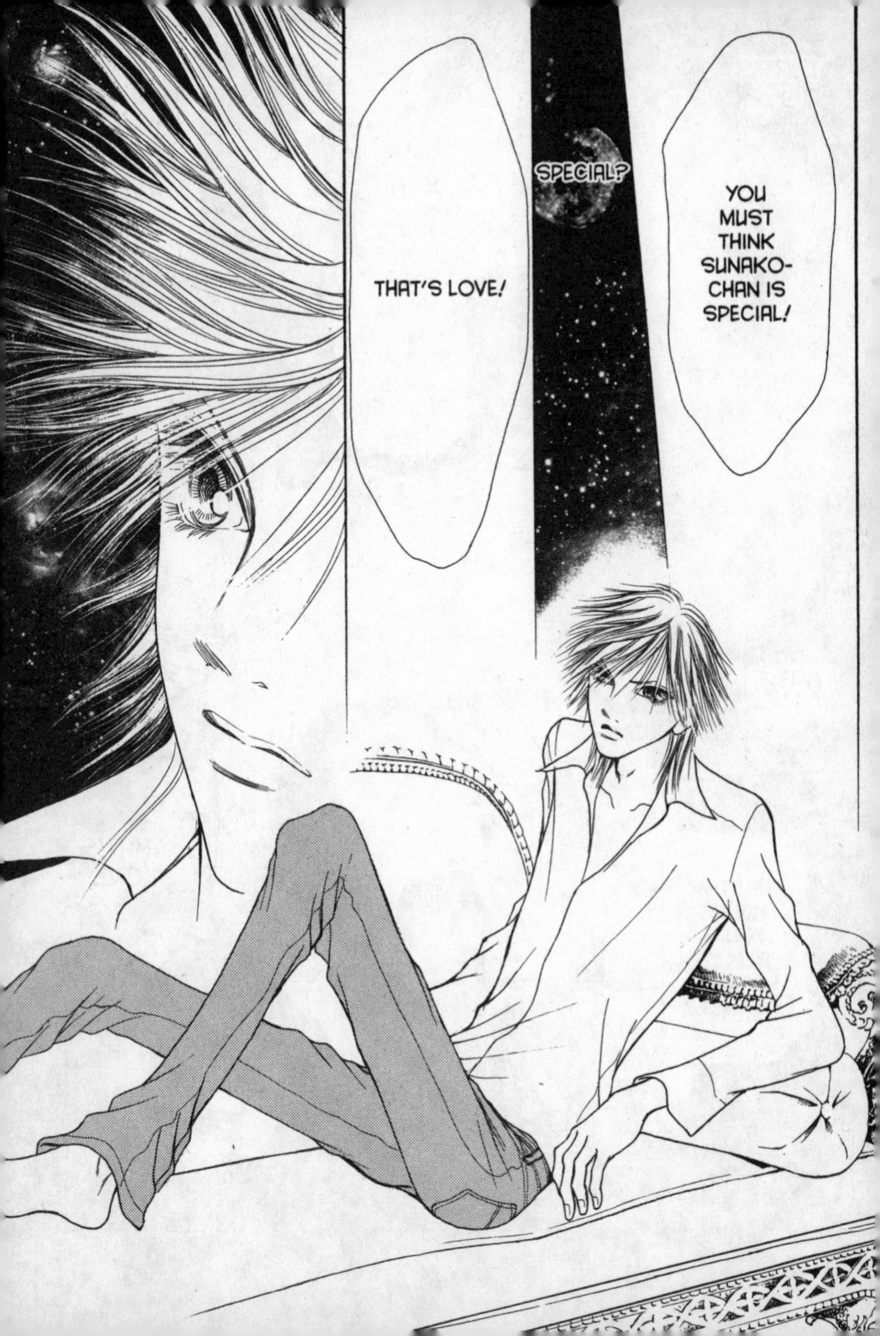
YOU MUST THINK SUNAKO-CHAN IS SPECIAL!
SPECIAL?
THAT'S LOVE!

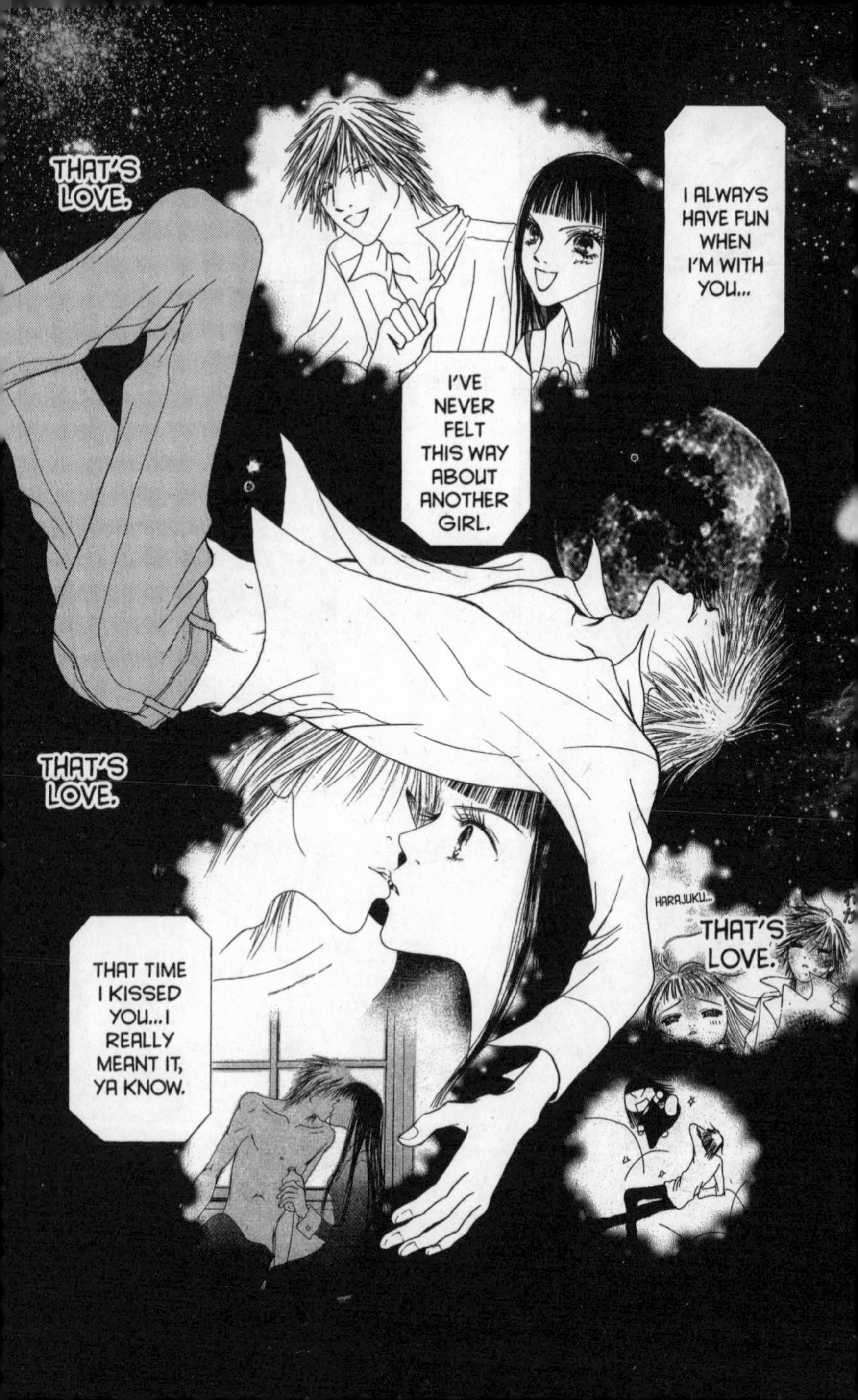
I ALWAYS HAVE FUN WHEN I'M WITH YOU...
I'VE NEVER FELT THIS WAY ABOUT ANOTHER GIRL.
THAT'S LOVE.
THAT'S LOVE.
HARAJUKU...
THAT'S LOVE.
THAT TIME I KISSED YOU...I REALLY MEANT IT, YA KNOW.

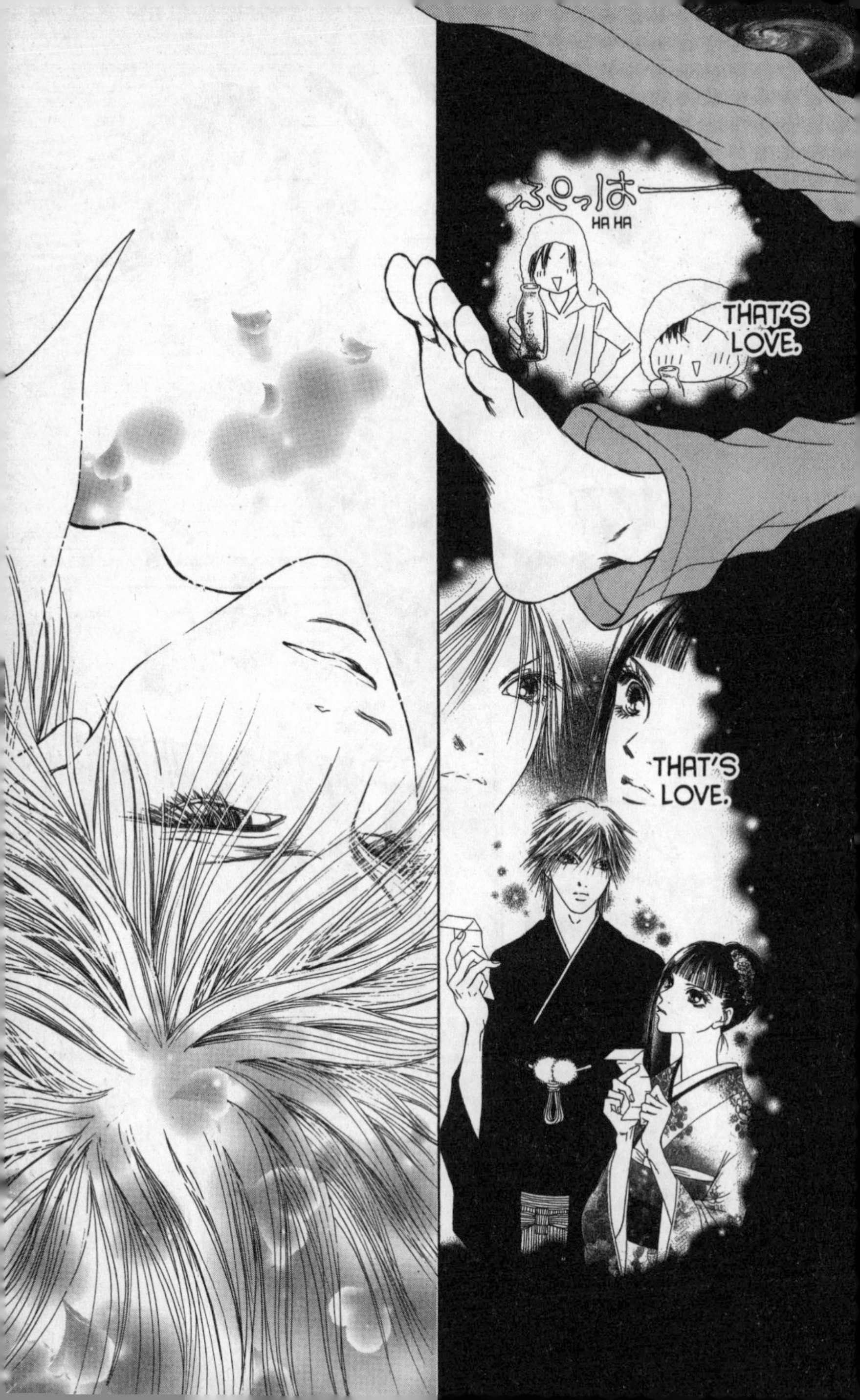
ぷっはー
HA HA
THAT'S LOVE.
THAT'S LOVE.

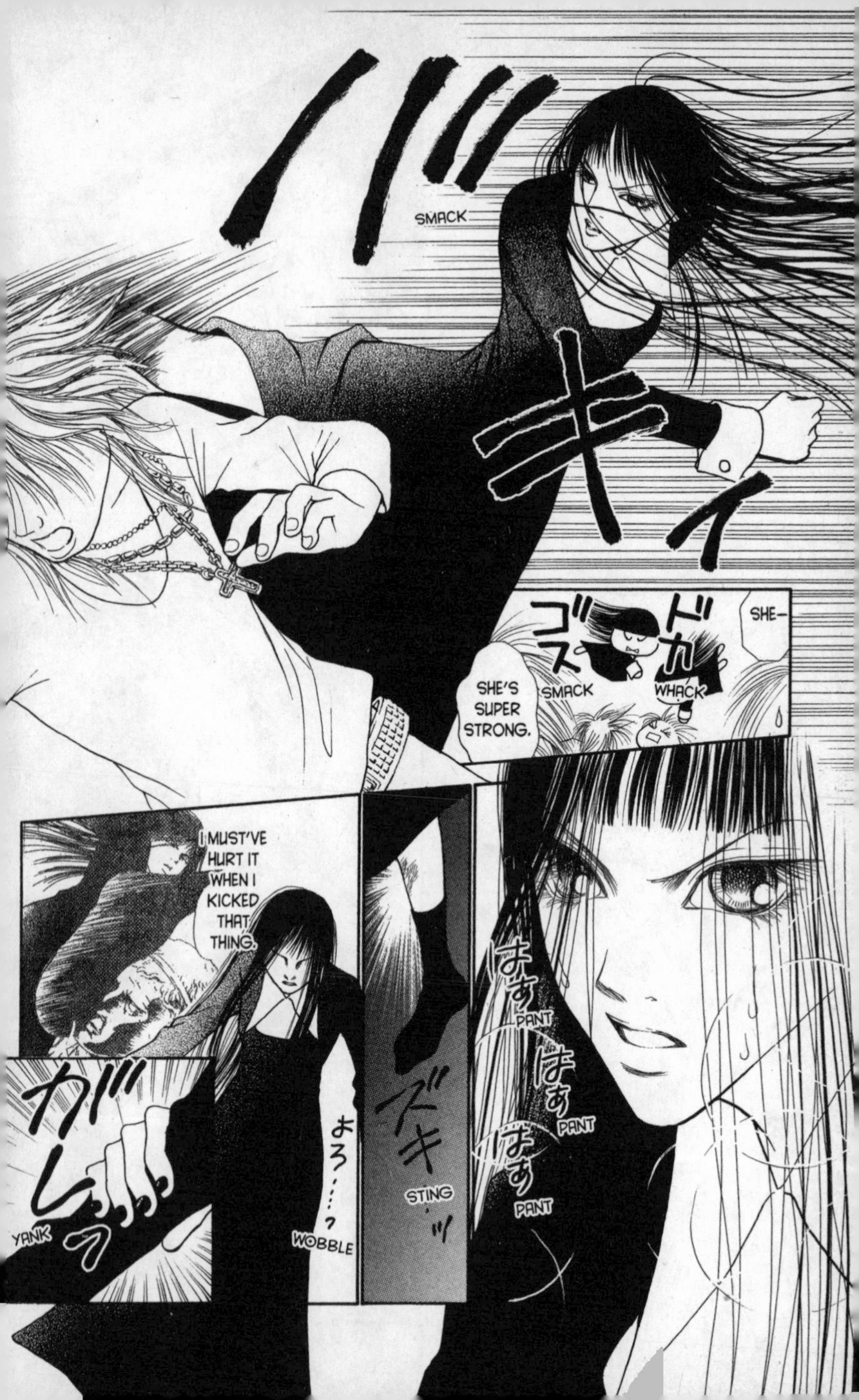
SMACK
キィ
SHE-
ドカ
WHACK
ゴス
SMACK
SHE'S SUPER STRONG.
はぁ
PANT
はぁ
PANT
はぁ
PANT
ズキ
STING
I MUST'VE HURT IT WHEN I KICKED THAT THING.
まろ…
WOBBLE
がしっ
YANK

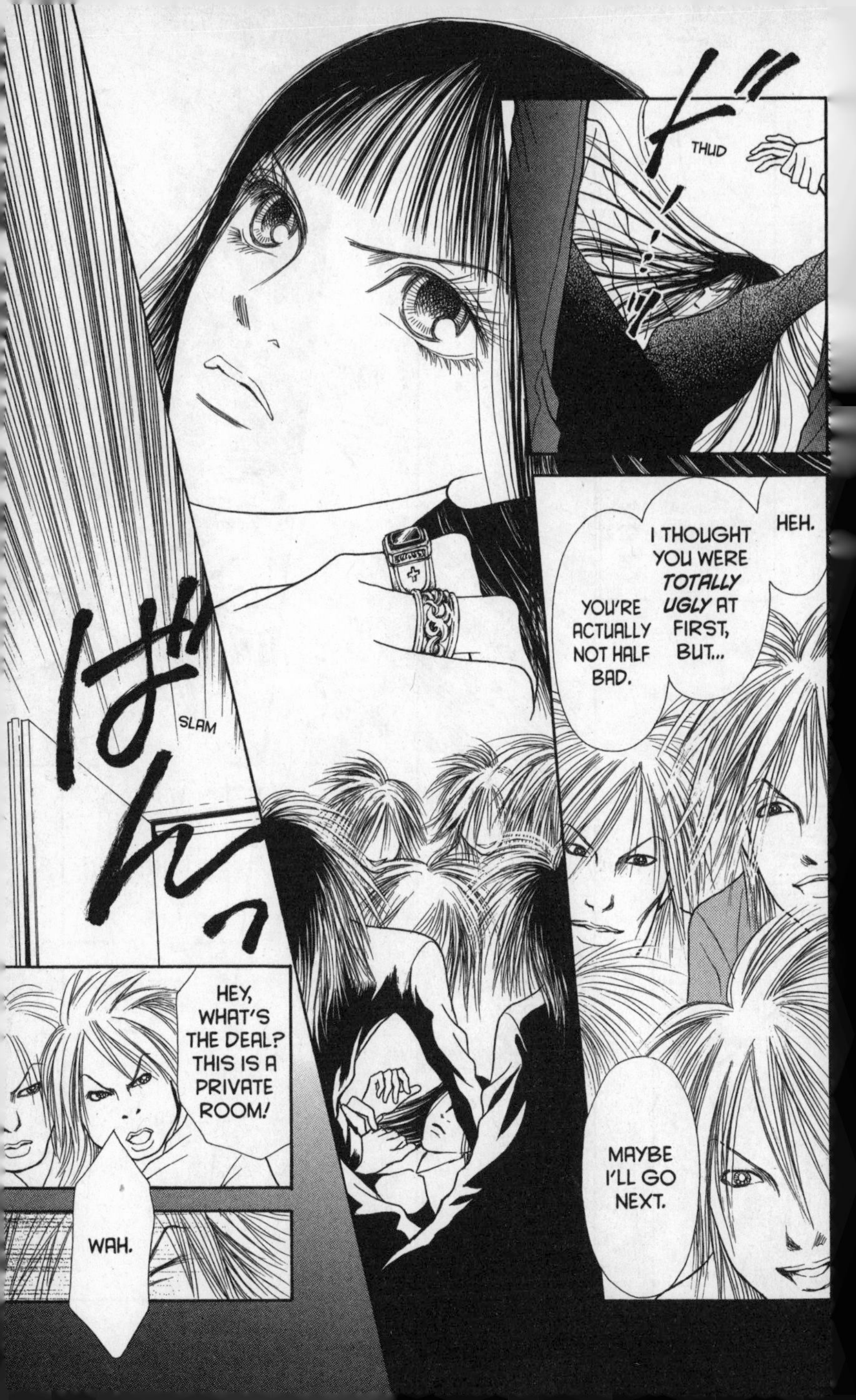
THUD
HEH.
I THOUGHT YOU WERE TOTALLY UGLY AT FIRST, BUT...
YOU'RE ACTUALLY NOT HALF BAD.
MAYBE I'LL GO NEXT.
ばんっ
SLAM
HEY, WHAT'S THE DEAL? THIS IS A PRIVATE ROOM!
WAH.

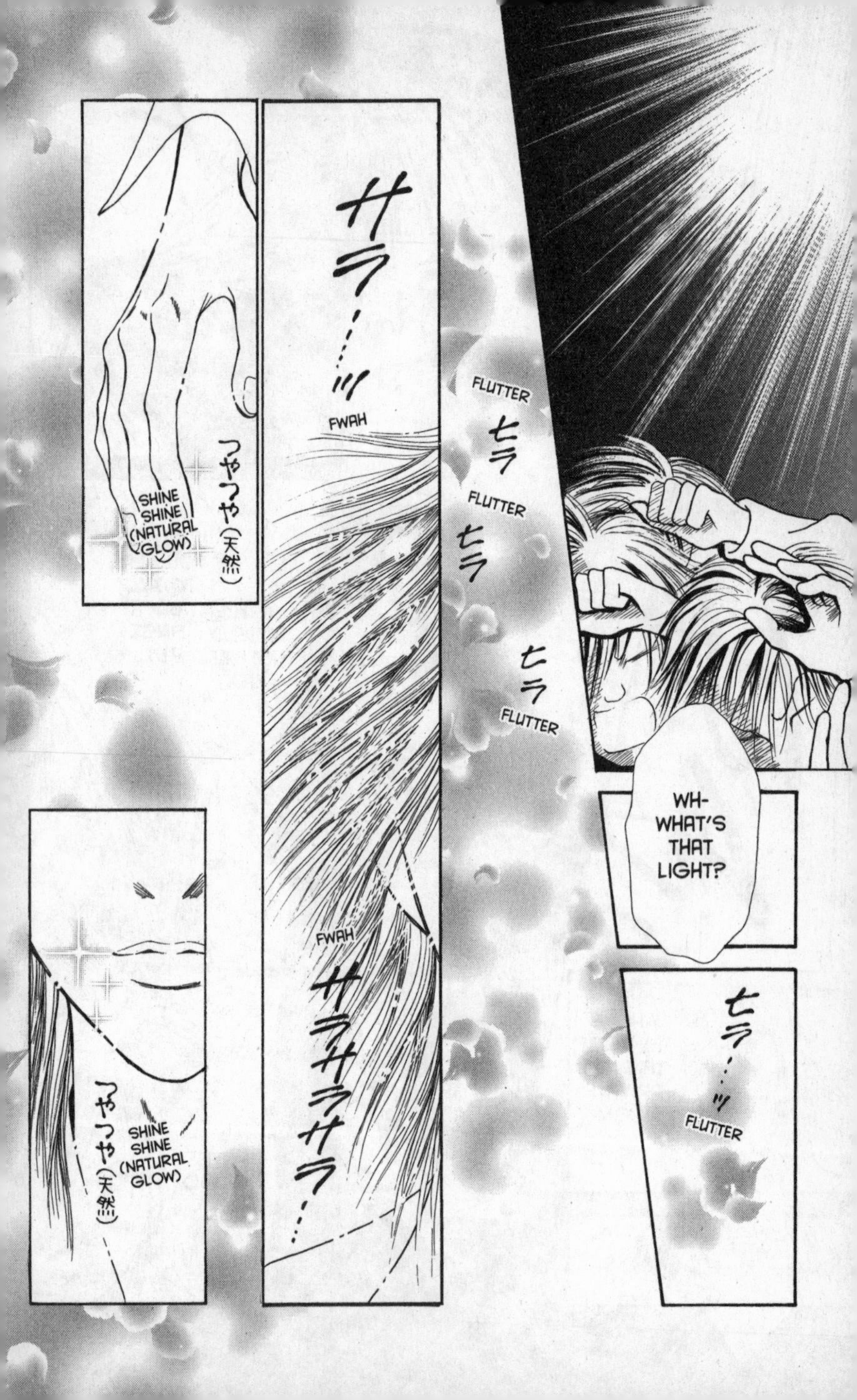
ヒラ
FLUTTER
ヒラ
FLUTTER
ヒラ
FLUTTER
WH-WHAT'S THAT LIGHT?
ヒラ…ッ
FLUTTER
サラ…ッ
FWAH
サラサラサラ…
FWAH
つやつや(天然)
SHINE SHINE (NATURAL GLOW)
つやつや(天然)
SHINE SHINE (NATURAL GLOW)

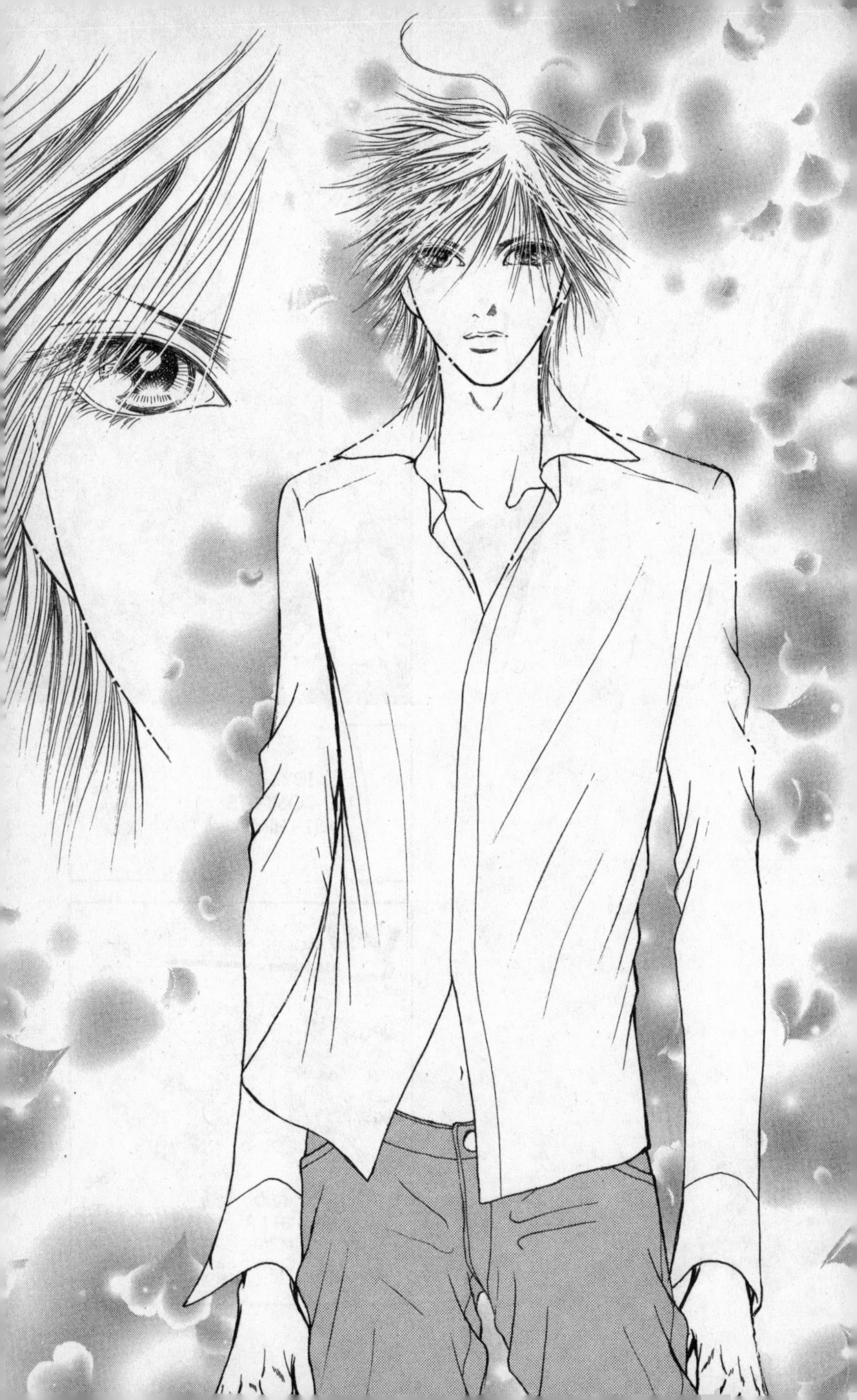

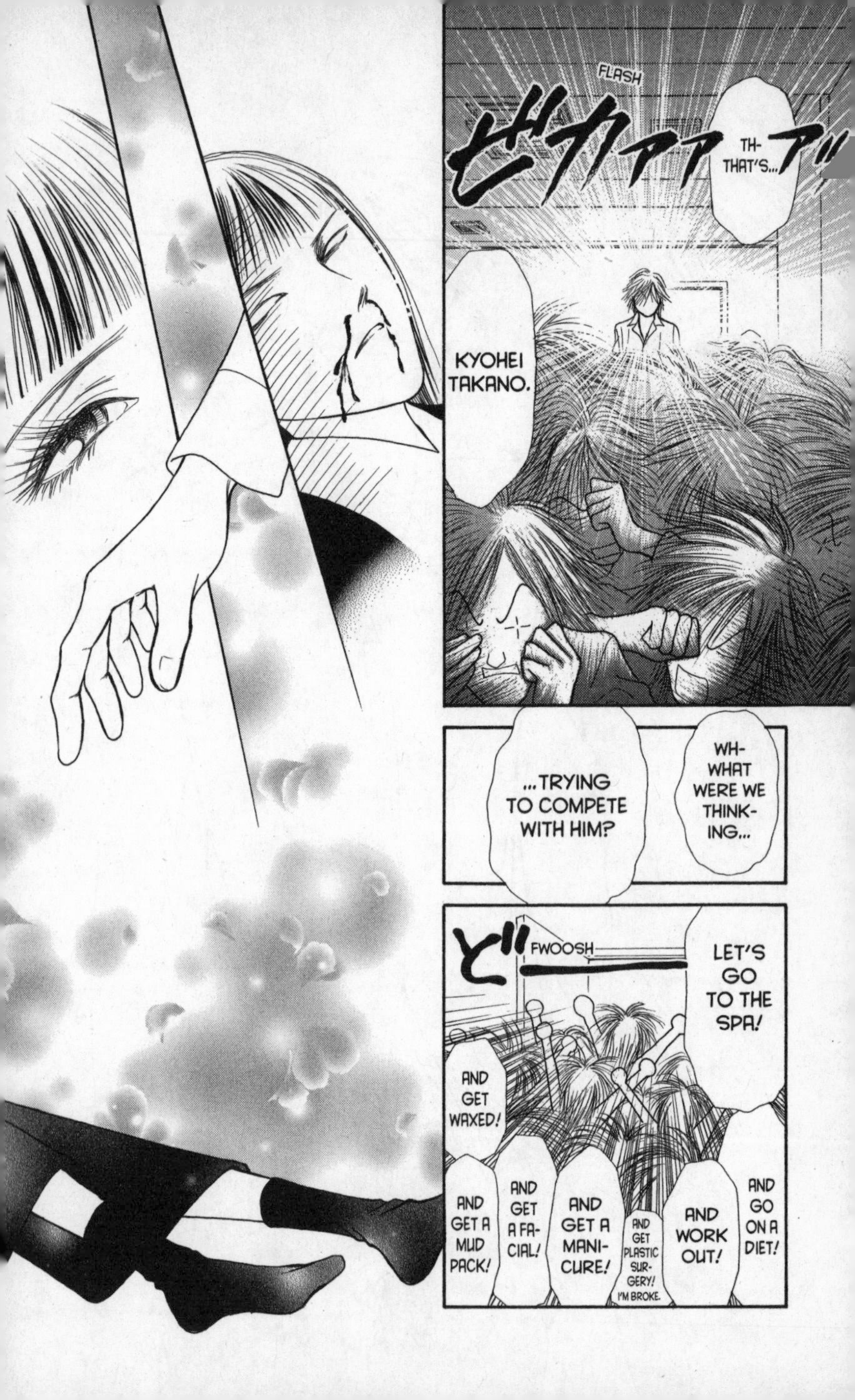
FLASH
TH-THAT'S...
KYOHEI TAKANO.
WH-WHAT WERE WE THINKING...
...TRYING TO COMPETE WITH HIM?
FWOOSH
LET'S GO TO THE SPA!
AND GET WAXED!
AND GO ON A DIET!
AND WORK OUT!
AND GET PLASTIC SURGERY!
I'M BROKE.
AND GET A MANICURE!
AND GET A FACIAL!
AND GET A MUD PACK!

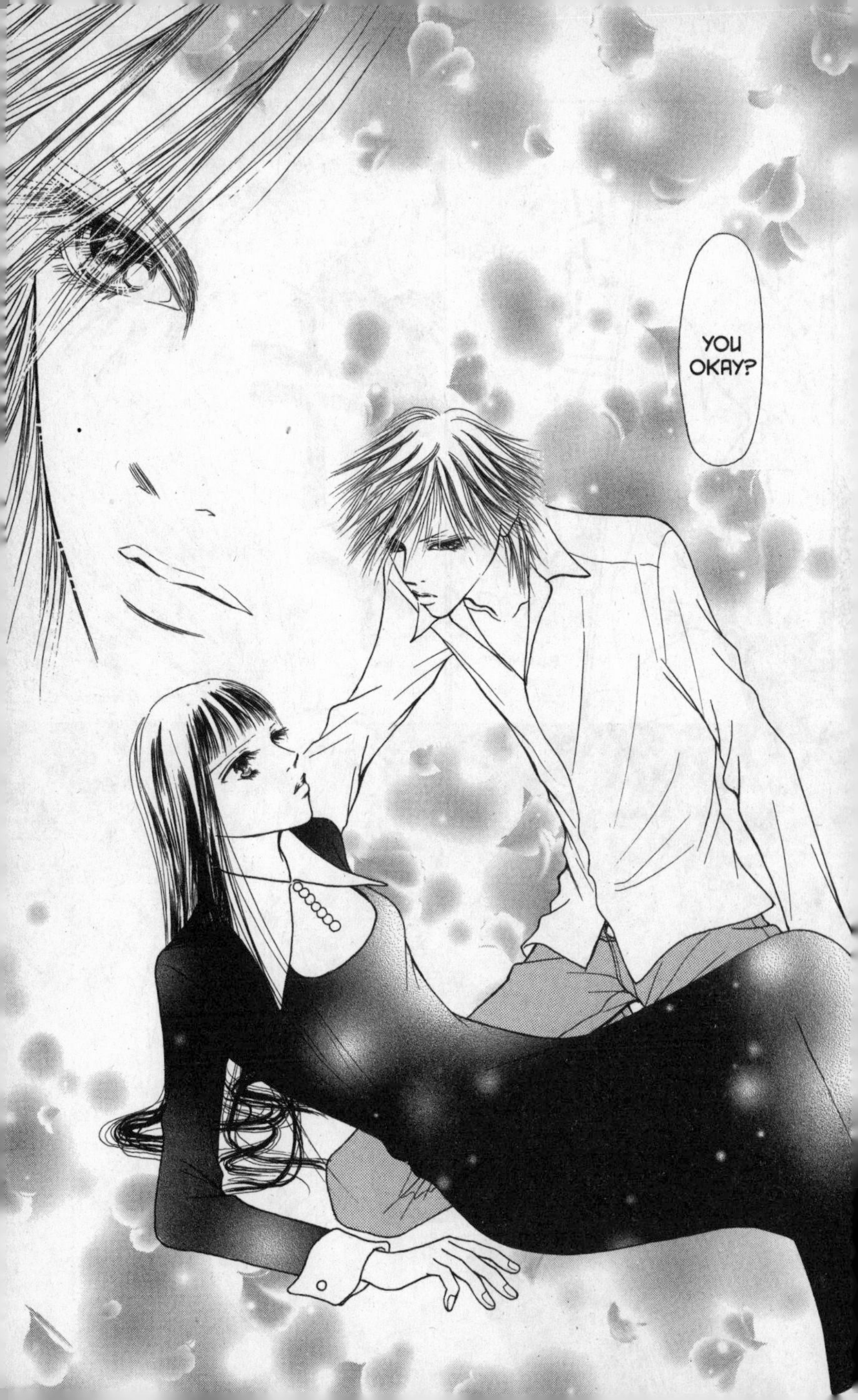
YOU OKAY?

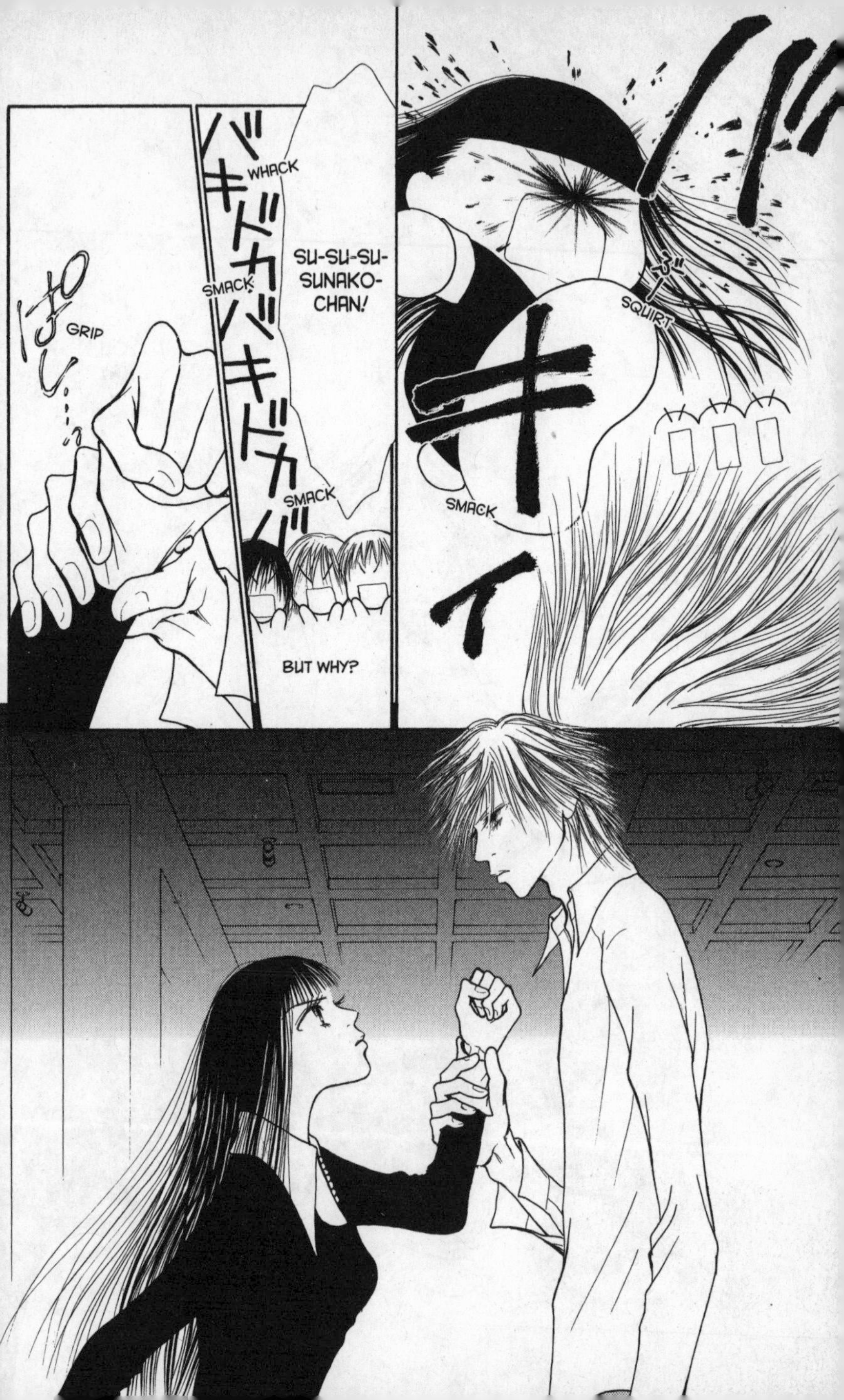

キイ
SMACK
ぶー
SQUIRT
バキドカバキドカバ
WHACK
SMACK
SMACK
SU-SU-SU-SUNAKO-CHAN!
BUT WHY?
ぱし…
GRIP

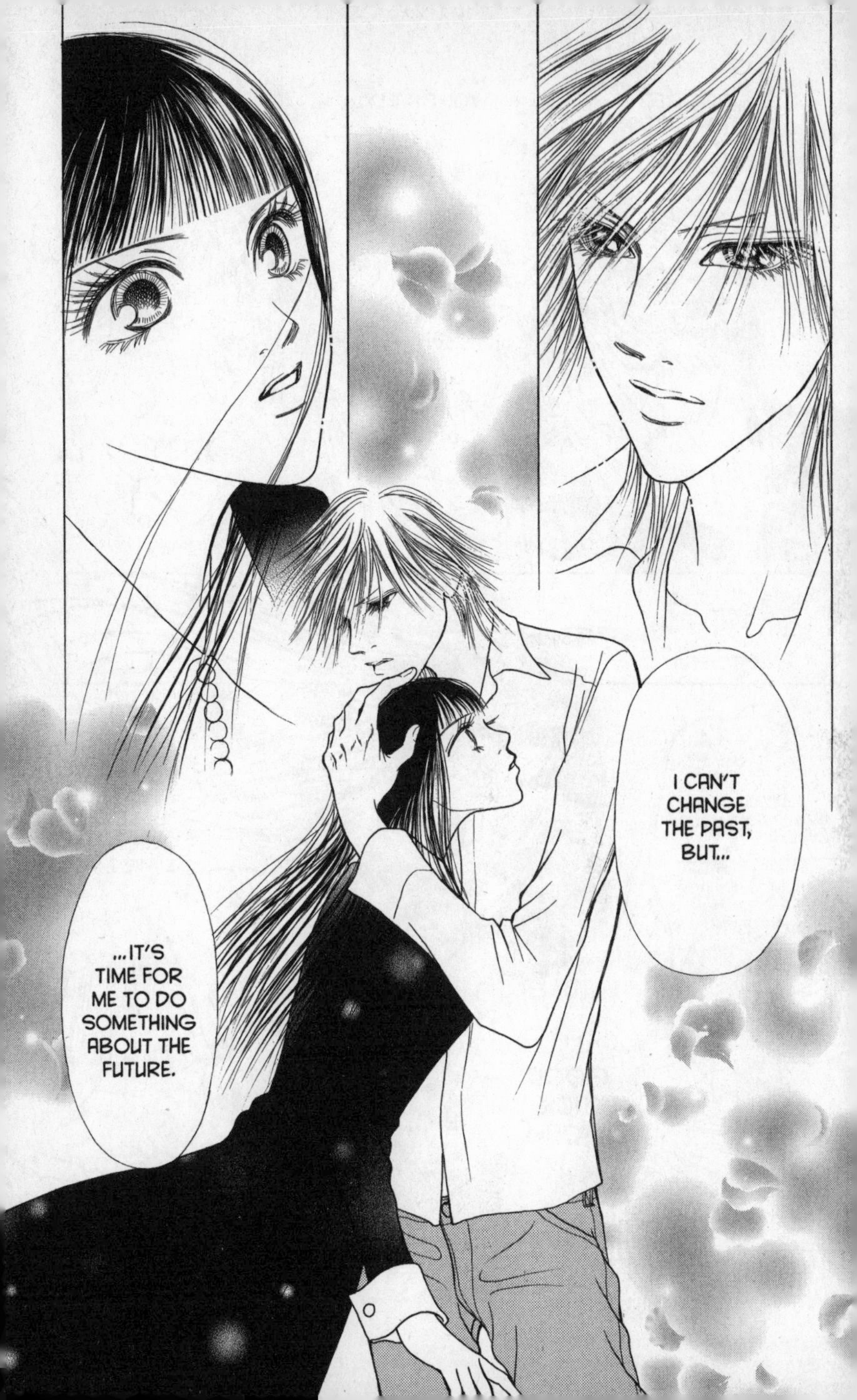
I CAN'T CHANGE THE PAST, BUT...
...IT'S TIME FOR ME TO DO SOMETHING ABOUT THE FUTURE.

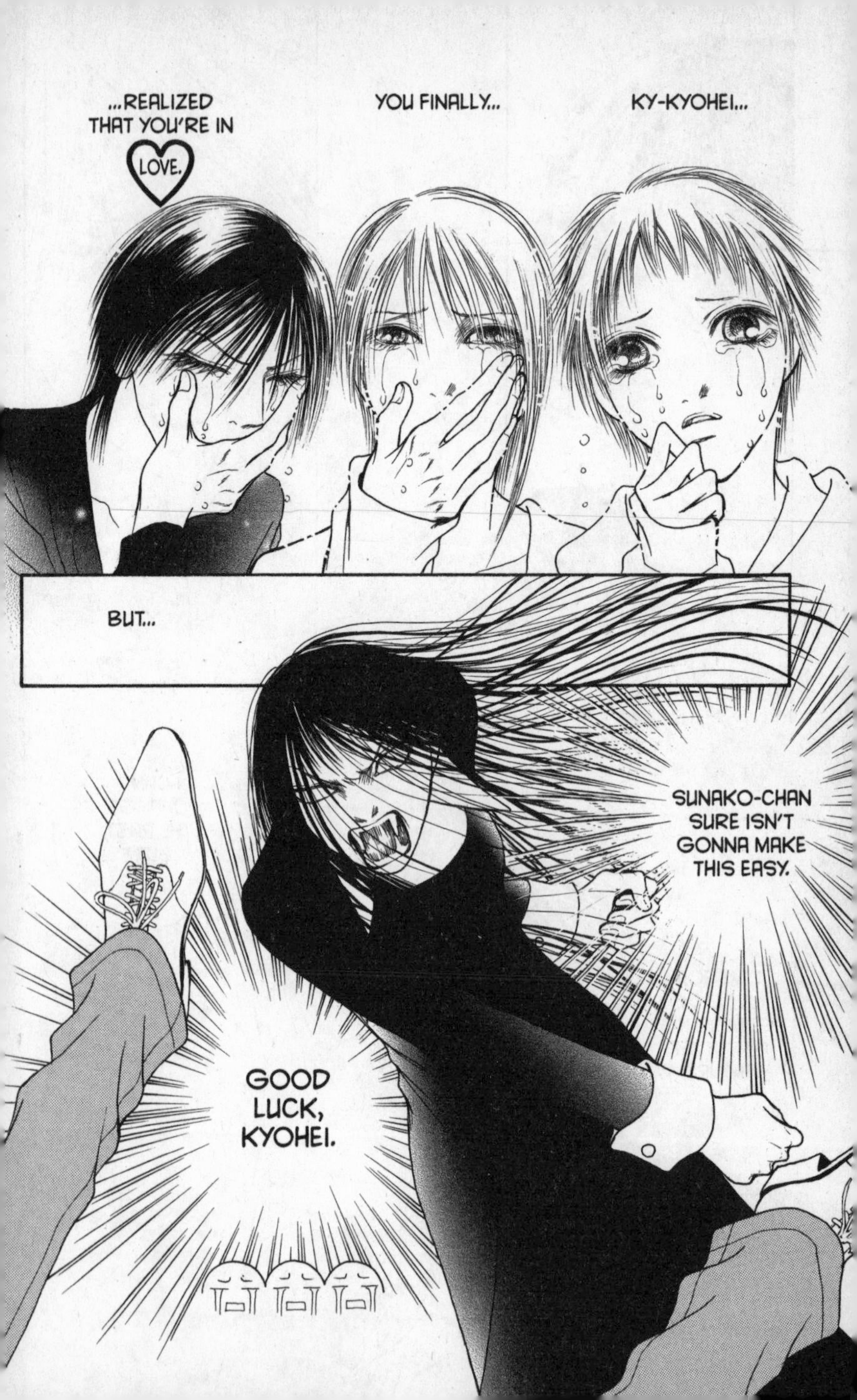
KY-KYOHEI...
YOU FINALLY...
...REALIZED THAT YOU'RE IN
LOVE.
BUT...
SUNAKO-CHAN SURE ISN'T GONNA MAKE THIS EASY.
GOOD LUCK, KYOHEI.

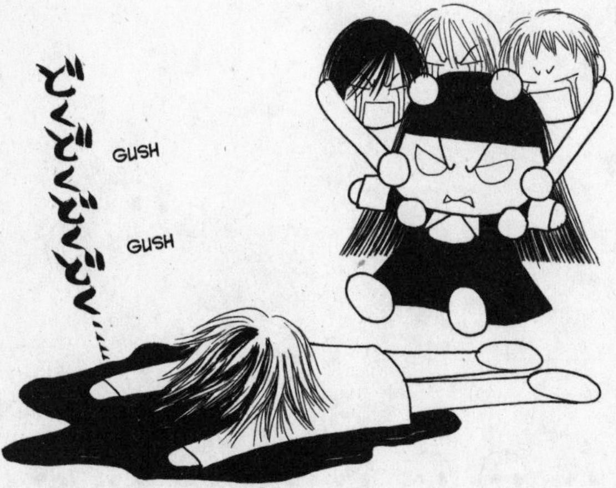
GUSH
GUSH

Chapter 87

SUNAKO AND THE MIRROR

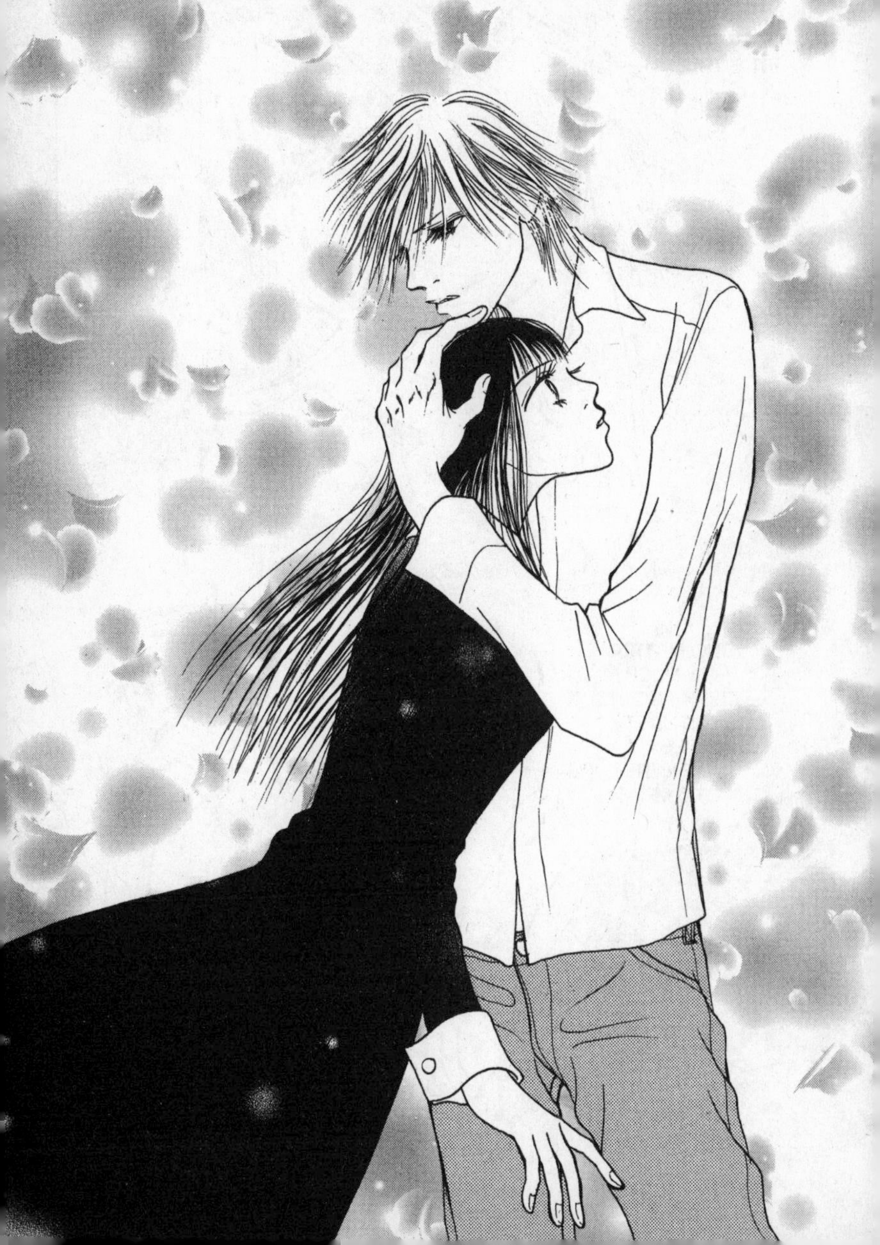

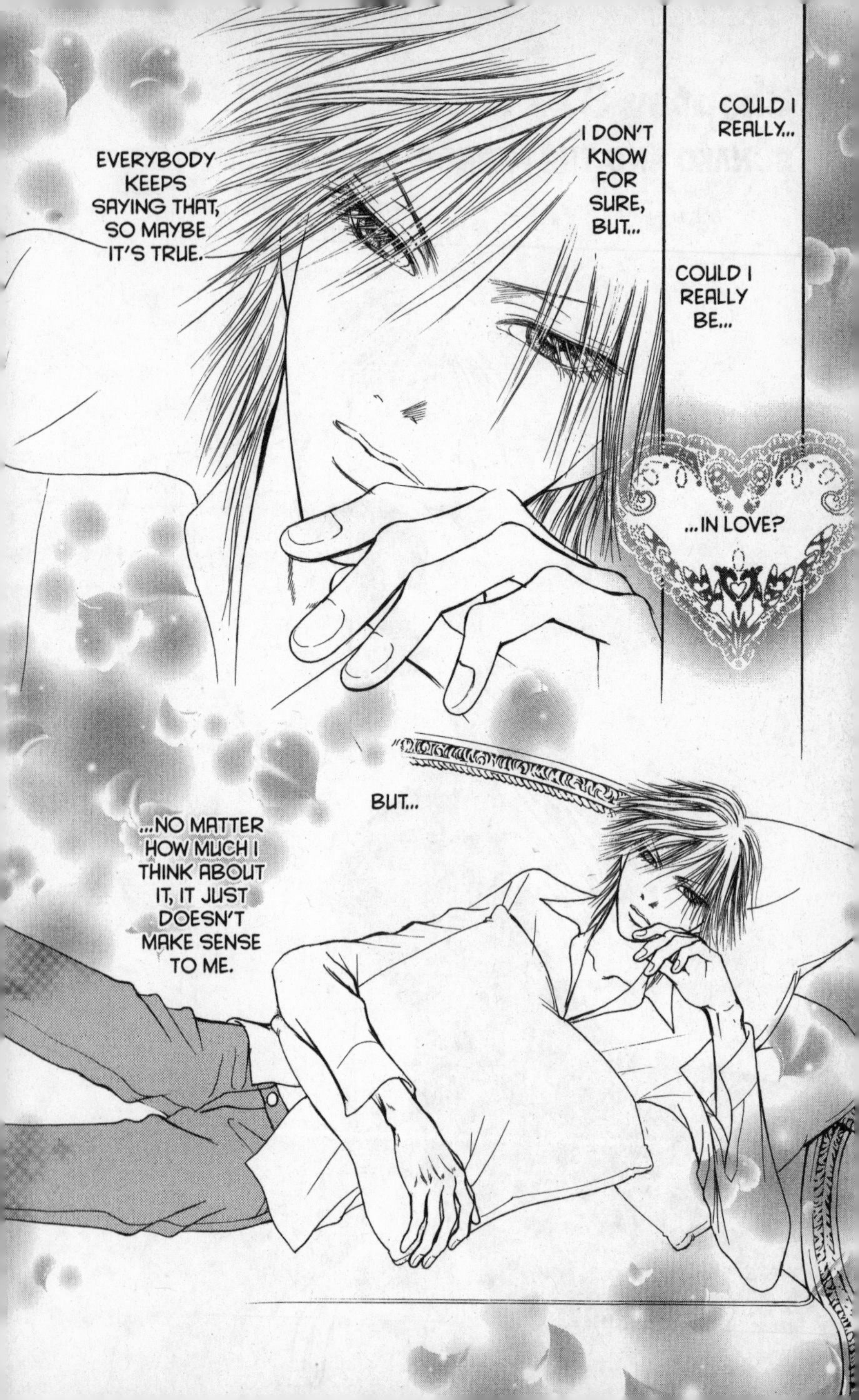
COULD I REALLY...
COULD I REALLY BE...
...IN LOVE?
I DON'T KNOW FOR SURE, BUT...
EVERYBODY KEEPS SAYING THAT, SO MAYBE IT'S TRUE.
BUT...
...NO MATTER HOW MUCH I THINK ABOUT IT, IT JUST DOESN'T MAKE SENSE TO ME.

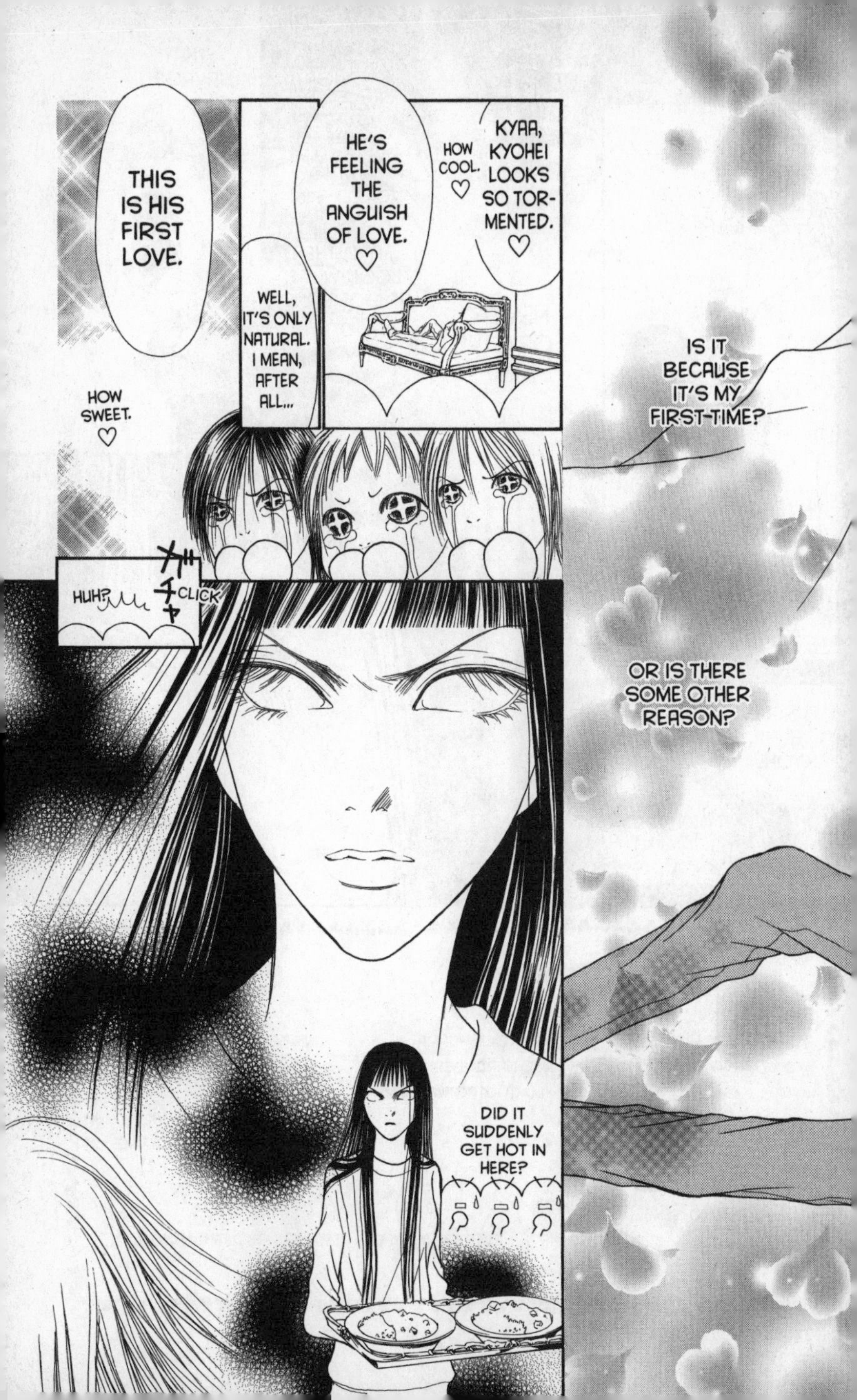
IS IT BECAUSE IT'S MY FIRST-TIME?
OR IS THERE SOME OTHER REASON?
KYAA, KYOHEI LOOKS SO TOR-MENTED. ♡
HOW COOL. ♡
HE'S FEELING THE ANGUISH OF LOVE. ♡
WELL, IT'S ONLY NATURAL. I MEAN, AFTER ALL...
THIS IS HIS FIRST LOVE.
HOW SWEET. ♡
ガチャ
CLICK
HUH?
DID IT SUDDENLY GET HOT IN HERE?

THAT SAVAGE...

I THOUGHT HE WAS JUST TRYING TO DRIVE AWAY THOSE CREEPS...

...AND THEN LOOK WHAT HE GOES AND DOES.

I'LL NEVER FORGIVE HIM!

HANG IN THERE, KYOHEI.

G- GOOD LUCK.

SPECIAL THANKS

YOUICHIRO TOMITA-SAMA
IYO MORI-SAMA

REN KOIUMI-SAMA
RYO NARUMI-SAMA
YUUKA KITAGAWA-SAMA

INNAN-SAMA
INO-SAMA
HOSOI-SAMA
EDITOR IN CHIEF-SAMA
EVERYBODY IN THE EDITING DEPARTMENT

MACHIKO SAKURAI
MIZUHO AIMOTO-SENSEI

EVERYBODY WHO'S READING THIS RIGHT NOW♡

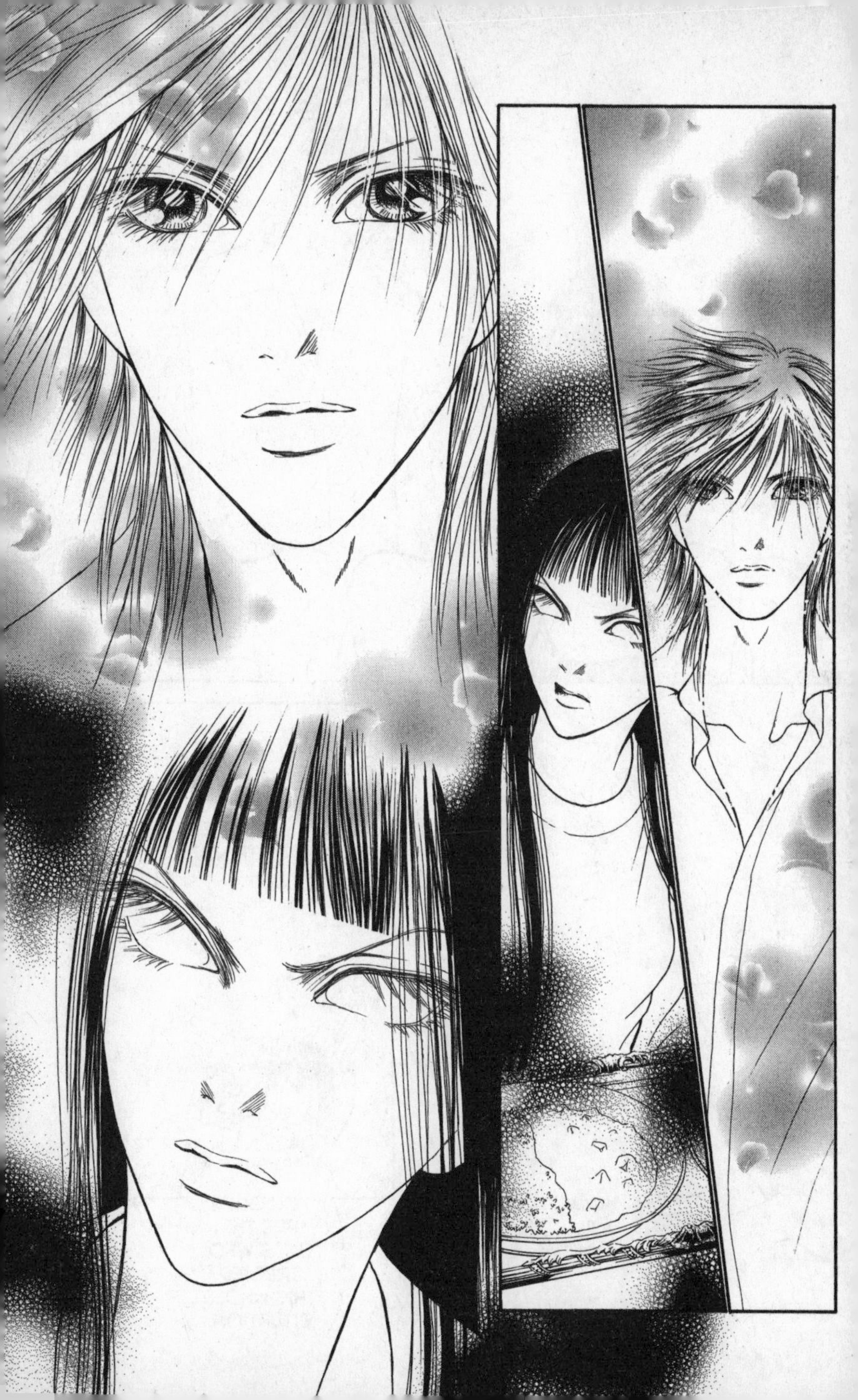

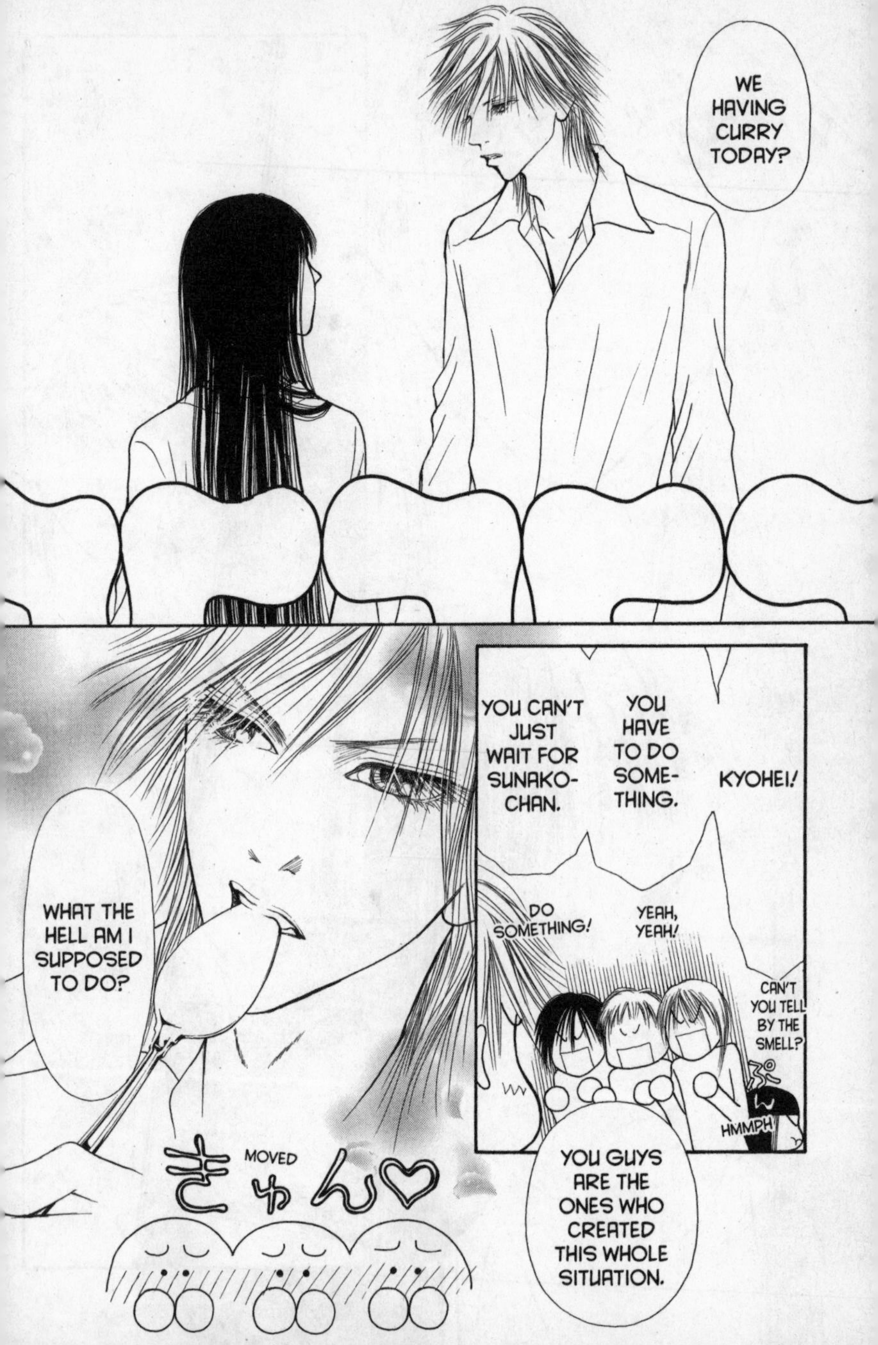

WE HAVING CURRY TODAY?
KYOHEI!
YOU HAVE TO DO SOMETHING.
YOU CAN'T JUST WAIT FOR SUNAKO-CHAN.
YEAH, YEAH!
DO SOMETHING!
CAN'T YOU TELL BY THE SMELL?
HMMPH
YOU GUYS ARE THE ONES WHO CREATED THIS WHOLE SITUATION.
WHAT THE HELL AM I SUPPOSED TO DO?
きゅん♡
MOVED

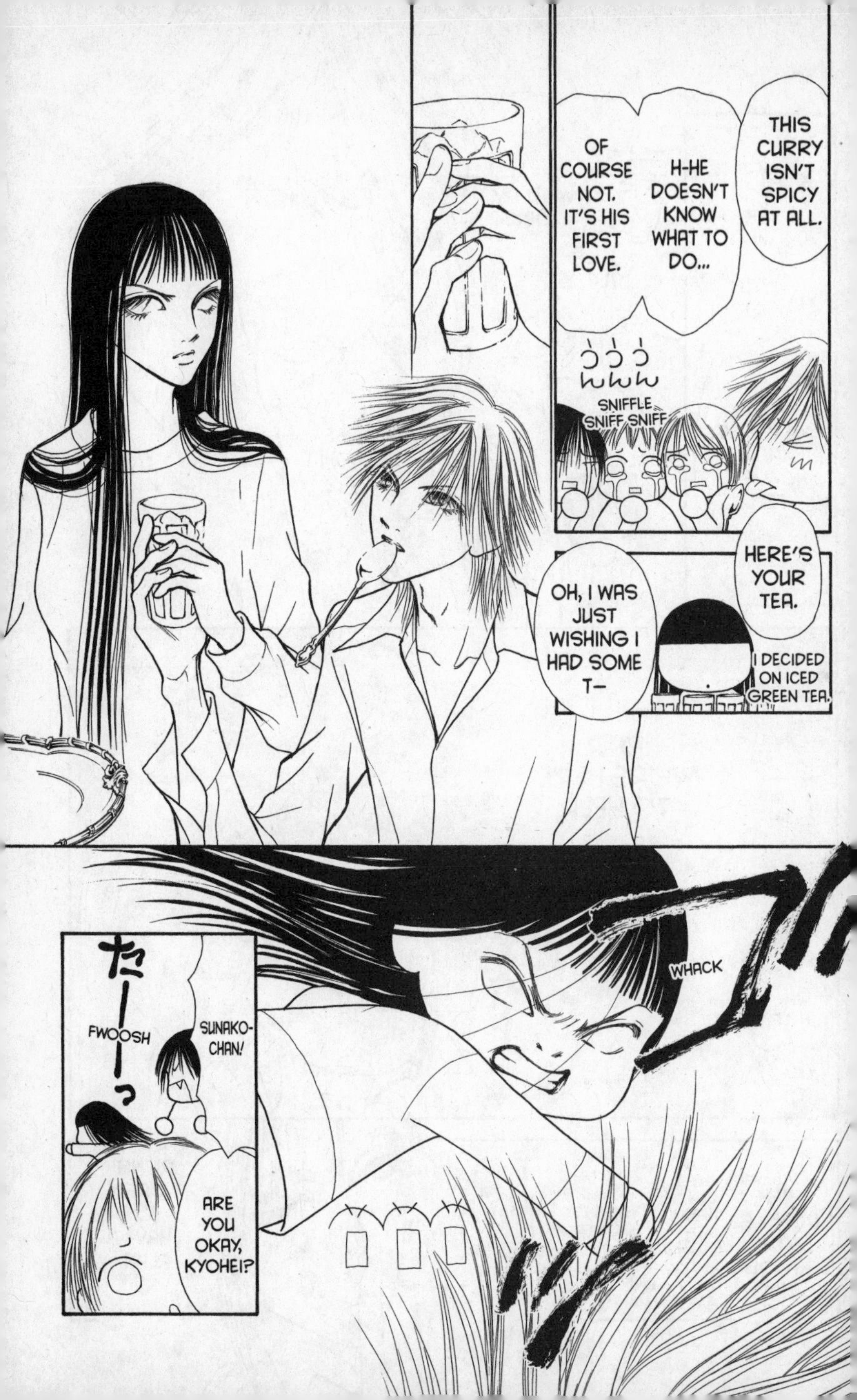
THIS CURRY ISN'T SPICY AT ALL.
H-HE DOESN'T KNOW WHAT TO DO...
OF COURSE NOT. IT'S HIS FIRST LOVE.
SNIFFLE SNIFF SNIFF
HERE'S YOUR TEA.
I DECIDED ON ICED GREEN TEA.
OH, I WAS JUST WISHING I HAD SOME T—
WHACK
たーーっ
FWOOSH
SUNAKO-CHAN!
ARE YOU OKAY, KYOHEI?

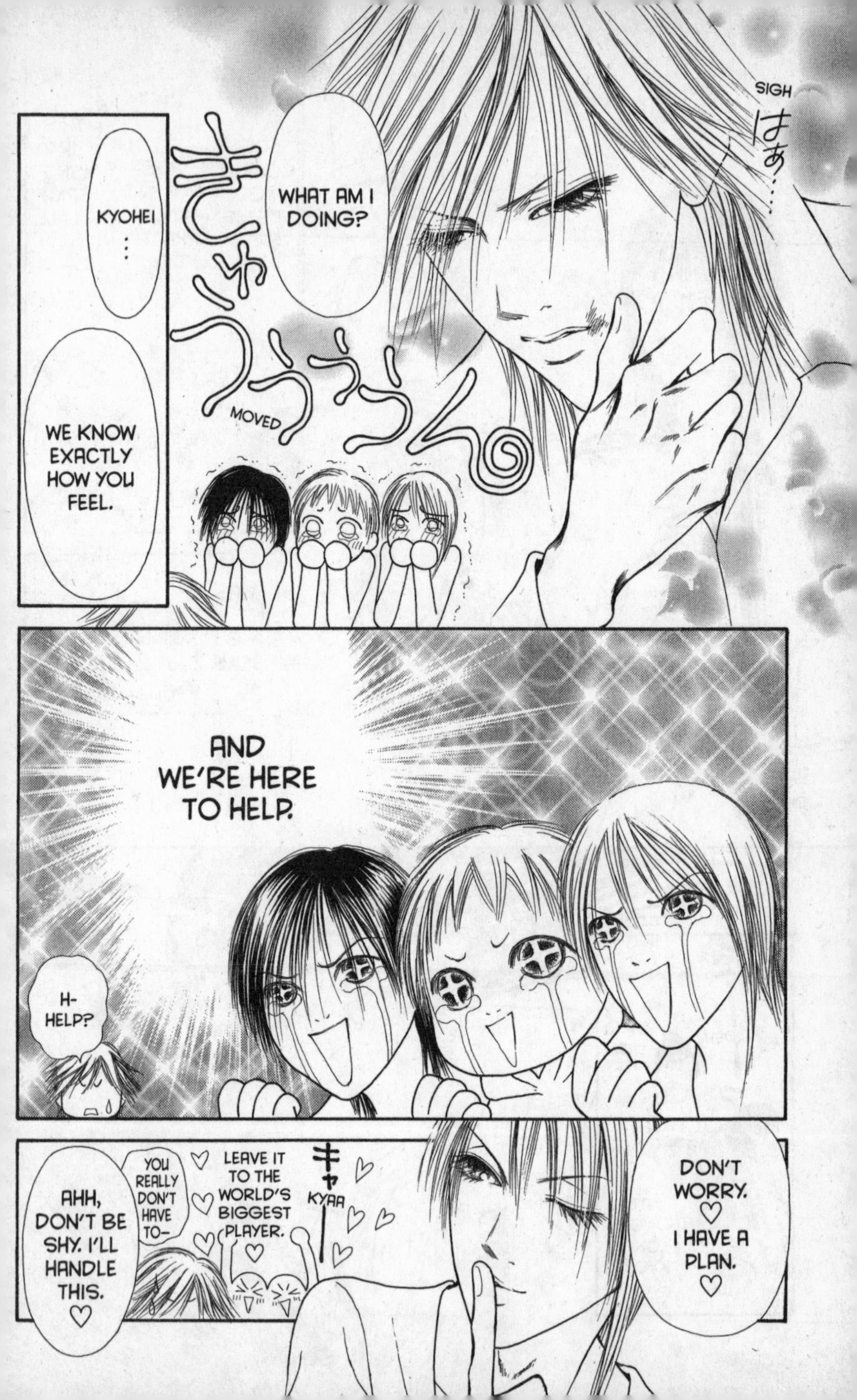
SIGH
はぁ…
WHAT AM I DOING?
きゅうううん
MOVED
KYOHEI …
WE KNOW EXACTLY HOW YOU FEEL.
AND WE'RE HERE TO HELP.
H-HELP?
DON'T WORRY. ♡ I HAVE A PLAN. ♡
キャー
KYAA
LEAVE IT TO THE WORLD'S BIGGEST PLAYER.
YOU REALLY DON'T HAVE TO—
AHH, DON'T BE SHY. I'LL HANDLE THIS. ♡

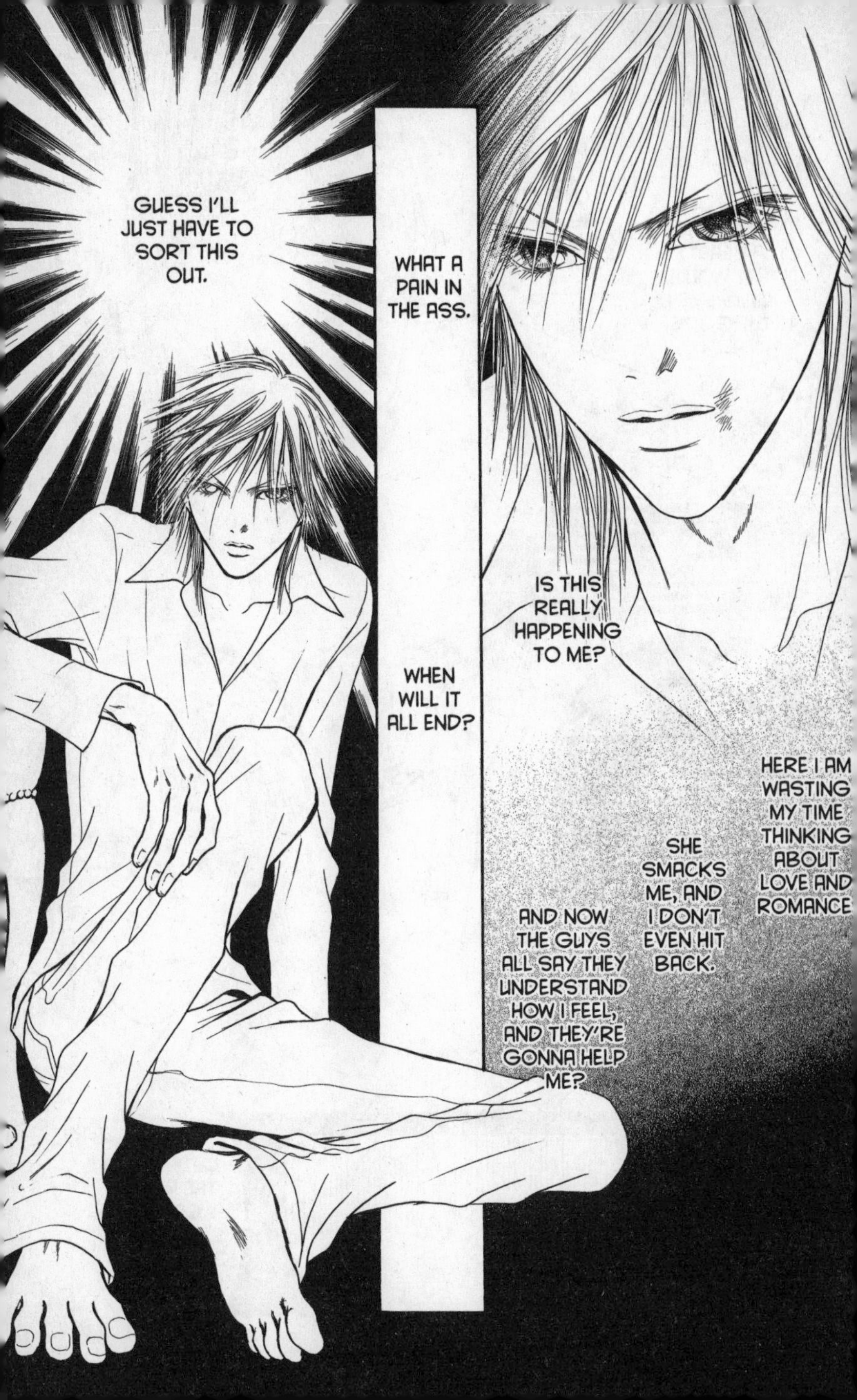
HERE I AM WASTING MY TIME THINKING ABOUT LOVE AND ROMANCE
SHE SMACKS ME, AND I DON'T EVEN HIT BACK.
AND NOW THE GUYS ALL SAY THEY UNDERSTAND HOW I FEEL, AND THEY'RE GONNA HELP ME?
IS THIS REALLY HAPPENING TO ME?
WHAT A PAIN IN THE ASS.
WHEN WILL IT ALL END?
GUESS I'LL JUST HAVE TO SORT THIS OUT.

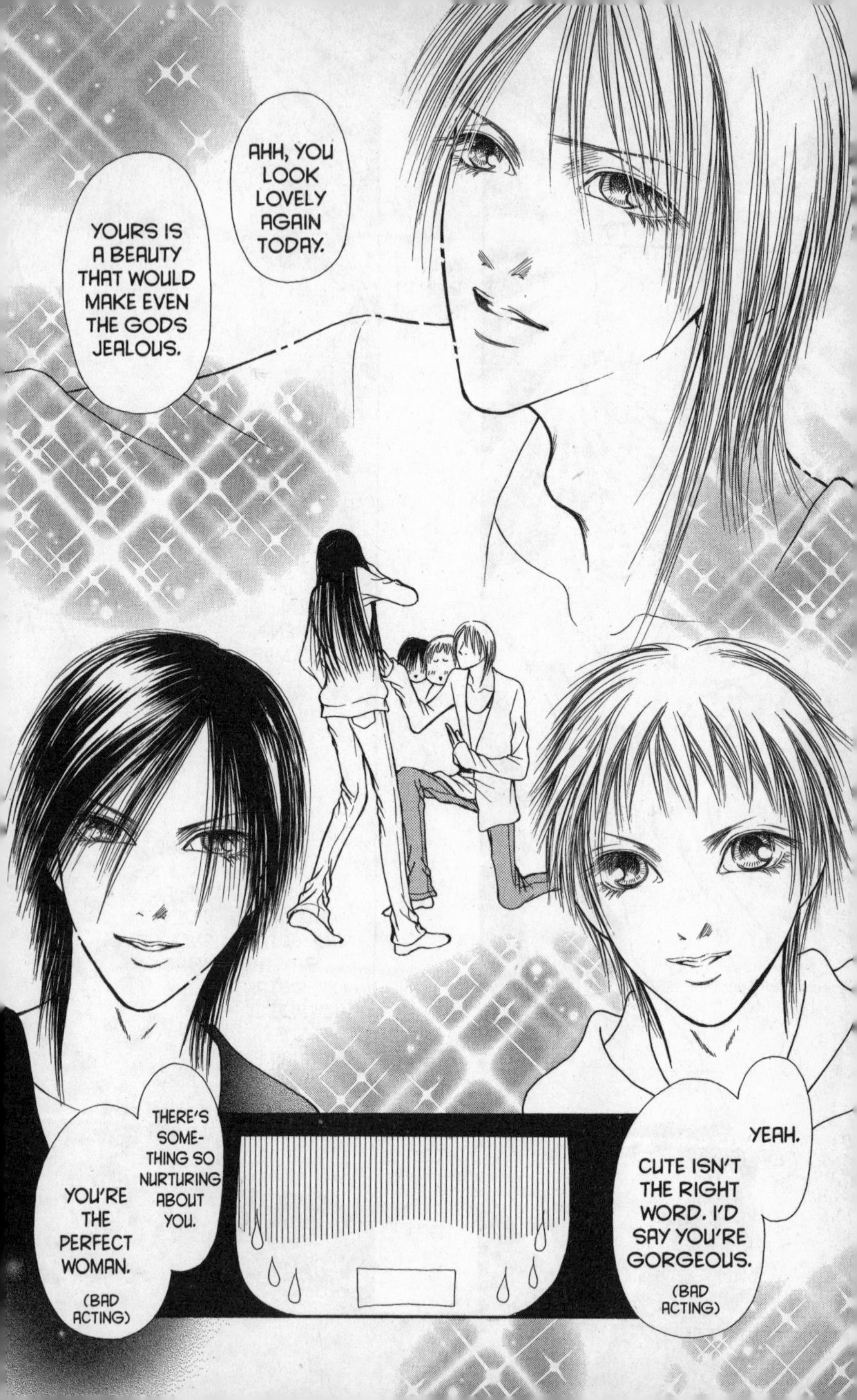
AHH, YOU LOOK LOVELY AGAIN TODAY.
YOURS IS A BEAUTY THAT WOULD MAKE EVEN THE GODS JEALOUS.
YEAH.
CUTE ISN'T THE RIGHT WORD. I'D SAY YOU'RE GORGEOUS.
(BAD ACTING)
THERE'S SOME-THING SO NURTURING ABOUT YOU.
YOU'RE THE PERFECT WOMAN.
(BAD ACTING)

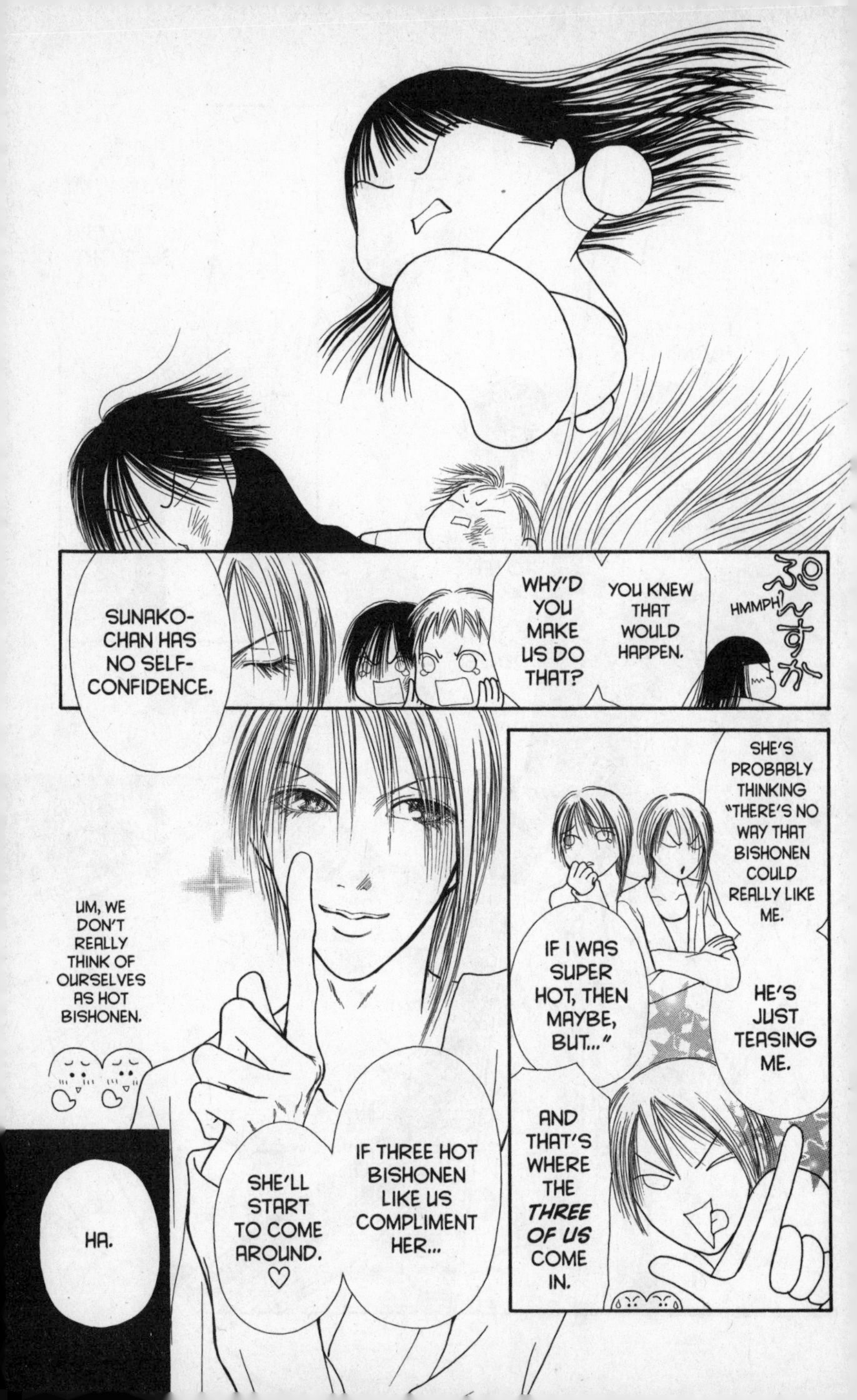

ふんすか
HMMPH!
YOU KNEW THAT WOULD HAPPEN.
WHY'D YOU MAKE US DO THAT?
SUNAKO-CHAN HAS NO SELF-CONFIDENCE.
SHE'S PROBABLY THINKING "THERE'S NO WAY THAT BISHONEN COULD REALLY LIKE ME.
IF I WAS SUPER HOT, THEN MAYBE, BUT..."
HE'S JUST TEASING ME.
AND THAT'S WHERE THE *THREE OF US* COME IN.
IF THREE HOT BISHONEN LIKE US COMPLIMENT HER...
SHE'LL START TO COME AROUND. ♡
UM, WE DON'T REALLY THINK OF OURSELVES AS HOT BISHONEN.
HA.

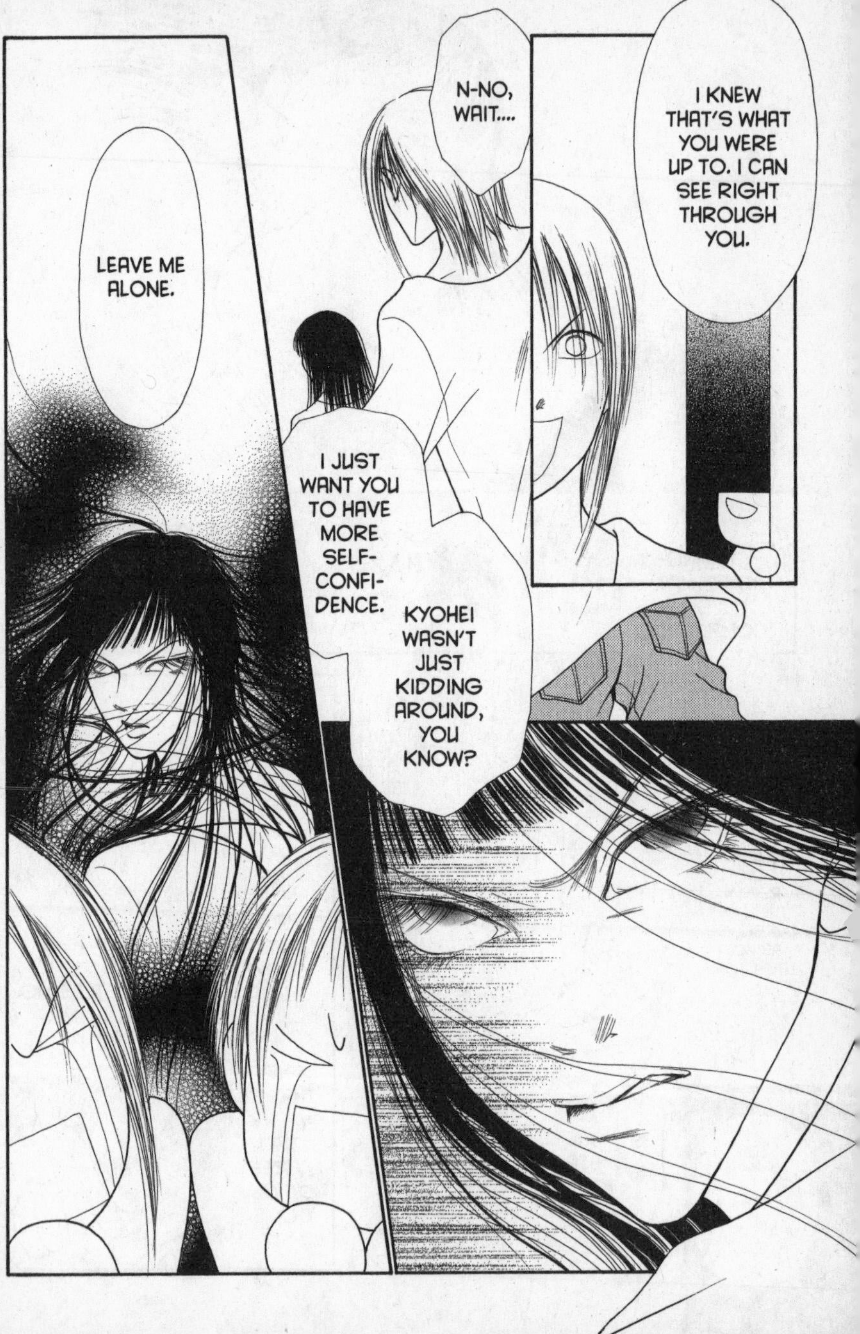
I KNEW THAT'S WHAT YOU WERE UP TO. I CAN SEE RIGHT THROUGH YOU.
N-NO, WAIT....
I JUST WANT YOU TO HAVE MORE SELF-CONFIDENCE.
KYOHEI WASN'T JUST KIDDING AROUND, YOU KNOW?
LEAVE ME ALONE.

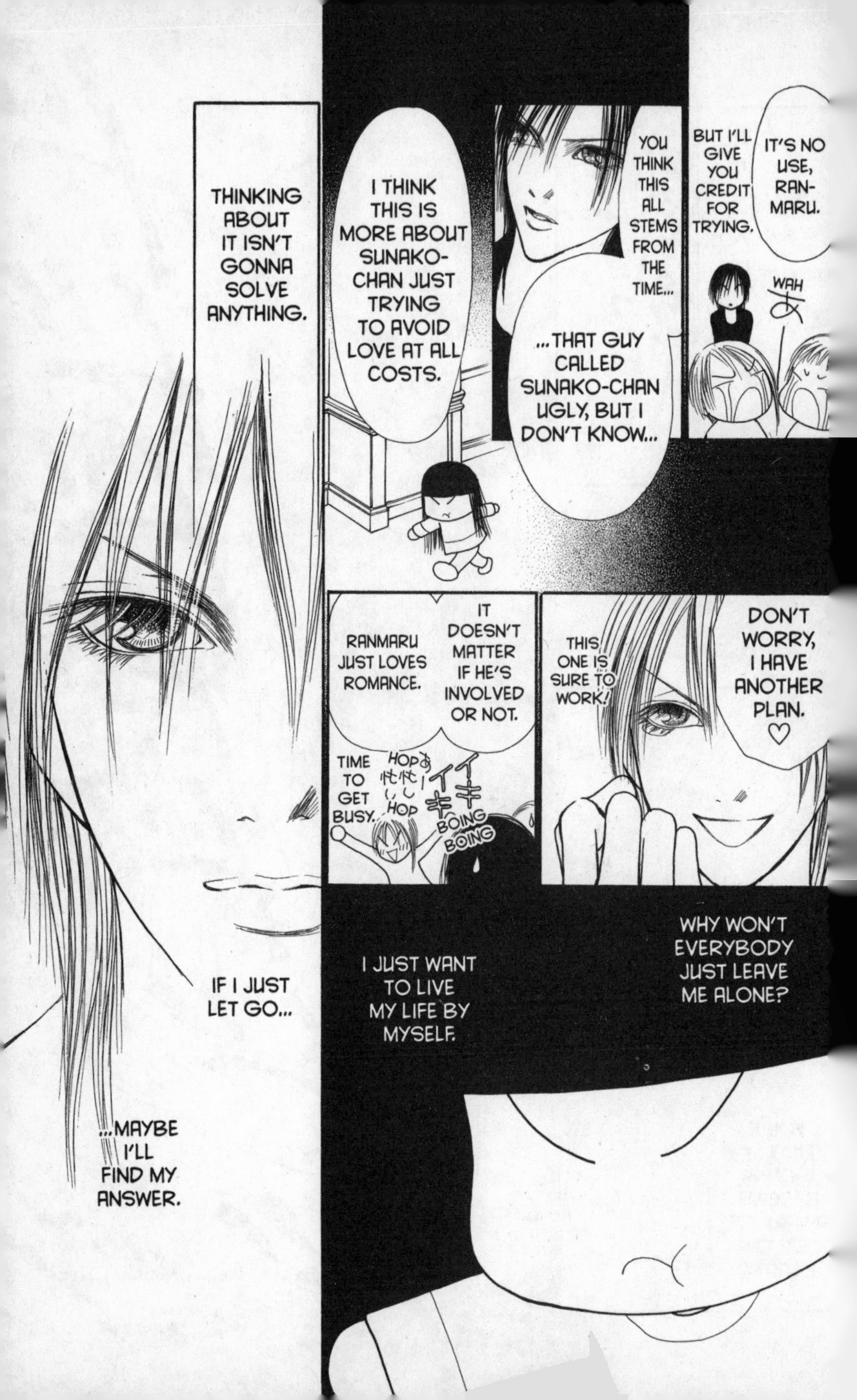
IT'S NO USE, RAN-MARU.
BUT I'LL GIVE YOU CREDIT FOR TRYING.
WAH
YOU THINK THIS ALL STEMS FROM THE TIME...
...THAT GUY CALLED SUNAKO-CHAN UGLY, BUT I DON'T KNOW...
I THINK THIS IS MORE ABOUT SUNAKO-CHAN JUST TRYING TO AVOID LOVE AT ALL COSTS.
DON'T WORRY, I HAVE ANOTHER PLAN. ♡
THIS ONE IS SURE TO WORK!
IT DOESN'T MATTER IF HE'S INVOLVED OR NOT.
RANMARU JUST LOVES ROMANCE.
HOP HOP
BOING BOING
TIME TO GET BUSY.
WHY WON'T EVERYBODY JUST LEAVE ME ALONE?
I JUST WANT TO LIVE MY LIFE BY MYSELF.
THINKING ABOUT IT ISN'T GONNA SOLVE ANYTHING.
IF I JUST LET GO...
...MAYBE I'LL FIND MY ANSWER.

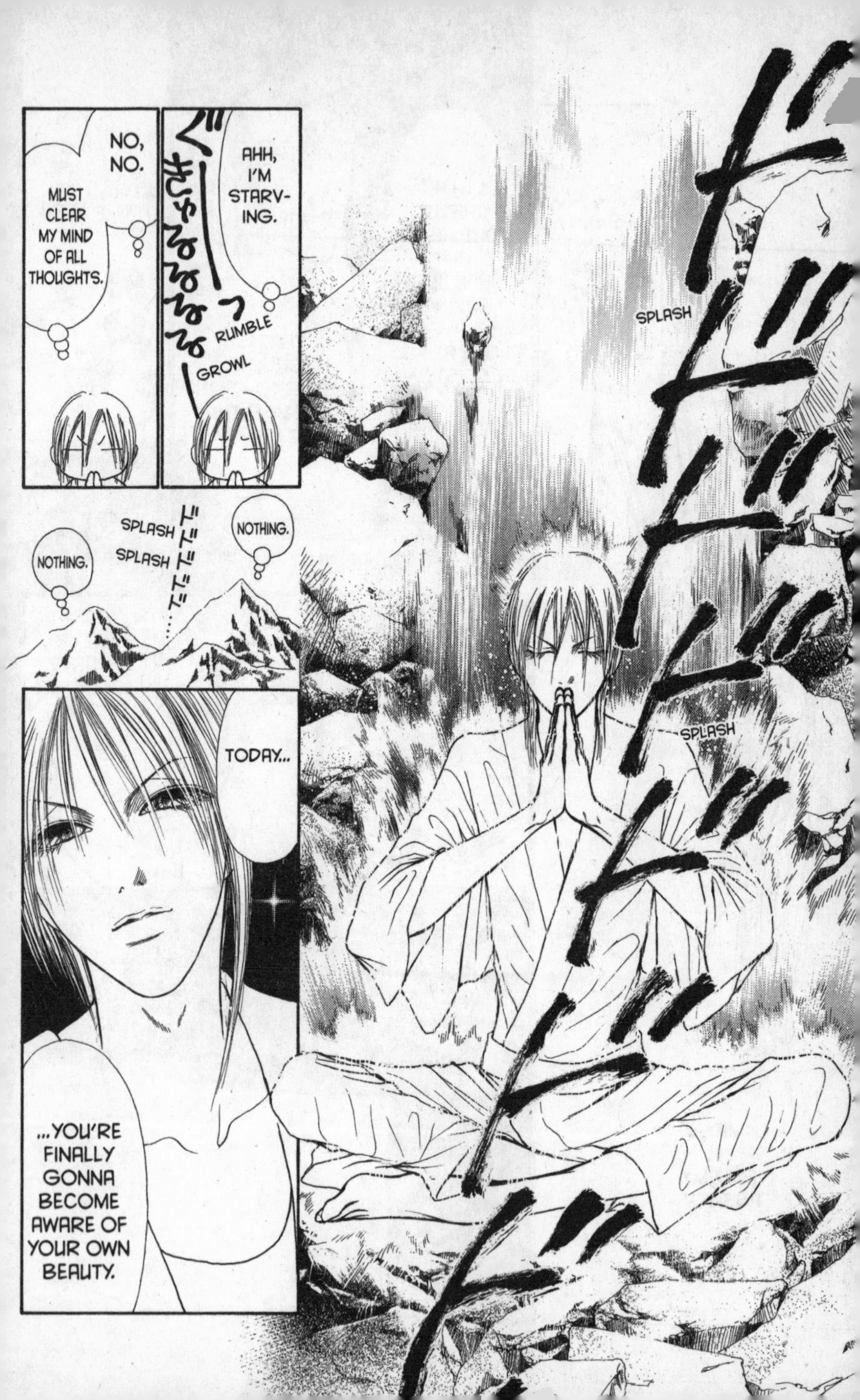

ドドドドドド
SPLASH
SPLASH
AHH, I'M STARV-ING.
ぐきゅるるるる~
RUMBLE
GROWL
NO, NO.
MUST CLEAR MY MIND OF ALL THOUGHTS.
NOTHING.
ドドドド…
SPLASH
SPLASH
NOTHING.
TODAY...
...YOU'RE FINALLY GONNA BECOME AWARE OF YOUR OWN BEAUTY.

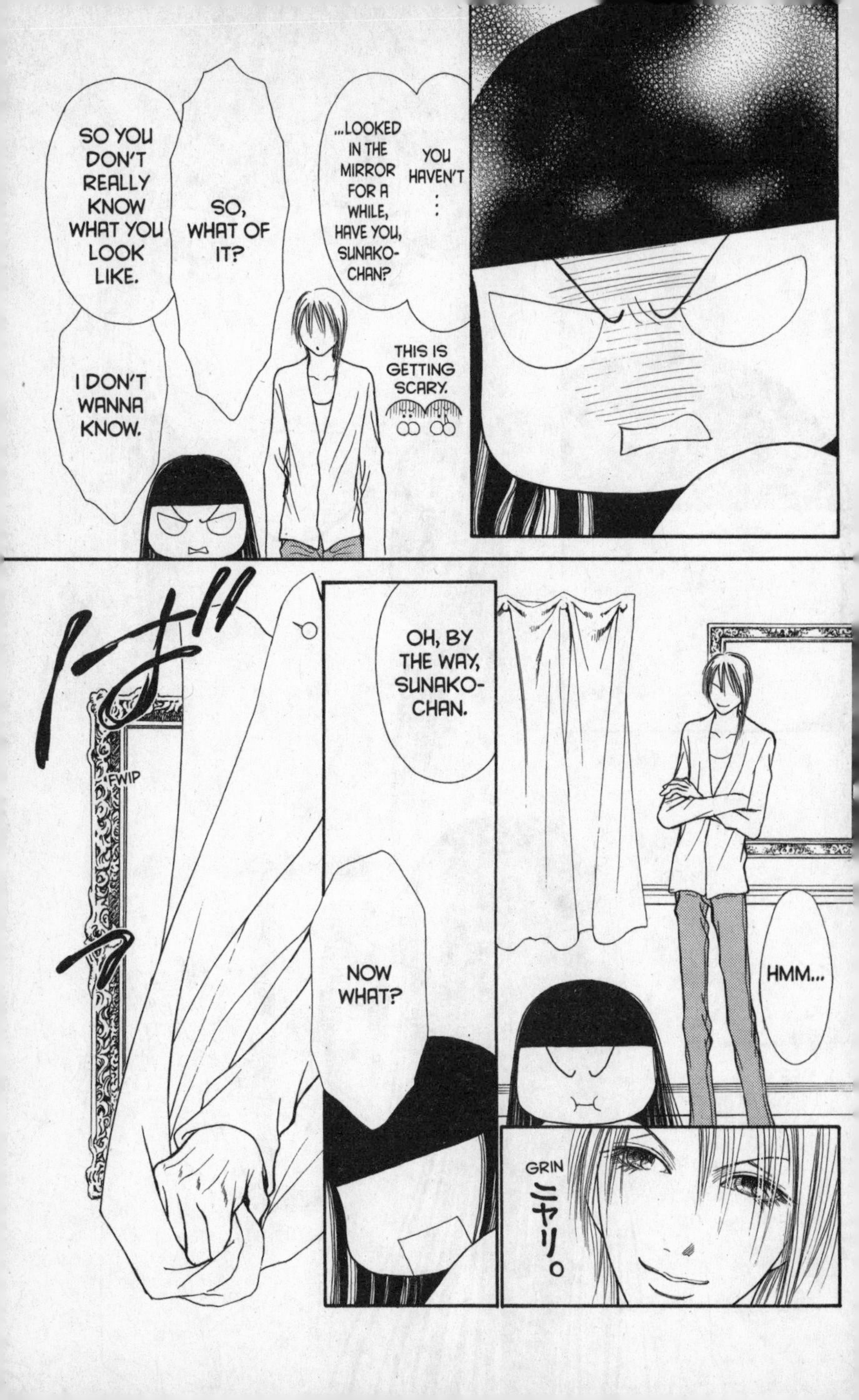
YOU HAVEN'T ...
...LOOKED IN THE MIRROR FOR A WHILE, HAVE YOU, SUNAKO-CHAN?
THIS IS GETTING SCARY.
SO, WHAT OF IT?
SO YOU DON'T REALLY KNOW WHAT YOU LOOK LIKE.
I DON'T WANNA KNOW.
HMM...
GRIN ニヤリ。
OH, BY THE WAY, SUNAKO-CHAN.
NOW WHAT?
FWIP

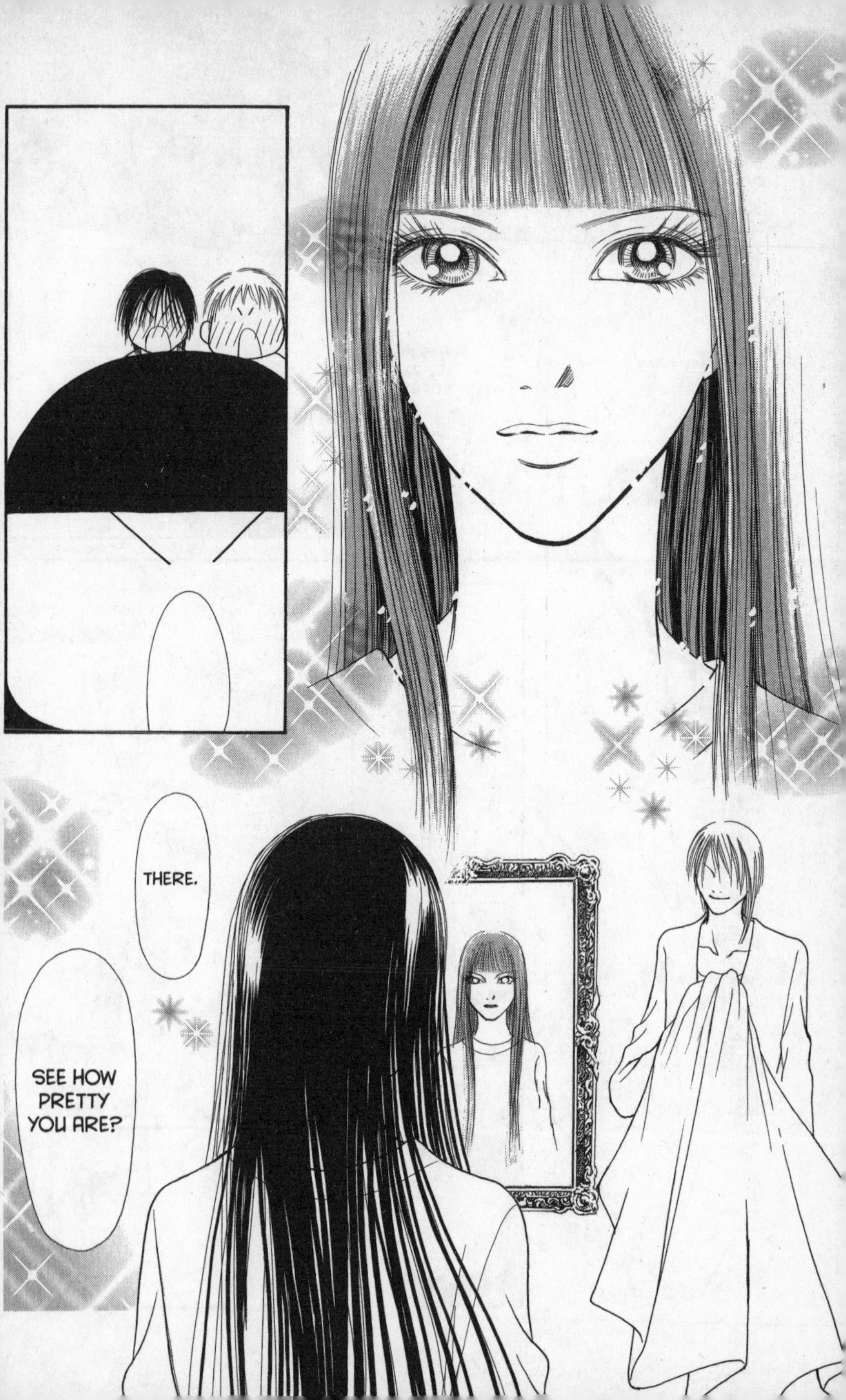
THERE.
SEE HOW PRETTY YOU ARE?

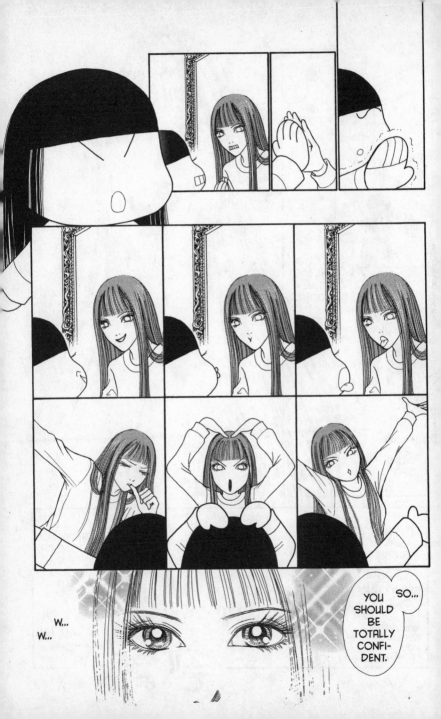

W...
W...

SO... YOU SHOULD BE TOTALLY CONFIDENT.

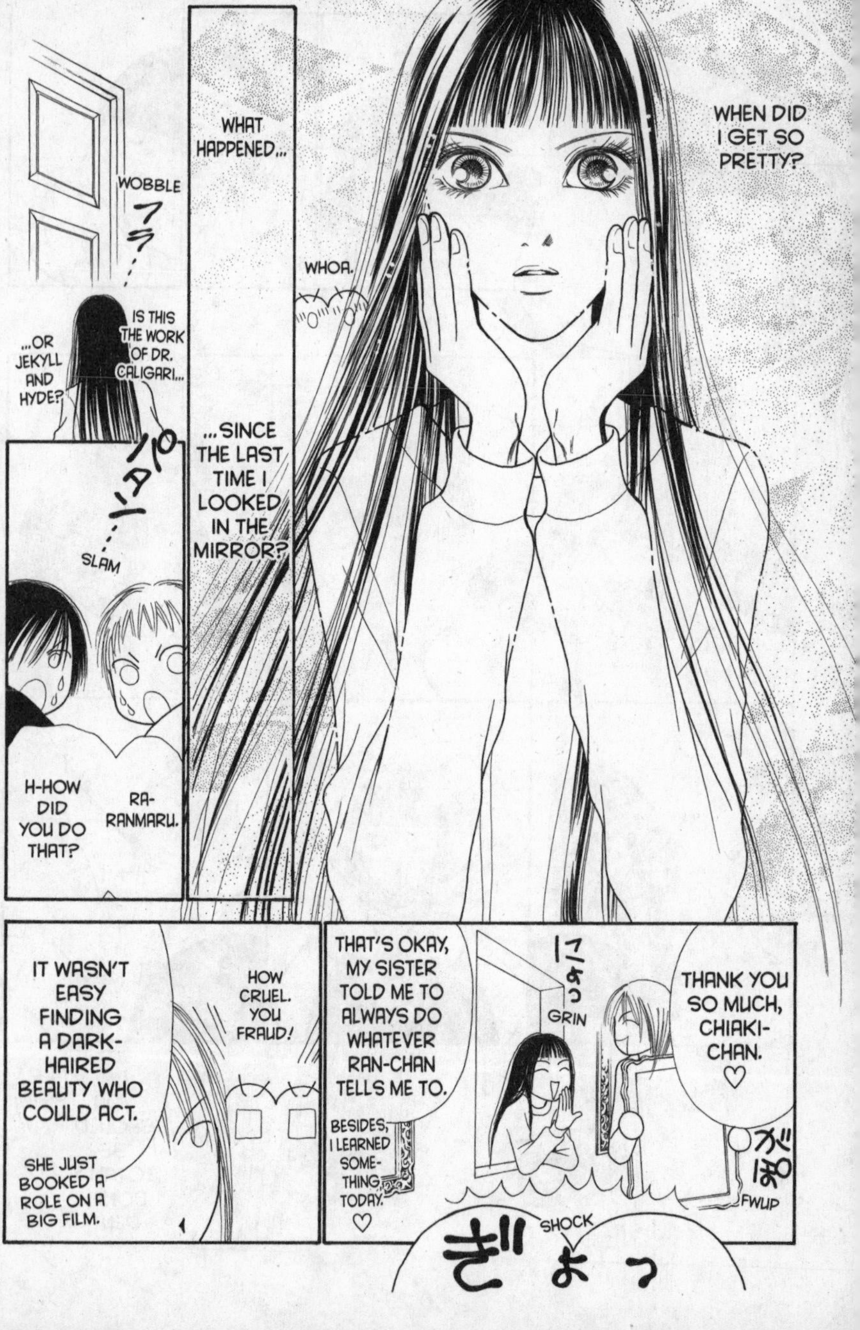
WHEN DID I GET SO PRETTY?
WHOA.
WHAT HAPPENED...
...SINCE THE LAST TIME I LOOKED IN THE MIRROR?
フラ
WOBBLE
IS THIS THE WORK OF DR. CALIGARI...
...OR JEKYLL AND HYDE?
パタン
SLAM
RA-RANMARU.
H-HOW DID YOU DO THAT?
THANK YOU SO MUCH, CHIAKI-CHAN. ♡
にょっ
GRIN
THAT'S OKAY, MY SISTER TOLD ME TO ALWAYS DO WHATEVER RAN-CHAN TELLS ME TO.
BESIDES, I LEARNED SOMETHING TODAY. ♡
がぽ
FWUP
ぎょっ
SHOCK
HOW CRUEL. YOU FRAUD!
IT WASN'T EASY FINDING A DARK-HAIRED BEAUTY WHO COULD ACT.
SHE JUST BOOKED A ROLE ON A BIG FILM.

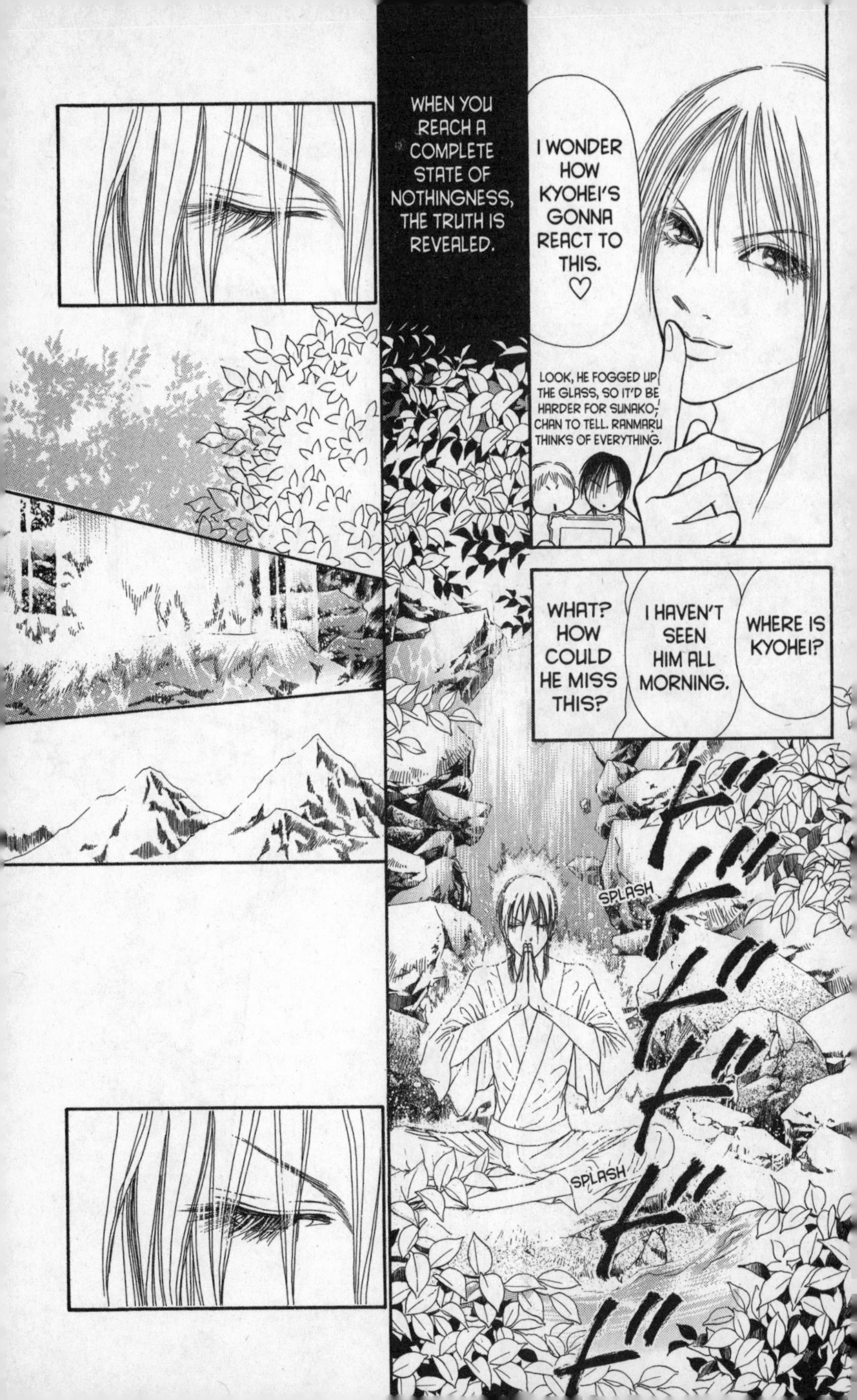
I WONDER HOW KYOHEI'S GONNA REACT TO THIS. ♡
LOOK, HE FOGGED UP THE GLASS, SO IT'D BE HARDER FOR SUNAKO-CHAN TO TELL. RANMARU THINKS OF EVERYTHING.
WHEN YOU REACH A COMPLETE STATE OF NOTHINGNESS, THE TRUTH IS REVEALED.
WHERE IS KYOHEI?
I HAVEN'T SEEN HIM ALL MORNING.
WHAT? HOW COULD HE MISS THIS?
SPLASH
SPLASH

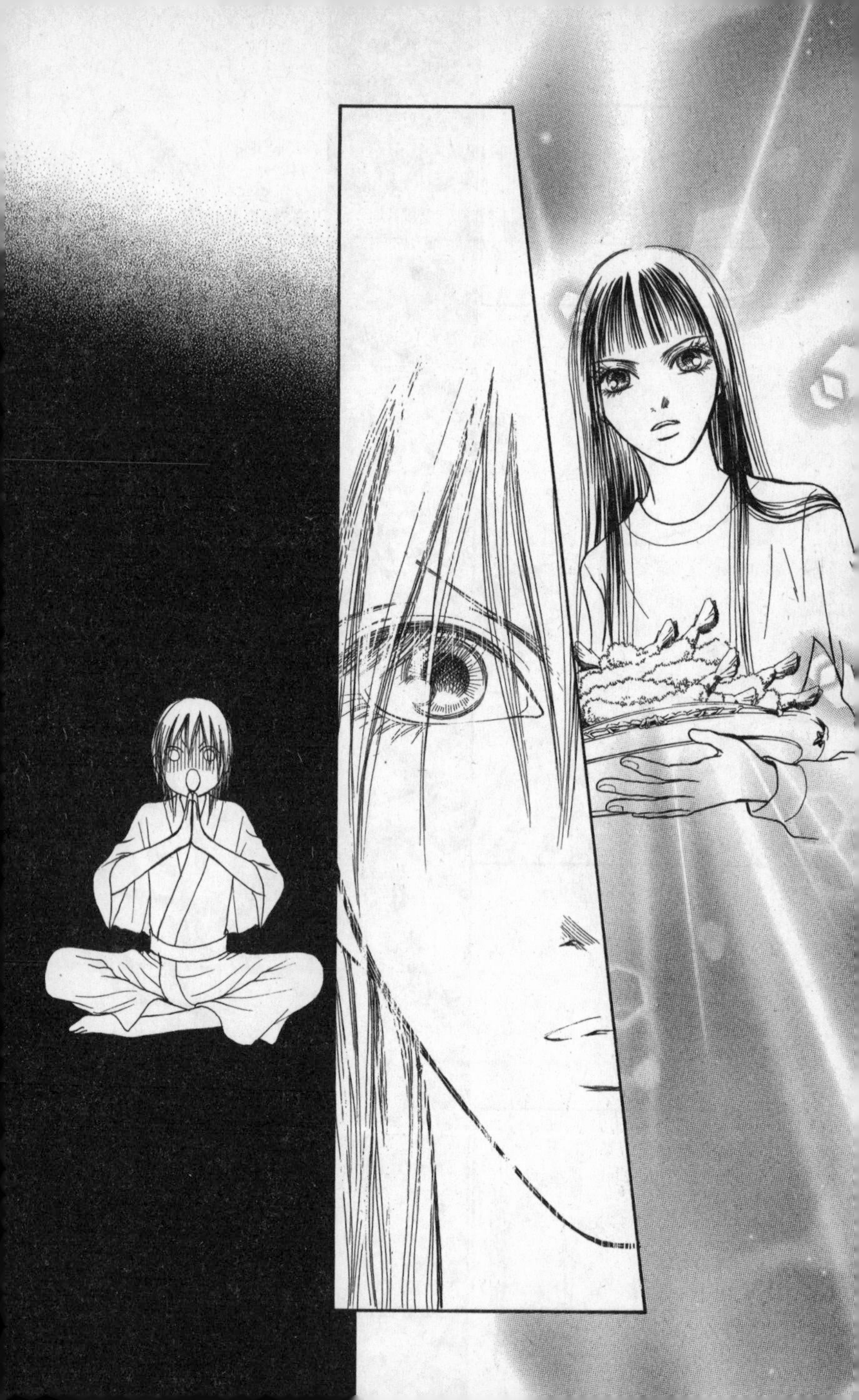

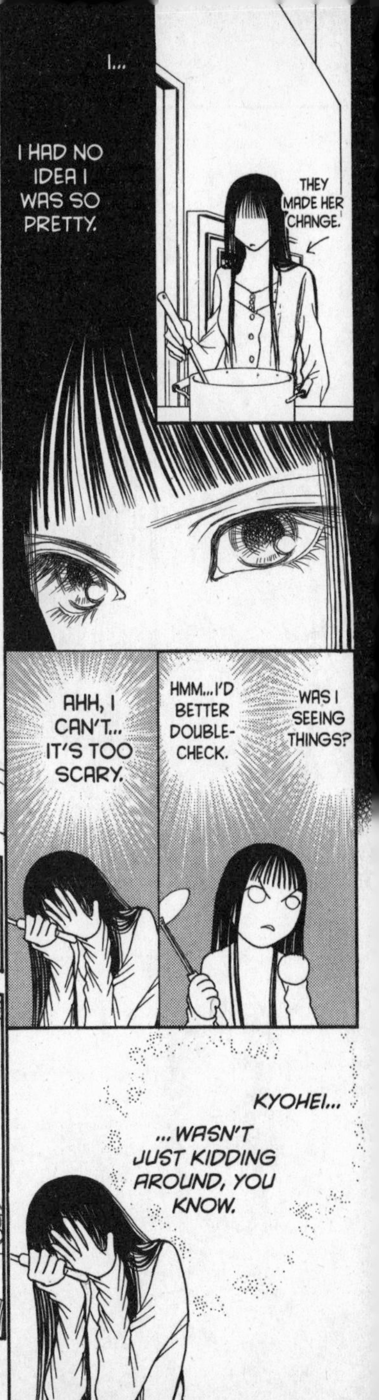
I...
THEY MADE HER CHANGE.
I HAD NO IDEA I WAS SO PRETTY.
WAS I SEEING THINGS?
HMM...I'D BETTER DOUBLE-CHECK.
AHH, I CAN'T... IT'S TOO SCARY.
KYOHEI...
...WASN'T JUST KIDDING AROUND, YOU KNOW.
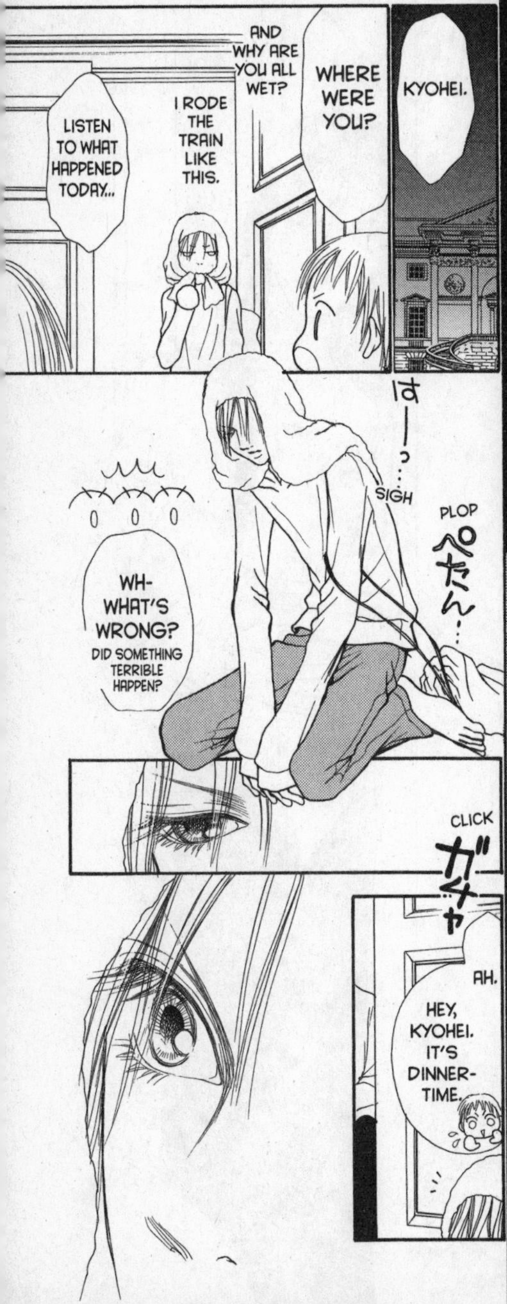
KYOHEI.
WHERE WERE YOU?
AND WHY ARE YOU ALL WET?
I RODE THE TRAIN LIKE THIS.
LISTEN TO WHAT HAPPENED TODAY...
はーっ…
SIGH
ぺたん…
PLOP
WH-WHAT'S WRONG? DID SOMETHING TERRIBLE HAPPEN?
ガチャ
CLICK
AH.
HEY, KYOHEI. IT'S DINNER-TIME.

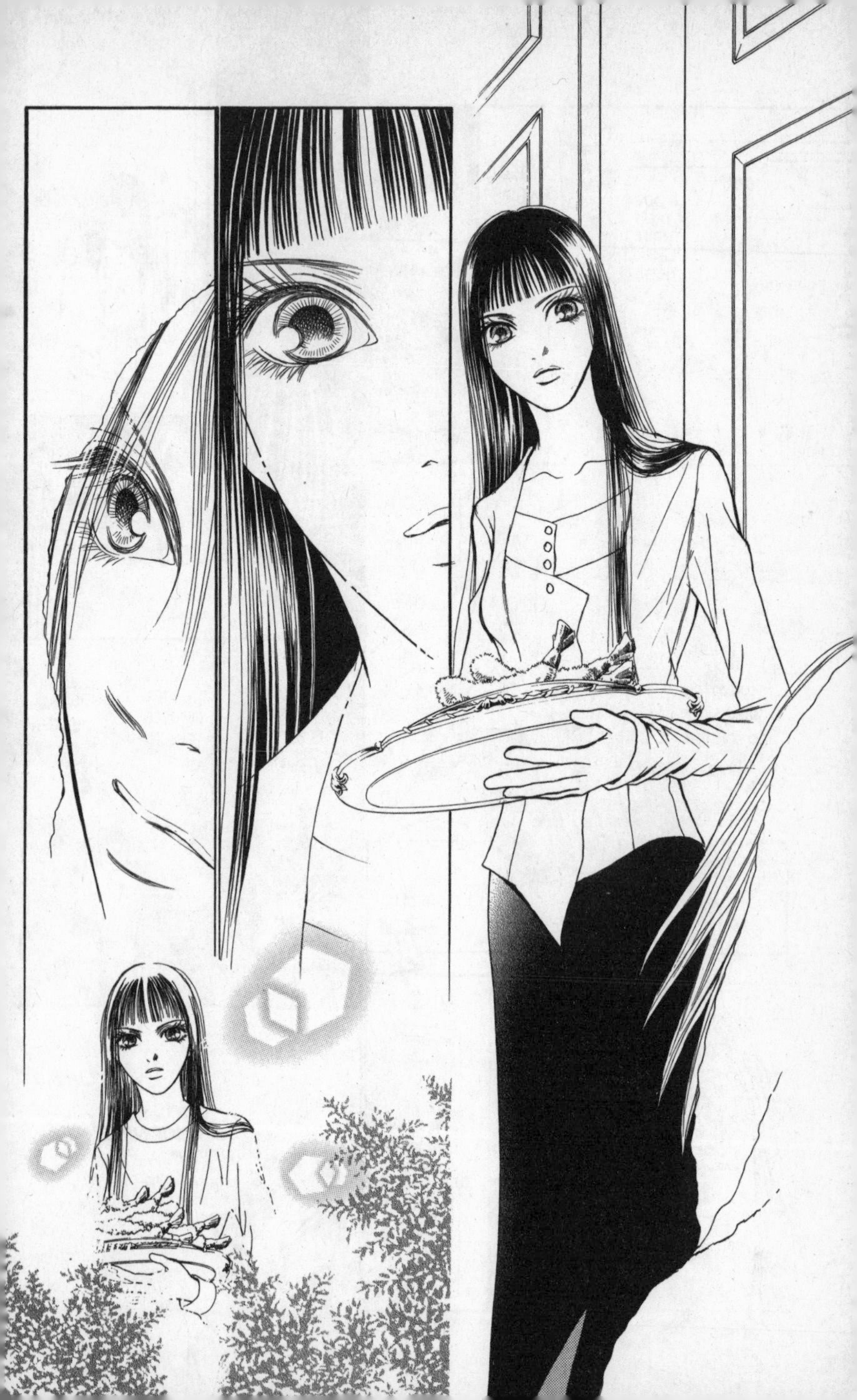

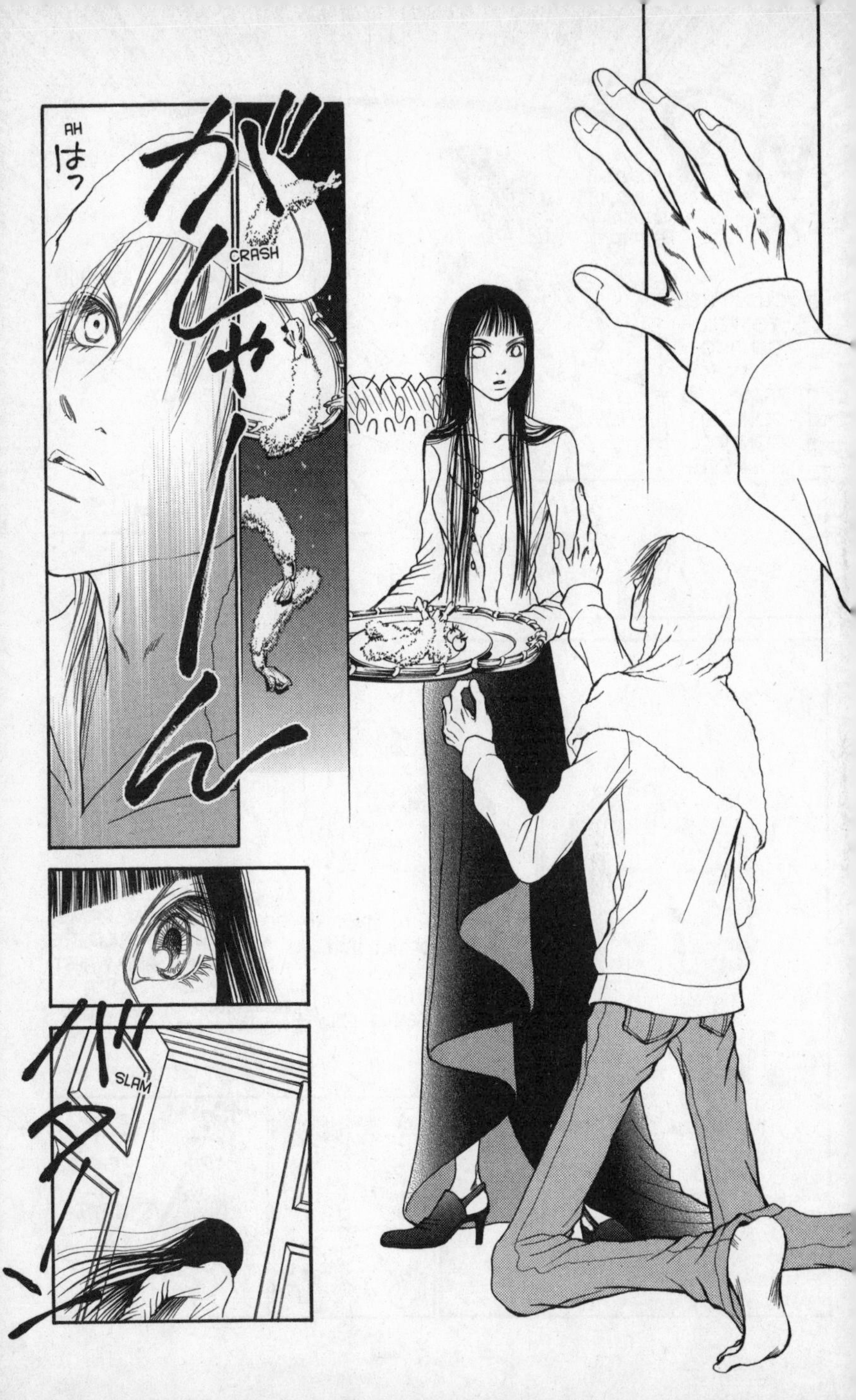
がしゃーん
CRASH
はっ
AH
バタン
SLAM

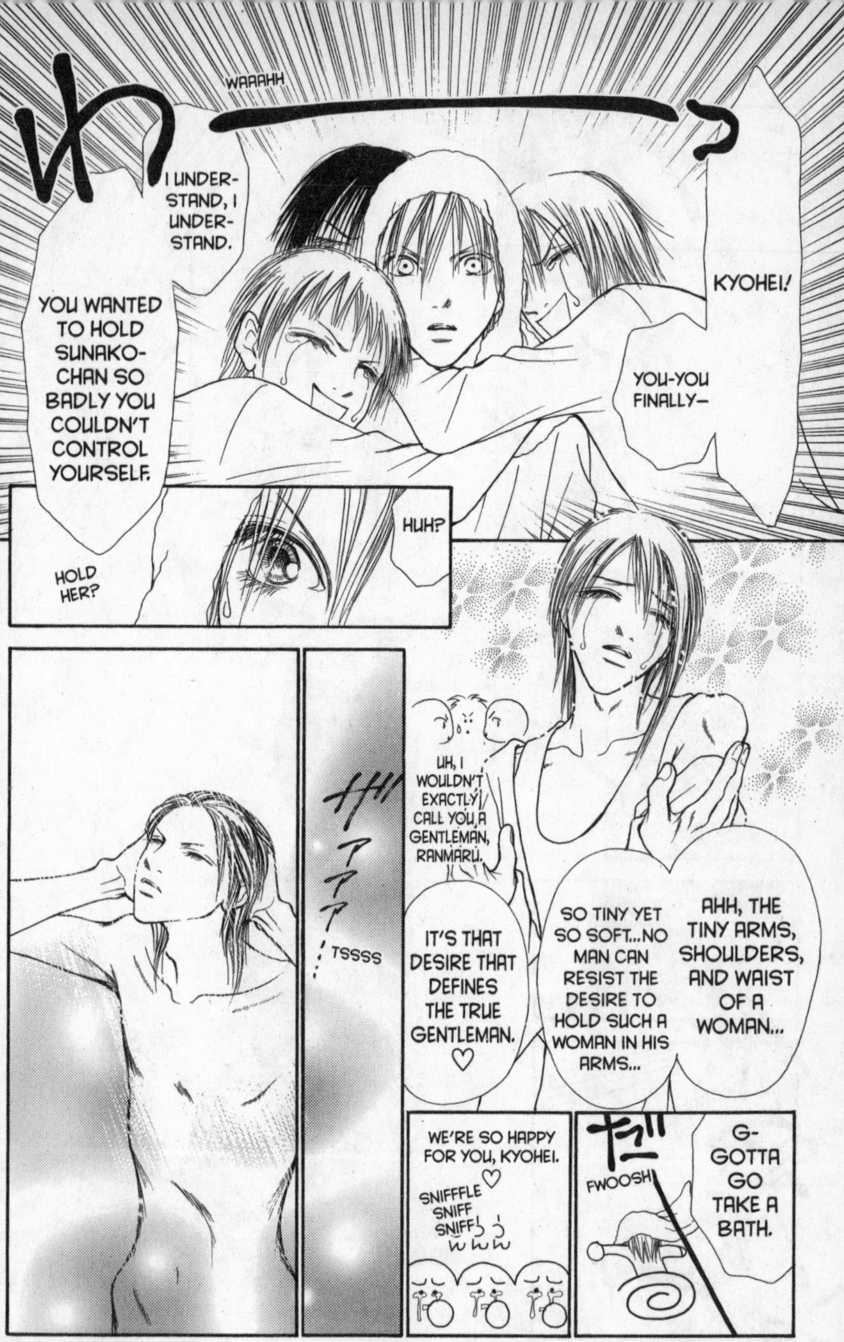
WAAAHH
KYOHEI!
YOU-YOU FINALLY—
I UNDER-STAND, I UNDER-STAND.
YOU WANTED TO HOLD SUNAKO-CHAN SO BADLY YOU COULDN'T CONTROL YOURSELF.
HUH?
HOLD HER?
AHH, THE TINY ARMS, SHOULDERS, AND WAIST OF A WOMAN...
SO TINY YET SO SOFT...NO MAN CAN RESIST THE DESIRE TO HOLD SUCH A WOMAN IN HIS ARMS...
IT'S THAT DESIRE THAT DEFINES THE TRUE GENTLEMAN. ♡
UH, I WOULDN'T EXACTLY CALL YOU A GENTLEMAN, RANMARU.
G-GOTTA GO TAKE A BATH.
FWOOSH
WE'RE SO HAPPY FOR YOU, KYOHEI. ♡
SNIFFFLE SNIFF SNIFF!
TSSSS

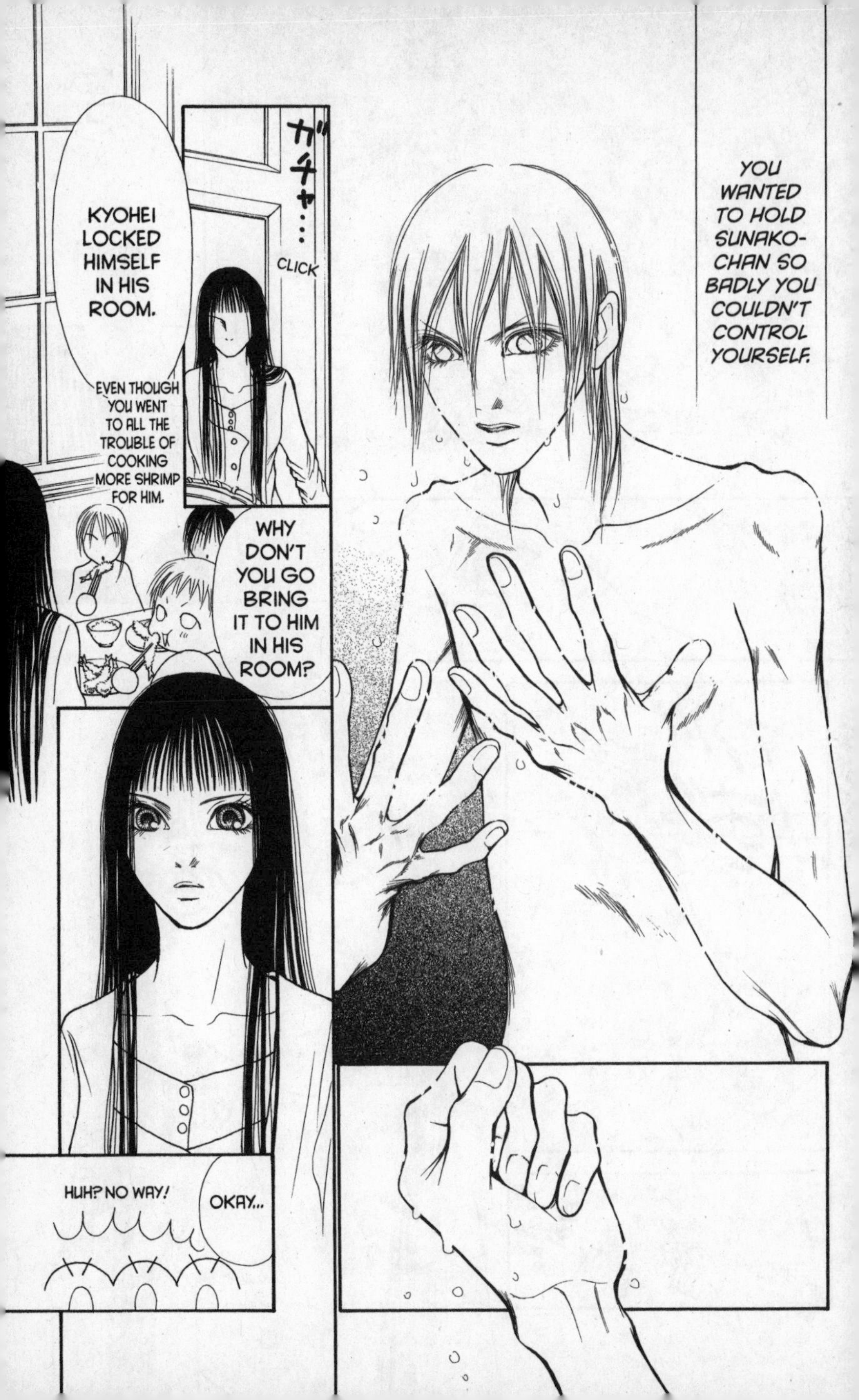
YOU WANTED TO HOLD SUNAKO-CHAN SO BADLY YOU COULDN'T CONTROL YOURSELF.
ガチャ…
CLICK
KYOHEI LOCKED HIMSELF IN HIS ROOM.
EVEN THOUGH YOU WENT TO ALL THE TROUBLE OF COOKING MORE SHRIMP FOR HIM.
WHY DON'T YOU GO BRING IT TO HIM IN HIS ROOM?
OKAY...
HUH? NO WAY!

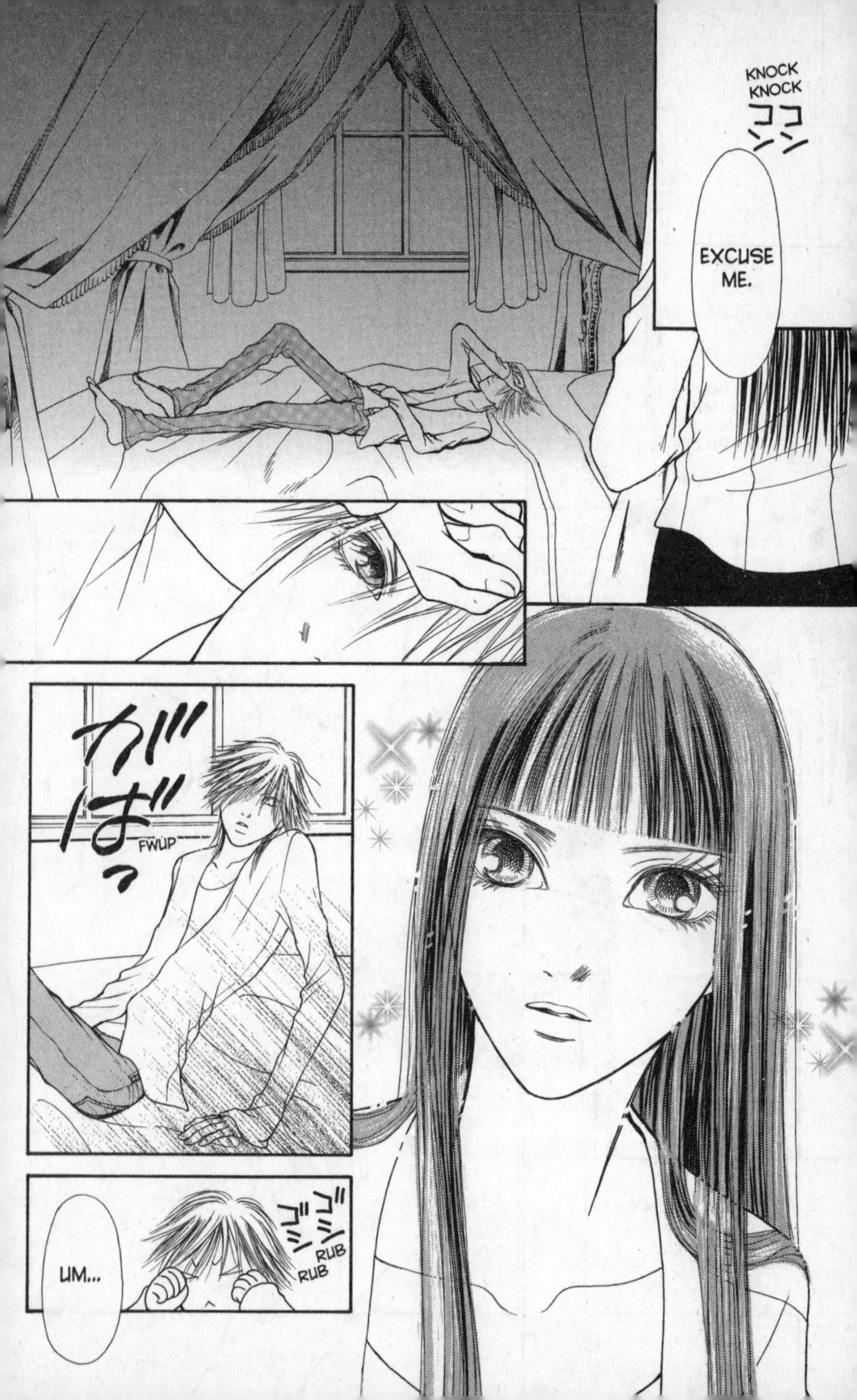
KNOCK KNOCK
ココン
EXCUSE ME.
がばっ
FWUP
ゴシゴシ
RUB RUB
UM...

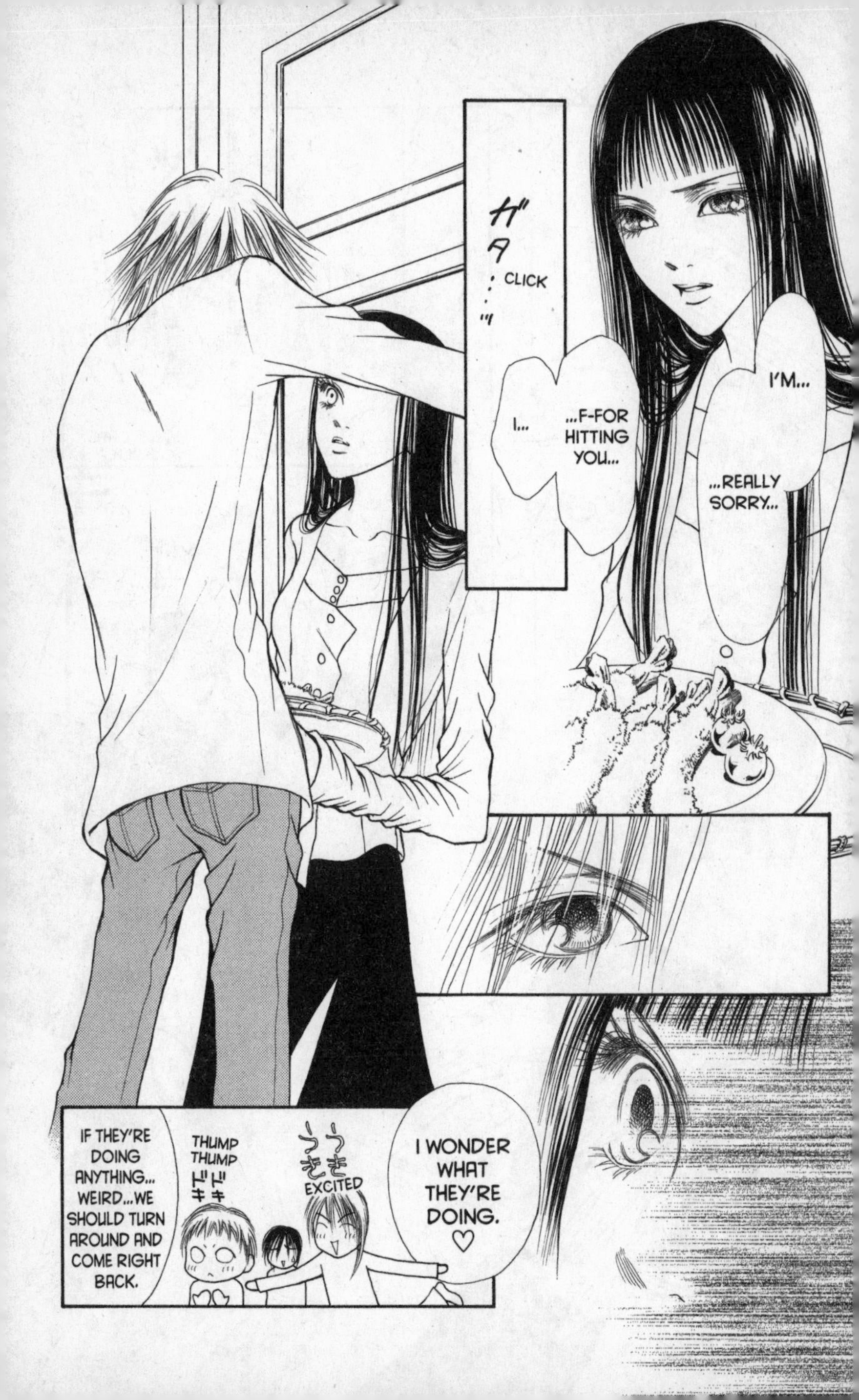

I'M... ...REALLY SORRY...
I... ...F-FOR HITTING YOU...
ガタ...ッ CLICK
I WONDER WHAT THEY'RE DOING. ♡
うきうき EXCITED
THUMP THUMP ドキドキ
IF THEY'RE DOING ANYTHING... WEIRD...WE SHOULD TURN AROUND AND COME RIGHT BACK.

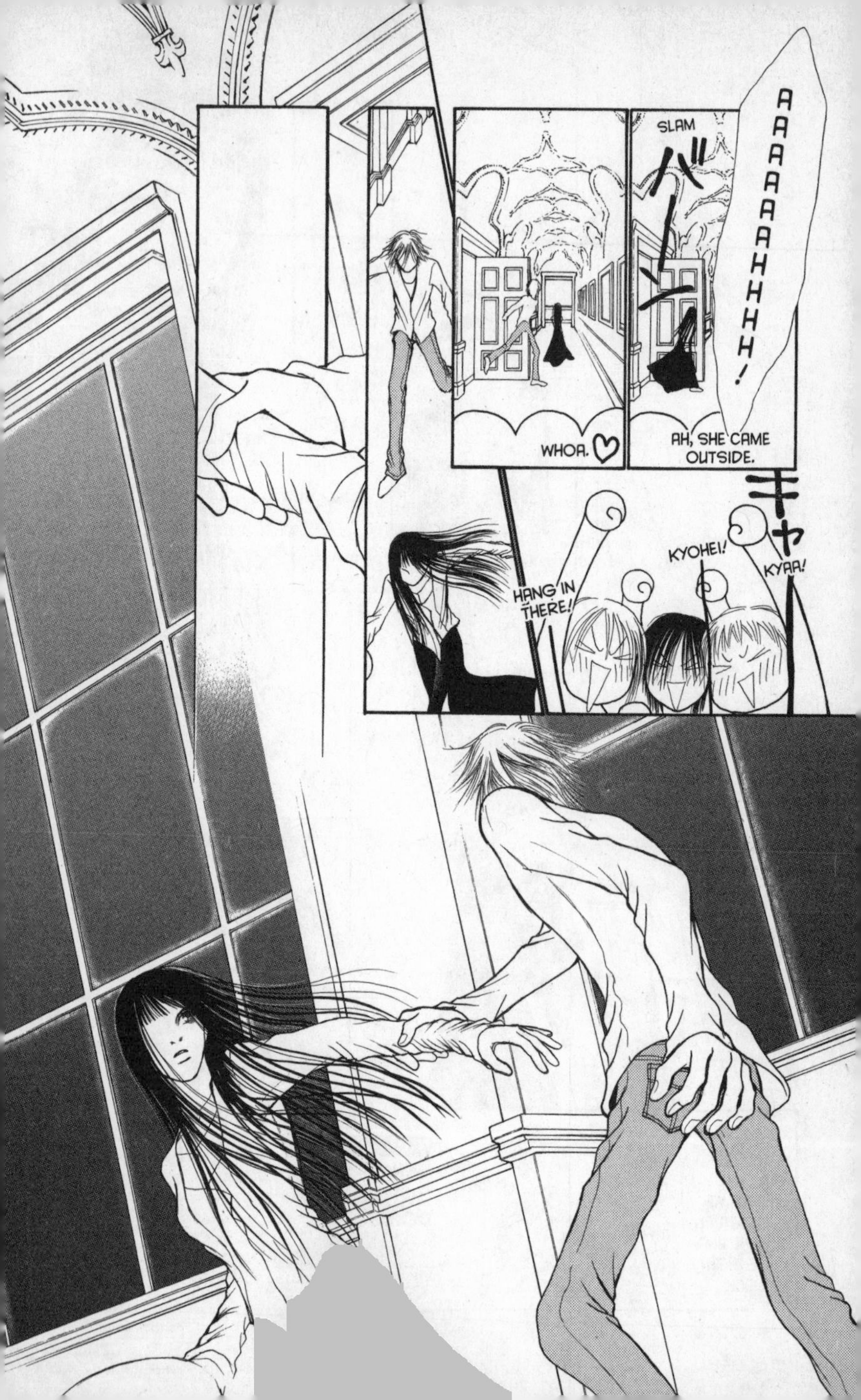
AAAAAAAHHHHH!
SLAM
バーン
AH, SHE CAME OUTSIDE.
WHOA. ♡
キャ
KYAA!
KYOHEI!
HANG IN THERE!

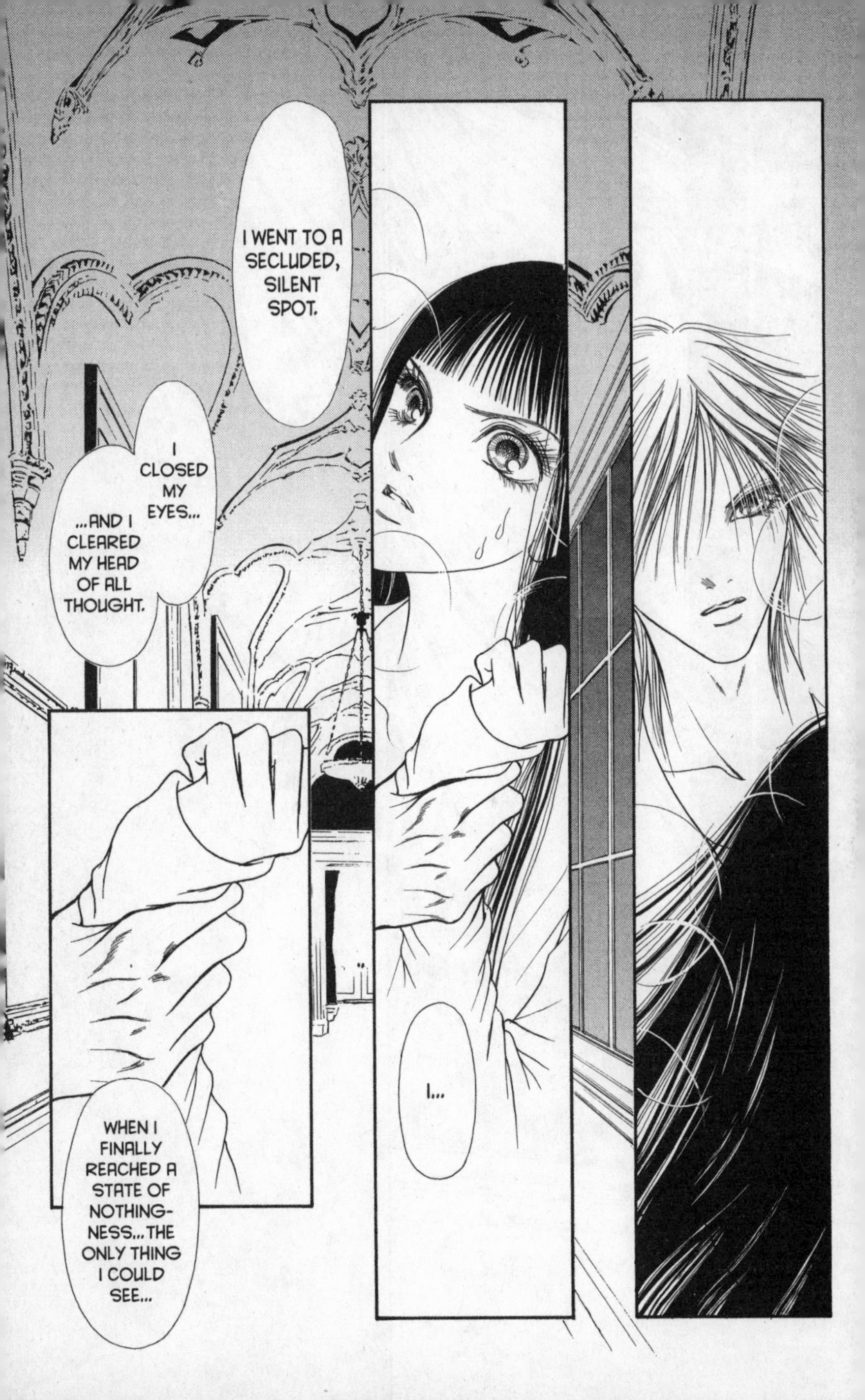
I...
I WENT TO A SECLUDED, SILENT SPOT.
I CLOSED MY EYES...
...AND I CLEARED MY HEAD OF ALL THOUGHT.
WHEN I FINALLY REACHED A STATE OF NOTHING-NESS...THE ONLY THING I COULD SEE...

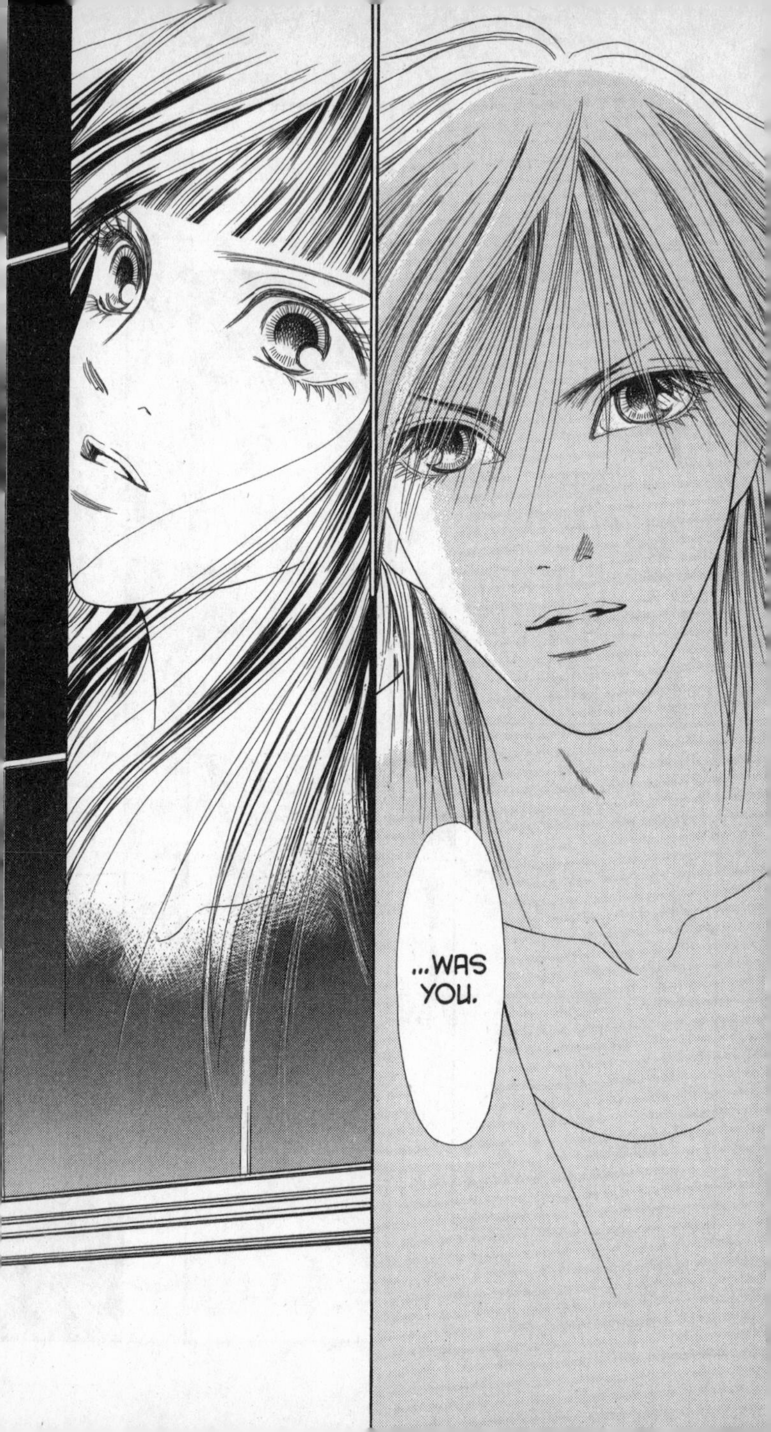
...WAS YOU.

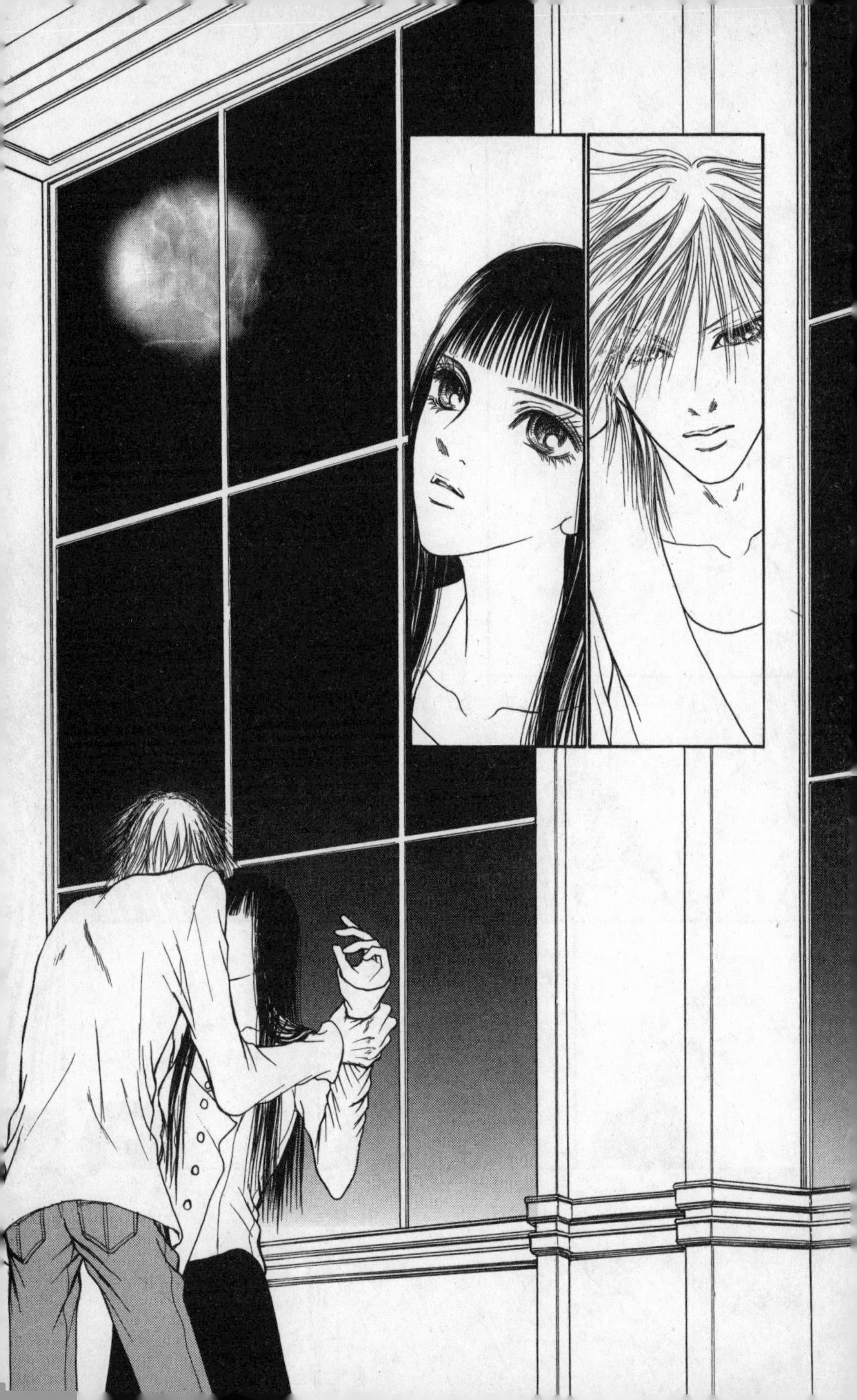

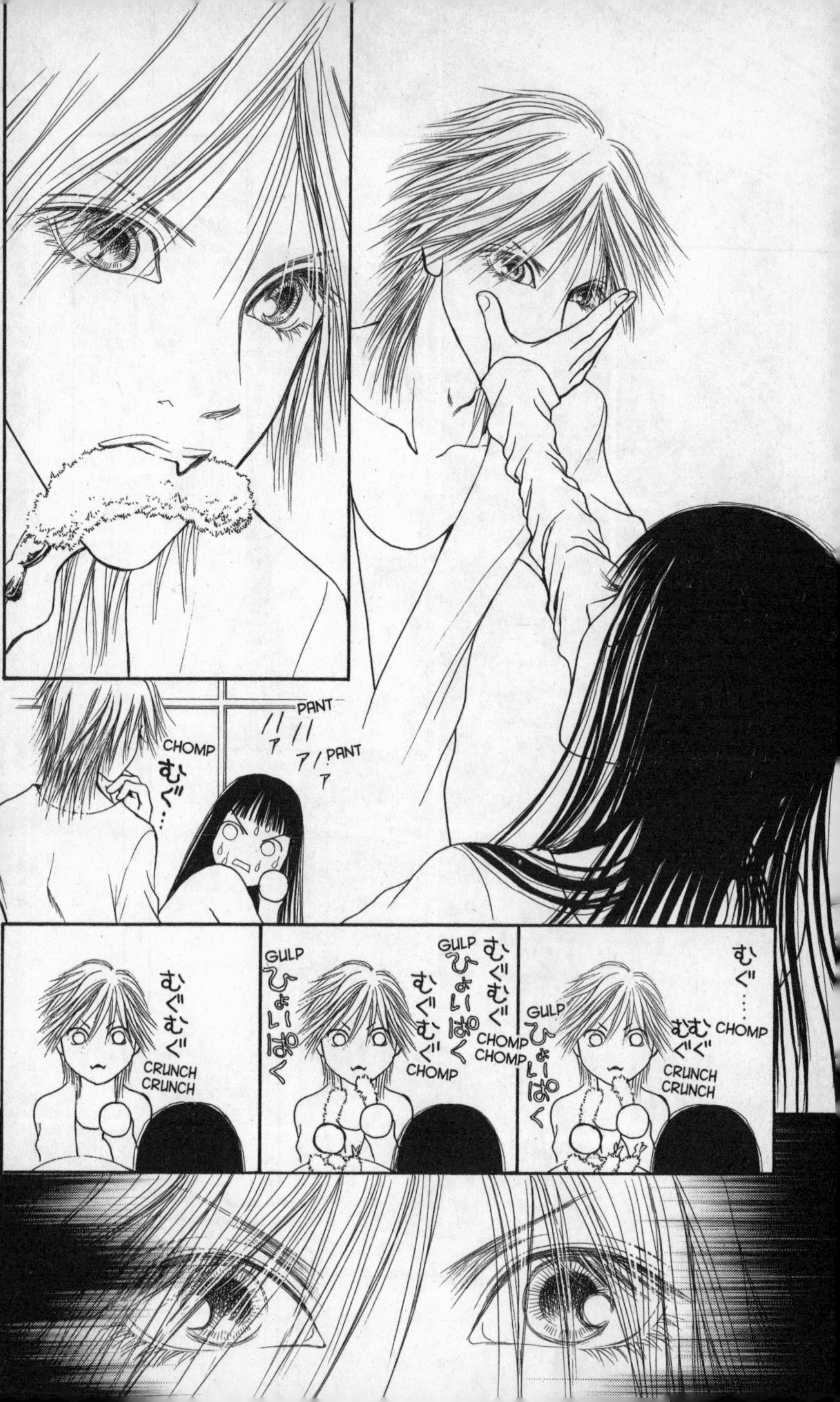
ハァ PANT
ハァ PANT
むぐ… CHOMP
むぐ…… CHOMP
むぐむぐ CRUNCH CRUNCH
ひょいぱく GULP
むぐむぐ CHOMP CHOMP
ひょいぱく GULP
むぐむぐ CHOMP
ひょいぱく GULP
むぐむぐ CRUNCH CRUNCH

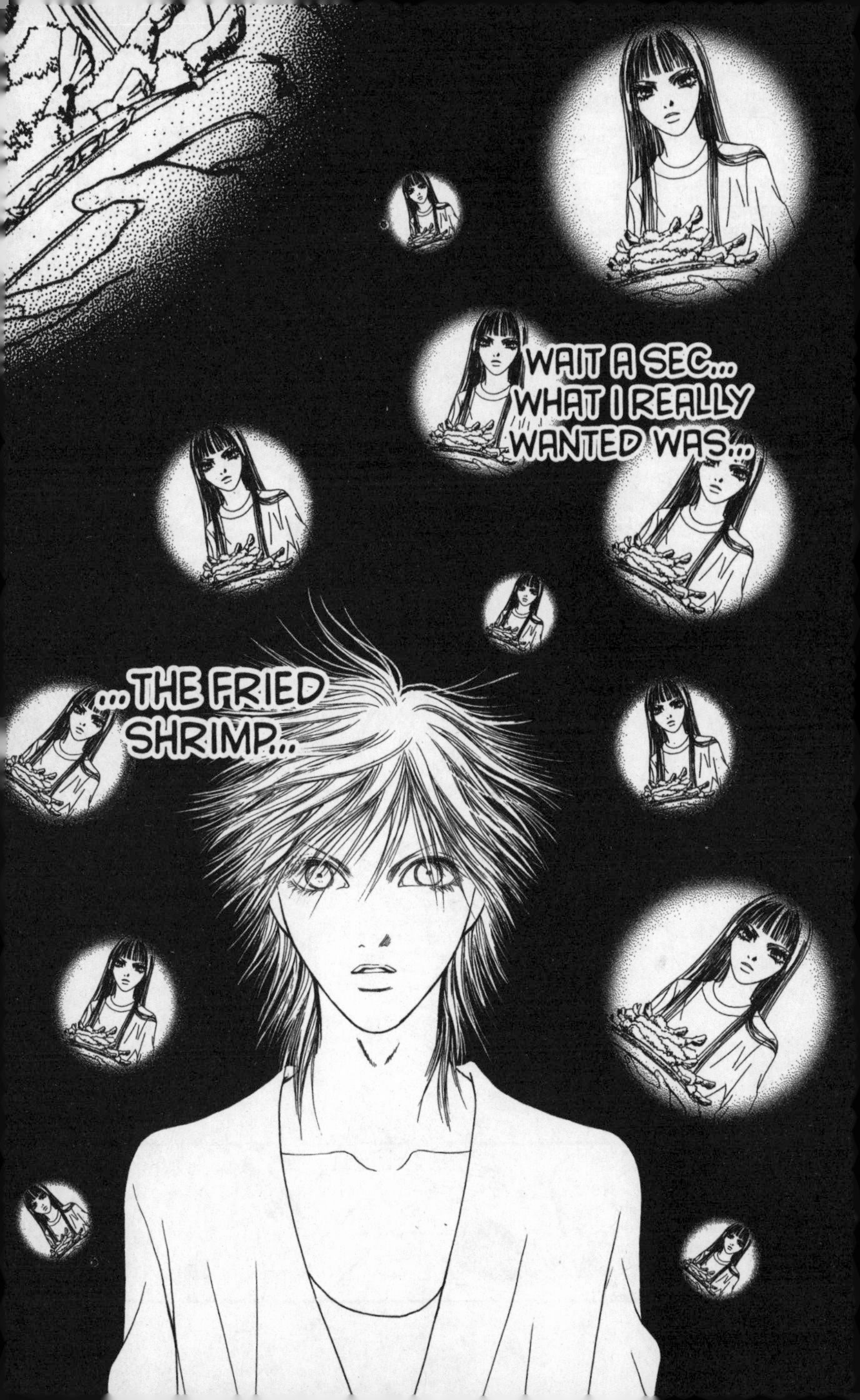
WAIT A SEC... WHAT I REALLY WANTED WAS...
...THE FRIED SHRIMP...

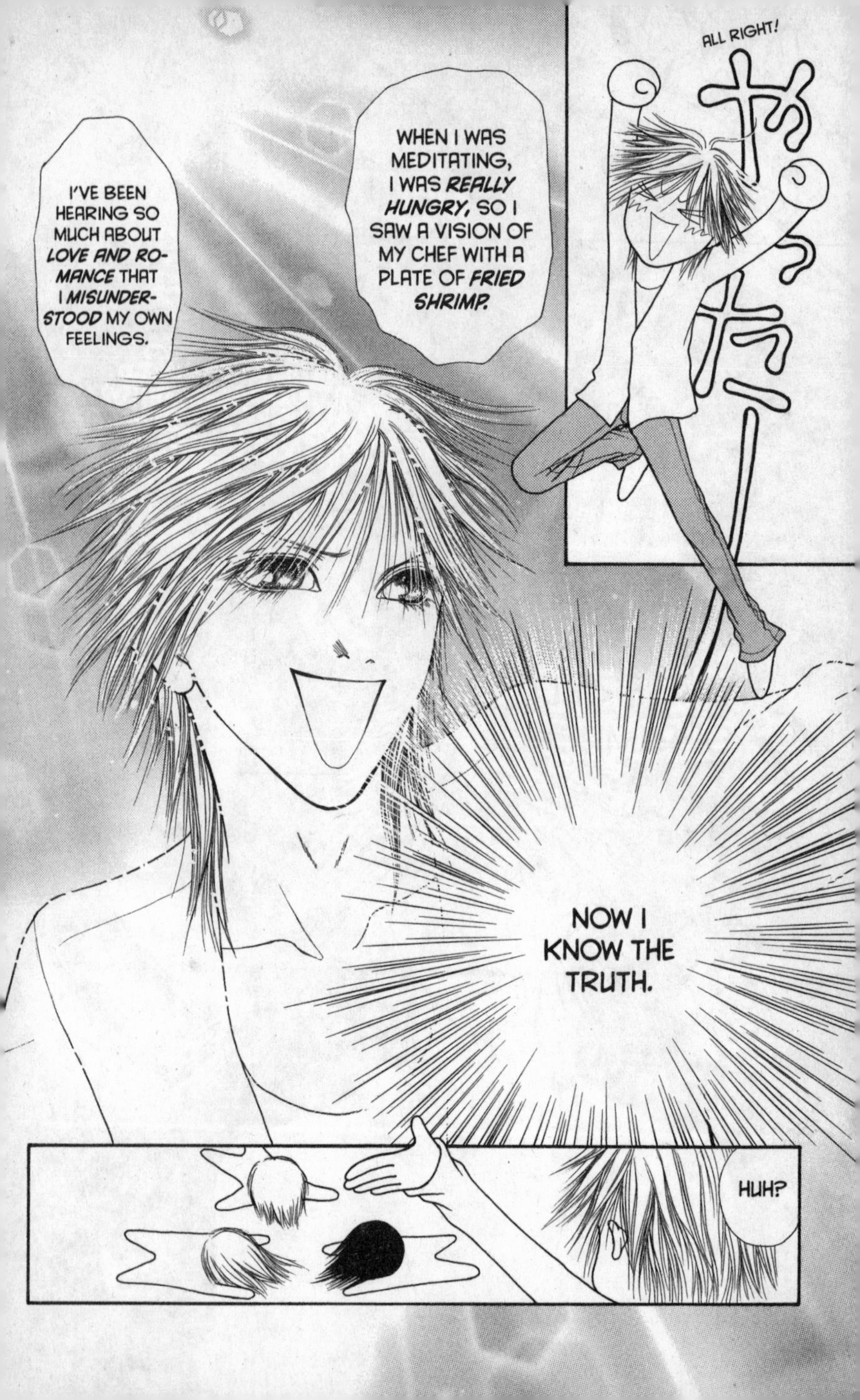
ALL RIGHT!
やったー
WHEN I WAS MEDITATING, I WAS *REALLY HUNGRY,* SO I SAW A VISION OF MY CHEF WITH A PLATE OF *FRIED SHRIMP.*
I'VE BEEN HEARING SO MUCH ABOUT *LOVE AND ROMANCE* THAT I *MISUNDERSTOOD* MY OWN FEELINGS.
NOW I KNOW THE TRUTH.
HUH?

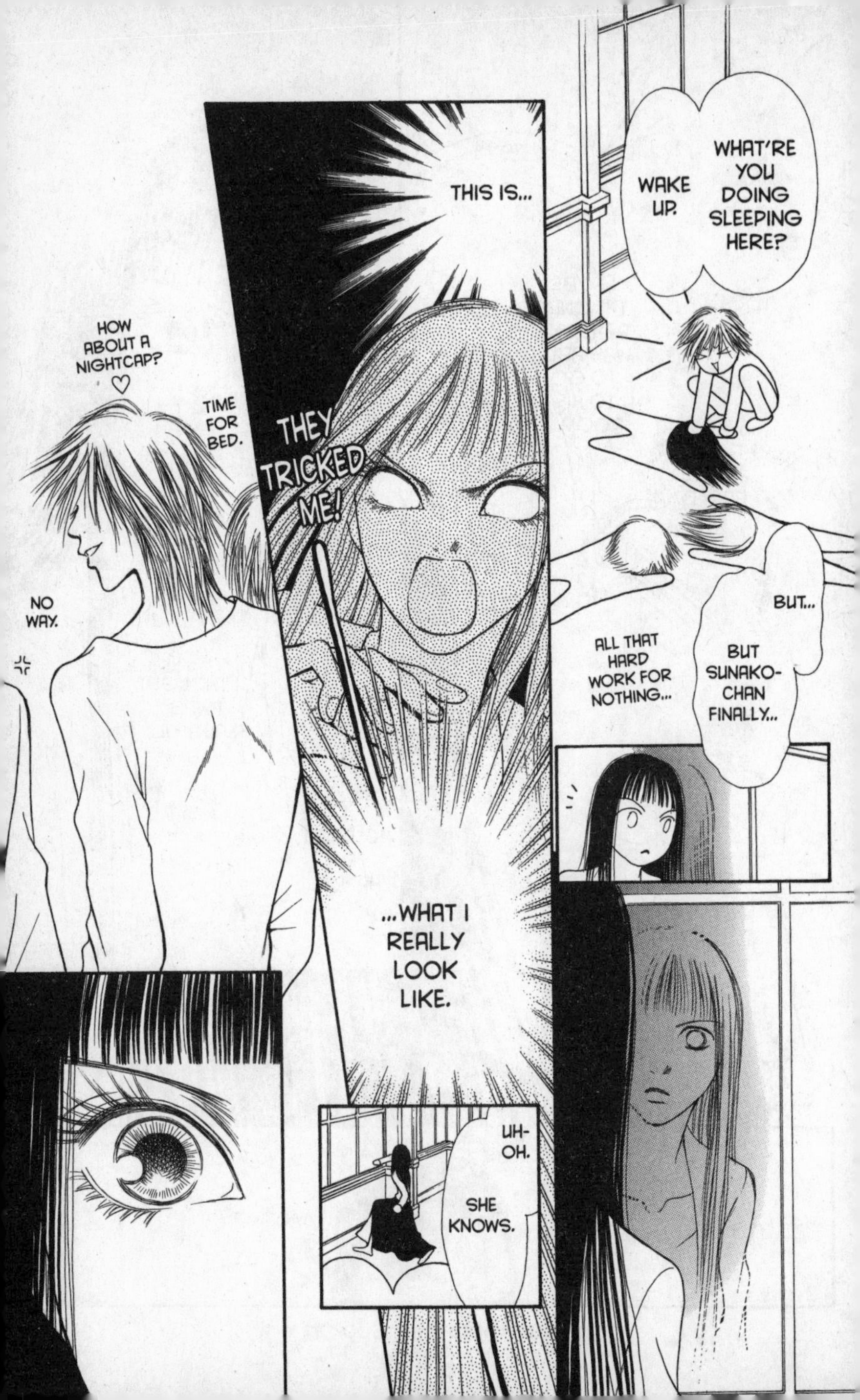
WHAT'RE YOU DOING SLEEPING HERE?
WAKE UP.
BUT...
BUT SUNAKO-CHAN FINALLY...
ALL THAT HARD WORK FOR NOTHING...
THIS IS...
THEY TRICKED ME!
...WHAT I REALLY LOOK LIKE.
UH-OH.
SHE KNOWS.
TIME FOR BED.
HOW ABOUT A NIGHTCAP? ♡
NO WAY.

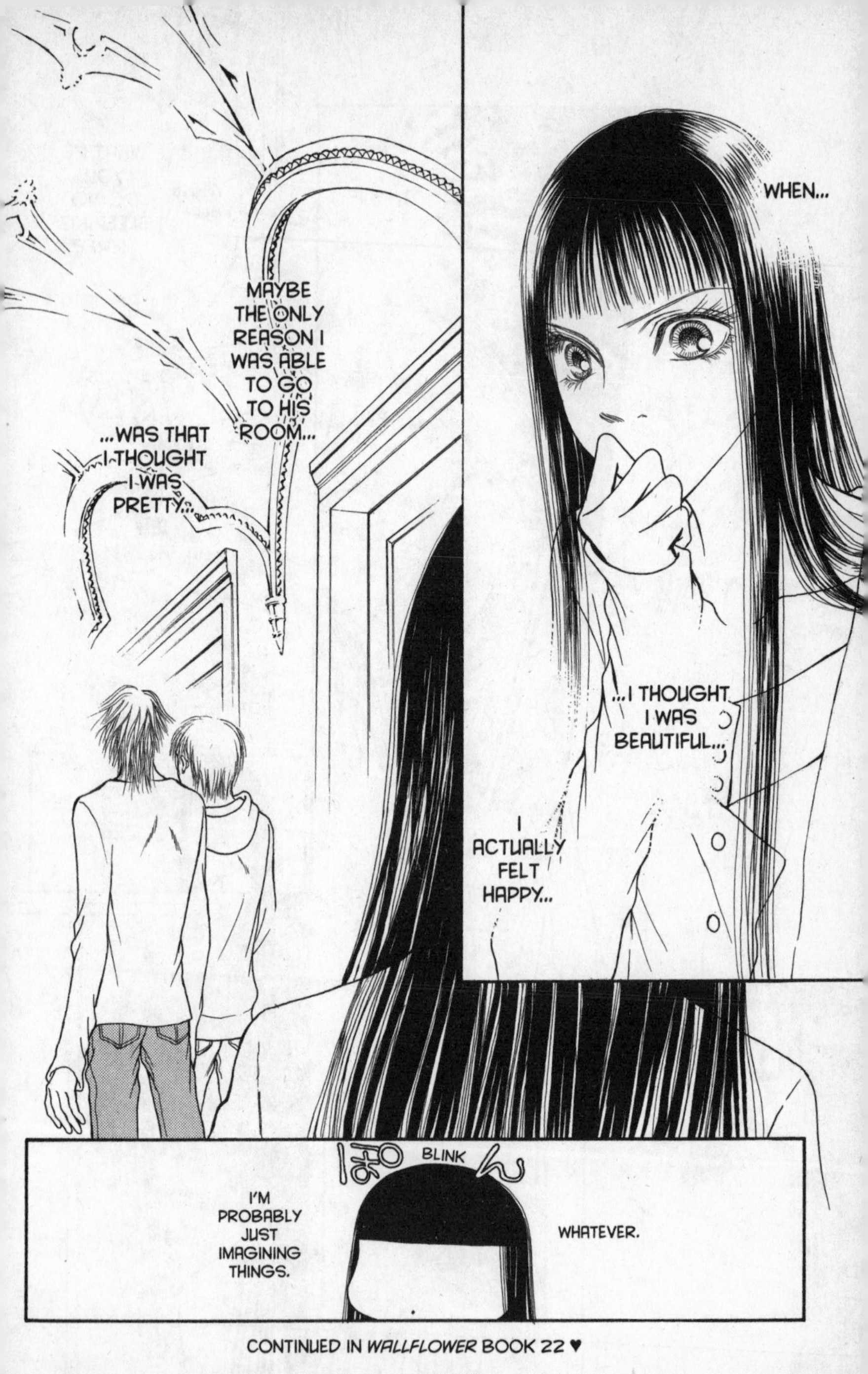
WHEN...
...I THOUGHT I WAS BEAUTIFUL...
I ACTUALLY FELT HAPPY...
MAYBE THE ONLY REASON I WAS ABLE TO GO TO HIS ROOM...
...WAS THAT I THOUGHT I WAS PRETTY...
BLINK
WHATEVER.
I'M PROBABLY JUST IMAGINING THINGS.

CONTINUED IN *WALLFLOWER* BOOK 22 ♥

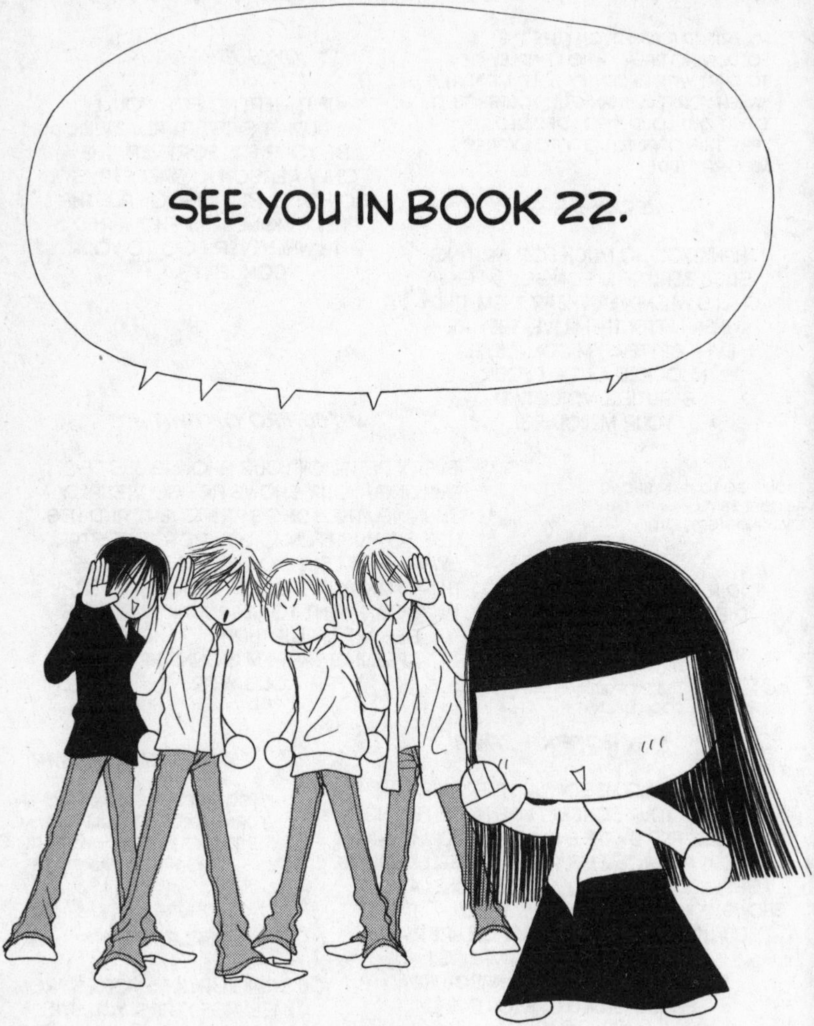
SEE YOU IN BOOK 22.

♥♥♥♥♥♥♥♥♥♥♥♥ I'D LIKE TO THANK YOU ALL. ♥♥♥♥♥♥♥♥♥♥♥♥

MY FRIEND RYON RYON (SEE THE FOLLOWING PAGE) WHO I FINALLY GOT TO CHAT WITH RECENTLY TOLD ME THAT "WHEN YOU FEEL THANKFUL, YOU SHOULD SAY IT OUT LOUD." SO I DECIDED TO TAKE THIS OPPORTUNITY TO EXPRESS MY GRATITUDE.

KIYOHARU-SAMA

IF IT WEREN'T FOR YOU, I WOULDN'T EXIST AT ALL. I WILL BE YOUR FAN FOREVER. THE ONLY REASON KYOHEI STAYS SO HOT IS BECAUSE OF ALL THE PHEROMONES I'M SHOWERED WITH WHENEVER I GO TO YOUR CONCERTS. ♡

MERRY-SAMA

THANK YOU SO MUCH FOR WRITING SUCH BEAUTIFUL SONGS. ♡ I GET CHILLS WHENEVER I HEAR THEM, AND WHEN I HEAR THEM LIVE, THEY'RE EVEN BETTER. I'M COMPLETELY KNOCKED OUT BY YOUR BEAUTIFUL VOICE AND YOUR MELODIES.

MITSUHIRO OIKAWA

EVERY DETAIL OF YOUR SHOW IS JUST SO AMAZING! YOUR SHOWS ARE SO VISUALLY STUNNING, THE SONGS ARE GREAT, AND IT'S JUST SO MUCH FUN. ♡ YOU'RE A TRUE STAR. WHENEVER I SEE YOU LIVE, IT MAKES ME THINK "OKAY, I'VE GOTTA WORK HARDER!" IN 2008, I WENT TO SEE MICHII TWO DAYS BEFORE MY BIRTHDAY. ♡ I HAVE A FEELING THAT I'M GONNA HAVE A FABULOUS YEAR. ♡

I DON'T GO TO THEIR SHOWS AS OBSESSIVELY AS THE OTHER SIX BANDS HERE, BUT...

DIR EN GREY
D'ESPAIRSRAY

I GO SEE THEM PRETTY OFTEN. THEY'RE REALLY COOL. ♡♡♡

NEW ROTE'KA-SAMA

YOU GUYS BRING ME SO MUCH PLEASURE. ♡♡♡ I WENT TO YOUR CONCERT WHEN I WAS FEELING DEPRESSED, AND BY THE END OF THE SHOW, I FORGOT ALL ABOUT MY PROBLEMS, AND I WAS FEELING GREAT. I GET ENERGIZED EVERY TIME I SEE ONE OF YOUR SHOWS. YOU MAKE ME LAUGH SO HARD. ♡ IT'S JUST SO MUCH FUN. ♡ AND THE SONGS ARE REALLY COOL. YOU GUYS'RE AMAZING! ATSU-CHAN, KATARU-KUN, NABO-CHAN, SHIZUO-SAN, I LOVE YOU GUYS. ♡♡♡♡♡

BOOGIEMAN-SAMA

I'M SO HAPPY TO SEE BANSAKU-SAN (FORMERLY OF BAROQUE) PLAYING BASS IN THIS BAND. I'M SUCH A BIG FAN OF YOURS!

D'ERLANGER

YOU BRING BACK MEMORIES FROM MY TEENAGE YEARS. YOU STILL SOUND AMAZING. ♡ I LOVE THE NEW SINGLE. ♡ KYO-SAN'S BAND BUG IS ALSO REALLY COOL. ♡♡♡

WITHOUT ALL OF YOUR CONCERTS I'D NEVER HAVE MADE IT THIS FAR IN LIFE.

RYON RYON

SHE'S A VOCAL TRAINER WITH MANY STUDENTS. I'M SO THANKFUL THAT SHE FINDS TIME TO HANG OUT WITH ME. ♡ SHE'S CUTE, ♡ AND I HAVE A TON OF RESPECT FOR HER. WHEN I WAS REALLY DEPRESSED, SHE GAVE ME GREAT ADVICE THAT MADE ME FEEL SO MUCH BETTER. ♡ I'M REALLY, REALLY THANKFUL FOR THAT. ♡♡♡ I LOVE YOU SO MUCH. ♡♡♡

WRITER N-SAMA

SHE'S A POPULAR WRITER WHO ALWAYS GETS ME OUT OF THE HOUSE, AND TAKES ME TO COOL PLACES. ♡ SHE'S INTRODUCED ME TO A TON OF PEOPLE. THANKS SO MUCH. ♡ SHE HUNG OUT WITH ME ON MY BIRTHDAY IN 2008. ♡ SHE'S SUCH A BEAUTIFUL TOMBOY. ♡ I TOTALLY ADMIRE HER. ♡

SHE WAS THE ONE WHO INTRODUCED ME TO RYON RYON. ♡

MY FRIENDS

BOTH MY FEMALE FRIENDS AND MY MALE FRIENDS...I LOVE YOU GUYS! ♡♡♡

MANGA ARTISTS I LOOK UP TO

THANK YOU SO MUCH. ♡♡♡ ESPECIALLY, MIZUHO AIMOTO-SENSEI...THANK YOU FOR EVERYTHING YOU'VE DONE FOR ME.

MY FAMILY

THANK YOU FOR YOUR KIND SUPPORT. I RESPECT AND LOVE YOU ALL. ♡♡♡ LOVE ♡♡♡

EVERYBODY WHO SENT ME LETTERS

THANK YOU SO MUCH. ♡ YOUR LETTERS ARE THE SOURCE OF MY STRENGTH. ♡ THANK YOU SO MUCH FOR READING MY MANGA. ♡

TENNOSUKE

LOVE 100% ♡♡♡

THANKS FOR READING ALL OF THIS. ♡

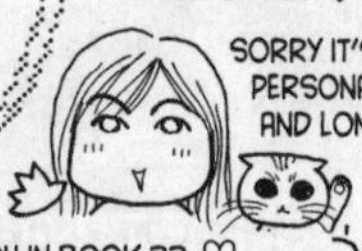

SORRY IT'S SO PERSONAL... AND LONG

SEE YOU IN BOOK 22. ♡

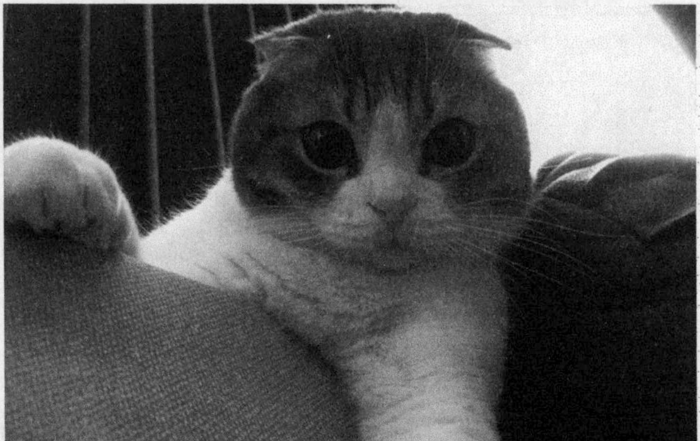

CHARACTER POPULARITY CONTEST!

I WILL NOW ANNOUNCE THE RESULTS OF THE POPULARITY CONTEST THAT WAS HELD TO COMMEMORATE THE 20TH VOLUME OF *WALLFLOWER*. BOTH MYSELF AND THE EDITING STAFF WERE ALL VERY MOVED BY YOUR POSTCARDS. I HOPE YOU'LL CONTINUE TO READ *WALLFLOWER*.

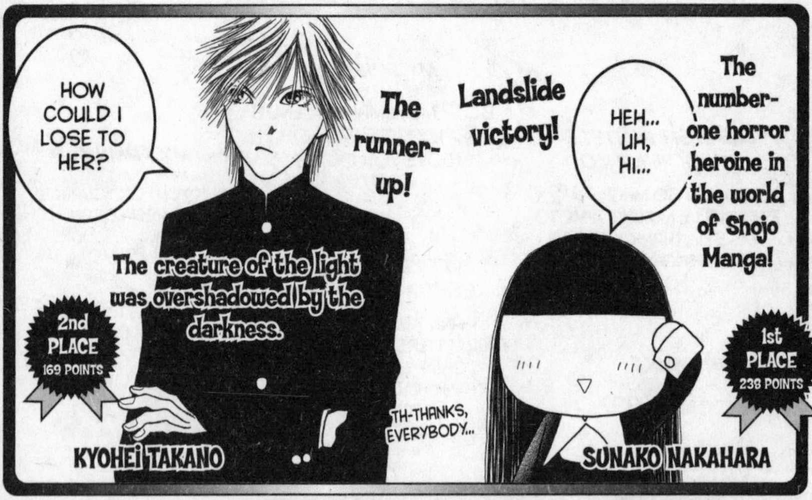
The number-one horror heroine in the world of Shojo Manga!
HEH... UH, HI...
Landslide victory!
1st PLACE 238 POINTS
TH-THANKS, EVERYBODY...
SUNAKO NAKAHARA
The runner-up!
HOW COULD I LOSE TO HER?
The creature of the light was overshadowed by the darkness.
2nd PLACE 169 POINTS
KYOHEI TAKANO

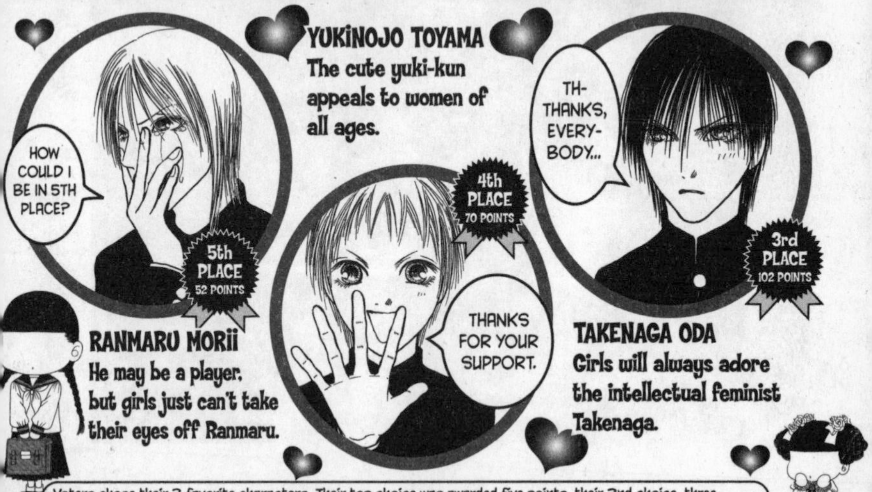
TH-THANKS, EVERY-BODY...
3rd PLACE 102 POINTS
TAKENAGA ODA
Girls will always adore the intellectual feminist Takenaga.
YUKINOJO TOYAMA
The cute yuki-kun appeals to women of all ages.
4th PLACE 70 POINTS
THANKS FOR YOUR SUPPORT.
HOW COULD I BE IN 5TH PLACE?
5th PLACE 52 POINTS
RANMARU MORII
He may be a player, but girls just can't take their eyes off Ranmaru.

Voters chose their 3 favorite characters. Their top choice was awarded five points, their 2nd choice, three points and their 3rd choice, one point. The total number of points was 756.

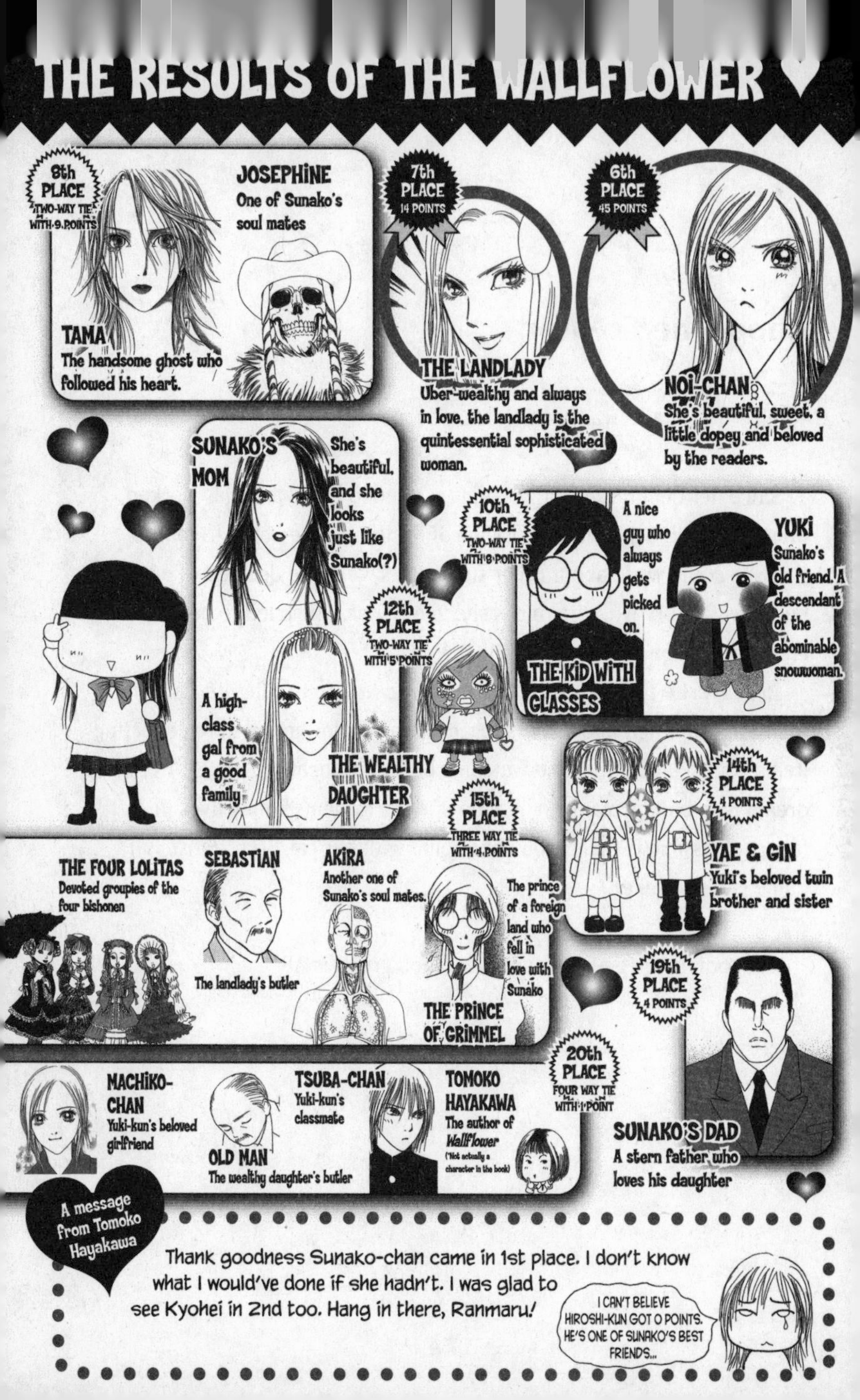
THE RESULTS OF THE WALLFLOWER ♥
6th PLACE 45 POINTS
NOI-CHAN
She's beautiful, sweet, a little dopey and beloved by the readers.
7th PLACE 14 POINTS
THE LANDLADY
Uber-wealthy and always in love, the landlady is the quintessential sophisticated woman.
8th PLACE TWO-WAY TIE WITH 9 POINTS
JOSEPHINE
One of Sunako's soul mates
TAMA
The handsome ghost who followed his heart.
10th PLACE TWO-WAY TIE WITH 8 POINTS
YUKI
Sunako's old friend. A descendant of the abominable snowwoman.
A nice guy who always gets picked on.
THE KID WITH GLASSES
SUNAKO'S MOM
She's beautiful, and she looks just like Sunako(?)
12th PLACE TWO-WAY TIE WITH 5 POINTS
THE WEALTHY DAUGHTER
A high-class gal from a good family
14th PLACE 4 POINTS
YAE & GIN
Yuki's beloved twin brother and sister
15th PLACE THREE WAY TIE WITH 4 POINTS
THE PRINCE OF GRIMMEL
The prince of a foreign land who fell in love with Sunako
AKIRA
Another one of Sunako's soul mates.
SEBASTIAN
The landlady's butler
THE FOUR LOLITAS
Devoted groupies of the four bishonen
19th PLACE 4 POINTS
SUNAKO'S DAD
A stern father who loves his daughter
20th PLACE FOUR WAY TIE WITH 1 POINT
TOMOKO HAYAKAWA
The author of Wallflower
(*Not actually a character in the book)
TSUBA-CHAN
Yuki-kun's classmate
OLD MAN
The wealthy daughter's butler
MACHIKO-CHAN
Yuki-kun's beloved girlfriend
A message from Tomoko Hayakawa
Thank goodness Sunako-chan came in 1st place. I don't know what I would've done if she hadn't. I was glad to see Kyohei in 2nd too. Hang in there, Ranmaru!
I CAN'T BELIEVE HIROSHI-KUN GOT 0 POINTS. HE'S ONE OF SUNAKO'S BEST FRIENDS...

About the Creator

Tomoko Hayakawa was born on March 4.

Since her debut as a manga creator, Tomoko Hayakawa has worked on many shojo titles with the theme of romantic love—only to realize that she could write about other subjects as well. She decided to pack her newest story with the things she likes most, which led to her current, enormously popular series, *The Wallflower*.

Her favorite things are: Tim Burton's *The Nightmare Before Christmas*, Jean-Paul Gaultier, and samurai dramas on TV. Her hobbies are collecting items with skull designs and watching bishonen (beautiful boys). Her dream is to build a mansion like the one the Addams family lives in. Her favorite pastime is to lie around at home with her cat, Ten (whose full name is Tennosuke).

Her zodiac sign is Pisces, and her blood group is AB.

Translation Notes

Japanese is a tricky language for most Westerners, and translation is often more art than science. For your edification and reading pleasure, here are notes on some of the places where we could have gone in a different direction in our translation of the work, or where a Japanese cultural reference is used.

24, page 3

The American TV drama *24* is wildly popular in Japan, where a subtitled version is available on DVD.

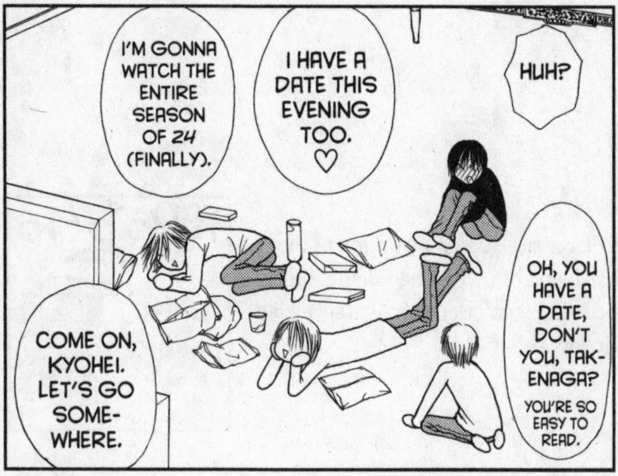
HUH?
I HAVE A DATE THIS EVENING TOO. ♡
I'M GONNA WATCH THE ENTIRE SEASON OF *24* (FINALLY).
OH, YOU HAVE A DATE, DON'T YOU, TAKENAGA? YOU'RE SO EASY TO READ.
COME ON, KYOHEI. LET'S GO SOMEWHERE.

Yakimo, page 37

Grilled sweet potatoes, called *yakimo*, are a popular treat sold by street vendors during Japan's chilly fall and winter.

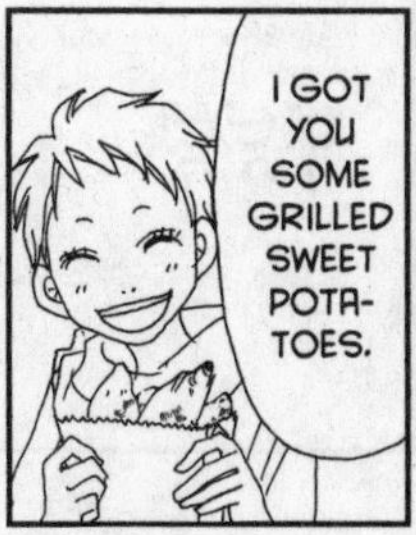
I GOT YOU SOME GRILLED SWEET POTATOES.

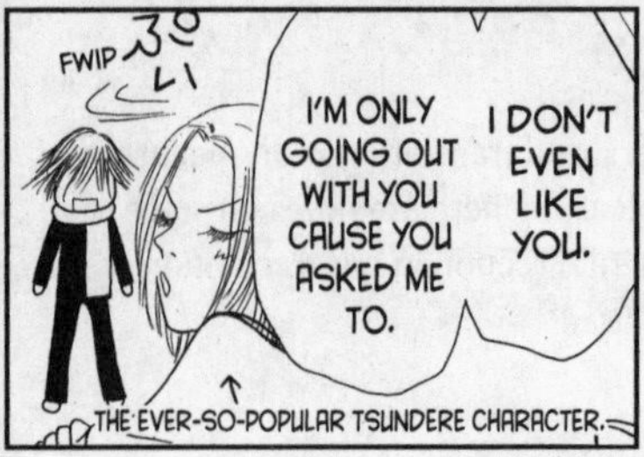
FWIP ぷい
I'M ONLY GOING OUT WITH YOU CAUSE YOU ASKED ME TO.
I DON'T EVEN LIKE YOU.
THE EVER-SO-POPULAR TSUNDERE CHARACTER.

***Tsundere*, page 37**

Tsundere is an otaku term for a type of anime/manga character. It usually refers to a girl who starts out mean, and then suddenly turns sweet and lovey-dovey.

***Furikake*, page 61**

The guys are putting *furikake* rice seasoning on top of their rice. *Furikake* is usually a blend of savory ingredients such as nori seaweed, sesame seeds, and dried fish. It is sprinkled over white rice to give it flavor.

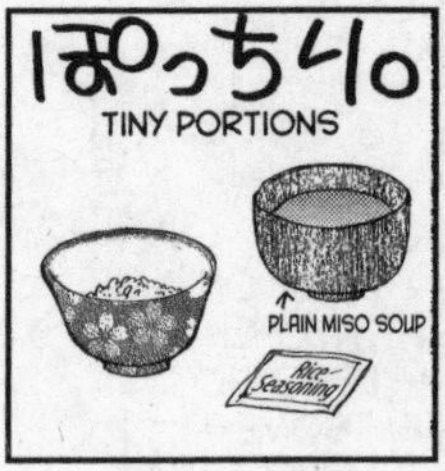
ぽっちん。
TINY PORTIONS
PLAIN MISO SOUP
Rice Seasoning

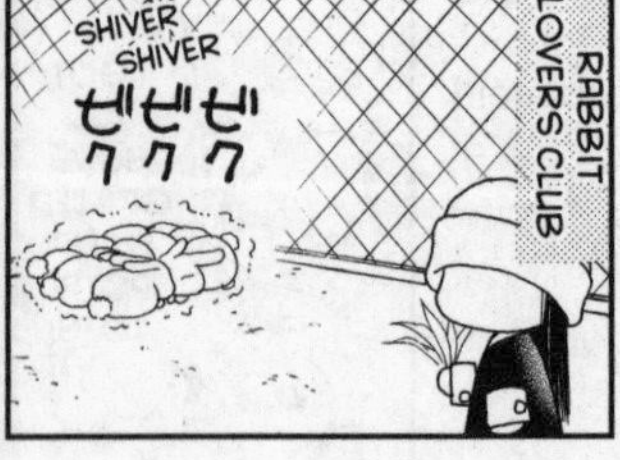
RABBIT LOVERS CLUB
SHIVER SHIVER
ぜぜぜ

Rabbits, page 75

It's very common for Japanese schools to keep pet rabbits on the grounds, particularly in elementary schools. Students are put in charge of caring for the rabbits.

Inside shoes, page 101

In Japanese schools, each student has a special pair of shoes used for walking inside the school.

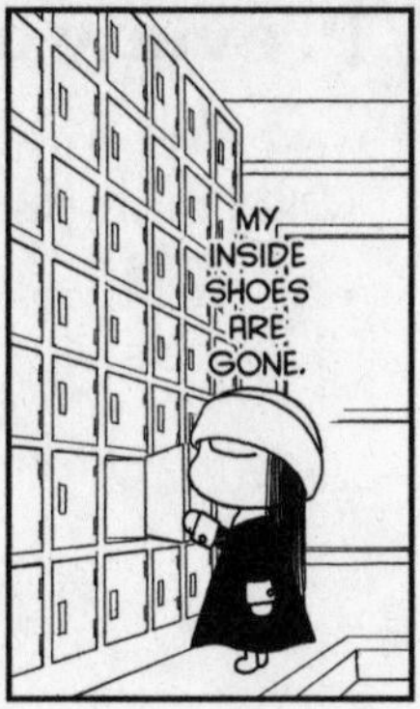
MY INSIDE SHOES ARE GONE.

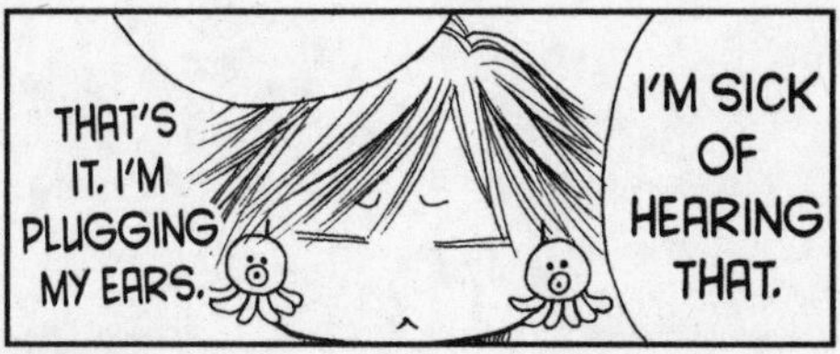
I'M SICK OF HEARING THAT.
THAT'S IT. I'M PLUGGING MY EARS.

Octopus ears, page 114

Perhaps you're wondering why Kyohei has octopi in his ears. The Japanese phrase, "mimi ni tako," literally means "calluses on the ears" and means that one has heard something so much that their ears are getting callused. However, the word for calluses, "tako," also means octopus. Hence the visual pun of octopi clinging to Sunako's ears.

Preview of Volume 22

We're pleased to present you a preview from volume 22. This volume is available in English, but for now you'll have to make do with Japanese!

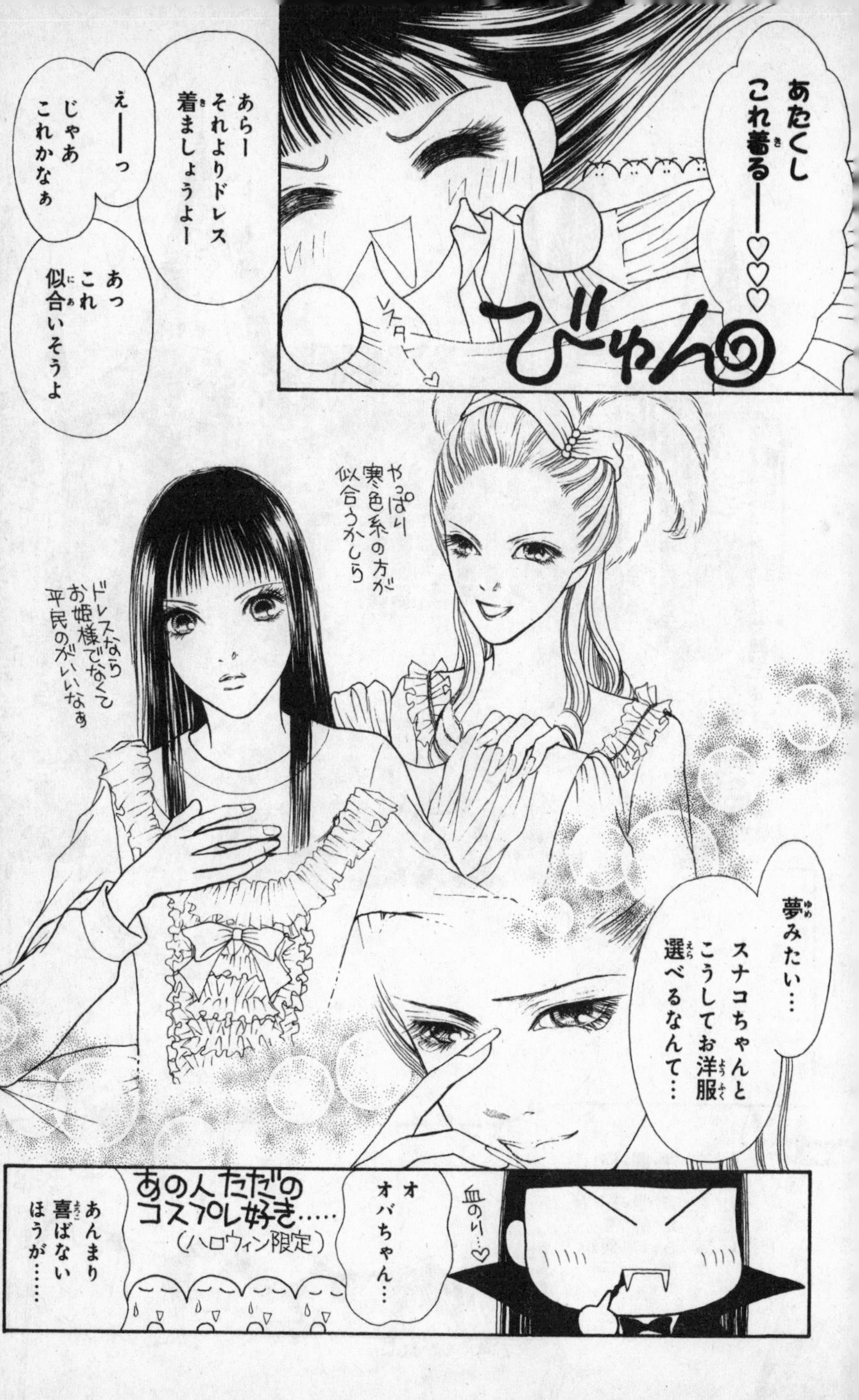
あたくし
これ着るーー♡♡♡
びゃん
あらー
それよりドレス
着ましょうよー
えーーっ
じゃあ
これかなぁ
あっ
これ
似合いそうよ
やっぱり
寒色系の方が
似合うかしら
ドレスなら
お姫様でなくて
平民のがいいなぁ
夢みたい…
スナコちゃんと
こうしてお洋服
選べるなんて…
血のり…♡
オ
オバちゃん…
あの人ただのコスプレ好き…..
(ハロウィン限定)
あんまり
喜ばない
ほうが……

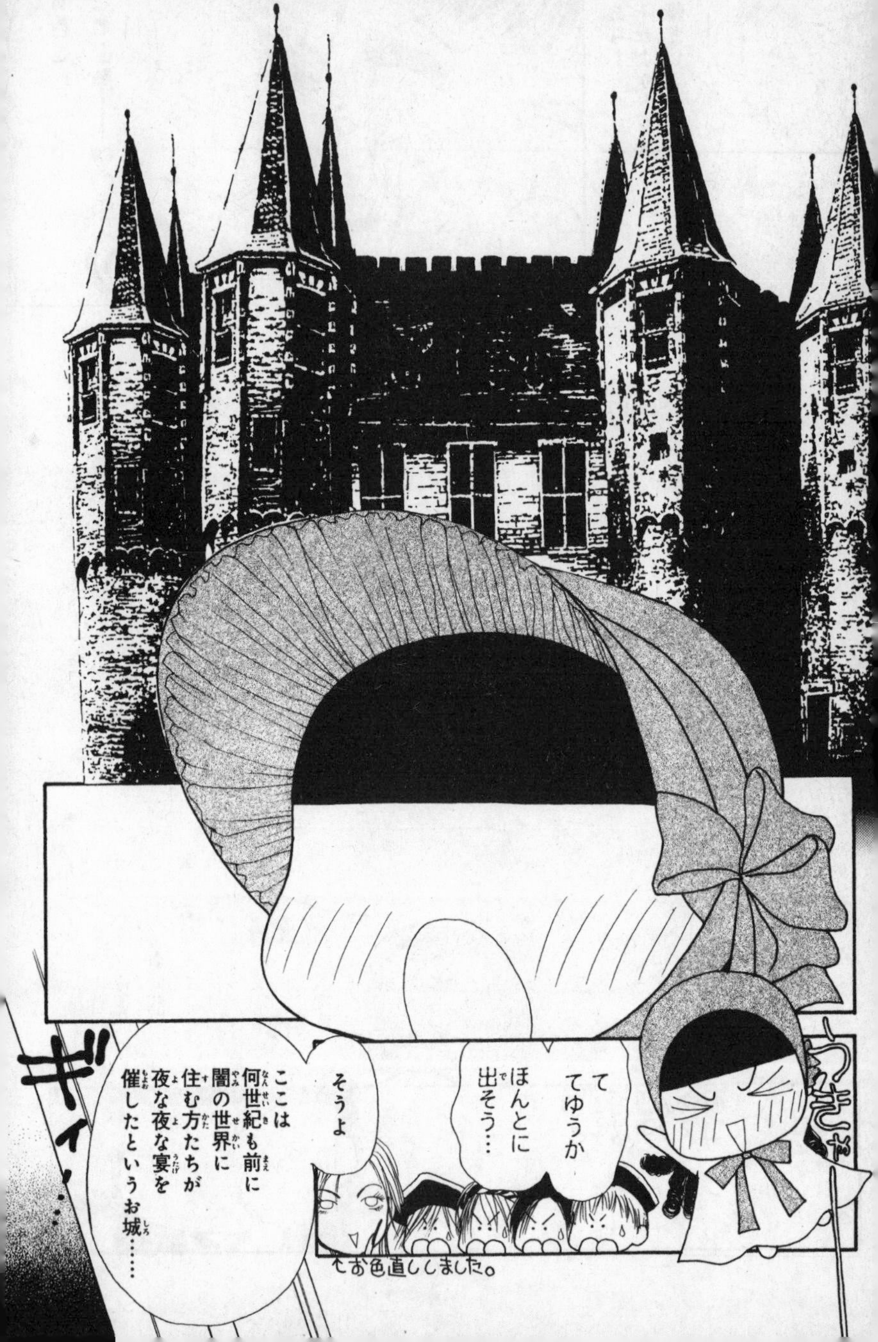
うきゃ
て
てゆうか
ほんとに
出そう…
そうよ
ここは
何世紀も前に
闇の世界に
住む方たちが
夜な夜な宴を
催したというお城……
ギィ…
↑お色直ししました。

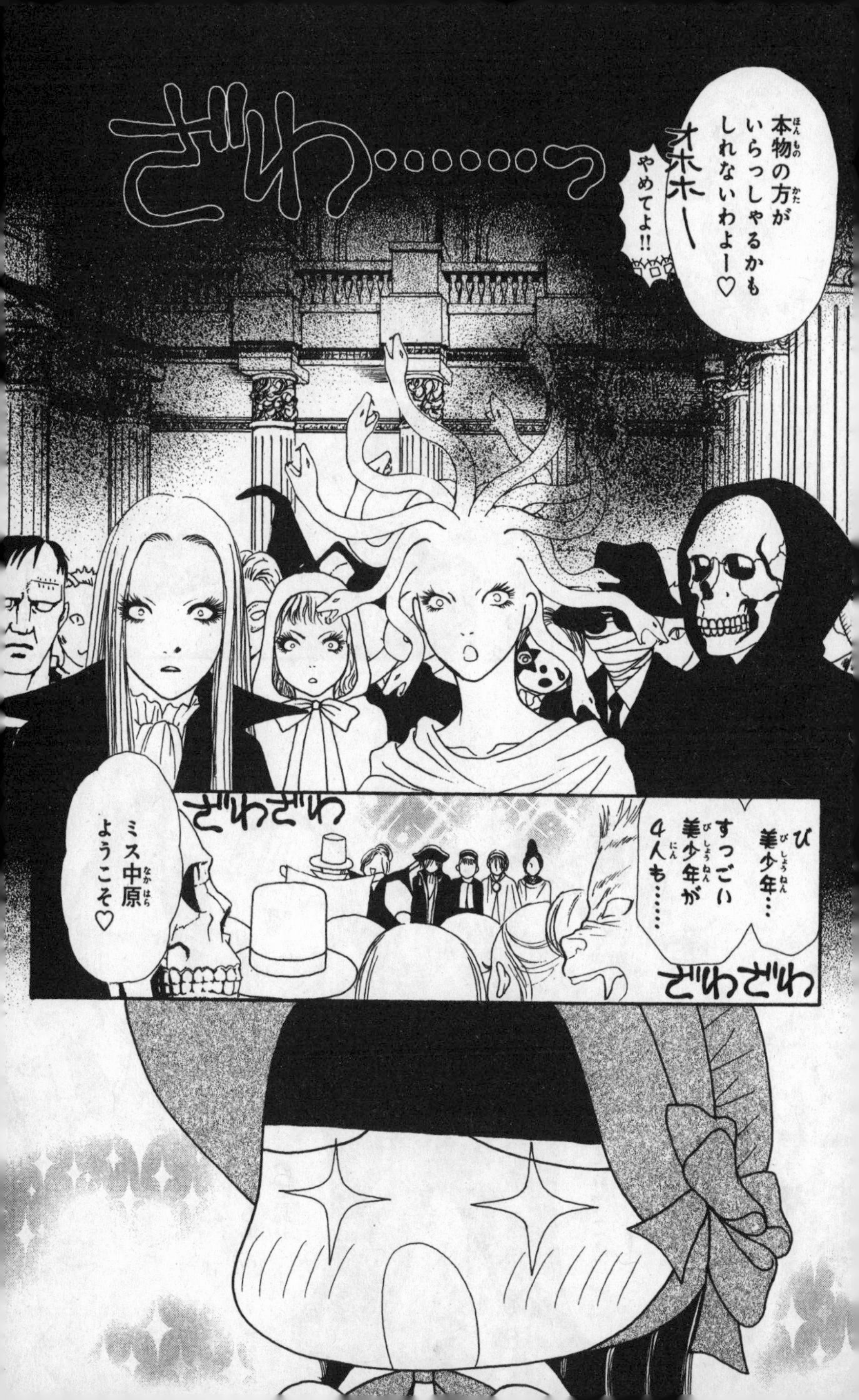
本物の方がいらっしゃるかもしれないわよー♡
オホホー
やめてよ!!
ざわ………っ
び　美少年……
すっごい美少年が4人も……
ざわざわ
ざわざわ
ミス中原ようこそ♡

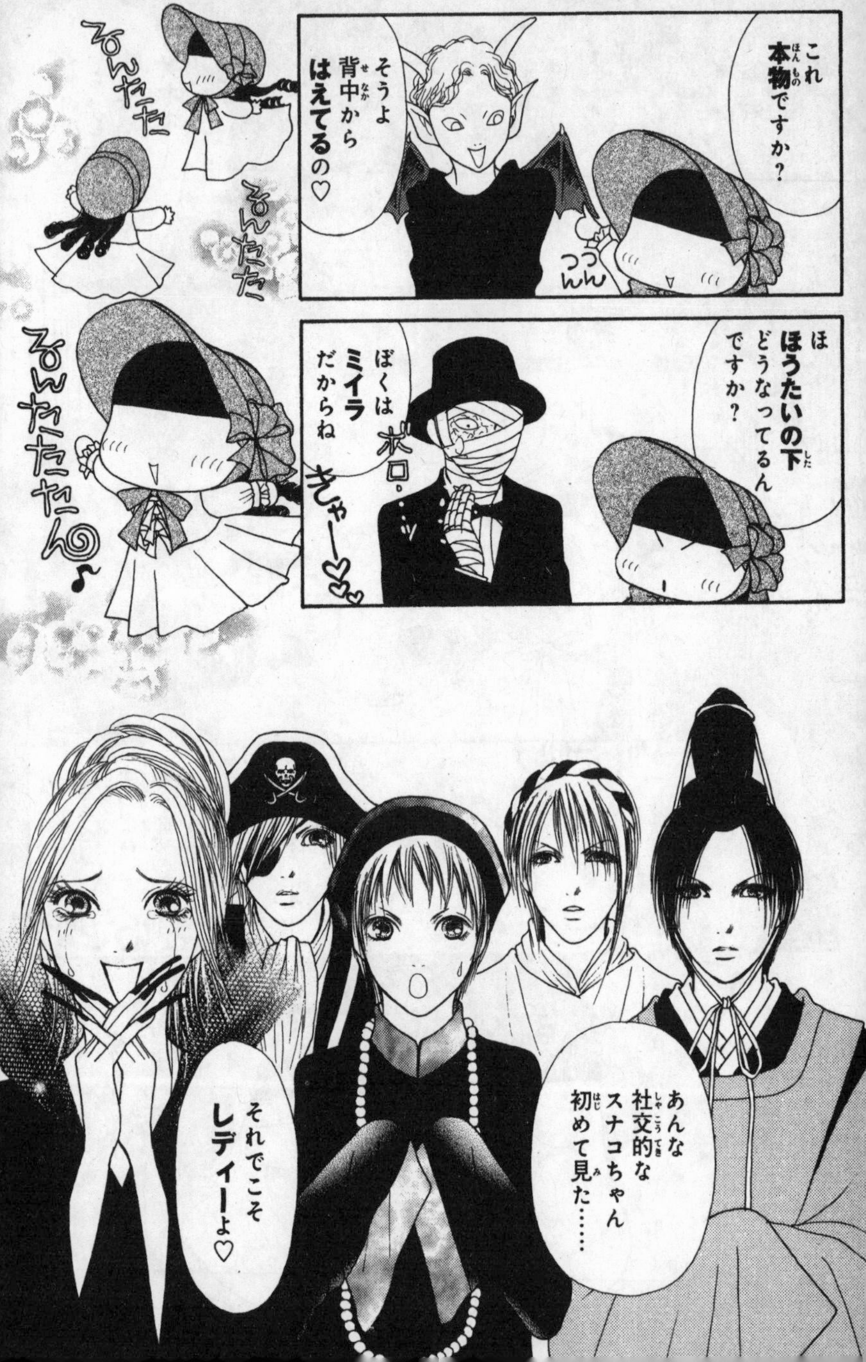
これ本物ですか？
つんつん
そうよ背中からはえてるの♡
ほうたいの下どうなってるんですか？
ぼくはミイラだからね
ポロ。
きゃー♡
るんたった
るんたった
るんたったったん♪
あんな社交的なスナコちゃん初めて見た……
それでこそレディーよ♡